THE LETTERS OF
ST. CYPRIAN OF CARTHAGE

Letters 55–66

ANCIENT CHRISTIAN WRITERS

THE WORKS OF THE FATHERS IN TRANSLATION

EDITED BY

JOHANNES QUASTEN   WALTER J. BURGHARDT
THOMAS COMERFORD LAWLER

No. 46

THE LETTERS OF ST. CYPRIAN OF CARTHAGE

TRANSLATED AND ANNOTATED

BY

G.W. CLARKE

Deputy Director
Humanities Research Centre
Australian National University

Volume III
Letters 55–66

NEWMAN PRESS
New York, N.Y./Mahwah, N.J.

Library of Congress
Catalog Card Number: 83-80366

ISBN: 0-8091-0369-9

Published by Paulist Press
997 Macarthur Boulevard
Mahwah, N.J. 07430

PRINTED AND BOUND IN THE UNITED STATES OF AMERICA

CONTENTS

*Conciliar letters, sent jointly by Cyprian and other African bishops

INTRODUCTION

PREFATORY

The letters in this volume cover the period from the time when Cornelius was well enough established as bishop within Rome to be able to convene a Council of Italian Bishops—by (say) mid-251 or so—to about the period when Stephen was replacing Cornelius' successor, Lucius, in the late spring of 254. Or to put it from the imperial point of view, they start with the principate of Gallus, last through the usurpation of Aemilian (and others), and end when Valerian and his son Gallienus have been now well and truly confirmed in their accession to power (securely there from autumn 253 onwards). This introduction merely aims briefly to sketch this setting—imperial and ecclesiastical—against which these letters were composed and therefore should be read. Detailed documentation is reserved for the commentary but attention is also drawn here in a general way to some special features of church life of the time which this correspondence particularly reveals, notably persecution under Gallus and the African Council meetings over the years 251–53.

IMPERIAL EVENTS

By the end of June 251 the unnerving news would have spread to most parts of the Roman world that Emperor Decius and his elder son, Herennius Etruscus, lay dead in the marshlands of the Dobrudja, their army disastrously defeated by the Goths at Abrittus. Even Cyprian registers (as he so seldom does in his letters) the impact of so stunning an imperial event in the opening letter of this volume

1

(*Ep.* 55.9.2 *ad fin.*). And those invading Goths, laden with plunder from their marauding of the Danubian provinces and boasting a valuable train of captives, taken especially from the pillaged city of Philippopolis, had now richly compensated themselves for the series of reverses they had suffered in Decius' campaign against them.[1]

The military governor of nearby Moesia (if that indeed was his office), C. Vibius Trebonianus Gallus, seized his opportunity swiftly (as beneficiary after the fact he is found in our sources accused of active treachery—no less than abetting the imperial defeat: which is not impossible). He promptly had himself proclaimed emperor by his troops (his son Volusianus was to be assistant Caesar) and with that authority he did what the situation compelled him to do if he was to have any hopes of consolidating his imperial pretensions. He reversed Decius' policy, which had been to block off and then annihilate the Gothic intruders; instead, he allowed them free passage out of Roman territory over the Danube, leaving intact their rich baggage trains and long lines of high-born prisoners (with their great potential for future income from ransom negotiations), and even throwing in an annual subsidy as a bond for satisfactory behaviour. For far more important to Gallus than military laurels and victories was the menacing threat to his position in Rome. Decius' younger son, Hostilian, was resident there and his obvious claims to the succession (he had recently been made Caesar) would be pushed strongly by the partisans and supporters of the Decian *factio* in Rome.[2]

A compromise was reached with impressive speed—Gallus had the military initiative, Hostilian the more legitimate claims and a party backing with strong vested interests: Hostilian was confirmed in his status as Caesar and then soon raised to the status of co-Augustus whilst Gallus' own son Volusianus was to be content with the lower rank of Caesar. In accordance with this conciliatory policy, the deceased Decii were piously enrolled among the *Divi*. But the placatory alliance was awkward and uneasy, and by the autumn of 251 Hostilian was dead—whether fortuitously from the disastrous plague which had now hit Rome or from deliberate treachery. The memory of Decius and his sons could now be erased from public monuments and inscriptions, and avoided in official documents, as Gallus and Volusianus (advanced to the status of Augustus) sought to obliterate traces of the short-lived dynasty they had replaced and to promote their own regime.[3]

Gallus and his son now proceeded to reside in Italy for the remainder of 251 and throughout the following year 252. But whilst they there sought to conciliate—or eliminate—the former party of Decius and to establish their own following in positions of power (and no doubt lay preparations for restoration work on the frontiers), reports of invasions and disasters kept coming in. Goths, Borani, and Carpi were again on the move in the northern lands, some robber bands even raiding by sea coastline cities across the Black Sea (penetrating as deep inland as Pessinus) and down along the shores of Asia Minor as far as Ephesus. It is into such a context of military upheaval and disarray that the African barbarian raids revealed by *Ep.* 62 could naturally fit (though the dating for them remains imprecise), and Scythians are found reported as penetrating into mainland Greece as well.[4]

But as likely as not, the scene was even more devastating in the more easterly provinces. Though chronology is controversial, there are strong grounds for believing that it was about the period of Decius' death that the renascent Sassanid dynasty under Sapor in Persia seized this season of uncertainty and confusion for cutting its deep swathe across Roman territory, boldly penetrating as far as Antioch (betrayed by one Mareades) and leaving an appalling catalogue, it could be claimed, of no fewer than thirty-seven devastated cities and their territories in its wake. The polyonomous usurper Lucius Julius Sulpicius Uranius Antoninus of Emesa in Syria may well have successfully established his illegitimate regime for several years in the aftermath of this incursion.[5] No wonder that Cyprian at this period is prepared to expatiate on the wars that arose more frequently, and the famines and pestilences that raged so savagely in his day (e.g. *Ad Demet.* 2, 5; *De mort.* 2), and the thirteenth book of the Sibylline Oracles with full confidence can predict for Gallus and his son that "famines, pestilences, mighty thunderbolts, fearsome wars, and anarchies in cities shall suddenly come" (lines 106 ff.).

For as if these catastrophes were not enough, virulent plague had now struck, taking heavy toll of the civilian population and calling for the customary expiatory rites (? *Ep.* 59.6.1) and even scapegoats

(? the Roman bishops, *Epp.* 60 and 61, for the Christians were popularly blamed as being the cause of the dire visitation). The lurid scenes enacted in Carthage as the disease spread, which we have depicted in Pontius' *Life* of Cyprian (cc. 9 f.), were being repeated in urban centres all over the Mediterranean (for contemporary Rome, Victor, *De Caes.* 30.2, where the emperors themselves see to the burial of the poor *anxie studioseque*). The auguries for success for this new regime were far from hopeful.

And, ironically, it was that scarce commodity of military success (although partial only) which brought this lacklustre regime to its end. For the governor of Moesia, Aemilius Aemilianus (who had probably replaced Gallus in the post), was encouraged by some successes against the Goths to try out his hand at overturning the new dynasty. Haste was essential, and with haste that bid on Italy succeeded; and by about mid-253 the regime of Gallus came to a quick and miserable end at Interamna. But the sources are clear: Aemilian enjoyed the fruits of his victory for no more than three short months. For Valerian had moved from the Germanic frontier (in which area he held a military command) to come to the assistance of Gallus— and he had little option (even if he wanted it otherwise) but to keep on coming now that Gallus had been defeated. By the autumn of 253 Valerian along with his son Gallienus were both together in Rome, legitimated in imperial power, and setting about their initial task of rewarding their supporters and conciliating those disaffected with the preceding regime. Pope Lucius and his companions in exile may have received their liberty to return to Rome as the result of some such general gesture of conciliation (see *Ep.* 61). But military events to the north (Gallienus) and in the east (Valerian) will certainly have preempted the attention of the new Augusti.[6]

PERSECUTION UNDER GALLUS[7]

Two letters in this present volume (*Epp.* 57, 58) record major fears of coming persecution and indeed major modifications in penitential discipline in the face of those ominous fears; another two letters (*Epp.* 60, 61) record dangers, arrest, and exile for two bishops of

Rome, Cornelius and his successor, Lucius (whose exile is shared by *comites*); a fifth letter (*Ep.* 59) registers threatening perils as the result of the recent publication of an edict requiring the population to offer sacrifice. These witnesses from the Cyprianic correspondence have all been conflated together and combined with a passage in the letters of Dionysius of Alexandria which refers in vague and general terms to the banishment under Gallus of holy men (*ap.* Euseb. *H.E.* 7.1): the result is confidently to deduce a serious outbreak of persecution under Gallus, menacing and world-wide. In other words, these five letters (one conciliar, the others from Cyprian) form the basis for drawing such a deduction and it is, therefore, important to review what facts can be established precisely for this episode and in particular to sieve a little more finely what these letters of Cyprian can indeed tell us about the scale, spread, and rhythm of difficulties experienced by the Christian communities during this period. But at the outset one should note the disquieting fact that most of our ancient authorities fail to make the deduction drawn by modern authorities. Not a word, for example, in Lactantius' *De mortibus persecutorum* (though Gallus would have provided a theme congenial to his purpose) nor even in Orosius despite his manifest hostility to Gallus (e.g. *hac sola pernicie* [= plague] *insignes Gallus et Volusianus*, 7.21.5 CSEL 5.480, cf. Eutrop. 9.5). The Byzantine historian Zonaras is exceptional in the tradition ("He [= Gallus] proved troublesome to the Christians no less than Decius, stirring up persecution against them and eliminating [*anelōn*] many," 12.21 ed. Dindorf 3.136 f.), but as a compiler of the twelfth century he is most unlikely to be independent of the primary sources to be discussed below.

1. *The evidence, apart from Cyprian's correspondence*

There are valuable documents surviving for this period by or about five bishops contemporary with the principate of Gallus, viz. Cornelius and Lucius in Rome, Cyprian in Carthage, Gregory Thaumaturgus in Pontus, and Dionysius in Alexandria.

1.A. Firstly, Dionysius.

Eusebius *H.E.* 7.1 records an extract from a letter of Dionysius of Alexandria addressed to Hermammon in which we are told that

Gallus, after a season of success and prosperity, "drove away [*ēlasen*] the holy men [*tous hierous andras*] who were supplicating God for his peace and health, and so along with them he banished [*ediōxen*] also their prayers on his behalf." Further material from the same letter is quoted by Eusebius at 7.10.2 ff. concerning, in retrospect, Valerian (with Gallienus' name carefully suppressed) and the Macriani; a summary (which alludes to a lengthy account of the wickedness of Decius) and an additional extract from the same letter occur at 7.22.12 ff. on the triumph of the god-loving Gallienus over his wicked foes (Macrianus). Clearly the letter dates to about a decade after Gallus' brief reign; indeed, to be precise, apparently to shortly before Easter of the year 261 or 262[8] during the "peace of Gallienus," *H.E.* 7.22.12. The unoriginal theme of the letter can without difficulty also be divined: the events of the 250s demonstrate that emperors enjoy peace, health, and prosperity whilst they engage the favour and prayers of Christians; they suffer wars, plagues, and disasters (Decius–Gallus–Valerian) when they persecute them. Gallienus' peace is coincident with the Church's peace. Consistent with this reading of the past decade, Gallus is blessed—tendentiously—with an initial period when "his reign was prospering and things were going according to his mind" (*ap.* Euseb. *H.E.* 7.1.).

Gallus' reign and Egypt are very much associated with the disastrous and (it was to prove to be) long-lasting plague, and Dionysius has elsewhere very full descriptions of the course of the disease both in another Easter letter addressed generally to the brethren (*H.E.* 7.22.l ff.) and in an Easter letter directed to Hierax (*H.E.* 7.21.9 ff.), but there is no mention anywhere in these two documents of Gallus. Some have pressed these fragments into chronological service for the persecution of Gallus—unwisely, for in fact the general festal letter appears almost certainly to date to the early 260s, the other (to Hierax) is as likely as not to come from about that same date.[9] In all events, they need not be describing sufferings confined to the early 250s and to the time of Gallus at all. *H.E.* 7.22.1 (written to the brethren "when the war was followed by a pestilential disease") is hardly to be regarded, therefore, as has been asserted, as the only document to be precise about the chronology of the plague and of the outbreak of the persecution of Gallus.[10]

Indeed, it is open to serious doubt—against most modern

authorities[11]—that from the words of Dionysius of Alexandria at Eusebius *H.E.* 7.1 we *must* conclude that "the holy men" who were driven away by Gallus have to be (clerics) from Egypt and that Egypt itself should accordingly figure on the list of areas known to have been affected by this "persecution." If true, that would help considerably to add up towards an atmosphere of *general* persecution and troubles. But Dionysius is addressing "Hermammon and the brethren in Egypt," *H.E.* 7.22.12. His language is curiously, and unwontedly, vague and undetailed for referring to local Egyptian heroes (contrast, for example, the twenty-seven names for Egyptian sufferers, during or immediately before the time of Decius, that happen to be preserved in other fragments of Dionysius' letters); the anonymous reference would be much more understandable for distant confessors somewhere overseas (Italy?).[12] And were that elsewhere indeed Italy, we cannot expect any such interpretation to be annotated in Eusebius. For he proceeds to write *H.E.* 7.2 (on contemporaneous events in Rome, immediately following the extract from Dionysius on Gallus) apparently quite unaware of the fate of Cornelius and the vicissitudes of Lucius and his companions in Italy under Gallus.

1.B. Secondly, Gregory Thaumaturgus.

Another area for which we can hope to form some continuous picture in this period is Pontus. Gregory of Nyssa, in his "vita" of Gregory Thaumaturgus (a rhetorical and unreliable panegyric), has lengthy descriptions of the persecution of Decius (MG 46.944 ff.) and of the plague (*ibid.* 956 f.), but there is no word in the appropriate context of any danger, compulsory sacrifices, exiles, etc. under Gallus. To the knowledge of Gregory of Nyssa "the persecution of Gallus" clearly passed this area by; perhaps the same applied for Egypt. The rate of probability heavily depends on what can be claimed for the situation in Africa, for, apart from Italy, that is the only other area from which we can expect, given our surviving material, contemporary evidence for the Church during this period of Gallus.[13] And for Africa the evidence is by far the fullest.

1.C. Thirdly, the treatises of Cyprian.

A close scrutiny of the 12 (or 13) authentic treatises of Cyprian yields little that can be categorised as definite. There are two tractates in particular, the *De mortalitate* and the *Ad Demetrianum*, which between them contain much about the plague and much about a Church facing persecution.[14] They are post-Decian. But I cannot find anything in them[15] which compels one to believe that the intended audience was actually at the time undergoing immediate persecution. The prospect of persecution is definitely anticipated. After Decius, that is not an unreasonable attitude of mind (on the unexceptional premise that what happened once could readily happen again), and with the constant and strident talk of Antichrist—more than mere emotive rhetoric—persecution, as one of the signs of the cataclysmic times, was, properly, only to be expected.[16] But what there is about persecutions (by no means an obsessive theme in these works) is consonant with a *general* hortatory tone and homiletic purpose, and, simply on the evidence of these treatises, one could not deduce anything secure about an *actual* persecution occurring between Decius and Valerian. What could be asserted is that if Cyprian at the time of writing had a persecution under Gallus in prospect, nothing specific was known, or at least divulged; and that these treatises were neither written during the course of an actual persecution under Gallus nor do any of his other treatises reflect back upon such a persecution. By a reading of the treatises alone, one would have to conclude that if a persecution was a reality for Cyprian under Gallus in Africa, it did not provide a sufficiently traumatic experience to pierce the generalities of Cyprian's rhetorical mode in these works.[17]

It ought to be noted that the chronology of these treatises is at once a vague and a delicate matter;[18] their (imprecise) dating is heavily dependent on that of the letters of Cyprian, and to these we now turn for a more detailed study.

2. The Correspondence of Cyprian and the Church in Africa in the Time of Gallus

Of prime importance as a terminus is *Ep.* 56. This is written shortly before an Easter festival (§3), to be followed subsequently by a Council of African Bishops (§3). Is the year 252 or 253? Four of the five other letters concerning the period of Gallus could well hinge on our decision. And the difference the decision makes to our picture of the persecution of Gallus is categorical; for to decide that the year was the later of the two, viz. 253, would reduce the exile of Pope Cornelius under Gallus (the major event in fact known of the persecution) to the duration of five or six weeks at the very most; all fears would have been over with the return of Lucius, the successor of Cornelius, from his (unknown) place of exile—possibly but a few months later. But more on this later.

A close inspection of *Ep.* 56—see introduction to the commentary on this letter—shows that one cannot be categorical about *either* 252 *or* 253 as its correct dating, but that the crucial phrase *per hoc triennium* in §1.1 (lapsed have been loyally doing penance since their trial and fall under Decius in 250 over such a period) pushes the choice decidedly towards 253. It should also be observed that the contents of *Ep.* 56 unmistakably imply that the general amnesty which was in fact granted to repentant and faithful lapsed in view of a coming persecution (announced in *Ep.* 57) has not yet taken place. Were such a persecution already in prospect[19] and were Cyprian contemplating such a general policy (a major concession in church penitential discipline) in view of the dangers ahead, it is extremely odd for him not to make mention of these highly relevant facts in his letter. Indeed, it is very clear that his thinking is still far from adopting such a general conciliatory policy; he circumspectly details the special nature of the particular cases under discussion (after an initial and unusually brave confession, lapse under extreme tortures, followed by a *triennium* when *iugiter et dolenter . . . cum summa paenitentiae lamentatione planxerunt,* §2.1; they are in a different category from the ordinary *sacrificati,* §2.2).

If the date of *Ep.* 56 is indeed 253, it entails a swift timetable, with apprehension of an impending persecution seizing Carthage *after* Easter 253 (April 3)—that is to say, after *Ep.* 56 was penned—but before or in the course of the Council meeting that followed (early May?) and at which a policy of reconciliation was accordingly adopted (*Ep.* 57). After that meeting, Pope Cornelius was written to twice, once not yet personally endangered, *Ep.* 57, a second time in trouble (but apparently not yet exiled), *Ep.* 60. He was dead, dismissed to Centumcellae, in the course of June that same year,[20] not many weeks later. The storm of persecution will have blown up very suddenly.

Ep. 57 undoubtedly emanates from the Easter Council adumbrated in *Ep. 56* (observe the *iugiter et dolenter* repeated from *Ep.* 56.2.1); it was in fact attended by 42 (named) bishops. It is a conciliar letter to Pope Cornelius informing him of a major decision taken by that Council concerning penitential discipline: lapsed Christians who have been loyally performing penance continuously since the time of their lapse (§1.2), after individual scrutiny (§5.1), are now to be readmitted to full communion. It is revealed that a new dimension has been added to the previously existing situation and this has brought about the change in policy. The threat of a coming persecution is now being keenly sensed—*diem rursus alterius infestationis adpropinquare coepisse, certamen quod nobis hostis indicit, necessitate cogente, proelium quod imminet, impendentis proelii tempore, urgente certamine, diem certaminis adpropinquasse, hostem violentum cito contra nos exurgere, pugnam non talem qualis fuit sed graviorem multo et acriorem venire, futuram . . . pugnam.*

The curious feature is that though the sense of danger is acute and heavily stressed (by the time this letter was written *pax* had already been dispensed, and the bishops could speculate on the stance which the reconciled might now have taken up, §3.2), the nature of that danger and the source of the information is vague and disturbingly inexact. The *fons et origo* of the new knowledge is described consistently in terms of visions and signs—*crebris adque adsiduis ostensionibus admoneamur, obtemperandum est namque ostensionibus adque admonitionibus iustis, sancto spiritu suggerente et Domino per visiones multas et manifestas admonente ut quia hostis nobis imminere praenuntiatur et ostenditur . . . , hoc nobis divinitus frequenter ostendi, de hoc nos providentia et misericordia Domini saepius admoneri.* No word of informants, even of rumour, or of deductions made from established facts. No hint that Rome or the bishop of Rome himself (the addressee) is thought to be under threat in any way, and, most significantly, only the most passing of suggestions that Rome should adopt a similar policy.[21] On the face of it, the sense of danger appears to be quite local.

The modern rationaliser is naturally reluctant to admit the possibility that no facts lay behind the Africans' premonitions, despite the way in which those sentiments are in fact couched. But at least one can say that it does not surpass credence that the particular case of the three repentant lapsed confessors (imbedded in *Ep. 56*), when raised, as promised, at the Council, brought to light the general problems associated with the repentant lapsed and that in the light of *ostensiones*, *admonitiones*, and *visiones* already experienced (from whatever source) they were solved in the way outlined in *Ep.* 57. The letter may tell us something about the minds and moods (the taut nerves and high-strung fears) of the Africian bishops but, on a sceptical view, need not necessarily provide any factual information at all about a persecution of Gallus. Certainly the contents of the letter make it quite clear that there was no *actual* suffering taking place either in Africa or in Rome at the time *Ep.* 57 was being written.

It is worth observing, however, that the sentiments of danger were certainly real enough and that the visions were at the least experienced by Cyprian himself (if not exclusively his). For in *Ep.* 58, the following letter, Cyprian cancels a projected visit to the inland proconsular town of Thibaris because of the many divine warnings he has personally received (*cum Domini instruentis dignatione instigemur saepius et admoneamur*) and instead of his presence he sends to the Christian community there a lengthy and general hortatory sermon on steadfastness in the face of *pressurae* ahead. The language closely echoes that of the conciliar epistle, *Ep.* 57: *pressurae diem super caput esse coepisse, gravior nunc et ferocior pugna imminet, futurae persecutionis metu, aciem quae nobis indicitur, si . . . supervenerit persecutionis dies.* There is the additional sentiment of the approach of the times of Antichrist, much repeated.[22] But the danger is no more immediate, there is no more factual information, than in *Ep.* 57. *Ep.* 58 brings, therefore, no further light to the chronological question, and the reality of any "persecution of Gallus" is not brought by it into any sharper focus.

Ep. 59 is an important letter for our problem: it is addressed by Cyprian to Pope Cornelius and it is written quite some time after a Council meeting had been held on May 15 (§10.1); the year is, beyond question, 252.[23] What must now be determined is the relationship between the contents of the Council referred to in this letter (firmly dated to 252) and those of *Ep.* 57 (still left undetermined as spring 252 *or* 253). Are they identical or different meetings?

Ep. 59 is a lengthy document in which Cornelius is at first praised for having in the past excommunicated the Carthaginian rebel Felicissimus but afterwards reproved for showing temerity in the face of a more rowdy collection of Carthaginian dissidents. Cyprian stoutly and somewhat heatedly rehearses the history of these dissensions at considerable length, insisting (understandably) on his own orthodoxy and legitimacy, which Cornelius' hesitancy could be construed as impugning, and on the rights of the African Church to deal with these domestic disputes. There is totally absent throughout its length any sense of official trouble brewing for or actually confronting Cornelius in Rome (note esp. §19: *florentissimo illic clero tecum praesidenti*); there is no sense of an urgent and general persecution deflecting Cyprian's concentration away from his own ecclesiastical troubles in Africa—indeed (§18.2) he can describe these troublesome *haeretici* as those who *ipsam pacem persecutione peiorem fratribus faciunt*, "who are making peace itself more perilous a time for the brethren than the persecution (ever was)." That is to say, it looks as if he regarded the time of writing (summer 252) basically as a period of peace, not of persecution. *Persecutio* in the letter in fact refers to the *past* (e.g. §10.3, §12.2, §13.1).

And yet, at the time of writing, Cyprian has this to say of himself: . . . *his ipsis etiam diebus quibus has ad te litteras feci ob sacrificia quae edicto proposito celebrare populus iubebatur clamore popularium ad leonem denuo postulatus in circo*, §6.1 ("in recent days, also, just as I am writing this letter to you, there has been once again popular outcry in the circus for me to be thrown to the lion: this has been occasioned by the sacrifices which the people have been ordered by a public edict to celebrate").

Cyprian in a Pauline mode (2 Cor. 11.23 ff.) is hotly defending the role he has played in his episcopate, highlighting the special way in which he was chosen as bishop, the special divine protection he has received in persecution, the special graces he has been accorded in being singled out for attack (proscription, *totiens ad leonem petitus in circo*, etc.). The above citation provides the climax of this catalogue.[24] The Adversary is naturally concentrating his assaults on the (true) leader of the flock.

Many discordant deductions have been drawn from these phrases.[25] Cyprian is clearly talking of a very recent danger (*his ipsis etiam diebus*) but the atmosphere of the entire letter demonstrates that it is not overwhelming. And the manner of description—addressed to Cornelius in Rome—very strongly suggests (but does not prove) that the *edictum* was simply a local one (a public expiation against the plague proclaimed by the proconsul?).[26] The *populus* was required to participate (at a ceremony in the circus?) and the absence from it of Cyprian, as a *persona insignis*, was noted with evident popular disfavour.[27] And it certainly did not constitute—contrary to the view of many modern authorities—to Cyprian's mind a "persecution" proper at all.

Prima facie the tone of *Ep.* 59 (referring to events of spring and summer 252) and that of *Ep.* 57 (? spring 252 or 253) are very different, the latter epistle being strident in its sense of impending hostilities, violent conflicts, and bitter fighting under persecution on the point of arriving. This general observation is confirmed by the contents of *Ep.* 59.13 ff. (cf. §9.3). From these chapters it is perfectly clear that no general moratorium has yet been declared for the *paenitentiam facientes;*[28] and yet this was the central message of *Ep.* 57. The deduction is inescapable. *Ep.* 57 must be referring to a spring meeting later than mid-May 252; it must accordingly date to early 253.

The position in Carthage can now be made plainer.

By the time of the spring Council meeting of 252 there has been no trouble (reconciliation of the repentant *sacrificati* etc. did not figure on the agenda); sometime later in the course of 252 an edict (certainly at least in Carthage) required *sacrificia* on the part of the *populus* generally. Plague had come to Rome by late the previous year; Carthage cannot have escaped its virulent attack by summer 252. It is a fair surmise (but surmise only) that this epidemic occasioned the *edictum*. Cyprian was, once again (*denuo*), *ad leonem postulatus*, but the danger generally passed the Christian community by. At the time of Easter (April 3) the following year (*Ep.* 56), 253, Cyprian is still talking of persecution as a possibility in the future (*si acies etiam denuo venerit*, §2.2), but when the Council was convened after Easter (second week of May?—in the previous year there was an interval of 34 days between Easter and the Council on the Ides of May), there was a pressing, indeed overwhelming sense of conflict approaching and the African Church made preparations accordingly. Cyprian personally had certainly been vouchsafed divine monitions (*Ep.* 58). The relevant letters which follow (notably *Epp.* 60, 61, 66) and Pontius' *Vita* demonstrate conclusively that this peril never became actual in Carthage. (These are discussed below.) Patently the Church there passed through a period of extreme apprehension, but did not in fact undergo "a persecution of Gallus."

We must now turn to Rome, the remaining area on which we are informed.

3. Rome

When Cyprian refers incidentally in *Ep.* 59.6 (summer of 252) to the *edictum* which enjoined *sacrificia* on the *populus*, he does not suggest there or elsewhere in the epistle that he understands that the Roman Christians are currently being troubled in a similar way: there is no word of fraternal sympathy and unity in suffering, and the Roman Church is considered to be flourishing and able to adhere to its normal procedures (*Ep.* 59.19). As far as these hints can be taken, Roman Christians would seem to be free of trouble, in Cyprian's perception.[29]

We must be into May of the following year, 253, when the conciliar letter (*Ep.* 57) was despatched to Cornelius; there was still no knowledge at that time in Carthage of any danger to the Roman bishop and people. Later (*Ep.* 60), word came that Cornelius has publicly confessed; he is in the vanguard of a projected army of Roman confessors (*Ep.* 60.1), but only he (so far) has fallen into peril (§2: *unum primo adgressus*), and the trouble arrived, it is strongly emphasised by Cyprian in a subsequent letter to Cornelius' successor, Lucius, with great unexpectedness (*illic* [= Rome] *repentina persecutio nuper exorta sit unde contra ecclesiam Christi et episcopum Cornelium beatum martyrem, vosque omnes, saecularis potestas subito proruperit, Ep.* 61.3.1). Cyprian voices to Cornelius once again that he has already been himself the recipient of inspired warnings that troubles are about to visit Africa—or himself—also (*Ep.* 60.5.1: *providentia Domini monentis instruimur et divinae misericordiae consiliis salubribus admonemur adpropinquare iam certaminis et agonis nostri diem*).

We know—as Cyprian apparently did not at the time he wrote *Ep.* 60 (for he is anxious to catalogue fully Cornelius' confessional honours)—that Cornelius was despatched to nearby Centumcellae. And there he died, but was not put to death,[30] whilst apparently still holding office, at least before June 25, 253 (the commencement date of his successor's pontificate).[31] His exile can have lasted at the very longest five or six weeks.

We are left, without resources, to conjecture the reason for his sudden relegation. Despatch of bishops out of Rome was not without precedent,[32] and certainly the question need not have concerned Emperor Gallus personally (who had troubles enough to occupy his attention).[33] We do not know with complete certainty if any others, as Cyprian projected, were officially made to share his deportation.[34]

Our next information concerns Lucius, Cornelius' successor, elected to office in late June 253. His *relegatio* (*Ep.* 61.1.2) followed so closely his election that Cyprian had been able to write in the one and the same letter doubly congratulating him on his preferment and on his confession (*Ep.* 61.1.1). Now, in *Ep.* 61, Cyprian is writing *cum collegis* to congratulate Lucius once more, this time on his return from exile. Lucius had been accompanied by *comites* (§1.1) who also share in his release. Again the wording in this letter (§3: *illic repentina persecutio nuper exorta sit*) plainly shows that at Carthage the feared *persecutio* had failed to materialise.

When did Lucius return? The persecution broke out *nuper* (§3); Lucius was elected *nuper* (§1). That is not particularly helpful. Lucius died in early March 254,[35] before Easter of that year (April 23). Many have suggested that because Cyprian is writing *cum collegis* (cf. *Ep.* 61.4.2 *vicarias vero pro nobis ego et collegae et fraternitas omnis has ad vos litteras mittimus*), *Ep.* 61 must derive from a Council meeting; that meeting cannot be that of spring 254 (by which time Lucius was dead); therefore, it must be dated to autumn 253, and this is the season for Lucius' return. Unfortunately the only autumn Council meeting we know of during Cyprian's episcopate was that convened on September 1, 256 on the critical issue of rebaptism; we know of no such urgent question which would require a special autumn session in 253. There may have been none, for it was standard Cyprianic practice to confer *ad hoc* with local or visiting *collegae*; to write *cum collegis* does not necessarily imply the holding of a full Council of African bishops. What might be said is that in *Ep.* 61 Cyprian gives no sense at all of any long-suffering and languishing period of exile having been endured; there was only preparedness to face *supplicium* and *poena*, §2.2; *e silentio* Lucius and his *comites* were not *foris* (§4.2), that is to say, away from Rome, for very long. Their recall may possibly lie behind Valerian's (much exaggerated) reputation for initially regarding Christians with favour, witnessed by Dionysius of Alexandria, *ap.* Eusebius *H.E.* 7.10.3. Valerian would seem to be safely in power sometime about September-October 253. But they may not have had to wait even until Valerian's accession.

4. Conclusion

For Pontus, our source is notably silent on any "persecution of Gallus." For Carthage, we have an incidental reference to an *edictum* enjoining *sacrificia* on the *populus* (252) accompanied by popular hostility against Cyprian but without any apparent additional aftermath. It is only at the post-Easter Council meeting of (? early May) 253 that we find desperate apprehension of a coming persecution. Our sources show that it never eventuates in Carthage. And so when Pontius writes the *vita* of his bishop, though he is eloquent about the plague and the role Cyprian played in the conditions in Carthage during it (§9), he, too, is notably silent about any persecution between Decius and Valerian (even though he appears to echo the language of *Ep.* 59.6.1 in §7.2—*suffragiis saepe repetitis ad leonem postularetur*). And though Cyprian defended *fuga* at this time (*Ep.* 58.4), there is no sign in the *vita* or the correspondence that he felt the need to leave Carthage himself. So, too, when in about the year 254 Cyprian defends, in *Ep.* 66, against attack, his personal role and integrity as bishop, especially under persecution, and the treatment of *lapsi* which he, as bishop, has advocated, there is no sign in that letter of any persecution under Gallus (whereas there is much that refers to the period of Decius); but at the same time Cyprian indignantly upholds the validity of the *somnia* and *visiones* which have guided his policies and actions (§10). It is now not too difficult to reconstruct a context for this particular attack.

For Rome, we have the relatively brief exiles of Cornelius and of Lucius and his companions. They seem, not unnaturally, to have shared—in exile—Cyprian's apprehensions for general trouble and to have granted accordingly a general penitential amnesty along the African lines (*Ep.* 68.5.1: *illi* [= Cornelius and Lucius] *enim pleni spiritu*

Domini et in glorioso martyrio constituti dandam esse lapsis pacem censuerunt et paenitentia acta fructum communicationis et pacis negandum non esse litteris suis signaverunt).[36] It would be helpful to be sure how far the erstwhile *lapsi* had in reality redeemed themselves by "confession" in *Ep.* 60.2.5.

From Egypt, we have the claim that after a season of success and prosperity Gallus drove away (*ēlasen*) the holy men who supported by their prayers the emperor's peace and good health. Are these now to be identified as the *Roman* clerics whose exile (to be dated to mid-253) coincided with the collapse and downfall of Gallus' principate?

All subsequent reconstructions of "a persecution of Gallus," ancient and modern, appear to be based on this meagre factual basis, often assisted by interpreting premonitions into facts and usually lengthened by an arbitrary (and often erroneous) dating of Cyprian's correspondence.[37] When obscurity lies so deep over this period, the minor details of Cyprian's letters are to be ignored at one's historical peril.

THE CHURCHES IN COUNCIL

The churches everywhere in 251 were faced with the vexatious issue of penitential discipline. How were they to treat the large numbers who had apostatised in one way or another under the persecution of Decius? And those churches had postponed reaching a final resolution on that matter until they were at last free to meet in Council together. No doubt, on the pattern of what we can discern for Carthage (see the summary in *Ep.* 20.2 f.) as well as for Rome (*Ep.* 30.8), Sicily (see *Ep.* 30.5.2), and Alexandria (Dionys. Alex. *ap.* Euseb. *H.E.* 6.44.4), working guidelines had been drawn up, where circumstances allowed, for dealing interim with urgent cases until such collegiate resolutions were physically possible. But the remarkable feature we can discern in many churches of the time is this habit of conciliar consultation which the stirring ecclesiastical events of the 250s are everywhere to disclose, in the east as in the west; it is a reflex which must have become habitual over the preceding half-century or so.[38]

We can catch only tantalising glimpses of earlier conciliar decisions taken in North Africa itself: they dealt with a wide spectrum of matters, ranging from major issues of principle—the treatment of adulterers, *Ep.* 55.21.1 (where see nn. 87 and 93), the question of "rebaptism," *Epp.* 70.1.2, 71.4.1, 73.3.1—through more localised disciplinary action (*Ep.* 59.10.1, the heretical church of Privatus), down to quite minor general regulations (with penalties imposed for infringement), *Ep.* 1.1.1, 1.2.1 (clerics not to be nominated as legal guardians or trustees). And a Council meeting was possibly planned for 250, but the persecution intervened: the turbulent presbyter Novatus thus escaped "the judgment of bishops" (*iudicium sacerdotum*—note the plural—*Ep.* 52.3). But partial as our view is, we can see enough to appreciate that Cyprian inherited a pattern of consultation and conciliar resolution that had been set in a preceding generation (though we remain in simple ignorance of the frequency, normal attendance, and usual timing of such gatherings). These present letters, however, do permit us the invaluable opportunity of inspecting for the first time in close detail the sorts of agenda and activity that had by now become customary at these meetings.

Before Easter of 251, now that the persecution had died down (*Ep.* 55.6.1), invitations had gone out (in a lost festal letter?) to North African bishops to attend a Council at Carthage (*Ep.* 43.7.2). No doubt the bishops were given at the same time some indication of the major items featuring on the agenda to be dealt with—and were given themselves an opportunity to raise questions for resolution (cf. *Ep.* 56.3, *Ep.* 64). Cyprian, as bishop of Carthage, appears to be in charge of arranging such matters (cf. *Ep.* 56.3).

After celebrating the great Easter festival with their own people (cf. *Ep.* 56.3), bishops, accompanied perhaps by one or two of their presbyters and deacons (see *Ep.* 59 n. 76), set out on their journey—often an arduous and lengthy affair (cf. *Ep.* 62 n.1)—down to the great city. About a month was needed to allow all those wishing to attend time to complete their travels (cf. *Ep.* 59 n. 49). For 251 we do not know the attendance figures. All we do know is that the questions facing the assembly were pressing and urgent, and that Cyprian stresses on a number of occasions the generous tally of venerable bishops who gave their approval to the resolutions passed in this year (see *Ep.* 55 n. 20, *Ep.* 59 n. 2). All the same, a number of bishops may have been preoccupied with difficulties they were encountering in their home area, having only just emerged themselves from their own places of safe concealment: such absentees would receive copies of the conciliar resolutions after the meeting itself was over (*Ep.* 55.6.1). And whilst it is clear that the bishops were the ones who sat in debate and passed those resolutions (cf. *Ep.* 59.14.2), we must also remember that their attendant presbyters and deacons (*Ep.* 59.15.1) and a large body of the laity were present as well (*Ep.* 1 n. 3). These were assemblies that could run into several hundreds.

On a reasonable calculation it was late in April 251 (Easter Sunday having fallen on March 23) that the travellers began to make their way into Carthage for the deliberations. We do know that the debates on the penitential question could be described (somewhat defensively) as having been full and lengthy (*Scripturis diu ex utraque parte prolatis*, *Ep.* 55.6.1; cf. *Ep.* 54.3.3: *diu multumque tractatu inter nos habito*), but there is no word to suggest that the business in hand could not all be dealt with at this spring sitting (an additional autumn session is often conjectured, but unnecessarily).[39] We also know that whilst the bishops were in the course of their assembly, conflicting reports reached them on the episcopal elections in Rome (*Ep.* 45.2.1). The bishops resolved to suspend judgment on that issue and to despatch two of their number to Italy to investigate the truth of the matter (*Epp.* 44.1.2, 48.2.1, 48.3.2). But it seems clear that the assembly of bishops was already over and dispersed by the time the two episcopal envoys could report back with their findings. For letters had to go out to individual bishops all over Cyprian's *provincia* informing them of the outcome (*per provinciam nostram haec eadem collegis singulis in notitiam perferentes*, *Ep.* 45.1.3) and all those bishops, in turn, were expected to send over to Rome individual letters of recognition to Cornelius (*per omnes omnino istic positos [sc. episcopos] litterae fierent, sicut fiunt*, *Ep.* 48.3.2, cf. *Ep.* 55.1.2). It is plain that recognition of Cornelius could not be made by the bishops assembled together in Council (and Cyprian would never have missed the opportunity of appealing to such a conciliar motion in his attempts to deflect criticism of his embarrassing procrastination in *Epp.* 44, 45, 48—or in his attempts to convince Antonianus in *Ep.* 55). It also follows that any formal condemnation of Novatian cannot have taken place either at these particular proceedings in spring 251 (on this, see below).

The bishops so assembled in Carthage (where did they meet?) were faced with a series of disciplinary matters. Felicissimus and his five rebel presbyters (Felicissimus having already been excluded from the Carthaginian congregation, *Epp.* 41 and 42) were now formally excommunicated by the African bishops, after their case had been given a hearing (*auditis eis*); a full document was drawn up recording the bishops' *sententiae* and resolutions, and prepared for sending over to Rome (*Ep.* 45.4.1)—doubtless in the hopes of ensuring that they would be excluded from communion there also (cf. *Ep.* 59.1.1, 59.9.1). It was essential to staunch the spread of the breakaway movement. Similar excommunication was successfully sought for two lapsed bishops who had now allied themselves with the heretical church of the Numidian Privatus; they had already been condemned by a group of nine fellow bishops (drawn, at a guess, from their own Numidian locality), *Ep.* 59.10.2 And we may reasonably take the case of Repostus of Satunurca (*Ep.* 59.10.2) as a typical sample of what was now regulated about those lapsed bishops who refused to submit to penitence. In 252 he can be included by Cyprian amongst those bishops "whom we had excommunicated" (*a nobis abstentis, Ep.* 59.11.2). Their cases would have now come up for firm resolution, so that the way would be made clear for the appointment of a replacement bishop if need be (cf. *Ep.* 65: the lapsed Fortunatianus replaced by Epictetus at Assuras). This would seem to be the appropriate setting for the conciliar confirmation of the rule, recorded in *Ep.* 67.6.3 (? 256) as having been passed *iam pridem* and agreed to also by Cornelius, that lapsed clerics could be admitted to penitence only on terms of laicisation; they are to be excluded from "clerical appointment and priestly honours" (thus *Epp.* 65.1.1, 64.1.1; cf. *Ep.* 55.11.3 [Rome]). There remained one further disciplinary matter that called for clarification: to whom properly belonged the jursidiction for dealing with penitential cases, especially given the wide scattering of the brethren that had taken place before the onslaught of the persecution? It was resolved, in the interests of justice, that cases should be heard where the delict was alleged to have occurred (*Ep.* 59.14.2).

All the remaining items that we know were discussed at this Council of 251 concerned directly the central issue of penitence for apostates. *Ep.* 55 helpfully rehearses (to an African bishop who was not in attendance) those resolutions, as well as the reasoning that lay behind them: the decisions there recorded are tabulated in the introduction to *Ep. 55*. Cyprian makes no bones about the nature of the outcome of the debate: it was a "healthy compromise" (*temperamentum salubri moderatione libravimus, Ep.* 55.6.1) between the extremes of harsh and unrealistic rigorism and sinful and polluting laxity. And the debate itself was no mere formality: its quality, earnest concerns, and high seriousness emerge clearly and impressively from the résumé presented in *Ep. 55*. Cyprian, for one, would appear to have shifted ground significantly as a result of it, moving substantially away from the somewhat severer line of the formal tractate he had composed, the *De lapsis* (where there is no hint of the special concessions to *libellatici* that were approved as a major resolution of this Council). Indeed, in *Ep. 55*, he feels obliged openly to defend, and at length, that shift in stance, now plainly visible and under criticism (§§3.2—7.3).

Copies of these important resolutions were promptly communicated to Rome (*Ep.* 55.6.2), where the equivalent Italian Council had yet to meet (it could hardly be summoned until the dispute over the episcopal chair in Rome was further clarified). It would be reasonable to suppose that copies would find their way also to churches in Spain and in Gaul with whom Cyprian is later seen to be in communication in *Epp.* 67 and 68 (he has received a copy or synopsis of at least one conciliar document from Gaul in *Ep.* 68.1.1): after all, the churches there were confronted with the identical problems. No doubt such copies came with covering letters voicing the sort of sentiment which we find expressed in *Ep.* 57.5.1: there the African bishops inform Cornelius of further penitential concessions passed by them at a later Council (253) and urge: "we believe that you too, being sensible of God's paternal compassion, will agree with our decision."

When the Council did eventually meet in Rome in the course of 251 (see *Ep.* 49 intro. on the timing), it numbered "sixty bishops and a still greater number of presbyters and deacons" (Euseb. *H.E.* 6.43.2). Cyprian could triumphantly declare that the resolutions it reached on the penitential question harmonised with their own (*Ep.* 55.6.2). We do know that it dealt with one additional and major item: "it was unanimously decreed that Novatus [i.e. Novatian], together with the partners of his arrogance, and those who decided to agree with the man's brother-hating and most inhuman opinion, should be considered as strangers to the Church, but that such of the brethren as had fallen into the misfortune should be treated and restored with the medicines of repentance" (Euseb. *H.E.* 6.43.2, trans. Oulton). Eusebius adds vaguely on this excommunication that "in the rest of the provinces [*eparchias*] the shepherds in their different areas individually considered what was to be done [sc. about Novatian]" (*loc. cit.*). This appears to refer to bishops in the vicinity not present at the Italian Council but who were solicited for their views on the standing of Novatian and his followers. For Cornelius was able to append to a letter he wrote to Fabius of Antioch "a catalogue of the bishops present at Rome who condemned the stupidity of Novatus [i.e. Novatian], indicating at once both their names and the name of the community over which each one presided; and of those who were not present, indeed, at Rome but who signified in writing their assent to the judgment of the aforesaid, he mentions the names and, as well, the city where each lived and from which each wrote" (Euseb. *H.E.* 6.43.21 f., trans. Oulton). We should probably deduce that bishops from the Gallic, Spanish, and African provinces [*eparchias*] were included in this catalogue, with Cyprian figuring prominently amongst them. For Eusebius saw a copy of a (now lost) letter of Cyprian's which Cornelius also sent on to Antioch; in it Cyprian voiced the carefully guarded opinion that "it was reasonable and proper [*chrēnai eulogōs*] that the leader of the heresy should be excommunicated from the catholic Church and likewise all those who were led away with him" (Euseb. *H.E.* 6.43.3). Cyprian was doubtless giving his own personal view to Cornelius after having received his copy of the minutes of the Italian Council of 251 and having been asked for an expression of assent; he cannot yet cite in support any African conciliar resolution which had formally ostracised the Novatianists from communion.

Cornelius also included in the dossier he despatched over to Fabius in Antioch a copy of the minutes not only of the Italian Council of 251 but of the African Council that year as well (Euseb. *H.E.* 6.43.3). In this way, the findings of this African Council will have been disseminated widely in turn amongst the eastern churches, Fabius being in active communication with the major churches there (Euseb. *H.E.* 6.46.3)—just as Dionysius of Alexandria can later be well informed on the African stance over the "rebaptism" issue (*ap.* Euseb. *H.E.* 7.7.5). Despite the tyranny of long distances and the delays in hazardous communications, the churches everywhere were busily seeking to keep in close contact and, if possible, harmonious step with one another, freely exchanging their own views and passing on others' and putting especial weight upon resolutions that had been arrived at in Council together. Our sources do not happen to disclose any major eastern synod held in 251 but there was already one in preparation, on the twin issues of Novatianism and penitence, to be convened at Antioch (Euseb. *H.E.* 6.46.3, cf. 7.4 f.). There had certainly been a brisk exchange of (divergent) opinions amongst the bishops in the region (see Euseb. *H.E.* 6.43.3), and Dionysius of Alexandria can be viewed starting up a flurry of activity, communicating far into the east (Armenia) as well as over to the west with his fellow bishops and church leaders—even with our very fragmentary knowledge, we can trace nearly a dozen of his letters on these particular issues (see *Letters of Cyprian* 2 [ACW 44] intro. pp. 11 f.).

One item remains: when was Novatian excommunicated by the African churches meeting in Council? For in *Ep.* 68.2.1 Cyprian can write to Stephen in Rome sharply reminding him that "when Novatian . . . sent envoys to us in Africa desiring to be admitted to communion with us, he went away instead from our Council here (we were a large company of bishops) taking with him the following verdict: he was now outside and no one of us could therefore be in communion with him; for whereas Cornelius had been appointed bishop within the catholic Church by the judgment of God and by the choice of clergy and laity, he had attempted to set up a profane altar, to establish a spurious chair, and to offer sacrilegious sacrifices in opposition to the true bishop. And so, if he sought to return to sanity of mind and sound counsels, let him undertake penitence and return to the Church as a suppliant." For good measure Novatian is further characterised as *nuper retusus et refutatus et per totum orbem a sacerdotibus Dei abstentus* (*Ep.* 68.2.2).

When was this African *concilium plurimorum sacerdotum qui praesentes eramus* which rejected Novatian's overtures so summarily? We have seen that it cannot be the spring meeting of 251 (when the issue between Novatian and Cornelius was still left undecided by the African bishops in Council). Neither would it appear to have taken place when Cyprian was writing *Ep.* 55: nowhere can Cyprian talk of Novatian in the same terms as he does (say) of Privatus who, in *Ep.* 59.10.1, is flatly, and effectively, dismissed as having been *nonaginta episcoporum sententia condemnatum.* Rather, in *Ep.* 55, it is Novatian who has put himself outside the Church by breaking himself the bonds of charity (*Ep.* 55.8.5 f.; 24.1 ff.)—he hasn't yet been excommunicated (the word *abstentus* is not used) by the united verdict of the college of African bishops meeting in Council.

We are left, accordingly, with three conjectures.

(i) In *Ep.* 68.2.1 Cyprian is referring—tendentiously—to an *ad hoc* gathering of bishops in Carthage who in the course of 251 were called in to help pass judgment on the reports of their episcopal envoys, Caldonius and Fortunatus, when they came in from Italy; they then informed their fellow African bishops (by letter) of their conclusion and sent the Novatianist legation in Carthage packing (i.e. Maximus, Longinus, and Machaeus, *Ep.* 50.1.1, where see n. 2). The wording in *Ep.* 68.2.1 seems to be echoed closely in *Ep.* 44.1.2 f.: *ego et collegae plurimi qui ad me convenerant expectavimus adventum collegarum nostrorum Caldoni et Fortunati . . . nec necesse fuerit audiri ultra eos qui a Novatiano venerant missi*, where the personal note (*ego/ad me*) decidedly suggests not a formally convened Council at all (see *Ep.* 44 n.6 and cf. *Ep.* 1.1.1 *ego et collegae mei qui praesentes aderant*). On the other hand, in *Ep.* 68—whether misleadingly or not—Cyprian seems to be using language appropriate for an official motion (*sententia*) carried unanimously at a well-attended Council (*concilium*).

(ii) Cyprian is referring to a second (autumn) Council sitting of 251: that is otherwise unattested and not otherwise needed, but it must remain a distinct possibility (the envoys could then be the second Novatianist legation to Africa as reported in *Ep.* 50.1.1).

(iii) Cyprian is referring to the African Council meeting of spring 252. The Novatianist Maximus, after his earlier expulsion, sometime returned to Carthage (he is there by summer 252, *Ep.* 59.9.2): he sought (we might speculate) an audience with the African bishops when they next convened in mid-May 252 in order to present Novatian's case before them—just as Privatus attempted to present his own cause also (*Ep.* 59.10.1). But Maximus' delegation met with the same brusque reception as Privatus; they were rejected, sent away with a stinging condemnatory motion instead. Novatianism certainly figured on the agenda of that meeting in 252: to draw up the register of genuine African bishops (to be forwarded to Cornelius, *Ep.* 59.9.3) would have involved some formal decision on the status of Novatianist sympathisers. There seems to be nothing against such a setting for the meeting which Cyprian can cite to Stephen in *Ep.* 68, and I therefore incline (with due hesitation) to this third possibility.

In the year 252, an African Council meeting was certainly in session in Carthage on the Ides of May (*Ep.* 59.10.1), a little over a month after the Easter celebrations (April 11). Two items are known for sure: (i) Privatus' attempt to have his case reconsidered was firmly rejected (*Ep.* 59.10.1); (ii) a list was drawn up of the orthodox bishops in North Africa (tainted neither by lapse nor heresy) to be sent over to Cornelius for his guidance and information (*Ep.* 59.9.3). To compose such a list, a review (however summary) of all the bishoprics in the North African *provincia* (over the hundred mark) would have been called for. The tightness of the ecclesiastical organisation and discipline is remarkable: it was a time for stocktaking in the face of a number of schisms (those of Novatian, Felicissimus, and Privatus being prominent, but other rebels are known, e.g. Fortunatianus of Assuras, *Ep.* 65). Clearly, Council meetings provided a valuable opportunity for the exchange and dissemination of information. Cornelius, in his turn, was apparently expected to distribute that list further afield—not only he but his colleagues as well (*tu et collegae nostri*) would then be in a position to know with whom it was proper to communicate (*Ep.* 59.9.3).

Furthermore, it is argued in the introduction to *Ep.* 64 that nothing precludes that the items reported in that letter should not also be fitted into the context of this Council meeting—indeed any other suitable place for them at a *known* Council meeting is impossible to find: attendance figures at the other known Council meetings do not square with the sixty-six who were present for these items of *Ep.* 64. In which case, Fidus, for whatever reason unable to attend, had written requesting that two matters be drawn to the attention of the Council: (i) an infringement of the new penitential regulations and (ii) the propriety of baptising newborn infants before the eighth day (Fidus being inclined to the "old law of circumcision"). On the first question, the bishops after lengthy debate (*librato apud nos diu consilio, Ep.* 64.1.2) resolved to reprimand the bishop responsible but to allow that the illicit reconciliation, now that it had been effected, should stand. The bishops write plainly conscious of the weight of their collective authority—they might have gone much further than mere reprehension (*satis fuit obiurgare Therapium*, *Ep.* 64.1.2); and they are fully aware of their powers to police the regulations they establish in Council (the bishop is instructed never to do it again—*instruxisse ne quid tale de cetero faciat*, *Ep.* 64.1.2). On the second question, concerning the baptism of the newborn, the *sententia* (§6.1) of the collective bishops was firmly opposed to Fidus' own views (*longe aliud in concilio nostro visum est*, §2.1). Fidus was obviously expected to yield to the majority view of his episcopal colleagues.

In all, 66 bishops were in attendance (*Ep.* 64 *init.*) but the names are not recorded. It is more than likely that Cyprian sent on a copy of their *placita* to Rome (as he did in 251 and is to do again in 253): they may lurk under the *cetera quae in notitiam tuam perferenda hinc* of *Ep.* 59.9.4 (where see n. 45), one of which, at least, was an item that figured in this Council's minutes (the rejection of Privatus, *Ep.* 59.10.1).

Just as Fidus signified by letter to his fellow bishops points that were disturbing him and which thus became, in every likelihood, items on the Council agenda in 252 (see *Ep.* 64), so in *Ep.* 56 six bishops wrote to Cyprian drawing his attention to an anomalous penitential case and requesting that he discuss the matter fully with many of his colleagues: Cyprian promised that a firm ruling (*firma sententia*) would be reached at the meeting of bishops to be convened after Easter was over (§3). It has been argued above that this should be Easter 253 (April 3), and the case which the six bishops raised should, therefore, have figured at the Council meeting that was probably in session by very early May 253. Forty-two bishops were then in attendance, drawn heavily (if not exclusively) from proconsular sees and largely from districts not too far distant from Carthage (see *Ep.* 57 n. 1). Haste and apprehension may have dictated the (somewhat limited) size and distribution of this attendance: the question of relaxing penitential rigour for the penitent lapsed demanded quick and urgent resolution in the face of a feared renewal of persecution, and, besides, Carthage was a city doubly to be avoided, with not only persecution but plague as well hanging heavy in the air over its crowded alleyways. But the bishops manifest no sense at all of any diminution

in the authority of their collective decision: they write *Ep.* 57 informing Cornelius that they have profoundly modified agreed policy, in
obedience to the suggestions of the Holy Spirit and the promptings
of divine inspiration, and as their own consciences, under the circumstances, have dictated (e.g. §§5.1 f.). We know of no further matters that were discussed; after reaching this conclusion they may have
dispersed promptly in order to get back to their own threatened
flocks and to prepare, if need be, for battle or for flight. Cyprian himself proceeded to cancel his planned trip to Thibaris so as not to be
any distance or length of time away from his own people (*Ep.* 58.1.1).

But any conciliar follow-up in Italy proved not to be possible:
Cornelius was soon in exile, and so was his successor Lucius. Both
are associated by Cyprian with firmly upholding a policy whereby
"they decreed (*censuerunt*) that reconciliation was to be granted to the
fallen and in their letters they indicated (*litteris suis signaverunt*) that
when penance was complete penitents should not be denied the rewards of communion and reconciliation" (*Ep.* 68.5.1). They may well
have written from exile to their comprovincial bishops, expressing
approval of the new conciliatory policy initiated (so far as we know)
by this African Council of 253.[40]

Any Councils held in the other western provinces over these
years are lost to our view. We can say, however, from the evidence
of *Ep.* 67, that Spanish bishops could meet together for the ordination
of Sabinus, or write in with their approval: they, therefore, appear
to be organised on a similar regional and cooperative basis (*Ep.*
67.5.2). Similarly for the Gallic provinces: Cyprian could be written
to more than once (*semel atque iterum*), informed of decisions taken by
Faustinus of Lyons and "by the rest of our fellow bishops established
in the same province," *Ep.* 68.1.1. That should imply that they are
accustomed to holding similar conciliar discussions and shaping similar conciliar policies.

Over in the east a large assembly of bishops had long been
planned and was now at last mustering at Antioch, to discuss "the
innovation of Novatian." Dionysius of Alexandria writes to Lucius'
successor in Rome, Stephen, pointedly reminding him of the (recent)
event and its happy (though unexpected) outcome: "Let me assure
you, my brother, that all the churches in the east and still further
distant, which were previously divided, are now as one, and all their

presidents everywhere are agreed together, being overjoyed at the peace they have unexpectedly reached—Demetrian at Antioch, Theoctistus at Caesarea, Mazabanes at Aelia, Marinus at Tyre . . . , Heliodorus at Laodicea . . . , Helenus at Tarsus with all the churches of Cilicia, Firmilian with all Cappadocia. I have given the names of the most distinguished of the bishops only, to avoid making my letter too long and its contents tedious. All the same, the whole of the Syrias and Arabia . . . along with Mesopotamia and Pontus and Bithynia, and, to put it briefly, everyone everywhere is exceedingly delighted with the harmony and brotherly love they have attained, and give glory to God for it" (*ap.* Euseb. *H.E.* 7.5.1 f.).[41] Even over these few years church Councils were proving themselves to be a vital—and generally speaking, mutually accepted—instrument for reaching settlement on vexatious disputes. The question, however, still remained unanswered: what was to be done when such regional Councils came to sharply divergent conclusions?

CHRONOLOGY OF THE LETTERS

The relative dating of each letter is discussed in some detail under the heading "Date and Circumstances" in the commentary on the individual letters. But the reader would be well advised to read the letters not in their numerical order but in chronological sequence (insofar as it can be ascertained), if anything approaching an unfolding view of events is to be obtained from this correspondence.

First, *Ep.* 55, written after the death of Emperor Decius (? early June of 251) and after the African and Italian Councils of 251 have been held. It reviews many of the decisions taken at those Council meetings which Cornelius' rival, Novatian, has now put under serious challenge. It should be followed by *Ep.* 65: this discloses the ecclesiastical disarray and disharmony left in the wake of the persecution of Decius in a small inland town of Africa Proconsularis (there are rival bishops, one of whom had lapsed but is still commanding loyalty from some of his old congregation). Both of these letters fit into a context of the second half of 251/early 252.

Ep. 64 is best construed (though this is controversial) as emanating from the next African Council meeting, held in mid-May of 252: it starts off dealing with an infringement of the rules for penitential discipline which had been drawn up at the Council meeting in the previous year. It should be followed by *Ep*. 59, written well on in the summer of 252, when a hotly indignant Cyprian rehearses to Cornelius the misdemeanors, past and present, of Felicissimus and his followers, now allied to old heretics and formed into a breakaway church subsequent to the Council meeting of 252.

We then move into the year 253. *Ep*. 56 comes round about Eastertime (April 3) raising questions on penitence which were to be reviewed at the subsequent Council meeting (? early in May). The result we can then see in *Ep*. 57, a conciliar document which declares that a major shift in penitential discipline has been taken under fears of coming persecution: *Ep*. 58, cancelling a trip to Thibaris in the expectation of those advancing dangers, follows shortly. Word then comes of the arrest of Cornelius in Rome: *Ep*. 60 on that event will date to later on in the same month of May 253. Sometime further down this same year Cyprian has occasion to write to Cornelius' successor, Lucius, on his return from his (? brief) sojourn in exile, *Ep*. 61.

That leaves three letters whose placement is more insecure. *Ep*. 66 could well come next, in early 254—Cyprian has been bishop for six years: it reveals the continuance of internal strife within Cyprian's community. But *Ep*. 63 (on the mixed cup in the Eucharist) is difficult to pin down so definitely: persecution has been experienced but it is not, at the time of writing, felt to be imminent. The same period of early 254 is not incompatible with such a setting (but precision is not possible). And *Ep*. 62 (on Christians held to ransom by barbarian captors) must be placed even more vaguely, within the general period of Cyprian's episcopate.

Therefore, read in order *Epp*. 55 and 65 [251/early 252]; *Epp*. 64 and 59 [252]; *Epp*. 56, 57, 58, 60, and 61 [253]; and, finally, *Epp*. 66, 63 [? early 254], and *Ep*. 62.

Text and Translation

I translate the standard text by Hartel (*Corpus scriptorum ecclesiasticorum latinorum* 3.2, 1871: there is a Johnson reprint, 1965). But I do indicate clearly in the commentary the points where I feel serious misgivings about the text before me. And I rely—not always with great faith—on Hartel's witness to his manuscripts; for my focus has been to elucidate the social and ecclesiastical setting of this correspondence, not to prepare for a new edition of the letters. (That long-needed new edition, for *Corpus christianorum*, is in the capable hands of Dr. G. F. Diercks, who was kind enough to read my manuscript and to provide invaluable comments on it.)

I also translate Hartel's text keeping as close as I can manage to the Latin. I know that this results sometimes in stilted and mannered prose, at other times in an unnaturally grand style, and from time to time in an ungainly and obscure turn of phrase. But to eliminate all these into the more even and matter-of-fact style of modern English prose would be to miss the modes in which Cyprian habitually cast his ideas and expressed himself; it would also be to make misleadingly precise and definite where Cyprian in fact remains ambiguously, and sometimes maddeningly, vague and imprecise.

I must thank many people for their help during the time this particular volume was composed, above all colleagues at the Institute for Advanced Study, Princeton, and Churchill College, Cambridge. The facilities and hospitality of those two institutions, affording gloriously undistracted study, made it possible during the year 1979 largely to write up the final draft of this book. I am most appreciative. And I must, as always, thank my wife, who in her generous nature continues loyally to believe that what I am working on must be worth the while. My thanks, too, to Walter J. Burghardt, S.J., for altruistically editing this volume.

As with the two preceding volumes, I fondly dedicate this book to the memory of my son Peter, who was accidentally killed in Cambridge in the course of 1979 while this book was being written. *Huius animam refrigeret interim Deus.*

THE LETTERS OF
ST. CYPRIAN OF CARTHAGE

55-66

LETTER 55

Cyprian sends greetings to Antonianus his brother.[1]

1.1 My dearly beloved brother, the first letter of yours which I received, unhesitatingly upheld the united opinion of the college of bishops, thereby declaring your own adherence to the catholic Church.[2] In it you indicated that you rejected communion with Novatian but rather that you followed our counsel[3] and were, therefore, in full accord with our fellow bishop Cornelius.

1.2 You also wrote in your letter that I should convey a copy of that letter of yours to Cornelius, our mutual colleague, so that he might be relieved of any further concern and could rest assured that you are in communion with him, that is to say, in communion with the catholic Church.[4]

2.1 But there has reached me subsequently a second letter of yours delivered through the services of our fellow presbyter Quintus.[5] In this letter I perceive your conviction has started to waver, swayed by letters from Novatian.[6] For whereas previously you had declared your counsel and your accord with firm resolution,[7] you now request in this second letter that I write back to you explaining what heresy it is which Novatian has introduced and how it is that Cornelius can be in communion with Trofimus and those who have offered incense.[8]

2.2 Now, if it is true that your worries derive from anxious concern for the faith, and if it is out of such concern that you are inquiring into the truth on a matter of which you have doubts, then there is no cause for reproach that you should now feel concern and indecision and hesitation when holy fear is your motive.[9]

3.1 But as it is, I do observe that it was after you had declared your verdict in your first letter that you were subsequently shaken by those letters from Novatian. Now, my dearly beloved brother, I must make one point clear at the very outset: men of gravity who have

33

been solidly established and firmly founded upon a rock[10] are not shaken even by gale and hurricane, let alone by some trivial breeze. They would not have their convictions constantly tossed to and fro by squalls and gusts of wind, left swinging in doubt and uncertainty before the blasts of contrary opinion, nor would they shift from their resolution, once reached, laying themselves open to reproach for fickleness of purpose.

Lest this should happen in your case or in the case of anyone else[11] through the letters of Novatian, I shall briefly set out, as you request, my brother, an account of the matter.

3.2 And as my conduct also seems to have caused you to be troubled, I must start by clearing my own case and character in your eyes. I do not want it thought that it was out of any fickleness that I have retreated from my earlier position. Nor do I wish to give the appearance that, whereas at the beginning I originally upheld the full rigour of the gospel, I have subsequently slackened my attitude from my former strictness and zealousness, in that I have come to the view that conditions for reconciliation ought to be made less stringent for those who have stained their consciences by obtaining certificates of sacrifice as well as for those who have actually committed the heinous act of sacrifice. Neither of these positions I adopted without careful deliberation and lengthy consideration.[12]

4.1 At the time of the persecution, when men were still locked in combat and in the heat of the glorious battle, what was incumbent on us was to arouse with all our might the fighting strength of our soldiers, using every resource of exhortation. In particular, we had to instill fresh spirit into the hearts of the fallen, rallying them by the trumpet call of our words in order to get them to pursue the route to repentance, but not just through prayer and lamentation. Since the opportunity was still there to rejoin the fray and to recover their salvation, they needed to be spurred on by the goad of our rebukes, to be stimulated to ardour for confession and zeal for the glories of martyrdom.

4.2 In fact, when my presbyters and deacons wrote to me that there were lapsed who could not be restrained and in their impatience were demanding to be admitted to communion, in the reply which I wrote (in a letter which you can still see) I ended with these words: "If they are in such excessive haste, they have what they are demanding within their own power—in fact present circumstances generously provide them with more than what they demand. The battle is still being fought; each day the contest is being staged. If they are genuinely and resolutely repentant of their fault and if the fervour of their faith is overpoweringly strong, he who cannot be deferred can be crowned."[13]

4.3 But, as to what was to be determined about the case of the lapsed, I postponed any decision. My idea was that when peace and tranquillity had been restored and God in His goodness allowed the bishops to gather together, then that was the time for everyone to contribute and exchange their views together and to deliberate upon them, and it was after that that we should determine what ought to be done. But should anyone have the presumption to admit the lapsed to communion without waiting for our deliberations and the ruling determined on the basis of that general deliberation, then he was himself to be excluded from communion.[14]

5. Moreover, I also wrote to this effect at some length to the clergy in Rome, who were at the time managing affairs without a bishop, as well as to the confessors there—the presbyter Maximus and the others who were then shut up in their prison but who are now united with Cornelius in the Church.[15] You can gather from their reply that I wrote to them in this vein. This is what they said in their letter: "However, on this major issue we are indeed in agreement with the opinion which you yourself have argued, namely, that we must wait first, until the Church has peace, and then, after bishops, presbyters, deacons, confessors, and the laity who have remained steadfast have exchanged views in conference together, we can deal with the question of the lapsed."[16] And at the conclusion to this letter (Novatian wrote it at the time, and when he read out aloud himself what he had written, Moyses, then still a confessor and now a martyr, gave to it his signature[17]) there was expressed the view that reconciliation should be granted to the lapsed who were sick and near death. This letter was distributed to all parts of the world and has reached the knowledge of all the churches and all the brethren.[18]

6.1 And, in accordance with what had been planned beforehand, when the persecution died down and opportunity offered for us to convene together,[19] there gathered in Council a generous number of bishops who had been preserved safe and unharmed thanks to their own staunch faith and the protection of the Lord.[20] Scriptural passages were produced, in a lengthy debate, on both sides of the issue[21] and eventually we arrived at a balanced and moderate decision, striking a healthy mean.[22] On the one hand, hopes for reconciliation and for admission to communion were not to be denied altogether to the lapsed, for there was the danger, otherwise, that in their despair they might fall away even further, and finding themselves shut out from the Church,[23] they might follow the ways of the world and start living no better than pagans. But in turn, on the other side, the strictness of the gospel teachings ought not be so relaxed that the fallen should be allowed to come rushing forward to communion pell-mell. Rather they should undergo prolonged penitence, and with grief and tears beg for indulgence from the Father; their various cases should be scrutinised individually, along with their personal attitudes and the special pressures under which they may have acted.[24]

All this is contained in the document which I am sure must have reached you; in it there are listed, in summary form, the various resolutions we passed.[25]

6.2 And in case anyone might regard the number of bishops who met in Africa to have been too few, you should know that we wrote to Rome also on this matter, to our colleague Cornelius.[26] And he, meeting in Council with a large number of his fellow bishops, has agreed upon the same verdict as ours, after debating with equal seriousness and striking the same healthy balance.[27]

7.1 I have felt compelled to write to you now on all this, so that you can be convinced that I have taken no action without grave consideration,[28] but that, according to the policy I had adopted in my earlier letters, I deferred all questions for determination at our debates together in Council. I certainly did not admit to communion any of the fallen before that time, for it was still possible for them to win not only pardon but even a martyr's crown.

7.2 But, afterwards, as the college of bishops harmoniously agreed[29] and as was demanded in the interests of gathering our scattered brethren together and of healing their wounds, I yielded to the urgent needs of the times and considered we ought to make provisions that would bring salvation to the many. And you should realise that today I am not deviating in any way from those measures which were resolutely adopted at our Council after we had debated together, however many may be the rumours that are now widely broadcast, and whatever the lies now in general circulation against the bishops of God—slanders that have in fact issued from the mouth of the devil in an attempt to rupture the bonds of catholic unity.

7.3 But your duty is clear. As a loyal brother and as a fellow bishop who is at one with us, you should not lend a ready ear to the words of apostates and slanderers; rather you should take care in judging the actions which your colleagues, men of moderation and sobriety, have taken, in the light of what you know about our lives and strict moral conduct.[30]

8.1 I now turn, my dearly beloved brother, to the character of our colleague Cornelius. My purpose is that you should have a more truthful appreciation of Cornelius, as we do, relying not on the lies of evil-tongued calumniators but rather on the judgment of God, who made him a bishop, and on the testimony of his fellow bishops, who, without exception the whole world over, have given him their approbation in unanimous accord.[31]

8.2 Firstly, what commends our dearly beloved Cornelius to God and to Christ and His Church as well as to all of his fellow bishops and what brings him particular credit and renown is this: Cornelius did not get to the episcopate by one sudden step; rather, having advanced through all the successive clerical offices and having served the Lord honourably in these services of religious administration, he reached the lofty pinnacle of the episcopacy by climbing up through every grade in the Church's ministry.[32]

8.3 In the second place, Cornelius neither solicited nor sought that office of bishop, much less did he come charging in and seize it, like some other people who are swollen and bloated with their conceit and arrogance. But he remained as ever gentle and meek, behaving precisely in the manner usually displayed by those who are chosen by God's will for such a position. As you would expect of a man of modesty and virginal chastity, a man of inborn humility and unfailing self-effacement, so far from resorting to violence in order to be made bishop, as certain other people have done, he actually suffered violence himself in that he had to be coerced into accepting that office of bishop.[33]

8.4 And bishop he was made, by a large number of our colleagues who were present at the time in the city of Rome and who have sent to us on the subject of his appointment testimonials which acclaim his honour and esteem and cover him with glory by their praises.[34] Moreover, Cornelius was made bishop by the choice of God and of His Christ, by the favourable witness of almost all of the clergy, by the votes of the laity then present, and by the assembly of bishops, men of maturity and integrity.[35] And he was made bishop when no one else had been made bishop before him, when the position of Fabian, that is to say, the position of Peter and the office of the bishop's chair, was vacant.[36]

But that position once having been filled by the will of God and that appointment having been ratified by the consent of us all,[37] if anyone wants to be made a bishop after that, it has to be done outside the Church: if a man does not uphold the Church's unity, it is not possible for him to have the Church's ordination. No matter who he may be, and however much he may sing his own praises, and whatever rights he may lay claim to, he is not one of us, he is an alien, he is an outsider. And in these cases there cannot be, after the first, any second appointment; should, therefore, anyone be appointed after the one who must be the only one appointed, he becomes then not even appointed to the second place, but nothing at all.

9.1 So, then, Cornelius took on this office of bishop, obtained neither through any corruption nor any extortion but through the will of God, who is the one who makes bishops.[38] Look at the courage he displayed in the very act of taking on that office, look at his resoluteness of spirit, the steadfastness of his faith; these are qualities we cannot fail to recognise, if we are honest, and admire. For he took his seat on his bishop's chair in Rome without a tremor of fear precisely at the time when that savage tyrant was menacing bishops of God with dire and dreadful horrors,[39] at a time when news that a rival emperor was being raised up against him he would receive with far greater patience and forbearance than word that a bishop of God was being appointed in Rome.[40]

9.2 There can be no doubt, dearest brother, that such a bishop deserves to be honoured with the highest commendation for his faith and courage. He must surely be accounted amongst the glorious confessors and martyrs, for he remained seated on his chair for so long a time, awaiting the executioners of his own body, the avengers of that enraged tyrant.[41] Cornelius had resisted his ferocious edicts,[42] in the vigour of his faith he had trampled underfoot all his threats and torments and tortures. They would come to attack him, sword in hand, to crucify him, to roast him in flames, to mangle his bowels and limbs in some exquisite form of punishment. It is true that the Lord, our protector, in His majesty and goodness did protect, after his appointment, the one who was appointed bishop according to His will. Yet, from the point of view of his readiness to sacrifice himself[43] and of the fears he endured, Cornelius suffered all that he could suffer.[44] The tyrant was later to be vanquished by the arms of battle; Cornelius had vanquished him already by his office of bishop.[45]

10.1 But don't be surprised, all the same, that there are in circulation some disgraceful and malicious stories concerning him. You must be aware that this is a work the devil is always engaged in, to lash the servants of God with lies and to disfigure their glorious reputation with fictitious rumours so that those who shine brightly in the light of their own conscience may be blackened by the reports of others.[46]

10.2 And you should also be aware that our colleagues have inquired into the matter[47] and have ascertained, beyond any shadow of doubt, that Cornelius has not been soiled with the stain from any certificate of sacrifice (a story which some are broadcasting), neither has he joined sacrilegiously in communion with bishops who themselves have sacrificed; rather he has united with us only those whose cases have been heard and whose innocence has been established.[48]

11.1 Indeed, in the case of Trofimus (on which you ask that I write to you), the situation is quite different from that reported to you by the rumour and lies purveyed by the spiteful. For our dearly beloved brother Cornelius has done no more than our predecessors also have often done: for the sake of gathering our scattered brethren together, he has made concessions in the face of necessity.[49]

11.2 Large numbers of Trofimus' congregation had seceded, following Trofimus. But Trofimus then proceeded to return to the Church and to acknowledge his former error, making amends for his offence and penitently begging for pardon. Indeed, he showed perfect humility and atonement by calling back the brethren whom he had so recently led away. His prayers were therefore heard and into the Church of the Lord were admitted not so much Trofimus as the large number of brethren who had remained with Trofimus, all of whom would have refused to return to the Church had they not come in the company of Trofimus.[50]

11.3 And so, after a large number of our colleagues there had debated the matter together,[51] Trofimus was received back; the return of the brethren and salvation restored to so many brought atonement on his behalf. Yet Trofimus was allowed in only on the condition that he be admitted to communion as a layman—it is not true (as letters from spiteful enemies have told you) that he now occupies the position of bishop.[52]

12. You also mention that it has been reported to you that Cornelius is admitting to communion, indiscriminately, those who have sacrificed; this, too, is one of those fictions and rumours originating with those apostates.[53] For those who withdraw from us are incapable of praising us, nor should we expect to find favour with those who reject favour with us,[54] who rebel against the Church, and who wildly fling themselves into the work of inciting our brothers away from the Church. And so, my dearly beloved brother, I do ask you not to listen too readily to whatever stories are being spread about concerning Cornelius, or myself, nor to give ready credence to them.

13.1 But the facts are as follows.

Should anyone fall seriously ill, in accordance with our resolution we bring comfort to them in their time of danger.[55] But once comfort has been brought to them and peace has been granted to them in that danger, we cannot then set about choking them or suffocating them or, by laying violent hands on them ourselves, forcing on their end. It is as if they absolutely have to die after so receiving peace, because it is to the *dying* that we grant peace! Whereas, in fact, we can see clear proof of God's loving-kindness and His paternal gentleness, should it so happen that those who receive the pledge of (eternal) life by being granted peace, then have their own lives prolonged here on earth after receiving that peace.[56]

And so, if, after the bestowal of peace, God should grant a reprieve, no one should find in that grounds for attacking their bishops, especially as it has been firmly resolved that we are to bring comfort to our brothers who are in danger of death.

13.2 What is more, my dearly beloved brother, you should not judge (as some do) that those who obtained certificates are to be put on a par with those who offered sacrifice. Why, even amongst those who actually sacrificed there is often to be discerned a great diversity in circumstances and conditions. For example, we should not put on a par the man who without hesitation sprang forward of his own free will to perform the accursed sacrifice, and another who after putting up a long struggle and resistance eventually approached that deadly task only under compulsion.[57] Equally different is the man who thrust forward his entire family as well as himself, and another who alone confronted the test on behalf of everyone else, thereby protecting his wife, his children, and his entire household at the cost of endangering himself.[58] Finally, the man who forced his own tenants and friends to perpetrate that criminal action is not to be equated with the man who spared his tenants and farmers,[59] who welcomed under the shelter of his own roof many brethren who were refugees in flight on their way to exile,[60] one who can present and offer before the Lord many souls alive and safe today to intercede for pardon on behalf on his one wounded soul.

14.1 There are, then, these great differences even amongst those who offered sacrifice. It is, therefore, manifestly callous and cruelly overrigid to insist on including amongst those who did offer sacrifice those who merely obtained certificates. For in the case of a person who acquired such a certificate[61] he may plead for himself: "I had previously read and I had learnt from my bishop's preaching[62] that we should not offer sacrifice to idols and that a servant of God ought not to worship images. And so, in order to avoid doing this action which was forbidden, I seized an opportunity which offered itself for obtaining a certificate (which I would certainly not have acquired had there not presented itself such an opportunity).[63] I either went up to the magistrate myself or I gave instructions to another who was on his way up to him. I declared that I was a Christian, that it was forbidden to me to offer sacrifice, that I could not approach the altars of the devil, and that I was, therefore, offering payment in order to avoid doing what was forbidden to me."

14.2 But as it is, the person who was thus tainted with a certificate has learnt from our admonitions that he ought not to have done even this and that, even though his hands remain undefiled and his mouth unpolluted by any contact with that deadly food, his conscience nonetheless has been polluted.[64] After hearing this advice from us, he is now in tears, and he is sorrowful, realising that he has sinned. But he thus gives clear assurance that, whilst in the past he went astray not so much out of wickedness as out of error, he is now ready and instructed for facing the future.

15.1 But if we are to reject the repentance of such people (who remain in some degree confident, and not overburdened, in their consciences), they will promptly follow the devil's invitation and dash off into heresy and schism,[65] taking along their wives and their children whom they had preserved in safety.

And as for us, on the day of judgment there will be found written down against our names that we failed to look after the sheep that was wounded, and that for the sake of one wounded sheep we lost many that were unharmed; and that, whereas the Lord left the ninety-nine sheep that were sound and went in search of the one which had strayed and was weary and having found it He carried it Himself on His own shoulders, we not only fail to seek out those that are weary[66] but we even drive them away when they approach us. It will be charged to us that precisely at the present time when false prophets are running amok in the flock of Christ, tearing it to pieces, we are presenting an opening to dogs and wolves to do their worst; those who were not destroyed through the attacks of the persecution, we are now destroying ourselves through our own callousness and inhumanity.[67]

15.2 And so, my dearly beloved brother, what will we have done about the words of the Apostle: *I please all men in all things, seeking not what is profitable to myself but profitable to the many, that they may be saved. Be imitators of me just as I also am of Christ?* And again he says: *To the weak I became weak that I might gain the weak.* As also he says: *If one member suffers, all the other members suffer with it, and if one member rejoices, all the other members rejoice with it.*[68]

16.1 But quite different, dearly beloved brother, is the thinking of philosophers, in particular of the Stoics:[69] they claim that all sins are equal and that it is quite wrong for a man of gravity to be easily moved to pity.[70] But the fact is that a vast distance separates Christians and philosophers, and we are warned by the Apostle: *Beware lest you fall prey to the empty wiles of philosophy.*[71] We ought, therefore, to shun any notions which do not issue from the clemency of God but which are rather begotten of the arrogance and rigidity of philosophy.

16.2 By contrast, we read of Moses in the Scriptures: *Now Moses was an exceedingly gentle man*. And in His own Gospel the Lord says: *Be merciful just as your Father has shown mercy to you*. And again: *The healthy have no need of a doctor but rather those who are sick*.[72]

16.3 What sort of healing art can a man practise who claims: "I look after only the healthy" (who do not require any doctor)?[73] Whereas it is to those who are wounded that we ought to provide our assistance and our healing remedies. And we should not regard those who we see were injured in the fatal persecution as dead but rather as lying unconscious. I say unconscious, for had they been completely dead, none of them would ever have become subsequently confessors and, indeed, martyrs.[74]

17.1 There is, therefore, still within them that which by subsequent penitence may be revived into faith. And moreover, penitence is the source which provides arms and strength for renewed valour.

17.2 But a man cannot be so rearmed if he falls away altogether out of despair. For if he has been cruelly and harshly excluded from the Church, he may turn to the ways of the heathen and the practices of the world;[75] or, being cast out from the Church, he may go over and join the heretics and schismatics, but even if he may subsequently be put to death for the sake of the Name, it will not be possible for him to merit a crown by his death, being as he is outside the Church and cut off from the unity of charity.[76]

17.3 In the light of all this, dearly beloved brother, it was our resolution that their cases should each be examined separately. For a start, those who had obtained certificates should be admitted to communion.[77] But in the case of those who had sacrificed, comfort should be brought to them at the hour of their death;[78] our reasoning was that in the grave there is no confession[79] and that we cannot insist that a man does penitence if the fruits of that penitence are withheld from him.

So now, should battle overtake him before his death, he will be found strengthened by us and armed for battle; if, on the other hand, he should fall desperately ill before any such battle, he departs with the solace of being restored to peace and to communion.[80]

18.1 But the Lord is the one who will come to judge; we pass no prejudgment ourselves. If He finds the sinner's repentance to have been fully and satisfactorily completed, then He can ratify the verdict which we have determined here on earth.[81] If, on the other hand, we have been fooled by someone's sham repentance, God, who is not mocked and who can see into the hearts of men,[82] will pass judgment on matters which we have discerned ourselves but imperfectly, and the Lord will emend the sentence of His servants.

Yet, for our part, my brother, we ought all the while to keep in mind the words of Scripture: 18.2 *A brother who helps a brother will be exalted*, and that the Apostle likewise has said: *Each one of you keep watch over yourselves lest you, too, fall into temptation; bear one another's burdens, and so you will fulfill the law of Christ.* We should further recall that he also warns in his epistle, by way of reproof to the proud and to break their arrogance: *And he who thinks he stands, let him take heed lest he fall*, as elsewhere he also says: *Who are you that you pass judgment on another man's servant? To his own master he stands or falls. But stand he shall, for God has power to keep him upright.* We should remember, too, the word of John when he demonstrates that Jesus Christ the Lord is our advocate and propitiator for our sins: *My little children, these things I write to you lest you fall into sin. But if anyone has sinned, we have as advocate before the Father Jesus Christ the Just: He is Himself the propitiation for our sins.* And the apostle Paul has similarly declared in his epistle: *If Christ died for us when we were still sinners, how much more surely, being now justified in His blood, shall we be rescued through Him from the divine wrath.*[83]

19.1 Bearing in mind this kindness and mercy which He shows, we have no right ourselves to be overrigid or harsh and callous in caring for our brothers. Rather we ought to mourn with those who mourn and weep with those who weep;[84] in so far as we can, we should set them on their feet again with the help and comfort of our love. We have no right to be so hardhearted and unyielding[85] as to knock back their repentance, but, on the other side, neither ought we to be so soft and easygoing as to slacken the rules and let all and sundry return to communion.

19.2 See, your injured brother lies there before you on the battlefield, wounded at the hands of our foe. On the one side is the devil, striving to have killed the man he has already wounded; on the other side is Christ, urging that the man whom He has redeemed should not be wholly lost. Which of these two do we assist? On whose side do we stand? Do we lend our support to the devil so that he can destroy him; do we simply walk past our brother lying there half-dead, like the priest and levite in the Gospel?[86] Or rather, being priests of God and of Christ, do we imitate Christ's teaching and example, snatch our wounded brother from the jaws of our foe, tend him, and keep him safe for God's judgment?

20.1 There is no reason for you to imagine, dearly beloved brother, that our brethren will be any the less courageous or that there will be a decline in the number of martyrs simply because repentance is made easier for the fallen and some hope of reconciliation has now been offered to those who do penance. For the strength of the true believers continues unshaken, the integrity of those who fear and love God with all their hearts remains as steadfast and as firm as ever.

20.2 Now even in the case of adulterers we allow a certain period for penitence and then peace is granted to them. Yet that has not caused any decline in virginity in the Church; the glorious ideal of chastity is not fading away simply because of the sins of others. The Church continues to flourish and bloom, crowned with the flowers of her many virgins; chastity and continence preserve their long-continued glory, the power of purity is not crushed because penitence and pardon are conceded to the adulterer.[87]

20.3 And you must realise that it is one thing for a man to stand by, awaiting the granting of pardon,[88] and quite another thing for him to achieve the heights of glory; it is one thing for him to be thrown into prison and not to emerge from it until he pays the very last farthing,[89] and quite another thing for him to receive all at once the rewards for faith and valour;[90] it is one thing for a man to be wracked by long grieving over his sins and to be purged and purified over a lengthy period of time by fire,[91] and it is quite another thing for him to have purged away all his sins by a martyr's death.[92] In a word, to hang in doubt on the day of judgment awaiting the verdict of the Lord is far different from being crowned by the Lord without a moment's delay.

21.1 And you must remember that even amongst our predecessors there were certain bishops here in our own province[93] who judged that peace ought not to be granted to adulterers and they, therefore, shut off completely any room for penitence in the case of sins of adultery. And yet that did not cause them to withdraw from the college of their fellow bishops, nor to shatter the unity of the catholic Church, obstinate in their harshness and rigour though they remained. Accordingly, he who refused to grant peace to adulterers did not separate himself from the Church simply because others were granting such peace. 21.2 Provided that the bonds of harmony remain unbroken and that the sacred unity of the catholic Church continues unimpaired,[94] each individual bishop can arrange and order his own affairs, in the knowledge that one day he must render an account to the Lord for his own conduct.[95]

22.1 For my own part, I am astonished that there are some who are so obstinate as to judge that no opportunity for penitence ought to be granted to the fallen and who consider that pardon must be denied to those who do penance. And yet it is written: *Remember whence you have fallen, do penance and perform your former good works.*[96] Now these words are certainly directed at a man who has undoubtedly fallen and whom the Lord is encouraging to rise up again through good works. For it is also written: *Almsgiving delivers from death,*[97] and, there, is clearly meant not deliverance from that death which the blood of Christ has quenched once and for all and from which the saving grace of baptism and of our Redeemer has delivered us,[98] but deliverance from that death which afterwards creeps in through sin.[99]

Furthermore, in another passage, an opportunity is indeed granted for penitence and the Lord actually threatens the person who fails to do penitence: *I have* (He says) *many things against you because you allow your wife Jezabel, who declares herself to be a prophetess, to teach and to seduce my servants, to commit fornication and to eat of foods offered in sacrifice, and I gave to her an opportunity to do penitence and she refused to repent of her fornication. See, I will cast her upon a couch, and those who have fornicated with her I will cast into great tribulation unless they do penitence for their deeds.*[100] Obviously the Lord would not have encouraged them to do penitence were it not the case that He promises pardon to the penitent. And to this effect in the Gospels He declares: *I say to you that likewise there will be rejoicing in heaven over a sinner who does penitence rather than over ninety-nine just who have no need of penitence.*[101]

22.3 We read in Scripture: *God did not make death neither does He take joy in the destruction of the living.*[102] Clearly, therefore, He who would have no one perish desires that sinners should do penitence and through penitence return again to life. Hence, too, through the prophet Joel He proclaims in these words: *And now the Lord your God says, return to me with all your heart, at the same time with fasting and weeping and mourning, and rend your hearts and not your garments, and return to the Lord your God because He is merciful and loving, slow to anger and full of kindness and He condemns the evil He has inflicted.*[103] 22.4 Similarly we read in the Psalms of both the strictness and the compassion of God, who is at once menacing and merciful, who punishes that He may correct and when He has corrected saves: *I will visit*, He says, *their wicked deeds with the rod and with the lash their iniquities. But my mercy I will not scatter away from them.*[104]

23.1 The Lord also illustrates the compassion of God the Father when He says in the Gospel: *What man is there among you who if his son should ask for bread would hand him a stone, or if he should ask for a fish would hand him a snake? If you, then, evil as you are, know how to give good gifts to your sons, how much more will your heavenly Father give good things to those who ask Him?*[105]

23.2 Here the Lord is drawing a comparison between a father according to the flesh and God the Father with His never-ending and boundless compassion. Now suppose that evil, earthly father has been gravely offended by his sinful and wicked son: even so, if later on he should see that this same son has now mended his ways, that he has put aside the iniquities of his past life, that by remorse and repentance he has been restored to sober and honest living and to the practice of virtue, why then he is glad and rejoices, and he welcomes back the son whom he has previously thrown out and with a father's joy and delight embraces his son.

But how much more must that one, true Father who is kind and merciful and compassionate, indeed who is Himself kindness and mercy and compassion, how much more must He take joy in the repentance of His own sons and no longer threaten them with His wrath if they are repentant or with punishment if they weep and mourn, but promise to them instead His pardon and forgiveness.

23.3 Hence, in the Gospel the Lord can call blessed those who mourn,[106] for he who mourns arouses His mercy, whereas he who is obdurate and proud heaps wrath upon himself and punishment in the judgment to come. 23.4 And that is the reason why, dearly beloved brother, in the case of those who do no penance, who give no evidence that they are wholeheartedly sorry for their sins, who make no public profession of their grief, we have determined that they ought to be altogether excluded from any hope of peace and communion if, on becoming dangerously ill, they should start to beg for them.[107] Obviously it is not repentance for their sin which drives them to ask but the warning of fast-approaching death; and he does not deserve to receive consolation in death who has failed to reflect that one day he must die.

24.1 Now as regards Novatian personally, dearly beloved brother, you ask that I write to you explaining what heresy it is he has introduced. In the first place I must make clear to you that it is not right for us even to want to know what it is he is teaching, since he is teaching *outside*. Whoever he may be, whatever his qualities, he can be no Christian who is not inside the Church of Christ. Sing his own praises for all he is worth, flaunt as he will in proud phrases his philosophy and his eloquence,[108] he has, nonetheless, failed to maintain charity with his brethren and unity with the Church, and he has therefore lost even what he had formerly been.[109]

24.2 Unless you really think that he is a genuine bishop who, at a time when a bishop had already been made within the Church by sixteen of our fellow bishops, goes to great efforts and intrigue to get himself made a bishop at the hands of renegades, and made a fake and foreign bishop at that![110] Moreover, there is but one Church founded by Christ but it is divided into many members throughout the world; likewise, there is but one episcopate but it is spread amongst the harmonious host of all the numerous bishops. And yet, despite this arrangement established by God, despite this unity in the catholic Church which is universally linked and locked together, he is now attempting to set up a man-made church and he is sending out to numerous cities upstart apostles of his own in order to lay down brand-new foundations for an establishment of his own devising.[111] And whereas in every one of the provinces and each of the cities there have been long since appointed bishops who are venerable in age, sound in faith, tested in tribulation, and proscribed in persecution,[112] he even has the effrontery to appoint over and above them a new set of spurious bishops.[113]

24.3 Fancy imagining that he could sweep the entire globe with this perverse novelty or that he could smash the framework of the

Church's body simply by scattering his seeds of discord. He fails to realise that though schismatics are always hot with enthusiasm at the very beginning, they are never able to expand or increase what they have unlawfully initiated but that, right from the start, they begin to fade away, they and all their evil rivalries.

24.4 Indeed he could not now retain the position of bishop even if he had been made bishop before anyone else, since he has broken away from the body of his fellow bishops and the unity of the Church. For the Apostle does warn us to give support to one another lest we depart from that unity which God has established. To quote his own words: *Supporting one another in love, striving to preserve the unity of the Spirit in the bond of peace.*[114] A man, therefore, who preserves neither the unity of the Spirit nor the bond of peace but cuts himself off from the ties of the Church and the college of bishops can have neither the power nor the dignity of a bishop, for he has chosen to maintain neither the unity nor the peace of the episcopate.

25.1 And what is more, look at the puffed-up arrogance of it all, the total disregard for meekness and humility, the supreme display of personal pride, that a man should dare to do or even imagine himself able to do what the Lord did not allow even the apostles to do, that he should think he is able to divide the tares from the wheat, or as if it was to him that had been granted power to wield the winnowing fan and to cleanse the threshing floor, that he should set about separating the chaff from the grain.[115]

25.2 And despite the fact that the Apostle says: *But in a great household there are not only vessels of gold and of silver but also vessels of wood and of clay*, he actually thinks he can pick out the vessels that are of gold and of silver but that he can despise, condemn, and cast away the vessels that are of wood and of clay, whereas the vessels of wood are to be burnt in the flames of the divine fire only on the day of the Lord and the vessels of clay are to be smashed only by the one to whom has been entrusted the rod of iron.[116]

26.1 But if he has really set himself up as the searcher of men's hearts and reins and as the judge of others,[117] then let him at least judge in all cases with complete fairness.[118] He must be fully aware of the words of Scripture: *See, you have been made whole; sin no more lest anything worse befall you.*[119] Let him, therefore, exclude from his company and following defrauders and adulterers.[120] For the case of one who has committed adultery is far graver and much more serious than the case of one who has obtained a certificate of sacrifice: the latter has sinned under compulsion, the former of his own choice;[121] the latter was the victim of error, thinking that it was enough to avoid offering sacrifice, the former has assailed another's marriage rights or he has visited some brothel, going down into the sewers and slimy stews of the rabble[122] and there his own sanctified body, God's temple, he has befouled with loathsome filth. To quote the Apostle: *Every sin that man commits is outside the body, but he who commits adultery sins against his own body.*[123]

26.2 Yet even to these sinners penitence is allowed and hope is still left to them if they show sorrow and make amends for their sin, just as the Apostle himself indicates: *I fear lest perchance when I come to you I may mourn over many of those who sinned before and have not repented of the foul deeds they have practised, of their acts of fornication and lust.*[124]

27.1 And there are no grounds for these upstart heretics to feel self-satisfied because, as they say, they have no communion with idolaters. For in their company are both defrauders and adulterers, and such sinners are guilty of the crime of idolatry if you follow the words of the Apostle: *Know this well and understand that no adulterer or fornicator or defrauder (for that is idolatry) has any inheritance in the kingdom of Christ and of God.* And again he says: *Mortify, therefore, your members which are on earth, laying aside fornication and impurity and evil desire and lust, which are all slavery to idols. Because of these things the wrath of God is coming.*[125]

27.2 Furthermore, as our bodies are members of Christ and we are, each of us, a temple of God, whoever by adultery violates that temple of God violates God; and whoever in committing sin does the will of the devil is being a slave to demons and their idols.[126] For evil deeds do not proceed from the Holy Spirit but from the promptings of the Enemy, and from the unclean spirit are born desires which drive men to act against God and be a slave to the devil.

It follows, therefore, that if they claim one man is polluted by another's sin and if, as they maintain and contend, the idolatry of the guilty passes on to the innocent, then, on their own argument, they cannot clear themselves of the guilt of idolatry, since it is established on the authority of the Apostle that adulterers and defrauders, with whom they are in communion, are idolaters.[127]

27.3 But this is not for us: we remain true to our faith, we follow the guidance set by God's teaching,[128] we are in agreement with the dictates of truth. We maintain that each person must be held responsible for the sin he commits himself and that no one can be made guilty for anyone else, for the Lord warns us with these words: *The just man's justice will be upon him, and the wicked man's wickedness will be upon him*, as likewise He says: *Fathers shall not die for their children and children shall not die for their fathers. Every man shall die for his own sin.*[129]

That is what we read and follow. We, therefore, certainly believe that no one ought to be debarred from the fruits of satisfaction and the hope of reconciliation. We put our faith in the divine Scriptures, we follow the authority and encouragement of God Himself; we are, accordingly, convinced that sinners are invited back to do penitence and that pardon and forgiveness are not denied to the penitent.

28.1 What a way to mock our brethren and to frustrate them, what a way to delude hapless sinners and to make their sorrows in vain, what a profitless and fruitless teaching that emanates from this heretical establishment! Imagine exhorting people to do penitence and make atonement, and at the same time taking away all healing power from that atonement. Fancy saying to our brethren: "Lament and pour forth tears and spend your days and nights in sorrow, and for washing away and cleansing your sin perform generous and frequent good works, but for all that you do it is outside the Church that you shall die. You should do whatever leads to reconciliation but never will you receive the reconciliation which you seek." Who would not be lost at once, who would not fall away in utter despair, who would not give up any thought of sorrowing for sin?

28.2 Do you think a farmer could carry on working if you said to him: "Use all your farmer's skill in working this land, do your very best to cultivate it, but no harvest will you reap, no vintage will you press,[130] no crop will you gather from your olive grove, no fruit will you pick from the trees"?

28.3 It is as if you were trying to encourage a man to own and run ships, and were to say to him: "My friend, purchase timber from the very best forests, fashion your keel with specially strong and hand-picked beams of oak, work away that your ship may be constructed and fitted with rudder and ropes and sails, but when you have done all this, no fruit will you see from its trading and its voyages."

29.1 This is tantamount to blocking off and cutting short the way to sorrow and the route to repentance. And whereas in the Scriptures the Lord God goes out of His way to welcome those who return to Him and who repent, yet we, by our callousness and cruelty in cutting off the fruits of repentance, we are totally destroying repentance itself. But if we find that no one ought to be prevented from doing penitence and that, in as much as the Lord is compassionate and merciful, reconciliation can be granted through His bishops to those who implore and call upon the mercy of the Lord, then we have no alternative but to recognise the sorrows of those who bewail their sin and we have no right to deny the fruits of repentance to those who grieve.

29.2 And because in the grave there is no confession and the rite of reconciliation cannot take place there,[131] those who are genuinely repentant and who ask ought for the time being to be accepted into the Church and there be kept for the Lord.[132] One day He will come to His Church and will surely pass judgment on those whom He finds inside within it. 29.3 But apostates and renegades, enemies and opponents, all those in fact who scatter the Church of Christ, even if they have been put to death for His name but outside the Church, they cannot, according to the Apostle,[133] be admitted to the peace of the Church, because they have not maintained the unity either of the Spirit or of the Church.

30. For the moment, dearly beloved brother, I have briefly run through, as best I can, these few points—although there is still much left to say—so that I could meet your request and might join you by ever closer ties to the fellowship of our body of bishops, your colleagues. But should you get the opportunity and the means to visit us, we could discuss at greater length together and confer more completely and fully on these matters in the hopes of furthering blessed concord.

I wish that you, dearly beloved brother, may ever fare well.

LETTER 56

Cyprian sends greetings to his brothers Fortunatus, Ahymmus, Optatus, Privatianus, Donatulus, and Felix.[1]

1. My dearly beloved brothers, you have written to me that when you were in the town of Capsa[2] for the ordination of a bishop,[3] our brother and colleague Superius drew your attention to the case of Ninus, Clementianus, and Florus.[4] These brothers of ours had previously been arrested during the persecution, and stoutly confessing the Name of the Lord had withstood the violence of the magistrate and the attacks of the frenzied mob.[5] Subsequently, however, whilst being subjected to savage tortures before the proconsul,[6] they gave way under their extreme torments, and through those protracted agonies fell from the heights of glory which they were scaling in all the vigour of their faith. Nevertheless, since this grave fall, incurred through compulsion and no choice of their own,[7] they have been doing penitence continuously over these last three years.[8] And so you judged that you ought to inquire whether by now it might be right to admit them back into communion.[9]

2.1 Now, in so far as my personal views are concerned, my own judgment[10] is that the Lord's mercies will not be wanting to those who, it is acknowledged, took their stand at the battlefront, confessed the Name of the Lord, and by their dogged and resolute faith withstood the violence of the magistrates and the onslaught of the raging mob; they endured imprisonment, and amidst the menaces of the proconsul and the roar of the crowd that pressed around put up a lengthy resistance against prolonged bouts of tortures that mangled and wrenched their limbs. Hence, their preceding merits help to excuse and compensate for their giving way, through the weakness of the flesh, at the very last. To have forfeited their glory is, therefore, enough to suffer for men of such calibre; we have no right to shut against them the door of pardon or to deprive them of their Father's compassion and of communion with us. As you said in your letter, they have passed three years in continuous and bitter mourning, in the most profound sorrow and repentance. That, in our estimation, may be sufficient for winning for them from the Lord His clemency.[11]

2.2 And I certainly do not think it would be rash and ill-considered to grant reconciliation to these men who we can see, thanks to their courageous fighting spirit, gallantly played their part in the battle previously and who can recover the glory that is theirs if the fighting should ever come again.[12]

It was resolved at our Council that comfort should be brought and reconciliation given to penitents who are in danger of death.[13] But, surely, they ought to take precedence over the dying in receiving reconciliation who we can see fell not through weakness of the spirit, but who, through infirmity of the flesh, proved unable to carry off the crown of their confession, all wounded as they were in the thick of the fighting. Above all, though they yearned for death, it was not granted them to be slain but the tortures went on mangling their wearied limbs. Yet, for all that time those agonies won no victory over their faith, which is unconquered; rather they wore out their flesh, which is weak.[14]

3. Be that as it may, your purpose in writing was that I might give this particular matter very full discussion with a number of our colleagues; it is an important question and demands, therefore, more mature and serious deliberation at a well-attended conference.[15] Seeing that it is the beginning of the solemn season of Easter,[16] almost all of our colleagues are at present away at home staying with their brethren. But as soon as they have fulfilled the solemn celebrations with their people and have begun to arrive here, I will discuss the matter fully with each of them. We can then come to a firm decision on the question you have raised and will write back to you a definitive opinion arrived at by the counsel and deliberations of many bishops.[17]

I wish that you, dearly beloved brothers, may ever fare well.

LETTER 57

Cyprian, Liberalis, Caldonius, Nicomedes, Caecilius, Iunius, Marrutius, Felix, Successus, Faustinus, Fortunatus, Victor, Saturninus, another Saturninus, Rogatianus, Tertullus, Lucianus, Sattius, Secundinus, another Saturninus, Eutyches, Ampius, another Saturninus, Aurelius, Priscus, Herculaneus, Victoricus, Quintus, Honoratus, Manthaneus, Hortensianus, Verianus, Iambus, Donatus, Pomponius, Polycarp, Demetrius, another Donatus, Privatianus, Fortunatus, Rogatus, and Monnulus send greetings to their brother Cornelius.[1]

1.1 Some time ago,[2] dearly beloved brother, we had determined, after sharing mutual counsel together,[3] that those who had been tripped up by the Enemy during the hostilities of the persecution, had fallen and defiled themselves with forbidden sacrifices, should continue to do full penitence for a long time;[4] but should they be seized by a dangerous illness, they might receive reconciliation at the very point of death.[5] For neither was it right nor did the compassion and clemency of God our Father allow us to shut the Church against those who knocked[6] or to deny the support which comes with the hope of salvation to those who sorrowed and supplicated; as they departed from this world they should not, therefore, be sent on to the Lord deprived of reconciliation and communion.[7] Indeed, the Lord Himself so permitted when He laid down the law that what had been bound on earth should be bound also in heaven but that in heaven there would be loosed what was loosed here before in the Church.[8]

1.2 But as things are now, we can see that the day is once again beginning to draw near bringing in a second outbreak of hostilities; we have been receiving repeated warnings and frequent signs[9] that we should be armed and be prepared ourselves for the warfare which the Enemy is declaring upon us, that by our exhortations we should be preparing also the people God has deigned to entrust to our care, and that we should be gathering inside the Lord's encampment every soldier of Christ, without exception, all who are eager for arms and cry out for battle.

Given no choice by this crisis,[10] we have decreed that reconciliation is to be granted to those who have never forsaken the Church of the Lord but who have continued to do penitence, mourning and entreating the Lord, without ceasing, right from the very first day of their fall, and that they ought to be armed and equipped for the now imminent battle.[11]

2.1 We are left no choice but to be obedient to reliable signs and warnings;[12] by them shepherds are directed not to abandon their sheep to danger, but rather to muster their entire flock together—the army of the Lord is to be armed ready for engagement on the spiritual battlefield.

So long as peace and tranquillity prevailed, it was right that grief and penitence should be prolonged over a more extended period, with comfort brought to the penitent when he fell ill and was in his last moments; under these circumstances it was possible long to delay those who wept and mourned whilst bringing comfort to them at a late hour, when they were sick and dying.[13]

2.2 But under the present circumstances reconciliation becomes a necessity not for the sick but for the strong, communion we must grant not to the dying but to the living. Those whom we stir and rouse to battle we must not leave all naked and unarmed; we must fortify and protect them with the body and blood of Christ. Since the Eucharist has been appointed for this purpose, to be a safeguard to those who receive it, those whom we would have safe against the Enemy we must now arm with the protection of the Lord's banquet. How, I ask, are we to teach and incite them to shed their own blood by confessing the Name of Christ, if we deny to them on the eve of going into battle the blood of Christ? How can we make them fit for the cup of martyrdom, if we do not first allow them the right of communion and admit them to drink, in the Church, the cup of the Lord?[14]

3.1 We need to draw distinctions, dearly beloved brother, between two kinds of lapsed. On the one hand, there are those who, after apostatising, returned to the world which they had renounced[15] and now live there as pagans, or who, becoming deserters to heresy, now take up each day impious arms against the Church. Far different, on the other hand, are those who have never left the threshhold of the Church, there with ceaseless lamentation begging for the con-

soling gifts of God their Father: they declare that they are now prepared for combat, ready to take their stand and to fight courageously
for the sake of the Name of their Lord and their own salvation.

3.2 At such a time as this, we are granting reconciliation not to
those who fall asleep but to those who keep awake,[16] we are granting
reconciliation not to men at their ease but to men at arms, we are
granting reconciliation not for repose but for combat. If, as we hear
tell of them, and as we hope and trust of them, they do take their
stand courageously and join with us in laying low the Enemy in the
encounter, we will have no regrets in having conceded reconciliation
to men of such courage. More than that; it confers signal honour and
glory on our episcopate to have granted reconciliation to martyrs, in
that as priests who offer up each day the sacrifices of God,[17] we are
thus making ready sacrificial victims and offerings for God.

But should any of the fallen mislead us (as I pray to the Lord
may never befall our brethren), should any one of them request reconciliation deceitfully and receive restoration to communion at this
time of impending battle though with no intention of joining that battle, then it is himself that he deceives and misleads by declaring one
thing in his mouth but concealing another thing in his heart.

3.3 In so far as we are gifted with sight and judgment, we see
every man's outward appearance, but their hearts we cannot search,
their thoughts we cannot scan. But He who searches men's secrets
and knows them, He is the judge of all these things: He is soon to
come and will pass judgment on what lies hidden and concealed in
men's hearts.[18] It is not right that the evil should obstruct the way of
the good (rather, they should be helped by the good).[19] There are no
grounds, therefore, for denying reconciliation to those who are about
to accomplish their martyrdom simply because there are some who
are going to deny.[20] After all, reconciliation should be granted to
everyone who is about to enter battle for just this reason that we must
not risk overlooking in our ignorance any man who is capable of winning his crown in the battle.[21]

4.1 It is not right for anyone to argue: he who takes up martyrdom is baptised in his own blood.[22] He has no need to receive, then,
peace from his bishop, for he is about to have the peace which is won
by his own glory and to receive a far richer reward from the Lord's
bounty.[23]

4.2 To this our immediate reply is that a man cannot be fit for martyrdom if he is not armed for battle by the Church; his heart fails if it is not fired and fortified by receiving the Eucharist. For the Lord says in His own Gospel: *But when they deliver you up, give no thought as to what you are to say. For it shall be granted to you at that hour what you are to say. It is not you who speak but the Spirit of your Father speaks within you.*[24]

Now when He says that the Spirit of the Father speaks in those who have been delivered up and are in the act of confessing the Name,[25] how is it that a man can be found fit and ready for such a confession if he has not first, by the reception of reconciliation, received the Spirit of the Father? For He is the one who gives strength to His servants and who Himself speaks and confesses within us.[26]

4.3 Then again, a man may abandon all his possessions, take to flight, and there lie hidden in the wilds; but by chance he may fall among robbers[27] or be overcome with fever and weakness and pass away. Will it not be charged to us that so good a soldier who abandoned all that he had, disregarded home and family and children, and chose to follow his Lord, departed this life deprived of reconciliation and communion? On the day of judgment will it not be found written against our names that we were lazy and negligent or callous and cruel: as shepherds we would neither, in time of peace, tend the sheep entrusted and committed to our care nor, in time of battle, equip them with weapons?

4.4 Will not the Lord heap upon us the reproach which He makes crying out through the mouth of His prophet: *Behold, you feed off their milk and with their wool you clothe yourselves; those that are fat you slaughter, yet my sheep you do not feed. The weak you have not strengthened, the sick you have not healed, the injured you have not comforted,*[28] *the strayed you have not recalled, the lost you have not sought, and the strong you have enfeebled with toil. And my sheep are all scattered, for there are no shepherds; they have become fodder for all the beasts of the field and there has been no one to search for them and call them back. This, therefore, is what the Lord says: Behold, I come against the shepherds and I shall seek out my sheep from out of their hands and I shall drive them away, so that they may not feed my sheep; no more will they feed them and I shall deliver my sheep from out of their mouths, and with justice shall I feed them?*[29]

5.1 We wanted, therefore, to prevent the Lord from demanding back the sheep entrusted to us, delivering them from out of our mouths by which we refuse them reconciliation and by which we confront them with the callousness and cruelty of man rather than with the goodness and gentleness of God our Father.[30] And so, prompted by the Holy Spirit and counselled by the Lord through many explicit visions,[31] we came to the decision, seeing that it is foretold and revealed that the Enemy is close upon us, to collect together the soldiers of Christ within the battlements, and after examining each case to grant reconciliation to the fallen, or, to put it another way, to supply with weapons all those who are soon to fight. And we believe that you too, being sensible of God's paternal compassion, will agree with our decision.[32]

5.2 But should there be any colleague of ours who considers that reconciliation ought not to be granted to our brothers and sisters even though the encounter presses close upon us, he will have to render on the day of judgment an account to the Lord for his unseasonable severity and his inhuman harshness.[33] But so far as we are concerned, we have acted as faith and charity and brotherly love demanded: we made public what was known to us in our hearts,[34] viz. that the day of the encounter has drawn near, that a ferocious enemy is soon to rise up against us, that there approaches a battle not like the one before but more vehement and violent by far. We made known that this is being revealed to us repeatedly through the power of God, that we are being warned about this time and time again through the foresight and mercy of the Lord.

We who put our trust in Him have every reason to feel confident of His help and His love. In time of peace He announces in advance to His fighting men the approach of battle; He will surely, then, grant to them when they do fight victory in that encounter.

We wish that you, dearly beloved brother, may ever fare well.

LETTER 58

Cyprian sends greetings to the laity dwelling at Thibaris.[1]

1.1 Dearly beloved brethren, I had certainly planned and long desired to make a personal visit to you should the state of affairs and the current circumstances permit; I wanted to fall in with your frequently expressed wishes, and by my presence there among you I had hoped, in so far as our poor powers of exhortation would allow, to bring support and encouragement to your community. But as things are, we are being detained here by the present critical state of affairs in such a way that I have no hope either of travelling any distance away from here or of absenting myself for any length of time from the people over whom, by God's favour, we have charge.[2] In the meantime, therefore, I am sending to you this letter to act as a substitute in my stead.[3]

1.2 We have been receiving numerous urgent warnings by which the Lord in His goodness seeks to instruct us. It is our duty, accordingly, to make known to you also the anxious warnings that are being communicated to us.[4]

You have to realise, you have to be utterly convinced, you have to hold as certain that the day of affliction is now dawning overhead: the demise of the world and the time of Antichrist are nigh.[5] Hence we must all take our stand, being at the ready to go into battle; we should have no thoughts other than for the glories of eternal life and the crown that is won by confessing the Lord. Neither should we regard what is coming as in any way comparable with what has already been; the battle that now looms over us is more serious and savage by far.[6] For it, the soldiers of Christ must equip themselves with the weapons of unblemished faith and valorous strength, reflecting that the reason why they drink each day the cup of the blood of Christ[7] is that they themselves may thus also be enabled to shed their blood for Christ's sake.[8]

1.3 For it proves our willingness to be found with Christ if we imitate what Christ did and taught. As the apostle John says: *He who says he abides in Christ ought himself also to walk just as He walked.* Likewise the apostle Paul teaches us with these words of exhortation: *We are sons of God, but if sons, heirs of God also and joint heirs with Christ—if, indeed, we share in His sufferings so that we may share in His glory.*[9]

2.1 These are the things upon which we must now reflect. There is no call for anyone to desire anything of the world now that that world is dying; instead, we must follow after Christ, who both lives Himself for ever and gives life to His servants who have faith in His Name. For the time is now at hand, dearly beloved brethren, of which long ago our Lord foretold, announcing its approach in these words: *There will come a time when all who put you to death will think that they are doing a service to God. And these things they will do to you, for they have not known the Father nor me. But I have told you these things so that when the time for them has come you may remember that I spoke of them to you.*[10]

2.2 And no one should feel surprised that we are being harried by constant persecution and hard pressed by incessant affliction and anguish, since the Lord has already foretold that these things would be so in the very last days, and He has already issued His instructions to us, His fighting force, through the teaching and encouragement of His word. Peter, His apostle, has also taught that persecutions come so that we may be tested and that if we follow after the just example of the just men who have gone before us,[11] we, too, may be united to the love of God through suffering and death. For he makes the following claim in his epistle: *Dearly beloved, do not feel surprised by the fiery trial which afflicts you: this has come to test you. And do not feel dismayed because something unexpected besets you. But as often as you have a share in the sufferings of Christ, be exceedingly glad, so that when His glory is revealed you may also rejoice and be glad. But if you are reviled for the Name of Christ, you are blessed; for the Name of the majesty and power of the Lord rests upon you. That Name is indeed blasphemed among them, but among us It is glorified.*[12]

2.3 But the apostles have taught us only what they in their turn have learned themselves from the precepts of the Lord and the commandments of heaven. Thus the Lord Himself strengthens us in these, His own words: *There is no man who leaves home and land, family and brethren, wife and children for the sake of the kingdom of God who shall not receive seven times more in this present time, and in the world to come life everlasting.* And again He says: *Blessed shall you be when men hate you and cast you out and expel you and curse your name as evil, for the sake of the Son of Man. Rejoice on that day and be glad, for, behold, great is your reward in heaven.*[13]

3.1 The Lord would have us, therefore, rejoice and be glad in times of persecution, for it is when persecutions come that the crowns of faith are awarded, that the soldiers of God are tested, and that the heavens stand open for the martyred.[14] After all, we have not enlisted for military service so that it should be our duty to think merely of peace, we have enlisted not in order that we should shirk and refuse military action. In such campaigning the Lord has Himself led the vanguard, and He is our instructor in humility and endurance and suffering: He sought first to do Himself what He has taught should be done and to suffer Himself first on our account, having encouraged us to suffer ourselves.

3.2 Dearly beloved brethren, let the thought be ever uppermost in your minds that He who alone has received all judgment from the Father[15] and who is the one who shall come to pass judgment has already pronounced His verdict in that trial and judgment that is to come: He has declared beforehand and He has testified that He will confess before His Father those who confess Him but those who deny He will deny.[16]

Now, were it possible for us to escape from death, then dying would sensibly be something we might fear. But as man, being mortal, has no option but to die, then let us grasp the opportunity that now comes thanks to God's promise and providence; let us bring our lives to an end, winning at the same time the reward of immortality; let us have no fear of being put to death, since we know it is when we are put to death that we win our crowns.

4.1 When you see our people scattered and driven to flight through fear of persecution, none of you, dearly beloved brethren, has reason for feeling distressed at no longer finding your community assembled together, at no longer hearing your bishops preach.[17] At such a time it is just not possible for everyone to be gathered in one place; they must needs be killed, even though they themselves may not kill.[18] In those days, whenever any of our brothers happens to be parted from the flock temporarily, by force of circumstances, and finds himself separated from them in body, but not in spirit, let him not be dismayed at the terrors of his flight; as he looks for refuge and concealment, let him not be alarmed at the loneliness of his desert region. He is not alone who has Christ as his companion in flight; he is not alone who by dint of preserving his temple of God[19] has God always with him wherever he may be.

4.2 And if, as he seeks flight among the lonely mountains, some brigand should overpower him, if some wild beast should attack him, if hunger, thirst, or cold should overcome him, or if, as he sails in desperate haste over the seas, storm and tempest should overwhelm him, Christ is there, watching over His soldier wherever the fighting may be. To all who die in persecution for the honour of His name, He presents the recompense which He promised He would give on the day of the resurrection.[20] Nor is the glory of such a martyrdom any the less because a man may not have died in the public gaze, witnessed by many: to die for Christ's sake is still the reason for his dying. That one Witness who puts martyrs to the test and gives to them their crowns provides adequate testimony for his martyrdom.[21]

5.1 Let us imitate, dearly beloved brethren, Abel, that just man who inaugurated martyrdom by being the first to be slain for justice' sake.[22] Let us imitate Abraham, the friend of God who did not hesitate to use his own hands in making a sacrificial offering of his son, acting in obedience and faithful devotion to God. Let us imitate the three youths Ananias, Azarias, and Misael: young as they were, they were not terrified, nor were they cowed by captivity. Judea had been conquered, Jerusalem had been captured, yet the king, even in his own kingdom, they conquered by the power of their faith. When bidden to worship the statue which King Nabuchodonosor had made, they proved themselves mightier than all the king's threats and the king's flames. Raising their voices, they bore witness to their faith with these words: *King Nabuchodonosor, there is no need for us to reply to you on this matter, for the God whom we serve has the power to rescue us from the blazing flames of the furnace, and He will deliver us out of your hands. And even if He does not, let it be known to you that we do not serve your gods neither do we worship the golden statue which you have erected.*[23] Such was their faith, they believed that they were able to escape, but they added "even if He does not," so that the king should know that they ere also able to die for the sake of the God whom they worshipped.

5.2 The strength of faith and valour is manifested in believing and knowing that God can deliver from immediate death and yet at the same time having no fear of death nor flinching from it and thereby proving one's faith all the more vigorously. From their lips there burst forth the Holy Spirit in all His undefiled and unconquerable might, thus revealing the truth of the Lord's pronouncement which He made in His Gospel with these words: *When they deliver you up, give no thought as to what you are to say; for it shall be granted to you at that hour what you are to say. It is not you who speak but it is the Spirit of your Father who speaks within you.* [24] He has said that what we may say and answer will be granted and presented to us at that hour through divine power and that at that time it is not we who speak but the Spirit of God the Father. And as He neither departs nor is parted from those who confess Him, He is the one who not only speaks but also is crowned in us. [25] Hence, too, in the case of Daniel, when he was under pressure to adore the idol Bel which the people and the king then worshipped, he boldly spoke forth in the fullness of his faith, championing the honour of his God and declaring: *I worship nothing save the Lord my God who founded heaven and earth.* [26]

6.1 In the Book of Maccabees we read of the cruel torments endured by the blessed martyrs, of all the different tortures to which the seven brothers were subjected, and of their mother who gave encouragement to her sons in the midst of those tortures and who died herself along with her sons. Do they not testify and demonstrate to us what is mighty valour and faith? [27] Do they not stir us by their sufferings to seek the triumphs of martyrdom? And what of the prophets whom the Holy Spirit quickened with foreknowledge of the future? What of the apostles whom Christ chose? [28] Have not the just, in being slain for justice' sake, taught us how we, too, might die?

6.2 No sooner was Christ born than there took place the martyrdom of the Innocents. For His name's sake all infants who were two years old or younger were slain; their tender years, though not yet fit for fighting, proved apt for crowns. For His name's sake innocent infants were slain, so that it could be seen that they are innocent who are put to death for Christ's sake. And it was further revealed that no one is protected from the perils of persecution when even the likes of these endured martyrdom. [29]

6.3 But it would indeed be a grave matter if the slave who bears the name of Christian refuses to suffer, whereas Christ, his Master, has endured sufferings before him, [30] and if we should refuse to suffer for our own sins whereas He, though without sins of His own Himself, has suffered for us. Moreover, the Son of God has suffered so that He might make us sons of God,[31] and yet the sons of man are loath to suffer in order that they may continue to be sons of God!

We may labour under the world's hatred; yet Christ endured that hatred of the world before us. We may be exposed to insults on this earth, we may undergo exile or tortures; yet the Maker and Lord of this earth experienced far worse things than this. And so He gives us these words of warning counsel: *If the world hates you, remember that it hated me first. If you were of this world, the world would love what is its own. But because you are not of the world and I have chosen you out of the world, the world, therefore, hates you. Remember the word I have spoken to you. The servant is not greater than his master. If they have persecuted me, they will also persecute you.*[32] Our Lord and God put into action Himself whatever He taught to others, so that any disciple who learns His teaching and does not put it into action is left without excuse.

7.1 And there is no reason for any of you, dearly beloved brethren, to be so panic-stricken by fear of the approaching persecution or by the imminent arrival of Antichrist that he be found without the weapons of the Gospel exhortations and the precepts and counsels of heaven which equip a man for every eventuality. The Antichrist comes, but Christ is coming after him. The Enemy runs riot and rampages, but the Lord is following immediately behind, on His way to avenge our wounds and sufferings. The Adversary rages and menaces, but there is One who has the power to deliver us from out of his clutches. 7.2 Only He is to be feared whose rage no man can evade, and He has forewarned us Himself in His own words: *Fear not those who kill the body but cannot kill the soul. But rather dread him who can kill both body and soul in hell.* And again He says: *He who loves his life in this world will lose it, and he who hates his life in this world will preserve it unto life everlasting.* 7.3 And the Apocalypse also forewarns us with these words of instruction: *If a man worships the beast and his image and receives his mark on his brow and on his hand, then he shall drink of the wine of God's wrath mixed in the cup of His wrath, and he shall be punished with fire and brimstone in the sight of the holy angels and of the Lamb, and the smoke from their torments will rise up for ever and ever, and no rest shall they have neither day nor night whosoever worship the beast and his image.*[33]

8.1 In the case of worldly contests men train away and practise, and they account it a great mark of honour for their reputation if they should have the luck to win their crowns watched by the people and in the presence of their emperor. But see! There is coming a magnificent and wonderful contest glittering with the prize of a heavenly crown; it is God who now watches us as we compete, and as He surveys with His gaze those whom He vouchsafed to make His sons He takes delight in the spectacle of our encounter. Whilst we struggle and fight in the battle of faith, we are being watched by God, we are being watched by His angels, we are also being watched by Christ. How resplendent must then be our glory, how deep our happiness, to engage in the contest with God presiding and to win our crowns with Christ judging!

8.2 Therefore, dearly beloved brethren, let us arm ourselves with all our strength, let us prepare ourselves for the contest with an unblemished heart, a sound faith, and a dedicated courage. Let the army of God march out to the battle that is now being declared on us. Let those who are still sound put on their arms lest they should lose the advantage of having lately stood their ground. Let those, too, who fell put on their arms so that even the fallen may regain what they have lost. Let honour challenge the one and remorse the other to battle. 8.3 The blessed Apostle in fact teaches us how to arm and prepare ourselves in these words: *Our wrestling is not against flesh and blood, but against powers and the princes of this world and of this darkness, against the spirits of evil on high. Therefore, put on full armour that you may be able to withstand on the most evil of days, so that when you have attended to all these things you may stand having your loins girt about with truth, having put on the breastplate of justice, having your feet shod with the preparation of the gospel of peace, taking up the shield of faith with which you can extinguish all the fiery darts of the most wicked one, and taking up the helmet of salvation and the sword of the spirit, which is the word of God.*[34]

9.1 Such are the arms we should now take up ourselves, with these spiritual and heavenly weapons we should now protect and defend ourselves so that on that most evil of days we may be able to withstand and repel the menaces of the devil. Let us now put on the breastplate of justice, so that our breast may be protected and defended against the darts of the Enemy. Let our feet be shod with the armature of the Gospel teachings so that when the serpent is being trampled and crushed under our feet he may not be able to trip or bite us. Let us carry with courage the shield of faith under the shelter of which we may be able to extinguish whatever darts the Enemy may hurl.

9.2 Let us take, in addition, as covering for our heads the spiritual helmet whereby our ears may be shielded from hearing the savage edicts,[35] whereby our eyes may be shielded from looking upon the abominable idols,[36] whereby our brow may be shielded so as to preserve intact the sign of God,[37] whereby our mouth may be shielded so as to confess Christ its Lord with triumphant tongue. Let us also arm our right hands with the spiritual sword so that they may boldly spurn the deadly sacrifices and that, being mindful of the Eucharist, those same right hands which now receive the Lord's body[38] may one day clasp the Lord Himself when they accept from Him hereafter heavenly crowns as their reward.

10.1 How grand and wondrous, dearly beloved brethren, will be that day when it comes, that day when the Lord sets about reviewing His people and when He will examine and weigh the deserts of each of us in His holy assessment! The guilty He will send to hell and our persecutors He will damn to the perpetual punishment of searing flames. But to us He will render the reward due for our faith and dedication. What glory, what bliss will be ours! To be let in to see God, to have the honour of sharing in the joys of salvation and of the eternal light in the company of Christ the Lord our God, to greet Abraham, Isaac, and Jacob, all the patriarchs, apostles, prophets, and martyrs, there in the kingdom of heaven to rejoice in the delights of the immortality bestowed upon us in the company of the just and the friends of God, to receive there *what eye has not seen, what ear has not heard, what has not entered into the heart of man.*[39]

10.2 That what we there receive far outweighs the labour or the sufferings we endure here on earth the Apostle declares in these words: *The sufferings of the present time are not worthy to be compared with the glory to come which shall be revealed in us.*[40] When that revelation has come, when that glory of God has shed its radiance over us, we will be as blessed and joyous in the honour and favour of the Lord as they will continue to be damned and wretched who have proved to be deserters from God or rebels against Him. They have done the will of the devil, and so together with the devil they must be tormented in unquenchable fire.[41]

10.3 Let these be the sentiments, dearly beloved brethren, that ever abide in your hearts. And may we thus make ready our arms by fixing our thoughts, day and night, on this reflection, by holding before our eyes and turning over constantly in our minds and our hearts what tortures are inflicted upon the wicked, what rewards are merited by the just, what the Lord threatens by way of punishment to those who deny, what, by contrast, He promises by way of glory to those who confess. If the day of persecution should come upon us whilst we meditate upon and contemplate these thoughts, then the soldier of Christ, being thus instructed by His precepts and counsels, shows no fear in the face of battle but is now ready for his crown.

I wish that you, most cherished brothers, may ever fare well.

LETTER 59

Cyprian sends greetings to his brother Cornelius.

1.1 I have read, my dearly beloved brother, your letter which you despatched by the hand of our brother, the acolyte Saturus.[1] Your letter was abundantly full of brotherly love and that spirit of church discipline and strict authority which bishops ought to exercise. For in it you informed me that you had rejected there in Rome Felicissimus who is no new enemy of Christ but has long since been excommunicated for his numerous and outrageous crimes, having been condemned not just by my own sentence but by the verdict of large numbers of my fellow bishops as well.[2]

1.2 And you informed me further that when he turned up there escorted by his pack of rebels and flanked by his troop of desperadoes you acted with all the decisive vigour which becomes our episcopal office, and that he was thrown out of the Church from which he and his fellows have long since been cast out by God the Almighty and by the strict censure of Christ our Lord and Judge. It could not be that this instigator of schism and division,[3] this defrauder of monies entrusted to him,[4] this violator of virgins, this defiler and despoiler of so many marriage beds[5] should any longer continue to outrage the bride of Christ, spotless, chaste, and holy as she is, by his foul presence and by contact with his obscene and vicious person.

2.1 However, I have also read, my brother, your second letter which you appended to your first letter. I am quite astonished by it, for I find that you were somewhat intimidated by the desperate menaces of these visitors of yours. As you describe it, they attacked you and threatened most violently that if you would not accept the letters they had brought[6] they would read them out publicly and they would produce as well much vile and disgusting matter—worthy, of course, of mouths like theirs.[7]

2.2 If, dearly beloved brother, things have really reached this point that men can be cowed by the insolence of the wicked and that what evildoers cannot achieve by lawful means they can get by uncontrolled violence, then we must despair of the strength of our episcopal authority and of that noble and God-given power which has been granted to us for governing the Church. No more can we persevere as Christians; indeed, no longer can we even be Christians if it has come to this, that we can be terrorised by the menaces and machinations of such a lawless rabble.

2.3 Menaced we are not only by Gentile and Jew[8] but by heretics as well; for all those whose hearts and minds have been seized by the devil daily manifest their envenomed and raving madness with their frenzied shouting. Yet, that is still no reason why we should retreat before them, simply because they are a menace to us, nor must the Enemy and Adversary necessarily be greater than Christ merely because he lays his hands on and seizes so much in this world. No, dearly beloved brother: we must preserve unshakeable strength of faith, and a courage that is unyielding and unassailable in order to withstand all the battering and assaults from the waves that come in roaring against us, beating them off with all the firmness of some massive opposing rock.

2.4 It is of no consequence what may be the source of the threat or danger which confronts a bishop; he lives his life exposed to threats and dangers—indeed, it is through those very threats and dangers that he rises to glory. And it is not only against the menaces of Gentiles and Jews that we should be alert and watchful; we can see that our Lord Himself was seized by His own brethren and betrayed by a man whom He had Himself chosen to be one of the apostles. So it was, too, in the very beginning of the world. The just Abel was slain by none other than his own brother; Jacob was pursued in flight by his enraged brother; Joseph as a boy was put up for sale with his very own brothers as the traders.[9] In the Gospel, too, we read it foretold that it will chiefly be from our own household that our enemies will come,[10] that those who have previously been united together by the sacred bond of fellowship will betray one another.

It is, I say, of no consequence who may be our betrayer, who may be our attacker, since it is God who gives leave that we should be betrayed—and thereby win our crowns. It can bring no disgrace upon us to suffer at the hands of our own brethren just as Christ Himself suffered, any more than it can bring glory upon them to act just as Judas did.

2.5 Look how high and mighty they make themselves! Look at the puffed-up and bladder-mouthed boasting that goes into their empty menaces—there, in Rome, they threaten me behind my back, whereas it is in their power to confront me face to face here in Carthage. 2.6 And their abuse, by which they are only tearing themselves and their own lives apart each day, holds no fears for us; their cudgels, stones, and swords, which they are brandishing with such bloodthirsty shouts, hold no terrors for us. So far as they are capable, such men are already murderers in the sight of God. But they cannot actually kill unless the Lord allows them to do so. And though we have to die but once,[11] yet they are guilty of slaying us each day through their words of hatred and their deeds of iniquity.

3.1 But, dearly beloved brother, there are still no grounds for abandoning church discipline or for being weak in the strict exercise of episcopal authority, just because we are being harassed with abuse or intimidated with threats. For we are confronted with these words of counsel from divine Scripture: *But the presumptuous and arrogant man, the man who brags of himself, he will accomplish nothing even though his greed is as insatiable as the grave.* And likewise we read: *And fear not the words of the sinful man, for all his glory shall become worms and excrement. Today he shall be held in high honour but tomorrow there will be no trace of him, for he will have returned to his dust and his schemes will have vanished.* And again: *I have seen the wicked man exalted on high, raised above the cedars of Lebanon. And I passed by, and lo! he was gone. I searched for him but I could not find where he had been.*[12]

3.2 Such pretentious self-importance, such arrogant and haughty self-aggrandisement has its origins not in the teachings of Christ, whose lesson is one of humility, but in the spirit of Antichrist, against whom the Lord issues these words of reproach through the prophet: *But you have said in your heart: I will rise into the heavens, I will set my throne above the stars of God, I will take my seat on a lofty mountain high above the lofty mountains to the north; I will rise above the clouds and I will be like the Most High.* But to this He added these words: *Yet you shall be brought down to hell, to the lowest depths of the earth. And those who see you will look upon you in astonishment.* Hence in another passage divine Scripture threatens such men with a similar fate in the following words: *The day of the Lord of hosts shall come upon everyone who is unjust and haughty, everyone who is high and mighty and exalted.*[13]

3.3 As a matter of fact, every man is instantly betrayed by the words that come from his own lips, for he reveals in his speech whether he has Christ in his heart or, in reality, Antichrist. As the Lord says in His Gospel: *You brood of vipers, how can your words be good when you are evil yourselves? For the mouth brings forth what comes from the overflowing of the heart. The good man brings forth good things from his store of goodness, but the evil man brings forth evil from his store of evil.* Likewise in the case of the sinful Dives: he begs for aid from Lazarus, who now rests on the bosom of Abraham in a place of repose, as he is himself racked with torments and is consumed in the heat of searing flames. Of all the parts of his body his mouth and tongue suffer punishment most, doubtless because it was by his mouth and tongue that he had sinned the most.[14] 4.1 And we must remember the words of Scripture: *Neither shall the evil-tongued possess the kingdom of God,* as well as the words which the Lord speaks in His Gospel: *Whoever shall say to his brother, You fool!, or shall say, Racha, to him, he will be liable to the fires of hell.*

How, then, can there be any escape from the condemnation and vengeance of the Lord for those who hurl such abuse not just at their brothers but even at their bishops on whom God has deigned to bestow such high honour? For whoever refused to obey God's high priest, the judge appointed here on earth for the time being, deserved instantly to be put to death. As our Lord God says in Deuteronomy:

And whatsoever man acts with such arrogance that he pays no heed to the priest or the judge, whoever he may be in those days, that man shall die, and when all the people hear of it they will be afraid, and they will desist henceforth from their wickedness. [15]

4.2 Similarly God said to Samuel, when he was being despised by the Jews: *They have not despised you but they have despised me.* So, too, the Lord says in the Gospel: *He who hears you hears me and him who sent me; and he who rejects you rejects me and him who sent me.* And when He had cleansed the leper, He said to him: *Go and show yourself to the priest.* Later on, at the time of His passion, when He had been struck a blow by a servant of the priest who said to Him: *Is this the way you reply to the high priest?*, the Lord uttered no word of reproach against the high priest nor did He debase in any way the honour due to the priest, but He merely said instead by way of establishing and demonstrating His own innocence: *If I have spoken ill, reprove me for the ill. But if I have spoken well, why do you strike me?* [16]

4.3 We also read in the Acts of the Apostles that it was subsequently said to the blessed apostle Paul: *Do you thus dishonour and revile God's priest?* And although those priests had now become guilty of desecration, sacrilege, and murder, for they had crucified the Lord and they therefore no longer preserved anything of their priestly honour and authority, yet Paul remained mindful even of the priestly name, however empty now and reduced to a mere shadow, and he therefore said: *I was unaware, my brothers, that he was a priest. For it is written: you shall not revile the leader of your people.* [17]

5.1 You can see that there are all these numerous and significant examples from the past in which God upholds with His blessing the authority and power of His bishops. What do you then think of those who make war on those bishops, who rise in rebellion against the catholic Church, who are not deterred by the warnings and threats of the Lord, not even by His vengeance in the judgment to come? In truth, heresies and schisms have their source and origin precisely in circumstances where people fail to obey God's bishop and where they forget the fact that in a church there is but one bishop and judge who acts in Christ's stead for the time being. [18]

5.2 But if all the brethren gave the bishop their obedience as God's teachings prescribe, no one would make any move against the college of the bishops; after God has made His choice and the people have cast their vote and fellow bishops have expressed their concurrence,[19] no one would set himself up to pass judgment not on the bishops now but on God Himself. No one would tear the Church of Christ apart by the destruction of her unity, no one would have the arrogant self-conceit[20] to establish a new heresy outside and beyond the Church. These things can only happen if there is anyone so irreligious, so irresponsible, so aberrant in mind as to believe that a bishop can be made without God's choice. And yet the Lord says in His Gospel: *Are not two sparrows sold for a farthing, and neither of them falls to the ground without the will of the Father?*[21]

So, as He declares that not even events of the least account take place without the will of God, would anyone suppose that events of the highest and greatest importance can take place in the Church of God without God's knowledge or permission? Is it possible that bishops, that is to say, God's own stewards, can have been appointed without His approval? 5.3 To be of such a view is to lack that faith by which we live our lives,[22] it is to deny honour to God even when we know and believe that all things are ruled and governed by His sovereign will and judgment.

Men may indeed be made bishops not according to the will of God, but only when they are made bishops outside the Church, only when they are made bishops in defiance of the teachings and ordinances of the gospel. It is just as our Lord Himself declares with these words in the Twelve Prophets: *They have set up a king for themselves, but not by my leave.* And again: *Their sacrifices are as the bread of mourning; all who eat of them shall be defiled.* And through the mouth of Isaiah the Holy Spirit also cries out, saying: *Woe to you, rebel sons! This is what the Lord says: you have made plans, but not by my leave; you have struck an agreement, but not by my inspiration, heaping sins upon sins.*[23]

6.1 But—and I now speak only under provocation, I speak in sorrow, I speak under compulsion—there is a man who is appointed bishop in the place of a deceased bishop; he is chosen in time of peace by the vote of the entire congregation;[24] he is protected in time of persecution by the help of God;[25] he is united with all his colleagues in mutual trust;[26] he has been held in esteem by his people for four years now as bishop;[27] in days of calm he has devoted himself to good order in the Church;[28] in days of storm he has been a victim of proscription, cited explicitly under his title of bishop;[29] many times in the circus have they shouted for him to be thrown to the lion, and he has been so honoured, too, in the amphitheatre, thereby attesting to the good favours of the Lord;[30] in recent days, also, just as I am writing this letter to you, there has been once again popular outcry in the circus for him to be thrown to the lion—this has been occasioned by the sacrifices which the people have been ordered to celebrate by a public edict.[31] 6.2 When such a man, dearly beloved brother, is publicly assailed by a pack of wild hooligans from outside the Church, it stands out clearly who is making that assault. Christ it cannot be, for He in fact appoints and protects His bishops. It can only be the adversary of Christ and the enemy of His Church who is hounding the appointed leader in the Church with his attacks. His object is that once he has removed the helmsman out of the way he may be able all the more fiercely to indulge his savage violence in making shipwreck of that Church.[32]

7.1 And, dearly beloved brother, no man of faith who is mindful of the gospel and heedful of the counsels and forewarnings of the Apostle should feel perturbed if in these days at the end of the world there appear certain headstrong and stiff-necked men who are hostile to God's bishops, who forsake the Church or work against the Church; for the Lord and His apostles have already foretold that such men would come in these days.[33] 7.2 Nor should any man feel surprised that the servant, who has been appointed as leader, should be deserted by certain people, seeing that the Master Himself was abandoned by His own disciples even though He worked the greatest wonders and miracles and by those works showed forth the power and might of God His Father. Even so He did not rebuke them as they turned away neither did He fulminate against them, but He merely turned to His apostles and said: *Will you, too, go away?*[34] Clearly He respected that law whereby man has been left to his own freedom and being thus gifted with his own choice is responsible himself for seeking his own death or salvation.[35]

7.3 But Peter, on whom the Lord had already built the Church, taking on himself to answer on behalf of them all, replied with the voice of the Church: *Lord, to whom shall we go? You have the word of eternal life, and we believe and know that you are the Son of the living God.* By these words he clearly signified and demonstrated that those who withdraw from Christ have only themselves to blame for their own destruction, whereas the Church, which believes in Christ and holds fast to the teachings it has learned, never departs from Him in any way. He indicated, furthermore, that they are the Church who remain in the house of God; but on the other hand they are no seedbed planted by God the Father who, we can see, stand with none of the strength and firmness of true wheat but who are blown about and scattered like so much chaff before the blasts of the Enemy. It is of these that John speaks in his epistle: *They went out from us, but they were not of us. If they had been of us, they would have remained with us.* 7.4 Likewise, Paul counsels us not to be distressed when the wicked perish away from the Church nor to be weakened in our own faith when the faithless withdraw from the Church. As he says: *What if some of them have fallen from faith? Do you imagine that their faithlessness has made void the faithfulness of God? Far from it. For God is true though every man be a liar.*[36]

8.1 For our own part, my brother, it is our clear duty in conscience to endeavour to see that no one should perish away from the Church through any fault of ours. But if anyone of his own volition and through his own wickedness does so perish, refusing to do penance and to return to the Church, then we shall be found blameless ourselves on the day of judgment. For we have made every effort to cure them; only those shall be left to suffer punishments who have refused to be cured by our saving counsels. 8.2 Equally we ought not to allow ourselves to be troubled by any abuse from these derelicts nor should they cause us to deviate from the right path and our guiding rules. For we have these words of caution from the Apostle: *If I should please men, I should be no servant of Christ.*[37] What is of vital importance, therefore, is whether we seek to serve men or God. If we please men, then the Lord is offended; but if we honestly struggle and strive to please God, then we have to be contemptuous of any abuse and insults that may come from men.

9.1 And I can explain, dearly beloved brother, why I did not write to you at once about that pseudo bishop Fortunatus who has been set up by a mere handful of chronic heretics.[38] The simple answer is that this was not a matter which needed to be brought to your attention at once and in great haste as being of the most formidable and gravest importance. And this was particularly so, as you were perfectly well acquainted with the name of Fortunatus: he is one of those five presbyters who some time back now became renegades from the Church and who were more recently excommunicated by the sentence of numerous bishops, our colleagues and the most conscientious of men.[39] It was last year that they sent you a letter on this matter. Likewise, you would be familiar with Felicissimus, that ringleader of rebellion, who is also included in that same letter which our fellow bishops lately sent to you. And he has been not only excommunicated by those bishops here: he has now been recently thrown out of the Church by yourself in Rome.[40]

9.2 Since I was confident that these matters had reached your attention and I was fully convinced that you would firmly remember them and would deal with them with proper strictness, I did not consider that there was any need for you to be apprised of the follies of these heretics as a matter of the utmost urgency. Indeed, the majesty and dignity of the catholic Church ought not to concern itself with what wild schemes insolent heretics and schismatics may be brewing up amongst themselves.

As a matter of fact, the faction of Novatian is also said to have now appointed here as their pseudo bishop the presbyter Maximus, who was lately sent over to us by Novatian as his representative and who was rejected from our communion.[41] 9.3 And yet I did not write to you on this subject either, for we are contemptuous of all such matters and, besides, I did send to you very recently the names of the bishops here in Africa who govern the brethren within the catholic Church with integrity and soundness of faith. Indeed, it was a unanimous resolution of our Council to write this list to you[42] for the express purpose that it would be a quick way for removing error and perceiving the truth clearly, and that, therefore, you and our colleagues would know to whom it is proper for you to write and from whom, in turn, it is proper for you to accept letters.[43] So, should there be anyone brazen enough to write to you who did not figure on that list in our letter, you would know either that he was tainted with sacrifice or some certificate of sacrifice, or that he was one of the heretics, in either case that he must obviously be unregenerate and unsanctified.

9.4 In fact, I did seize the opportunity provided by a close friend and cleric, the acolyte Felicianus whom you had sent over here in company with our colleague Perseus,[44] and through him I did write to you about other matters which needed to be brought to your attention from here, as well as about this fellow Fortunatus.[45] But whilst our brother Felicianus was being delayed here by contrary wind and was in fact held back by us so that he might take other letters,[46] Felicissimus dashed over to you and arrived there ahead of him. That's just the way with the wicked: they're always in a hurry, fancying that they might be able to prevail over the innocent if only they move fast enough.

10.1 Now I did let you know, dear brother, by this Felicianus that Privatus had come to Carthage; he is a veteran heretic from the colony of Lambaesis and was condemned a good number of years ago for his many grave sins by the sentence of ninety bishops[47] and, as you must be well aware, was most severely censured as well in a letter written by Fabian and Donatus, our predecessors.[48] Privatus declared that he wished to put his case before us at the Council meeting which was held on the Ides of May last,[49] but being refused admission he proceeded to make this fellow Fortunatus a pseudo bishop of his, being judged suitable to join Privatus' own college of bishops.

10.2 Privatus had been accompanied by a certain Felix, whom Privatus had himself appointed a long time ago as a pseudo bishop in his heresy outside the Church. Present, too, were Iovinus and Maximus, who also came along in the company of that heretic Privatus: they had been condemned by the sentence of nine of our colleagues for abominable sacrifices and other serious offences established against them and were then excommunicated a second time by very many of us in Council last year.[50] 10.3 And further, these four were joined by Repostus of Sutunurca: he not only fell himself during the persecution but by his sacrilegious counsels he caused the downfall of the majority of his own people as well.[51]

These were the five who along with a handful of people who are stained with sacrifice or have evil consciences appointed Fortunatus as their pseudo bishop.[52] Their iniquities harmoniously matching, the ruler so chosen might thus also match in character his subjects.

11.1 From these facts you can now assess, dearly beloved brother, the whole pack of lies which those lawless thugs have spread so freely over there in Rome; for whereas of those guilty of sacrifice or heresy there came to Carthage no more than these five pseudo bishops, and these were the ones who appointed Fortunatus to be their partner in derangement, yet as true sons of the devil and there-fore speaking nothing but lies, they have had the outrageous temer-ity, as you tell me in your letter, to boast that there were in fact present twenty-five bishops. They kept making this same lying boast here too, earlier on, to our own brethren, claiming that twenty-five bishops were going to come out of Numidia to make a bishop for them.[53]

11.2 But to their great embarrassment this lie of theirs was ex-posed when there foregathered only five and these five were ship-wrecked souls who had already been excommunicated by us. So they then set sail for Rome with their cargo of falsehoods, fancying that the truth could not sail after them to confound their lying tongues by establishing the facts of the matter. And this, my brother, shows gen-uine derangement, not to remember or be aware that lies cannot mis-lead for long, that night lasts only until day begins to dawn but that when the daylight has grown bright and the sun has arisen, darkness and shadows give place to the light, putting an end to the rapine which flourished under cover of the night.

11.3 And so, should you ask them for the names of these twenty-five, they would not be able to give such a list—even of fic-titious names. They are so hard up for numbers, even of sinners, that twenty-five cannot be rounded up to join them from amongst those guilty of sacrifice or heresy. But in fact they lie and inflate their num-ber in order to deceive the ears of honest souls or distant brethren—as if, even supposing this were the real number, the Church can be overcome by heresy or right can be overcome by wrong.

12.1 But at this point, dearly beloved brother, I must avoid re-turning blow for blow with them[54] by rehearsing in my letter all their many crimes both past and present. We must bear in mind what is befitting for God's bishops to say and write: what we speak must be dictated not by resentment but by modesty. Otherwise I run the risk of appearing to be heaping slanderous abuse upon them out of prov-ocation instead of simply producing a catalogue of their sins and of-fences.

12.2 And so I am going to refrain from mentioning the thefts they have committed from the Church, I am going to omit their schemings, their adulteries, and their wide assortment of crimes. There is one exception, however, a case which concerns not me nor my fellow men but God; and over this felony of theirs I do not consider I ought to pass in silence. And it is this: right from the very first day of the persecution,[55] at a time when the lapsed were still flushed from the criminal deeds they had just committed, when not only the devil's altars but even the hands and lips of the fallen were yet reeking with the foul sacrifices, they never ceased to be in communion with the fallen and to try and obstruct their repentance.

God proclaims: *He who sacrifices to the gods, unless it is to the Lord only, shall be totally destroyed.* And in His Gospel the Lord says: *Whoever has denied me, I shall deny him.* And in another passage God gives expression to His outrage and wrath with these words: *To them you have poured out libations and for them you have offered up sacrifices. For this shall I not be wrath? says the Lord.*[56] And yet these people obstruct them from petitioning God when God declares with His own lips that He is wrath; they obstruct them from entreating Christ through prayers and penances when Christ affirms that He denies those who deny Him.

13.1 For our own part, we wrote to them on this precise subject even whilst the persecution continued, but our words were not heeded.[57] Subsequently, at a well-attended Council meeting we agreed together to resolve (and we added a severe warning to our resolution) that the brethren should do penance and that no one should be so irresponsible as to grant reconciliation to those who refused to do penance.[58] And then these people, profaning God and raving in impious and headstrong opposition to the bishops of God, go and leave the Church and take up murderous arms against her, their mother; they are doing their very best to help the devil complete his works of malice and to prevent our merciful God from healing within His Church those who still lie wounded.

13.2 By their deception and lies they thus ruin any repentance which these poor wretches might do, and ensure that they do not appease the wrath of God. They obstruct the man who was previously ashamed or afraid of being a Christian from seeking out Christ his Lord afterwards, they hinder the man who had forsaken the Church from returning to the Church, they make every effort they can to stop them from atoning for their sins by adequate deeds of sorrow and reparation, from shedding the tears which can wash clean their wounds. True reconciliation they destroy by their false and fallacious reconciliation; the stepmother impedes them from reaching their true mother's healing embrace, anxious to prevent her from hearing any sobbing and weeping coming from the hearts and lips of those who have fallen.[59]

13.3 And what is more, they still have those lapsed under their power, forcing them this time to heap abuse upon their bishops with those same tongues and lips through which they have already sinned on the Capitol.[60] They hurl foulmouthed abuse after confessors and virgins, after all good men who are eminent for their distinguished faith and enjoy a position of glory within the Church. In reality, such attacks are tearing apart their own lives and hopes more than they can injure our own humble, modest, and self-effacing brethren. It is not the man who hears but the man who hurls abuse who is to be pitied; it is not the man who is struck by his brother but the man who strikes his brother who has offended before the law. In cases of injury when the wicked do harm to the innocent, they who think they are inflicting harm are the ones who suffer the real harm.

13.4 Hence, their minds have now become disordered, their consciences deadened, their senses deranged.[61] For God's wrath makes men unable to perceive their sins and therefore to repent of them, as it is written: *And God sent upon them the spirit of lethargy.* That is to say, they are prevented from coming back to be healed, from finding in adequate deeds of reparation and prayers of entreaty the cure for the sins they have committed. The apostle Paul also declares this in his epistle with these words: *They have not the love of truth so as to find salvation. God shall, therefore, put them under a delusion, so that they believe falsehood, so that they may all be brought to justice, all who have not believed the truth but take delight in wickedness.*[62]

Now the highest degree of blessedness is not to sin at all, the second is to recognise one's sins. In the one there races ahead a pure and unspoilt innocence which preserves us whole, in the other there follows close behind a remedy which can heal us. But both of these blessings those people have now lost by their offences against God: they no longer have that grace which is received through the sanctification of baptism, neither can they resort to the aid of repentance by means of which faults can be cured.[63] I cannot believe, my brother, that you imagine for a moment that they commit but slight offences against God, that their sins are only venial and minor, when,

thanks to them, men do not dread the anger of the Lord and the con-
suming flames on His day of judgment, when, even though the Antichrist is nigh at hand, the faith of our people is being stripped of its
weapons just as they are about to go into battle, for they disarm them
of that determined strength which comes from fear of the Lord.[64]

13.5 The laity must do what they can to cope with this disorder;
but upon the bishops falls the much graver task and duty of affirming
and forwarding the glory of our sovereign God. We must not be
found in any way neglectful of this duty, for we have these words of
warning from the Lord: *And now, my priests, this commandment is for
you: if you will not heed it, if you will not place it in your heart to give honour
to my name, says the Lord, then I shall send my curse upon you and your
blessings I shall curse.*[65] 13.6 But, I ask you, is honour then given to
God when men so flout the sovereignty and strictures of God? Even
though He declares that He is wrath and angered with those who
offer sacrifice, threatening them with everlasting punishments and
unending sufferings, yet these desecrators publicly proclaim that
they should disregard the wrath of God, that they should not fear the
Lord's judgment, that they should not beat at the door of Christ's
Church.[66] Rather, they do away with penitence, they dispense with
public confession of heinous sins, they scorn the bishops and trample
them underfoot, and instead, presbyters preach reconciliation to
them, but delusively; and in order to prevent the fallen from ever aris-
ing again and those now outside the Church from ever returning to
it, communion is then offered to them by men who are themselves
no longer in communion.[67]

14.1 And they were not even satisfied with having departed
from the gospel and with having deprived the fallen of the hopeful
prospect of doing penance and making reparation. It was not enough
for them to have dissuaded those entangled in frauds, befouled with
adulteries, or polluted with the deadly contagion of pagan sacrifices[68]
from petitioning God for mercy and making confession of their
crimes in the Church, and to have taken away from them every sentiment, and therefore every fruit, of repentance. It was not enough
for them to have set up for themselves outside and beyond the
Church and in opposition to the Church a cell for their lawless faction,[69] to which there might throng the guilt-ridden mob of those
who refused to entreat God's mercy and make Him reparation.

But they have gone further than that. They have had heretics set up for them a pseudo bishop, and on top of that they now have the audacity to sail off carrying letters from schismatics and outcasts from religion even to the chair of Peter, to the primordial church, the very source of episcopal unity;[70] and they do not stop to consider that they are carrying them to those same Romans whose faith was so praised and proclaimed by the Apostle,[71] into whose company men without faith can, therefore, find no entry.

14.2 But what, we might well ask, did they hope to gain from going over and announcing that a pseudo bishop had been apppointed in opposition to the bishops? Either they are satisfied with what they have done and persist in their wickedness, or, if they are dissatisfied and would back off from it, they know the place to which they should return. For it was a resolution enacted by us all—and it is eminently right and just—that a man's case should be heard in the place where his offence was committed;[72] and, besides, each individual shepherd has been assigned a portion of the flock to rule and govern, knowing that one day he will be called upon to render an account to the Lord for his actions.[73] It is, therefore, totally improper that these men over whom we have charge should go tearing about, seeking to break up the harmony and concord that prevails among the bishops by their underhand treachery and wild deceits. Rather, they ought to be pleading their case in that place where they can face up to their accusers and to the witnesses of their crime. It is possible, I suppose, that this handful of desperate outlaws fancies that the authority of the bishops who have been appointed here in Africa is too slight to deal with their case. And yet it so happens that those bishops have already given judgment on it; only recently after weighty examination they passed condemnation upon them as being grievously guilty of numerous offences.[74] Their case has, therefore, already been tried, sentence has already been pronounced on them. It would be scandalous if bishops, who ought to exercise strict justice, should be exposed to the reproach that they weakly vacillate and capriciously change their minds; for we have the Lord's own words to instruct us: *In what you say you should declare simply "yes" or simply "no."*[75]

15.1 And should you reckon up the number of those who passed judgment upon them last year, including the presbyters and deacons,[76] then there were present on that occasion at their trial and condemnation more people than these men in fact now number who are alleged to be in league with Fortunatus. For you ought to be aware, dearly beloved brother, that since being made a pseudo bishop by the heretics, Fortunatus has by now been deserted by nearly everyone. Previously people were hoodwinked by their clever tricks and taken in by their fraudulent talk, being told that they were all about to return to the Church together, but they woke up to the fact that they had been fooled and cheated when they saw that a pseudo bishop had been appointed out there.[77] And so they are daily making their way back and come knocking at the door of the Church. But we have to act with anxious caution, for we are to render an account to the Lord of our actions, as we weigh up and scrutinise with scrupulous care which of them ought to be allowed in and received back into the Church.[78]

15.2 In the case of some, either the offences they have themselves committed form such an obstacle or the brethren cannot be budged from their unyielding opposition that it proves totally impossible to let them in without causing scandal and peril to the majority of our brethren. Indeed, we have no right to gather in that which is putrid so as to harm those parts which remain sound and healthy; nor is he a useful or prudent shepherd who lets in among his flock sheep that are sickly and diseased so as to infest his entire flock by exposure to the disease they bring with them.[79]

15.3 Oh how I wish, dearly beloved brother, that you could be present here with us when those who make their way back from schism are warped and twisted sinners! Then you would see under what difficulties I labour to persuade our brethren to show forbearance, to stifle their feelings of bitter resentment, and to consent that these evildoers should be let in and given healing treatment.

They do indeed show joy and delight when those who come back are good enough people whose sins are less offensive; but, correspondingly, they put up noisy protest and resistance whenever those who would return to the Church are diehard and shameless sinners, men contaminated with adulteries or pagan sacrifices, and yet, to crown it all, still remaining arrogant, and there is, therefore, every likelihood of their corrupting the well-disposed souls within the

Church. It is with enormous difficulty that I manage to persuade my people—I really extort it out of them—that they allow the admission of such sinners.

15.4 And in fact the resentment our brethren have felt has proved all the more reasonable in that one or two, despite protests and objections from the people, were received in through my leniency and then turned out to be worse than they had been; for they proved incapable of faithfully keeping up their penitence, having come without genuine repentance.[80]

16.1 But words fail me adequately to describe those who have sailed across to you, sent as representatives by that pseudo bishop Fortunatus. They come in the company of Felicissimus, who has himself left no crime untried, and they bring to you letters as false as he himself is who wrote them. They come laden with the guilt of a rich variety of sins; and their lives are so foul and appalling that even if they had still been inside the Church, it would have been obligatory to cast such men out of the Church.

16.2 And so, being only too well aware of what is on their own consciences, they dare not come up to us or approach the threshold of our Church, but they have gone off roaming outside, seeking all over the province brethren they may ensnare and despoil.[81] And then becoming well known in time to everyone and finding themselves shut out everywhere for their notorious sins, they even sail off over to you. The fact is that they cannot possibly front up to approaching us or appearing before us, for they would face from the brethren a barrage of the most bitter and grievous of criminal charges. 16.3 If they are really prepared to experience the justice of our court, let them come to us. And then, if they can submit any sort of excuse or defence, let us examine what spirit of atonement they can show, what fruits of repentance they can produce. For the doors of this church here are closed to no one, no one is denied access to the bishop. All who approach may experience the help of our forbearance, leniency, and compassion. It is my fervent desire that all should come back inside the Church, that every one of our fellow soldiers should be mustered within the camp of Christ and the dwelling places of God the Father.

For my part, in my zeal and longing to reunite our brotherhood, there is nothing that I do not forgive, there is much that I deliberately overlook. Even sins committed against God I do not investigate with the full and rigorous scrutiny that religious duty demands:[82] by forgiving offences more than I ought, I even run the risk of becoming an offender myself. I give a ready welcome and an embrace of whole-hearted affection to all who return in a spirit of repentance, to all those who confess to their sins in a spirit of sincere and humble atonement.

17.1 But if there are any who imagine they can make their way back to the Church by means of menaces instead of by prayers of supplication or who suppose that they can force an entry for themselves by means of threats and intimidation instead of by tears of remorse and acts of reparation, then let them be convinced in no uncertain terms that the Church of the Lord stands shut in their faces. The camp of Christ stands strong and invincible, fortified by the protection of the Lord; it does not surrender to threats. The bishop of God who holds fast to the gospel can indeed be killed as he guards the precepts of Christ; but he cannot be defeated.

Here we are supplied and supported with a model in courage and faith by Zechariah the priest of God:[83] when he could not be cowed by threats of stoning, he was put to death in the temple of God, as he cried out repeatedly (just as we, too, cry out against the heretics), using these words: *Thus speaks the Lord: you have forsaken the ways of the Lord, and the Lord shall forsake you.*[84]

17.2 That, therefore, a mere handful of foolhardy criminals forsake the ways of the Lord that lead to heaven and salvation and are, accordingly, abandoned by the Holy Spirit for their unholy actions, this provides no reason why we, like them, must be forgetful of the divine teachings; there are no grounds for us to suppose that the crimes of these madmen can prevail over the judgments passed by bishops nor for us to believe that the efforts of mere men can be more powerful in attack than the providence of God shall be in defence.

18.1 And at this point, dearly beloved brother, must we push aside the dignity of the catholic Church, the unspoilt nobility of the faithful people who remain within that Church, even the powerful authority of her bishops? And all for this. So that these heretics now established outside the Church[85] can say they are ready to pass judgment upon one who is the rightful leader within the Church, that sick men may pass judgment upon one who is sound, the wounded upon one who is unharmed, the fallen upon one who stands upright, the accused upon their judge, the sacrilegious upon their sacred priest.

All that would then be left is for the Church herself to surrender to the Capitol, that the bishops should quit, taking away with them the altar of their Lord, and that at the same time the heathen images and idols and all their altars should move in to occupy the sacred and hallowed benches of our clergy.[86] And won't Novatian then be supplied with still more lavish and generous scope for his abusive attacks of rhetoric against us, if these men who have offered sacrifice and publicly denied Christ should not only be solicited to return and let back in without doing any penance but should then even turn round and tyrannise over the Church with their intimidating violence?

18.2 So, then, if peace is what they really want, let them lay down their arms. If they seek to make satisfaction, why do they need to menace us? But if they do in fact threaten us, let them remember that bishops of God are not frightened by the likes of them. Why, not even the Antichrist when he comes will win a way into the Church simply by uttering threats nor will men surrender to his armed violence simply because he declares that he will destroy those who resist him. These heretics are in fact putting weapons into our hands whilst they suppose we are being terrorised by their threats; for instead of casting us down upon our faces, they are in fact rousing us to stand at the ready and they are enflaming us with zeal, since they are making peace itself more perilous a time for the brethren than persecution.[87]

18.3 But we do fervently pray that they may not accomplish in iniquity what they wildly threaten in word, that whilst they may sin by their words of treachery and bitterness, they may not also offend by such deeds. And we further beseech and entreat the God whom they never cease to provoke and harass that their turbulent passions may grow calm, that they may cast off their frenzied madness and return to sanity of mind, that their hearts, now shrouded in the shadows of sin, may recognise the light of repentance, that they may beg their priestly minister to pour forth prayers and petitions on their behalf rather than themselves pour out the blood of their bishop.

But if they do persist in their madness, if they persevere in these savage plots and murderous threats of theirs, there is nowhere to be found a bishop of God who is so feeble, so prostrate, so abject, so infirm with the weakness of human frailty that he would not, with God's help, stand up to confront these assailants and enemies of God; he would find his lowliness and infirmity given fresh spirit and vigour from the strength of God who protects him.[88]

It matters not to us at whose hand or at what hour we may perish, being assured that we shall receive from the Lord the recompense for our lifeblood. But what must cause us to weep and mourn is their condition, for the devil so blinds them that they remain heedless of the unending torments of hell and even strive to imitate the coming of the Antichrist who fast approaches.[89]

19. I am well aware, dearly beloved brother, that ordinarily you read out our letters both to the clergy who greatly flourish there in Rome and who are seated there with you, as well as to your most pious and prosperous laity,[90] and that you do so as a mark of that mutual charity which we both owe and manifest to each other. And yet on this occasion I urge and request that what you would otherwise do out of courtesy without being asked you do for me now at my specific request, so that by reading out this letter of mine you may thereby wholly eradicate from the ears and hearts of the brethren any infection which may have found root there through their poisonous talk and noxious propaganda, and that there may thus be left no stain of heretical calumny to sully the sound and sincere affection of the faithful.

20.1 And as for the future, let our beloved brothers resolutely shun and avoid conversation and discourse with such men *whose speech spreads like a cancer.* As the Apostle says: *Evil talk corrupts good characters,* and again: *After you have admonished the heretic once, avoid him, recognising that a man of that sort has a perverted mind and that he has condemned himself in his sin.* And through Solomon the Holy Spirit speaks with these words: *The perverse man carries damnation in his mouth, he harbours fire on his lips.* Likewise He again counsels us: *Hedge in your ears with thorns and listen not to a wicked tongue,* as again: *The evil man listens to the tongue of the unrighteous but the just man heeds not lying lips.*[91]

20.2 I do realise that our brethren in Rome, being fortified as they obviously are by your foresight as well as being kept well alert by their own vigilance, can be neither ensnared nor deluded by the poisons of these heretics; and I also appreciate that their abiding loyalty to the teachings and precepts of God is equalled only by their fear of the Lord. Nevertheless, we do write these things to you all, however superfluously it may be, induced by our solicitude for your well-being, which is only an expression of the love we bear you. For there must be no commerce or fellowship formed with such characters, there is to be neither table nor talk shared with men of such iniquity, we are to be as far removed from them as they have separated themselves from the Church, for it is written: *But if he has scorned the Church, you should regard him as a heathen and a publican.* And the blessed Apostle not merely advises us, he expressly orders us to keep aloof from men of this kind: *We charge you,* he says, *in the name of our Lord Jesus Christ to keep aloof from every brother whose ways are irregular and who does not follow the tradition they have received from us.*[92]

There can be no fellowship between the faithful and the faithless. Whoever is not with Christ, whoever is an enemy of Christ, whoever is hostile to His peace and unity, cannot have a place in our company. If they come with prayers of supplication and works of reparation, let them be heard; if they hurl insults and threats, let them be driven away.[93]

I wish that you, dearly beloved brother, may ever fare well.

LETTER 60

Cyprian sends greetings to his brother Cornelius.

1.1 News has reached us, dearly beloved brother, of the glorious witness you have given of your faith and valour. It has indeed filled us with such jubilation to learn of your noble confession that we count even ourselves as having some share and partnership in your honours and achievements.[1] Between us we have but one Church; we are united in heart; we are inseparable in concord. What bishop would not, therefore, rejoice in the honours of his brother bishop as if they were his very own? Where is there a community of brethren who would not take delight in the joy of their fellows?

1.2 I have not powers adequately to describe the jubilation and rejoicing that followed here upon our hearing the happy news of your flourishing deeds of bravery; there you had established yourself as leader in confession for your brethren. Not only that. Those leader's confessional honours have become all the greater, for your brothers have shown that they all feel as one with you; by stepping forward, leading the way, to glory, you have made many your companions in glory. By showing yourself prepared to confess the first, on behalf of them all, you have induced your people to become confessors themselves.[2]

We are left, accordingly, in a quandary what we should first extol in you—the alacrity and steadfastness of your own personal faith or the love between brothers that permits no parting. There has been publicly displayed, among you, the bravery of the bishop, marching on ahead; but there has also been revealed the union between him and his brothers, who follow on behind his lead. As there is amongst you but one mind and one tongue, the whole of the church of Rome has in effect confessed the Lord.[3]

2.1 Brightly has there shone forth, dearly beloved brother, that faith which the blessed Apostle so extolled in you.[4] Even in those days he could foresee through the Spirit this glorious valour we can see today, this resolute strength; by his heralding of the future he was in fact testifying to your meritorious achievements, by his praising the fathers he was in fact spurring on the sons. Through your present display of unanimity and fortitude you have set up a splendid model for the rest of the brethren to follow. You have taught them to have a profound fear of God and to hold fast onto Christ. You have taught the people to be united with their bishops in peril and brother not to be separated from brother in persecution. You have taught that it is totally impossible to break a union bonded together by concord and that the God of peace bestows on the peacemakers whatsoever petition is put to Him by all in unison together.[5]

2.2 The Adversary had come hurtling forward, all violence and terror, to wreak havoc on the camp of Christ. But he was beaten back with a vehemence that was the match of his onslaught. He was confronted by courage and strength that was the equal of the dread and terror he had brought with him. He had supposed he could overthrow once again the servants of God[6] and in his usual way strike panic in them as in so many raw and inexperienced recruits, caught off their guard and all unprepared. And so, to start with he attacked one, like a wolf attempting to separate a sheep from the rest of the flock, like a hawk attempting to divide a dove from the column on the wing. For if an attacker has not strength enough to confront all his victims at once, he contrives to isolate and encompass them singly.

2.3 But being driven back by both the faith and vigour of the united army he encountered, he has realised that the soldiers of Christ are now keeping alert watch, that they are now standing at the ready for battle, that die they can but conquered they cannot be, and that they are unconquerable just because they are unafraid to die. They do not return the attack of their attackers since it is not lawful for the innocent to kill even the guilty,[7] but, instead, they readily surrender their lives and their blood so that they may withdraw all the more speedily from wicked and barbarous men who enjoy such scope for their wickedness and barbarity in this world today.

2.4 How glorious was that spectacle watched by the eyes of God, how great was the rejoicing of His Church witnessed by His Christ! They saw the fighting men advance to the combat offered by the enemy, not one by one; no, the entire camp came marching forth as a man. And it is evident that everyone would have come had they but heard, since whoever heard did come running up in such haste.

2.5 How many of the fallen were thereupon restored by a glorious confession![8] They stood their ground with bravery, having become all the braver for facing battle through the very anguish of their repentance. Hence, it is now clear that whereas in the recent past they had been taken by surprise and had panicked, terrified by the unexpected and unaccustomed event,[9] they did nevertheless recover themselves afterwards; now they have regained their true faith and their proper strength drawn from the fear of God, and they have reinforced them for facing every form of endurance with unflinching constancy. No longer do they stand by awaiting pardon for their sin; now they take their stand anticipating a crown for their martyr's sufferings.

3.1 And what, dearly beloved brother, does Novatian say to all this? Does he now abandon his error? Or rather—as is the way of the insane—is he driven to increased frenzy by our very gains and successes? Is it that as, on our side, the glory of our charity and faith keeps growing all the greater, so, on their side, the madness of quarreling and jealousy breaks out with renewed violence? The poor fool: so far from healing his own wound, he keeps on dealing even more grievous wounds both to himself and to his followers. Upon his own brethren he helps bring destruction by braying out with that raucous voice of his and by hurling the darts of his envenomed eloquence,[10] so intransigent has he become through the perverseness of his secular philosophy, instead of being made a lover of peace through the gentleness of the Lord's wisdom.[11] He is now a traitor of the Church, the enemy of compassion, the murderer of repentance, the teacher of pride, the corruptor of truth, and the destroyer of charity.

3.2 Does he yet recognise who is the bishop of God, which is the Church and the house of Christ, who are the servants of God, now being molested by the devil, who are the Christians, now being attacked by the Antichrist? For the Adversary does not seek out those whom he has already subdued, nor does he trouble himself to overthrow those whom he has already made his own. Rather, the enemy and foe of the Church despises and ignores as being captives and conquered already those whom he has succeeded in estranging from the Church and has led away outside the Church. Instead, he hastens on to harass those in whom he perceives that Christ still has His dwelling place.[12]

4. And yet, even should it so happen that someone among them is arrested, that person would still have no grounds for flattering himself as now being a confessor of the Name. It is all too evident that even if the likes of these are put to death outside the Church, there is still no crown of faith for them, only punishment instead for betrayal of faith; nor will they have any dwelling place in the house of God among brothers who are one in spirit, for, as we can see, their demented discord has driven them to forsake the sacred house of peace.[13]

5.1 We do earnestly exhort, dearly beloved brother, to the utmost of our endeavours, in the name of that mutual charity which unites us so closely one to the other, that we, along with all our people, should devote ourselves without ceasing to fastings and vigils and prayers; for we are being counselled and instructed by the Lord in His providence and we are receiving salutary warnings and advice from God in His mercy that the day is now approaching for our combat and contest.[14] Let us, therefore, be urgent and constant with tearful entreaties and frequent supplications; for us these are the heavenly arms which enable us to take our stand and to hold our ground with steadfast courage; these are our spiritual fortifications, these are the divine weapons which protect us.

5.2 And let us be mindful of one another, being united in heart and one in spirit; let us, on either side, pray constantly for one another; let us lighten the burden of our trials and tribulations by our mutual love. And if any one of us, blessed through God's favour with a speedy death, should go on ahead before the others, let our charity continue still before the presence of the Lord, let our prayers not cease on behalf of our brothers and sisters in the presence of our merciful Father.[15]

I wish that you, my dearly beloved brother, may ever fare well.

LETTER 61

Cyprian and his colleagues send greetings to their brother Lucius.[1]

1.1 It was only recently, dearly beloved brother, that we sent our congratulations to you, for through God's favour you had been honoured and blessed twice over in the administration of His Church, being appointed at once confessor and bishop.[2] But now we repeat our congratulations no less warmly to you and to your companions[3] as well as to all your brethren, for through the abundant and beneficent protection of the Lord you have now all been brought back to His people, with those praises and that glory of yours undiminished.[4] 1.2 And so the shepherd has been restored for feeding the flock, the helmsman for piloting the ship, the ruler for governing the people; it now becomes clear that your banishment was so ordained by divine providence not in order that the bishop should be parted from his church through expulsion and exile[5] but so that he might return to his church increased in greatness.

2.1 In the case of the three youths the dignity of their martyrdom was in no way diminished because they came forth safe and sound from the fiery furnace, having thwarted death. Nor were Daniel's honours incomplete because, though delivered up as prey to the lions, he lived on through the protection of the Lord, to enjoy great glory.[6] Among the confessors of Christ the fact that their martyrdom has been deferred does not detract from the merits of their confession; rather, it serves to make manifest the marvellous works of our divine Protector.

2.2 For we can see that in your own case there have been put into action the words which those courageous and celebrated youths proclaimed before the king.[7] They declared that for their part they were prepared to burn in the flames rather than to serve his gods or adore the idol which he had made; yet, they asserted, the God whom they worshipped (and whom we also worship) had the power to release them from the fiery furnace and to rescue them from the hands of the king and from their present sufferings.[8]

We can discern that all this has now been accomplished in your case, thanks to the faith which you displayed in your confession, and the protection of the Lord which He has cast about you. For whereas you showed yourselves ready and willing to undergo every kind of affliction, yet the Lord delivered you from suffering and preserved you for His Church.

2.3 And so, that you are all coming back does not mean that the bishop's dignity as confessor has been diminished; rather, it means that his authority as bishop has been increased. For at the altar there now takes his stand a priest[9] who not by his words but by his deeds exhorts his people to take up the arms of confession and to become martyrs. And in these days when the Antichrist is at hand[10] he trains his soldiers ready for the battle not merely with rousing words and speeches but with the example of his own faith and courage.

3.1 Now we understand, dearly beloved brother, and comprehend in our hearts with full clarity what have been the sacred and salutary purposes of our divine Majesty. We can recognise why this unexpected persecution lately broke out amongst you and why the secular powers suddenly launched out against the Church of Christ, against the bishop and blessed martyr Cornelius, and against all of you.[11] It was so that the Lord might rout and confound the heretics by making manifest which was His Church, who was its one bishop chosen and appointed by God,[12] who were the presbyters united with that bishop in the dignity of the priesthood,[13] who were the one, true people of Christ linked together by that bond of charity which distinguishes the Lord's flock—in a word, who were they whom the Enemy sought to assail and who, on the contrary, were they whom the devil spared as belonging already to him. 3.2 For the adversary of Christ pursues and assaults only the camp and the army of Christ; heretics, already laid low in the dust and now belonging to him, he passes by in scorn, seeking to cast down those whom he sees to be still standing.

4.1 How I wish we now had the opportunity, dearly beloved brother, whereby we who love you in reciprocal affection could be present there in Rome as you make your return! We might then ourselves partake with the others in the joyful excitement at your arrival. What elation must there be among all the brethren, how they must all surge forward to clasp each one of you as you come into sight. Scarcely can the people kiss you enough as they embrace you in welcome, scarcely can they satisfy their eyes with looking and gazing upon you, so jubilant are they at your arrival.[14] The brethren there in Rome now begin to get some notion of what the great joy will be like that will follow upon the Lord's coming. Given the fact that His arrival has so speedily drawn near, you have now projected an advanced image, as it were, of that coming. Just as John, by his coming as Christ's precursor and forerunner, preached that the Christ had come, so now it becomes evident by the bishop's returning as the Lord's confessor and high priest that the Lord, too, is now making His return.

4.2 Meanwhile in our stead, dearly beloved brother, my colleagues and I along with all of the brethren are now sending this letter to you. We wish to communicate to you through this message our own delight and to express our sincere and devoted affection. Here, too, we do not cease in our sacrifices and in our prayers to give thanks to God the Father and to Christ His Son our Lord, and likewise to pray and beseech that He who is Himself perfect and makes others perfect may preserve and bring to perfection in you the glorious crown of your confession. Indeed, it may be that He has recalled you from exile just so that your glory might not be left concealed had it been that your confession and martyrdom were brought to their fulfillment away from your people. For the victim which provides the brethren with an example in both courage and faith ought to be offered in sacrifice where the brethren are themselves present.[15]

We wish that you, dearly beloved brother, may ever fare well.

LETTER 62

Cyprian sends greetings to his brothers Januarius, Maximus, Proculus, Victor, Modianus, Nemesianus, Nampulus, and Honoratus.[1]

1.1 It has caused us the gravest anguish in our hearts, dearly beloved brothers, and indeed it brought tears to our eyes to read your letter which in your love and anxiety you wrote to us about our brothers and sisters who are now held in captive hands. Who would not be distressed at such a calamity or who would not reckon the distress which his brother feels as his own, remembering the words which the apostle Paul speaks: *If one member suffers, the other members also suffer with it; and if one member rejoices, the other members also rejoice with it.* And in another place he asks: *Who is weak and I am not weak also?*[2] 1.2 We must now, accordingly, reckon the captivity of our brethren as our own captivity also, and we must account the distress of those in peril as our own distress; for, I need hardly remind you, in our union we form but one body and, therefore, not just love but our religion also ought to rouse and spur us on to redeem brethren who are our fellow members.[3]

2.1 Now the apostle Paul further says: *Do you not know that you are the temple of God and that the Spirit of God dwells in you?*[4] And so, even if charity had failed to move us to come to the assistance of our brothers, we would still have needed to consider that in this case what have been taken captive are temples of God. It is our duty, therefore, not to allow such temples of God to remain long in captivity through any dilatory negligence on our part or indifference at their distress. Rather, we ought to act with all speed, exerting every possible effort, so that by our dutiful services we may earn the favour of Christ our Judge and of the Lord our God.

2.2 To quote the apostle Paul: *All of you who have been baptised in Christ, have put on Christ.*[5] And so we ought to behold Christ in our captive brethren and we ought to redeem Him from the peril of captivity who has redeemed us from the peril of death. Hence, just as He rescued us from the jaws of the devil, so too now He who abides and dwells within us is to be rescued from the hands of the barbarians,[6] and He who redeemed us on the cross through His blood is now to be redeemed by us through the payment of money. And for the present He allows such things to happen, for He is trying the strength of our faith, testing whether each of us would do for another what he would have done for himself[7] were he to be held captive among barbarians.

2.3 If a man preserves some sense of humanity, if he is at all mindful of mutually-shared affection, would he not imagine, if he is a father, that they who are now there are his own sons; or, if he is a husband, would he not fancy that his own wife is now held captive there, and hence be overcome at once with distress as with conjugal love?[8] But what must cause us all the most painful of harrowing grief is to think of the perils of the virgins who are being held there. We have to lament not only over the loss of their liberty but over the loss of their honour as well; we have to grieve not so much because they are enchained by those barbarians as because they may be debauched in brothels and abused by procurers, in dread lest those members which have been dedicated to Christ and vowed in modesty to the honour of perpetual chastity may have been violated and defiled by lustful outrages.[9]

3.1 Such were the painful thoughts and reflections which your letter prompted amongst our brethren here. And so they all forthwith contributed most willingly generous financial aid for their brothers. Being of such robust faith, they are ever ready to do the works of God; but on this occasion they were more than usually fired to perform such works of mercy by their awareness of these distressing circumstances.

Now the Lord says in His Gospel: *I was sick and you visited me.* But His words will be accompanied by a far greater reward for our good works when He says: I was captive, and you redeemed me. Again He says: *I was in prison, and you visited me.* But it will be far more advantageous for us when He proceeds to say: I was held captive and in prison, I lay among barbarians behind bars and in chains, but you freed me from my slavery and imprisonment; for we shall soon receive our recompense from the Lord when the day of judgment comes.[10] 3.2 And so we thank you most gratefully for wishing us to have a share in your anxious concerns and to be partners with you in so noble and necessary a work. You have offered to us fertile fields on which we might cast the seeds of our hope, in the expectation of the abundant and fruitful harvest that is produced by this heavenly and blessed labour.

Accordingly, we are sending in cash one hundred thousand sesterces[11] which have been collected from the contributions of the clergy and the laity who reside here with us in the church over which, by God's favour, we have charge. This is for you to distribute with your wonted diligence.

4.1 Our fervent wish is indeed that nothing similar should happen in the future and that our brothers, under the protection of the Lord's majesty, may be kept safe from all such perils. If, however, in order to test and examine the faith and charity in our hearts, anything of the kind should befall you, do not hesitate to write word of it to us; you can be fully confident and assured that whilst our church and all of the brethren here do pray that this should never occur again, yet, if it does, they will willingly provide generous assistance.

4.2 I have appended below the names of the individual contributors so that in your prayers you may be mindful of our brothers and sisters[12] who have so promptly and willingly undertaken this very necessary work. May you thus ensure that they may never fail to do such works of mercy, repaying them for their good works in your sacrifices and devotions.

Furthermore, I have added as well the names of our colleagues and fellow bishops who, being present in Carthage, also made contributions themselves on behalf of their own people[13] according to their resources. In addition to our own sum I have indicated their smaller donations as well,[14] which I am also sending.

All of these people you would do well to remember in your prayers and devotions, as faith and charity demands.

We wish that you, dearly beloved brothers, may ever fare well in the Lord and be mindful of us.

LETTER 63

Cyprian sends greetings to his brother Caecilius.[1]

1.1 I am fully aware, dearly beloved brother, that for the most part bishops who by the grace of God have been set in charge over the Lord's churches throughout the world adhere faithfully to the gospel truth and the Lord's teachings; they do not, by adopting any newfangled and man-made inventions, deviate from what Christ our Master both prescribed and practised. Notwithstanding, there are some who, whether through ignorance or naïveté, when they consecrate the Lord's cup and administer it to their people, do not follow the precepts and practices of Jesus Christ our Lord and God, the Author and Teacher of this sacrifice.

I have, therefore, considered it my solemn duty and obligation to write to you all a letter on this matter,[2] so that anyone still held captive by their error may see the clear light of truth and return to the fundamental and original doctrine handed down to us by the Lord.[3] 1.2 But we trust, dearly beloved brother, that you do not suppose that what we write are our own personal fancies or man-made opinions, or that we are foolhardy enough to take this task upon ourselves acting on our own initiative; for it is our way ever to be unassuming, preserving a humble and modest reserve. But when something is commanded by God's inspiration and instruction,[4] there can be no choice for a faithful servant but to obey his master; he must stand acquitted before all of undertaking anything himself out of arrogance, seeing that fear of offending the Lord obliges him to do what he is bidden.

2.1 And you should understand that the warning we have been given is this: in offering the cup the teachings of the Lord must be observed and we must do exactly as the Lord first did Himself for us—the cup which is offered up in remembrance of Him is to be offered mixed with wine.[5] For inasmuch as Christ says: *I am the true vine*,[6] it can never be supposed that the blood of Christ is water; it is wine. 2.2 And it is, therefore, obviously impossible that Christ's blood, by which we have been redeemed and quickened, should be present in the cup when in the cup there is no wine: wine signifies

the blood of Christ, as is foretold by sacred type and testimony to be
found throughout the Scriptures.[7]

3. For already in Genesis we find in the story of Noah a
prophetic anticipation of this very aspect of this sacred mystery;
Noah appears there as a type presaging the Lord's passion. For he
drank wine, he became inebriated, he went naked in his own household, he lay back with his thighs naked and exposed, his middle son
observed his father's nakedness and indeed made it known abroad
but it was covered over by the older and younger sons. There is no
need for me to pursue the rest of the story; it is sufficient to appreciate
this point alone, that in drinking not water but wine Noah exhibited
a symbol of the truth to come and thus prefigured the Lord's passion.[8]

4.1 Likewise in the case of the priest Melchizedek we see foreshadowed in mystery a type of the Lord's sacrifice, as the Holy Scriptures testify with these words: *And Melchizedek, the king of Salem,
brought forth bread and wine, for he was a priest of the most high God and
he blessed Abraham.* And the fact that Melchizedek indeed portrayed a
type of Christ is declared in the Psalms by the Holy Spirit speaking
in the person of the Father to the Son: *Before the daystar I begot you.
You are a priest forever according to the order of Melchizedek.* And this order
is doubtless that one which derives its source and origins from that
sacrifice of Melchizedek, for Melchizedek was a priest of the most
high God, he did offer bread and wine, and he blessed Abraham.
And who is more truly a priest of the most high God than our Lord
Jesus Christ, who offered sacrifice to God the Father and made the
very same offering as Melchizedek had done, viz. bread and wine,
that is to say His own body and blood?[9]

4.2 And that preceding blessing bestowed upon Abraham extended to our people likewise. For if Abraham believed in God and
that belief was credited to him as justice, then clearly everyone who
believes in God and lives by faith will be found a just man and is
revealed to have been long since blessed and justified in the person
of the faithful Abraham. This is proved by the words of the blessed
apostle Paul: *Abraham believed in God and this belief was credited to him
as justice. And so you can recognise that it is the men of faith who are the sons
of Abraham. And the Scripture, foreseeing that God would justify the nations
by faith, announced beforehand to Abraham that in him all the nations would*

be blessed. So it is that men of faith are blessed along with the faithful Abra-ham.[10]

And this is why in the Gospel we find that sons are raised to Abraham out of the stones—that is to say, are gathered in from the nations;[11] and so, too, in praising Zacchaeus the Lord said in response: *Salvation has come to this house today, for this man, too, is a son of Abraham.*[12]

4.3 And therefore, as we read in Genesis, it was in order that the blessing might be duly bestowed upon Abraham through Mel-chizedek the priest, that before it there preceded a symbol of Christ's sacrifice, consisting, of course, in the offering of the bread and the wine. And when the Lord brought to fulfillment and completion that symbolic action, He offered bread and a cup mixed with wine, and so He who is Fullness itself fulfilled the truth of that prefigured symbol.

5.1 Likewise, too, through the person of Solomon the Holy Spirit forecasts a type of the sacrifice of our Lord which is to come, referring to a victim offered in sacrifice, to bread and wine, and even to an altar and the apostles.[13] *Wisdom*, he says, *has built her own home, supporting it with seven pillars. She has slaughtered her own sacrificial victims, she has mixed in her bowl her own wine and she has prepared her own table.* 5.2 *And she has sent forth her own servants, with loud proclamation inviting men to partake of her wine bowl. Whoever is simple-minded, she says, let him come to visit me. And to those who lack understanding she has said: Come and eat of my bread, and drink the wine which I have mixed for you.* Solomon declares that the wine has been mixed, that is to say he pro-phetically foretells that the cup of the Lord is mixed with water and wine. Hence, it becomes evident that in the passion of our Lord that was accomplished which had already been predicted.[14]

6.1 In the blessing of Judah the same message is also signified, and there, likewise, a figure of Christ is portrayed. For Judah was to be praised and worshipped by his brethren; he was destined to press down upon the necks of his enemies as they turned and fled—using those very hands by which He bore the cross and conquered death; for He is Himself the lion of the tribe of Judah, He reclines in sleep during His passion, but then He arises to become Himself the hope of the nations. 6.2 To all of which the Holy Scriptures add these words: *He shall wash his raiment in wine and his robe in the blood of the grape.* And when the blood of the grape is mentioned, this can signify only that in the Lord's cup the blood is wine.[15]

7.1 Moreover, through Isaiah the Holy Spirit makes this same prophetic testimony concerning the Lord's passion, using these words: *Why is your clothing ruddy, and your apparel as from the treading of the full and well-trodden wine vat?*[16] Can water make clothing ruddy? In the wine vat is it water which is trodden by the feet and squeezed out by the press? Obviously, wine is deliberately referred to here, so that by wine we may be sure to understand the blood of the Lord, and so that what was afterwards manifested in the cup of the Lord might be foretold by the proclamation of the prophets. 7.2 And mention is likewise made to treading and pressing in the wine vat,[17] for just as it is impossible to prepare wine for drinking unless the bunch of grapes is first trodden and pressed, so neither could we drink ourselves the blood of Christ unless Christ had first been trodden upon and pressed, and had drunk before us the cup which He could then pass on to His believers to drink.

8.1 But you must realise that every time that water is named by itself in the Holy Scriptures, there is a prophetic allusion to *baptism.*[18] We can see this signified in Isaiah: *Remember not the things of the past nor consider the things of long ago. Behold, I am making new things; they shall now spring forth and you will recognise them. I will make a way in the wilderness and rivers in the waterless land to give water to my chosen people, my folk whom I took as my own that they might proclaim my powers.*[19] In that passage God foretold through the prophet that rivers should one day flow in abundance among the nations, in lands which before had been waterless, and that those rivers should water the chosen people of God, that is to say those who by the regeneration of baptism have been made the sons of God.

8.2 There is, likewise, another prediction and prophecy, concerning the Jews: if they should become thirsty and seek after Christ, they will find drink with us, that is, they will acquire the grace of baptism. *If they shall become thirsty,* he says, *in the desert places, he will provide them with water, he will produce it for them out of the rock; the rock will be split, water will flow forth, and my people will drink.* And this we find fulfilled in the Gospel when Christ, who is the rock, is split open during His passion by a blow from a lance.[20] 8.3 And Christ Himself reminded us of this prediction when He cried out with these words:

Whoever is thirsty let him come, and whoever believes in me let him drink. As the Scripture says, "out of his belly will flow streams of living water." And that it might be made even clearer that the Lord is speaking there not of the cup but of baptism, the Scripture has added these words: *But He spoke this of the Spirit whom those who believed in Him were to receive.*[21] For it is through baptism that we receive the Spirit and that is why it is only after we have been baptised and have obtained the Spirit that we proceed to drink the cup of the Lord.[22]

8.4 And no one should feel troubled by the fact that when the Holy Scripture speaks of baptism, it says that we thirst and drink, for even the Lord says in the Gospel: *Blessed are they who thirst and hunger for justice,* meaning simply that we drink all the more fully and abundantly that which we desire to receive eagerly and thirstily. It is just as the Lord says, in another passage, to the Samaritan woman: *All who drink of this water will thirst again, but he who drinks of the water which I shall give him will not thirst for all eternity.* And by these words, too, are signified the saving waters of baptism, which are indeed received but once and then never repeated, whereas the cup of the Lord we constantly thirst after and drink in His Church.[23]

9.1 But, dearly beloved brother, we have no need for a long list of proofs to establish that by the term "water" baptism is always signified and that is how we ought to interpret it, since the Lord at His coming has made manifest the full truth concerning baptism and the cup. He has directed that that never-failing water, the water of eternal life, should be given in baptism to believers.

But as for the cup, He has taught us by His own authoritative example that it should consist of the union of wine and water. 9.2 For on the eve of His passion He took the cup, blessed it, and gave it to His disciples, saying: *Drink all of you of this. For this is the blood of the covenant, which shall be shed for many, for the forgiveness of sins. I say to you, I shall not drink further of this fruit of the vine until that day when I shall drink with you new wine in the kingdom of my Father.* Here we find that the cup which the Lord offered was mixed and what He called blood was wine.[24]

9.3 It becomes, therefore, evident that the blood of Christ is not offered if there is no wine in the cup, and that the Lord's sacrifice is not duly consecrated and celebrated unless the offering and sacrifice we make corresponds with His passion. And how are we going to drink with Christ new wine from the fruit of the vine in the kingdom of the Father if in our sacrifice to God the Father we do not even offer the wine of Christ and if we do not mix the cup of the Lord as the Lord Himself has appointed?

10.1 Likewise, the blessed apostle Paul, who was especially chosen by the Lord and sent forth to preach the truths of the gospel, makes exactly this same assertion in his epistle with these words: *The Lord Jesus, on the night He was betrayed, took bread, gave thanks, broke it, and said: This is my body, which is for you. Do this in remembrance of me. In like manner He took the cup also, after He had supped, and said: This cup is the new covenant in my blood. Do this, as often as you drink it, in remembrance of me. For as often as you eat this bread and drink this cup, you proclaim the death of the Lord until He comes.*[25]

10.2 Now if the Lord directed, and those directions are confirmed precisely and repeated to us by His apostle, that as often as we drink we are to do in remembrance of the Lord what the Lord also did, then we must conclude that we fail to observe the instructions given to us if we do not also do exactly what the Lord did: it must be by mixing the cup in like manner that we do not depart from His divine teaching.

10.3 And in another passage the Apostle teaches us in even stronger and more urgent terms that we must never depart from the precepts of the gospel and that the disciples must observe and do exactly what their Master taught and did. Here are his words: *I am astonished that you turn so quickly away from Him who called you to grace, to follow another gospel. Not that there is another gospel; only that there are some people who disturb your minds, trying to pervert the gospel of Christ. But even if we or an angel from heaven should preach a gospel different from that which we have proclaimed to you, he is to be held accursed. And as we have said before, so I do say again now: If anyone proclaims to you a gospel different from that which you have received, let him be held accursed.*[26]

11.1 And so, since neither the Apostle himself nor an angel from heaven is at liberty to proclaim any doctrine different from that which Christ once taught and His apostles have proclaimed, I am truly astonished how this practice can have arisen whereby, contrary to the prescriptions of the gospel and of the apostles, in some places water, which by itself is incapable of signifying the blood of Christ, is offered in the Lord's cup.

11.2 And yet the Holy Spirit also gives expression to this sacred mystery in the Psalms, by alluding to the Lord's cup with these words: *Your cup which intoxicates is truly excellent.* And the cup which so intoxicates must clearly be mixed with wine; for no one can become intoxicated on water.[27]

11.3 Now the Lord's cup intoxicates just in the same way as we read in Genesis that drinking wine made Noah intoxicated. But the intoxication that comes from the Lord's cup and His blood is far different from the intoxication that comes from profane wine. For when the Holy Spirit spoke in the psalm of "your cup which intoxicates," He added the words "is truly excellent," since it is obvious that the Lord's cup intoxicates in such a way that drinking it makes men sober. It restores their minds to spiritual wisdom. By it everyone recovers his senses, turning away from a taste for these earthly things towards an appreciation of the things of God. And just as by drinking that ordinary wine we put our minds at ease, we become relaxed in spirit, and we lay aside all our troubles and cares, so, too, after drinking the blood of the Lord and His saving draught, we lay aside all memory of the old man, we forget his former worldly ways,[28] and our hearts, which before were troubled and distressed under the tormenting and crushing weight of sins, are put at ease and become joyful through God's merciful bounty. In brief, to drink this cup in the Church of the Lord can indeed bring us joy, but only if, when we drink it, we adhere to the true prescriptions of the Lord.

12.1 So you can appreciate the extent of our perversity and wrongheadedness if we should turn wine into water, whereas at the marriage feast the Lord turned water into wine, and that symbolic action, too, ought to warn and guide us that it is wine we should offer in the sacrifices we make to the Lord. And so it was that when the Jews had come to lack spiritual grace, they also lacked wine; *for the vineyard of the Lord of hosts is the house of Israel.*[29] 12.2 Now Christ has taught and revealed that the Jews are to be succeeded by the multitude of the Gentiles and that through the merits of our faith we are to take over that place which the Jews had forfeited. For He turned water into wine, that is, He revealed that upon the desertion of the Jews the peoples of the Gentiles should rather come flocking in together in their crowds at the wedding between Christ and His Church. For that waters signify the nations the Holy Scripture declares in the Apocalypse with these words: *The waters you saw, upon which that harlot sits, are the peoples and populations, the nations of the heathen and tongues.*[30]

And this we can plainly perceive to be contained in the sacred mystery of the cup. 13.1 For Christ bore the burden of us all, having borne the burden of our sins. And so we can see that by water is meant God's people,[31] whereas Scripture reveals that by wine is signified the blood of Christ. When, therefore, water is mixed with wine in the cup, the people are made one with Christ and the multitude of believers are bonded and united with Him in whom they have come to believe. 13.2 And this bonding and union between water and wine in the Lord's cup is achieved in such a way that nothing can thereafter separate their intermingling. Thus there is nothing that can separate the union between Christ and the Church, that is, the people who are established within the Church and who steadfastly and faithfully persevere in their beliefs: Christ and His Church must remain ever attached and joined to each other by indissoluble love.

13.3 Hence, when we consecrate the cup of the Lord, water alone cannot be offered, no more than can wine alone. For should anyone offer up only wine, then the blood of Christ will be there, but without us, whereas if there is only water, the people will be there, but without Christ. So it is only when both are mingled, bonded, united, and fused one with the other that this spiritual and divine mystery is accomplished. And just as the Lord's cup consists neither of water alone nor of wine alone but requires both to be intermingled together, so, too, the Lord's body can neither be flour alone nor water alone but requires that both be united and fused together so as to form the structure of one loaf of bread. 13.4 And under this same sacred image our people are represented as having been made one, for just as numerous grains are gathered, ground, and mixed all together to make into one loaf of bread, so in Christ, who is the bread of heaven, we know there is but one body and that every one of us has been fused together and made one with it.[32]

14.1 There are, therefore, dearly beloved brother, no grounds for anyone to suppose that he ought to follow the custom practised by some people who may in the past have imagined that water alone should be offered in the Lord's cup. We have only to ask who it is that they themselves have followed. And if in the sacrifice which

Christ offered we are to follow nobody but Christ, then it becomes our clear duty to heed and do only what Christ did and only what He prescribed should be done. And for this we have His own words in the Gospel: *If you do what I prescribe to you, no longer do I call you servants but friends.* And that Christ alone is to be heeded, the Father Himself testifies in His words spoken from on high: *This is my beloved Son, on whom my favour rests. Heed you him.*[33]

14.2 Accordingly, if Christ alone is to be heeded, it cannot be right for us to pay attention to what anyone else before us may have supposed should be done, but rather to attend to what Christ, who is before all, first did Himself. We are obliged to follow not the customs of men but the truth of God, as God declares through the prophet Isaiah in these words: *In vain do they worship me, for they teach the doctrines and precepts of men.* And the Lord repeats this same message in the Gospel in these terms: *You cast aside the precepts of God in order to establish a tradition of your own.* Again, He claims elsewhere: *If any man breaks even the very least of these precepts and teaches men to do the same, he will be accounted the very least in the kingdom of heaven.*[34]

14.3 If, then, we may not break even the very least of the Lord's precepts, how much more solemnly binding upon us must it be to make no transgression in matters of such gravity and importance which so closely concern the very mystery of the Lord's passion and our redemption. Just as equally we must make no fundamental change to what has been divinely instituted, relying on some man-made tradition. 14.4 For if Christ Jesus, our Lord and God, is Himself the great High Priest of God the Father and if He offered Himself as a sacrifice to the Father and directed that this should be done in remembrance of Him,[35] then without a doubt that priest truly serves in Christ's place who imitates what Christ did and he offers up a true and complete sacrifice to God the Father in the Church when he proceeds to offer it just as he sees Christ Himself to have offered it.

15.1 On the other hand, all the rule and order that safeguards the truths of our religion will be undermined if we do not loyally observe what is divinely prescribed.

15.2 It may be that some feel apprehensive at our morning sacrifices that if they taste wine they may exhale the smell of the blood of Christ.[36] That is the sort of thinking which causes our brethren to become reluctant to share even in Christ's sufferings in times of persecution, by thus learning in making their oblations to be ashamed of the blood that Christ has shed Himself.[37] 15.3 Whereas we have to remember the words of the Lord in the Gospel: *If any man is ashamed of me, the Son of man will be ashamed of him.* And the Apostle likewise says: *If I were wanting to please men, I should not be the servant of Christ.*[38]

How, I ask then, can we shed our blood for Christ's sake, if we blush for shame to drink Christ's own blood?[39]

16.1 But some may possibly deceive themselves with this comforting reflection that even while it is clear that water only is offered up in the morning, yet (they claim) "when we come to supper we offer a cup that is mixed."[40] But when we dine we cannot call all the people together to share in our meal; we cannot celebrate the full truth of this sacrament if we do not have all of the brethren present.[41]

16.2 Then again, it may be further objected, it was not in the morning but only after supper that the Lord offered the mixed cup. Are we, therefore, to celebrate the Lord's sacrifice after supper so that we may then offer a mixed cup with the brethren gathered all together at that time for the Lord's sacrifice?[42]

Now it was only proper that Christ should make His offering towards the evening of the day, so that He might signify by that hour at which He sacrificed the setting and evening of the world, as it is written in Exodus: *And all the people, the assembly of the children of Israel, shall put him to death towards evening.* And again in the Psalms: *Let the lifting up of my hands be an evening sacrifice.* Whereas for us, we celebrate the resurrection of the Lord in the morning.[43]

17.1 And because at every sacrifice we offer we mention the passion of our Lord (indeed, the passion of our Lord is the sacrifice we offer), then we should follow exactly what the Lord did. And Scripture confirms that as often as we offer the cup in remembrance of the Lord and His passion, we are doing what all are agreed the Lord did before us.[44]

17.2 Now, dearly beloved brother, someone among our predecessors, whether through ignorance or naïveté, may have failed to observe this and to keep to what the Lord has taught us to do by His example and instruction. That is his concern, and our Lord in His merciful kindness may indeed pardon such honest simplicity. But so far as we are concerned, there can be no excusing us, for we have now been warned and counselled by the Lord to offer His cup mixed with wine just as He Himself offered it, and we have been instructed as well to direct letters upon this matter to our colleagues. We are thus to ensure that the Gospel rule and the Lord's instructions are everywhere to be observed and that there is to be no departure from the teaching and example that Christ has given us.[45]

18.1 To continue now to scorn these instructions and to persist in former error must, therefore, entail incurring that reproof and rebuke which the Lord makes in the psalm with these words: *Why do you proclaim my laws and profess my covenant with your lips? For you hate my teachings, and my words you have cast behind you. On seeing a thief you hastened to join him and your lot you have shared with adulterers.* And so to proclaim the laws and covenant of the Lord and yet not to follow exactly what the Lord has done is precisely to cast the Lord's words aside; it is to scorn His teachings; it is to commit not carnal but spiritual thefts and adulteries. For he who like a thief steals away from the truth of the Gospel words and deeds of our Lord is guilty of adulterously corrupting His sacred commandments.[46] 18.2 It is just as it is written in Jeremiah: *What is chaff to the wheat? Therefore, behold I am hostile with the prophets, says the Lord, for they each steal my words from his neighbour and my people they seduce with their lies and their errors.* And in another passage in the same prophet we also read: *And she has committed adultery with wood and stone, and yet for all this she has not returned to me.*[47]

We must, therefore, stand in anxious watch and be alert with holy fear lest we, too, should ever fall foul of such thieving or adultery.

18.3 Now if we are indeed priests of God and of Christ, there is no one I know whom we ought to follow in preference to God and Christ, especially as He Himself expressly states in the Gospel: *I am the light of the world. Whoever follows me shall not walk in darkness but will have the light of life.* So that we may not, therefore, walk in darkness, we ought to follow Christ and to observe His commandments, since He Himself also declared elsewhere, as He sent forth the apostles: *All power is given me in heaven and on earth. Go, therefore, and teach all peoples, baptising them in the name of the Father, and of the Son, and of the Holy Spirit, teaching them to observe all things whatsoever I have commanded you.*[48]

18.4 And so, if we would walk in the light of Christ, let us not depart from His precepts and commandments, giving thanks all the while that whereas He does instruct us in what we should be doing in the future, He also pardons us for any errors we may have done in all good faith in the past. And since His second coming is now drawing near to us, in His generosity and loving-kindness He vouch-safes to shed the light of His truth ever more brightly into our hearts.[49]

19. It is, therefore, dearly beloved brother, incumbent upon us in our piety and fear of the Lord as well as upon the very office and station of bishop which we hold to guard the truth of our Lord's teachings to us by mixing the Lord's cup with wine when we offer it up. And it is our further duty to follow the Lord's warning counsel to us and to correct any error into which some in the past appear to have fallen, so that when He shall come in all His heavenly glory and majesty He may find us upholding what He has counselled, observing what He has taught and doing what He Himself has done.

I wish that you, my dearly beloved brother, may ever fare well.

LETTER 64

Cyprian and his other colleagues present at the Council, sixty-six in number, send greetings to their brother Fidus.[1]

1.1 We have to hand, dearest brother, your letter in which you informed us of the case of the former presbyter Victor:[2] before he had performed full penitence and made satisfaction to the Lord God against whom he had sinned, our colleague Therapius with rash and precipitate haste granted him reconciliation though the time for this was still premature.[3] This action has seriously disturbed us, for it marks a departure from the authority of our decree: reconciliation has been conceded to Victor before the full and proper period of satisfaction, without any petitioning or even knowledge of the laity, and even though no sickness made it urgently required nor any necessity forced his hand.[4]

1.2 Nevertheless, after weighing the issue in a lengthy debate, we concluded that it sufficed to reprimand our colleague Therapius for this rash action of his and to direct him to avoid such actions in the future. Yet we were of the opinion that however reconciliation had been granted, once it was granted by a bishop of God it ought not to be taken away,[5] and on this principle we have allowed Victor to enjoy the admission to communion that had been conceded to him.

2.1 As far as concerns the case of infants, you expressed your view that they ought not to be baptised within the second or third day of their birth; rather, the ancient law on circumcision ought to be respected and you therefore concluded that the newly-born should not be baptised and sanctified before the eighth day.[6]

Our Council adopted an entirely different conclusion. No one agreed with your opinion on the matter; instead, without exception we all formed the judgment that it is not right to deny the mercy and grace of God to any man that is born.[7] 2.2 But seeing that the Lord says in His own Gospel: *The Son of man has come not to destroy the souls of men but to save them*,[8] we must do everything we possibly can to prevent the destruction of any soul. We need to ask, what can be lacking to one who has been already formed by the hands of God in his mother's womb? To our way of thinking, indeed, and to our eyes infants after their birth appear to grow and increase as the earthly days go by; but as far as God their Maker is concerned, whatever has been made by Him is perfect and complete thanks to His handiwork and almighty power.

3.1 Moreover, the divine Scriptures in which we put our trust declare to us that all, whether infants or older, enjoy exactly equal shares in the divine bounty. For Elisha, with a prayer of supplication to God, stretched himself over the widow's infant son who lay there dead, placing head upon head and face upon face, spreading his limbs over each of the little child's limbs and joining feet with feet. Now if you think of this action in terms of different ages and bodily sizes, an infant could not possibly have the same dimensions as a fully-grown adult nor could his small limbs match and measure up to an older man's. But in this incident what is being illustrated is divine and spiritual equality,[9] according to which all men are equal and alike because they have all once been made by God; we may be different, so far as the world is concerned, in the development of our bodies depending on our various ages, but there is no difference between us so far as

God is concerned. Unless you are prepared to claim that even that very grace which is given to the baptised is distributed in greater or lesser degree according to the ages of the recipients! Whereas, in truth, the Holy Spirit is not measured out but is conferred equally upon all through the bounty and loving-kindness of the Father.[10] For just as God draws no distinction between persons, so neither does He between ages,[11] but He shows Himself a Father equally to all, being evenhanded in the distribution of His heavenly graces.

4.1 We now turn to your claim that the foot of an infant in the very first days after his birth is not clean, every one of us still recoiling in repugnance at the thought of kissing it.[12] In our view this too ought to be no reason for blocking the bestowal of heavenly grace. For it is written: *To the clean all things are clean.*[13] 4.2 Nor should anyone of us shudder in repugnance at that which God has deigned to make. The infant may indeed be still fresh from its birth; yet he is not such that anyone should shrink in repugnance from kissing him in the course of bestowing grace and conferring peace upon him.[14] When we kiss an infant, piety should tell each one of us that we ought to be thinking of the very hands of God from which that infant has so freshly come; in a sense, therefore, in a human being recently formed and newly born we are kissing those hands of God when we embrace what God has made.

4.3 And as for the fact that among the Jews circumcision of the flesh was observed on the eighth day, that was but a holy sign, an anticipatory image, a prefiguring given in prophecy which has been brought to reality and fulfillment with the coming of Christ.[15] Because the eighth day, that is to say the first day after the Sabbath, was going to be the day on which the Lord should rise again, bring us to life, and give us circumcision of the spirit, that eighth day, that is to say the first day after the Sabbath, the Lord's own day, preceded as an image of what was to come.[16] That image has ceased now that the reality has superseded it and we have been given circumcision of the spirit.

5.1 And that is the reason why, in our view, no one is to be prevented from obtaining grace by that law which was once in the past in force:[17] circumcision of the flesh ought not to block the way to circumcision of the spirit. Rather, every man without exception has the right to be admitted to the grace of Christ since Peter, too, in the Acts of the Apostles declares: *The Lord has said to me that no man is to be called impure and unclean.*[18]

5.2 Besides, if anything could stand in the way of obtaining grace, it would rather be adults, men of mature and more advanced years, who might have their way blocked by their more grievous sins. But remember this: even in the case of those who have sinned most grievously, offending many times in their past lives against God, they are granted remission of their sins, subsequently, on becoming believers.[19] No one is denied access to baptism and grace. How much less reason is there then for denying it to an infant who, being newly born, can have committed no sins. The only thing that he has done is that, being born after the flesh as a descendant of Adam, he has contracted from that first birth the ancient contagion of death. And he is admitted to receive remission of his sins all the more readily in that what are being remitted to him are not his own sins but another's.[20]

6.1 And so, dearest brother, our verdict at the Council was this: we ought not to be the cause for debarring anyone from access to baptism and the grace of God, for He is merciful, kind, and loving towards all men. 6.2 And whilst this is a rule which ought to be observed and maintained concerning the whole of mankind, it is our view that it should be observed most particularly in the very case of newborn infants; they have all the more claim upon our assistance and God's mercy for the reason that, right from the very first moment they are born, in their crying and wailing they are doing nothing else but imploring for our help.[21]

We wish that you, dearest brother, may ever fare well.

LETTER 65

Cyprian sends greetings to his brother Epictetus and to the laity dwelling at Assuras.[1]

1.1 Dearly beloved brethren, I was deeply upset and gravely disturbed to learn that Fortunatianus, your former bishop, even after his grievous lapse and transgression, should now want to act as if he were altogether without fault[2] and that he is, therefore, proceeding to lay claim to the position of bishop for himself. 1.2 In all this my primary distress is for the wretched man himself: he has been so utterly blinded by the darkness of Satan or so duped by the sacrilegious counsels of certain people[3] that whereas he ought to be making atonement and passing his days and nights in urgent prayers, supplications, and tears, seeking to appease the Lord, yet, in fact, he has the gall still to lay claim to the dignity of bishop, which he betrayed, as being his own.[4] It is as if there were no profanation in approaching the altar of God straight after leaving Satan's.[5] Indeed, it is as if on the day of judgment he should not rouse against himself special wrath and outrage from the Lord, even though, instead of having given guidance to his brothers in faith and courage, he shows himself an instructor in treason, recklessness, and foolhardiness,[6] and instead of teaching his brothers how to stand bravely in battle, he teaches those who have been overthrown and laid low not even to petition the Lord.

And yet the Lord says: *To them you have poured out libations and for them you have offered up sacrifices. For this will I not be wrath? says the Lord.* And elsewhere He says: *He who sacrifices to the gods, unless it is to the Lord only, will be totally destroyed.* Moreover, the Lord speaks again in these words: *They have worshipped those whom their own fingers have made, and the lowly man bows down and the great man does obeisance. And I shall not relent towards them.* And in the Apocalypse also we read of the wrath of the Lord who utters these menacing words: *If a man worships the beast and his image, and receives his mark on his brow and on his hand, he too will drink of the wine of the wrath of God, mixed in the cup of His wrath, and he will be punished with fire and brimstone in the sight of the holy angels and in the sight of the Lamb. And the smoke of their torments will ascend for ever and ever. And they shall have no rest, neither day nor night, they who worship the beast and his image.*[7]

2.1 Such, therefore, are the torments and punishments with which on the day of judgment the Lord menaces those who obey Satan and who sacrifice to idols. How then does he imagine he can act as a priest of God, seeing that he has obeyed and served the priests of Satan? How does he suppose that his hand can now be turned to the sacrifice of God and the solemn prayer of the Lord,[8] seeing that it has been in bondage to sacrilege and sin? For in the Sacred Scriptures God forbids from approaching the sacrifice even priests whose sin is far less grave, saying in Leviticus: *The man in whom there shall be any blemish or spot shall not approach to offer gifts to God.* Likewise in Exodus He says: *And let the priests who approach the Lord God be sanctified, lest perchance the Lord should forsake them.* And again He says: *And they who approach to serve at the altar of the Holy One shall not bring sin upon themselves lest they should die.*[9]

2.2 And so those who have indeed brought grievous sins upon themselves, that is to say, those who by sacrificing to idols have offered sacrilegious sacrifices, can lay no claim to the priesthood of God for themselves, neither can they offer on behalf of the brethren any solemn prayer in His sight. For in the Gospel it is written: *God hears not the sinner; but He does hear any man who worships God and does His will.*[10] And yet some hearts have been so blinded by a profound and enveloping darkness that they let in no ray of light from the saving precepts of God. But once having turned away from the straight path and the true way they go plunging forwards hurling themselves into the abyss as they wander lost in the night of their sins.

3.1 Nor should it cause any surprise if they who once denied the Lord now reject our counsels or the Lord's precepts. What they hanker after are the payments and presents and profits over which in times past they used to gloat so insatiably;[11] even now they gulp at the thought of the feasts and banquets which used to leave them for days afterwards hung-over and belching with indigestion. They now demonstrate with the utmost clarity that previously it was not their religion which they served; rather it was to the service of their own bellies and sordid gain that they were devoted with irreligious greed.[12]

3.2 Hence, it is our belief and judgment that this very censure of God has come down upon them as a result of His searching test:[13] they were so visited in order to prevent their standing any longer before His altar, and to stop there being any further contact between the impure and the chaste, the faithless and the faithful, the irreligious and the devout, the earthly and the godly, the sacrilegious and the holy. 3.3 We must, therefore, keep watch with all vigilance so as to prevent such men from returning once again to pollute that altar and to infect the brethren; we must strive with all our energies so as to put such restraints as we can manage upon their present insolence and wickedness, inhibiting their attempts to continue to act as bishops—whereas, in fact, they have gone hurtling down to the lowest depths of death, plunging so much lower than any of the fallen laity, for they are weighed down by a more grievous lapse.

4.1 But if these madmen should continue incurably insane and if they should remain in the blindness of their night in which they now find themselves upon the withdrawal of the Holy Spirit, then our counsel is clear: we will have to separate the brethren individually from their snares and cut them off from any contact with them in order to avoid the risk of their being trapped in the nets of their error. For the oblation cannot be sanctified where the Holy Spirit is not present, neither is the Lord able to grant His benefits to any man through the prayers and supplications of one who has himself outraged the Lord.[14]

4.2 And so, should Fortunatianus persist in his present lunacy, becoming forgetful of his own heinous offence through the blindness of Satan or even becoming an assistant and servant of Satan's in his work of deceiving the brethren, you must make every effort you possibly can to call back the hearts of the faithful from error, for they can be lost in these blinding mists spread by the ravening devil. You must stop them from giving unthinking assent to the delirium of others or from becoming accomplices in the crimes of desperate men. Rather, let them remain without corruption, adhering faithfully, as they have done, to the way of salvation; let them continue vigorously to preserve their innocence which they have hitherto guarded and protected.

5.1 As for the lapsed, they must recognise the enormity of their own offence and never cease to entreat the Lord; they must not abandon the catholic Church, for it is the one and only Church founded by the Lord. Rather, let them keep knocking at the door of that Church as they persevere in their acts of atonement, entreating the Lord for mercy, so that they can be let in again where once they were admitted[15] and thus return to Christ from whom they have departed. Let them give no heed to those who would deceive them with their fatally seductive lies, for it is written: *Let no man deceive you with empty words; for these things the wrath of God is coming upon the children of rebel-*

lion. Do not, therefore, become partners with them.[16] And so let no man associate himself with these rebels who are without fear of God and who abandon His Church entirely.

5.2 But should anyone be too impatient to entreat the Lord who has been so offended and refuses to obey our counsels, but chooses instead to take to the following of such desperate and ruined men, then he will have only himself to blame on the day of judgment. For when that day comes, how will he be able to entreat the Lord when not only has he denied Christ already, he has now even denied the Church of Christ into the bargain, and instead of obeying His bishops who are sound, whole, and living, he has given himself over to be an associate and partner with the dying?

I wish that you, my dearly beloved brothers, may ever fare well.

LETTER 66

Cyprian, also called Thascius, sends greetings to his brother Florentius, also called Puppianus.[1]

1.1 I had concluded, my brother,[2] that by now you had at long last turned to repentance for having in the past rashly heeded and even believed in such foul and vile abuse about us, to hear which causes even pagans to feel disgust.

But I do indeed observe from your letter[3] that you are even now totally unchanged from your character of the past, that you still continue to believe the same things about us, and that you have not budged at all from those beliefs you once formed. I also notice that in order to forestall any risk that the lustre of your bright and shining martyrdom might be tarnished by any communion with us,[4] you are conducting a painstaking inquiry into our personal character and that after God the Judge, who makes bishops,[5] you are wanting to set yourself up as judge, I won't say over me (for of what account am I?) but over the very judgment that God and Christ have passed.

1.2 Now Christ declares: *Are not two sparrows sold for a farthing and neither of them falls to the ground without the will of the Father?*[6] and thus the God of majesty and truth thereby establishes that even things of the least consequence do not come to pass without the knowledge and leave of God. In the face of this it is tantamount to disbelief in God, it is to declare yourself a rebel against Christ and His gospel, if, as you do, you hold the view that bishops of God can be appointed in His Church without His knowledge. For to believe that those who are so appointed are unworthy in character and vile in morals is precisely to maintain that it is neither by God nor through God that bishops are ordained in His Church.[7]

2.1 But can you possibly judge that the testimony I give of myself is of greater worth than God's? For the Lord Himself declares and teaches that if a man should set himself up to be his own witness, then the witness that he gives is not true; the simple reason is that, of course, every man is biased in his own favour and no one comes out with damaging and hostile reports against himself. By contrast, unprejudiced truth and trustworthy testimony is to be found when in the statements made about us it is another who makes them, acting as witness for us. As Christ says: *If I bear witness of myself, my witness is not true. For there is another who bears witness of me.*[8]

2.2 Now if the Lord Himself, who one day is to come and pass judgment on all things, was thus reluctant that He should be trusted for His own testimony about Himself but preferred instead to have the judgment and testimony of God the Father for His commendation, how much more strictly ought His servants to observe this rule, for it is upon the judgment and testimony given by God that they must rely for their commendation as well as for their glory.[9]

But in your own case, in spite of the judgment passed by God and in spite of our own clear conscience which is supported by the vigour of its faith, you have chosen to believe the fabrications of hostile and evil-tongued detractors, as if those who have apostatised and are now renegades outside the Church, from whose breasts the Holy Spirit has departed,[10] can offer anything but a wicked heart and a deceitful tongue, and, therefore, hatred and sacrilegious lies. The man who puts his faith in such as these must inevitably be found in their company when the day of judgment comes.

3.1 And in answer to your assertion that bishops ought to be humble because both the Lord and His apostles were humble, I reply that my own humility is perfectly well known and appreciated by all the brethren, no less than by the pagans themselves, and that you both knew and appreciated it yourself when you were still in the Church and in communion with me. 3.2 Moreover, I have to ask which one of us is the further removed from humility. Is it I who am each day to be found serving the brethren and who with expressions of delight and joy give a kindly and individual welcome to everyone who comes into the Church?[11] Or is it you who set yourself up to be bishop over your bishop and judge over the judge[12] whom God has appointed for the time being? And yet the Lord God says in Deuteronomy: *And whatever man acts with such arrogance that he pays no heed to the priest or the judge, whoever he may be in those days, that man shall die, and when all the people hear of it they will be afraid, and they will desist henceforth from their wickedness.* And again He speaks to Samuel in these words: *They have not despised you but they have despised me.* Furthermore, when in the Gospel it was said to Him: *Is that the way you reply to the high priest?*, He uttered no word against the high priest, thereby protecting the dignity of the priesthood and teaching us that it ought to be respected, but He said in reply, merely in order to clear His own innocence: *If I have spoken ill, reprove me for the ill. But if I have spoken well, why do you strike me?* 3.3 Likewise, when it was said to the apostle Paul: *Do you thus dishonour and revile the high priest?*, he answered with no word of insult against the high priest, even though he might have boldly launched out against those who had crucified God and who had now destroyed the Lord Christ, and the Temple and its priesthood. But instead, he remained mindful even of the empty shadow of the priestly name, though he was dealing with false priests who had been despoiled of their powers, and he, therefore, said: *I was unaware, my brothers, that he was a priest. For it is written: you shall not revile the leader of your people.*[13]

4.1 There is the possibility, I suppose, that you did regard me as a bishop before the persecution, when you were at the time in communion with me, but that I have ceased to be a bishop since the persecution.[14] The coming of the persecution certainly lifted you up to the sublimest heights of martyrdom, whereas it pulled me down under the heavy weight of proscription, for the public notice could be read: *If anyone holds in his possession any part of the goods of Caecilius Cyprianus, the bishop of the Christians.*[15] And so even those who did not believe that it was God who appointed me bishop should at least have believed that it was the devil who proscribed me as bishop.[16]

4.2 And these things I say not by way of boasting; I mention them only in sorrow, for you are now appointing yourself judge over God and Christ, and He did say to the apostles, and thereby to all the leaders who are successors to the apostles, appointed to replace them:[17] *He who hears you hears me, and he who hears me hears Him who sent me. And he who despises you despises me and Him who sent me.*[18]

5.1 One can now trace the source from which schisms and heresies have arisen and do arise:[19] they occur when the bishop, who stands alone and who is the appointed leader in the Church, is held in contempt by the proud and arrogant, and when the man whom God has deigned to honour as worthy of office is deemed unworthy by men.

What an insolent sense of swollen self-importance, the high and mighty presumption of it all! Fancy anyone issuing a summons to bishops, the appointed leaders, to attend his court of inquiry. And unless we are cleared before your bench and are acquitted by your verdict, the brethren will have had no overseer these last six years, the people no leader, the flock no shepherd, the Church no helmsman, Christ no priest, and God no bishop![20]

5.2 But only let Puppianus fly to the rescue! Let him issue his sentence and declare ratified the judgment God and Christ have already passed! Otherwise it could be thought that the great number of faithful who have been called away to their rest during our time may have departed without the hope of peace and salvation; it could be considered that a whole new flock of converts may have received through us no grace of baptism and the Holy Spirit;[21] it could be judged that the reconciliation and restoration to communion which we have conferred, after examination, upon so many of the penitent lapsed may be rendered null and void by the authority of your verdict.

Vouchsafe your approval at long last, we beg you! Condescend to issue a pronouncement upon our case, establishing our episcopate upon the firm foundation of your findings! God and His Christ can then be gratefully in your debt, for, thanks to your kind services, at one and the same time the priest will have been restored to Their altar and the ruler to Their people.

6. Bees have a queen bee and cattle a leader, which they faithfully follow;[22] robbers give humble and unquestioning obedience to

their captain. How far are they more upright and virtuous than you, brute beasts and dumb animals though they are; and likewise, brigands who live lives of bloodshed and turbulence spent in constant fighting and warfare. In the latter case their appointed leader is at least acknowledged and feared, and yet he has received his appointment not by the verdict of God but merely by the common agreement of a gang of desperadoes and a pack of criminals.

7.1 Now you have indeed remarked that you need to remove from your conscience a scruple which has proved a stumbling block to you.[23] Stumbled you certainly have, but thanks to your own brand of irreligious credulity; stumbled you have, but thanks to your own sacrilegious inclinations and will. For you lend a ready ear to and even willingly believe in calumnies of shame, impiety, and indescribable disgrace against your brother and your bishop; you stoutly defend these lies of others as if they were your own personal property; and you have forgotten the words of Scripture: *Hedge in your ears with thorns and listen not to a wicked tongue*, and again: *The evil man listens to the tongue of the unrighteous, but the just man heeds not lying lips.*[24]

7.2 And how is it that the martyrs did not stumble against this scruple, and yet they were filled with the Holy Spirit and were already, through their sufferings, very close to the vision of God and His Christ? For from their prison they sent letters addressed to Cyprian the bishop,[25] thereby acknowledging and bearing witness to him as being the holy priest of God. And how is it that so many of my fellow bishops and colleagues also failed to stumble against this scruple? And yet upon their retirement from public they were proscribed, or they were arrested and put in chains and cast into prison, or they were exiled and banished and so advanced toward the Lord by this illustrious route, or in certain places they were put to death and were glorified by the Lord, receiving their heavenly crowns.[26] And how is it that there also failed to stumble against this scruple all the many confessors who come from this people of ours here, the people who are with us now and have been committed to our care by the grace of God? And yet they were subjected to interrogation and tortures and are now held in glory through the memory of their illustrious wounds and scars.[27] Likewise, all the many spotless virgins failed thus to stumble, all the many virtuous widows, and, in a word, all the churches throughout the whole world such as are united with us by the bond of unity.

7.3 Unless, of course, it can be the case (as you claim in your letter) that every one of these, by being in communion with me, has become polluted by contact with our polluted lips[28] and they have, therefore, lost the hope of eternal life through this contagious communion of ours! Puppianus alone is immaculate, inviolate, holy, and chaste, for he would not associate himself with us, and in paradise and the kingdom of heaven, therefore, he will be found dwelling all by himself.

8.1 In your letter you also claimed that it is because of me that the Church now finds she has a portion of herself scattered and dispersed, whereas the whole of the faithful of the Church have in fact been gathered, united, and joined together in indissoluble concord and only they have remained outside who, even had they been inside, would simply have had to be cast out.[29] For the Lord, who is the protector and guardian of His own people, does not allow His wheat to be plundered from His threshing floor; it is only the chaff that can be separated off from the Church. 8.2 As the Apostle says: *What if some of them have fallen from faith? Do you imagine that their faithlessness has made void the faithfulness of God? Far from it. For God is true, though every man be a liar.* The Lord, too, in the Gospel, on the occasion when the disciples started to leave Him as He was speaking, turned to the Twelve and said: *Will you, too, go away? And Peter answered and said: Lord, to whom shall we go? You have the words of eternal life, and we believe and know that you are the Son of the living God.*[30]

8.3 Speaking there is Peter, upon whom the Church had been built, and in the name of the Church he is teaching and revealing that even when a whole host of proud and presumptuous people may refuse to listen and go away, the Church herself does not go away from Christ, and that in his view the Church consists of the people who remain united with their bishop, it is the flock that stays by its shepherd. By that you ought to realize that the bishop is in the Church and the Church is in the bishop, and whoever is not with the bishop is not in the Church. You must understand that it is to no avail that people may beguile themselves with the illusion that whilst they are not at peace with the bishops of God they may still worm their way in and surreptitiously hold communion with certain people.

Whereas, in truth, the Church forms one single whole; it is neither rent nor broken apart but is everywhere linked and bonded tightly together by the glue of the bishops sticking firmly to each other.[31]

9.1 Therefore, my brother, you would do well to reflect upon the majesty of God who appoints these bishops of Christ. You would do well to turn your thoughts, at long last, towards Christ who by His sovereign will and judgment and His saving presence guides both the Church leaders so appointed and along with those leaders the Church itself.[32] You would do well to become convinced that it is not the hatred of men but the judgment of God which determines the innocence of bishops. You would do well even at this late hour to start doing penitence for your foolhardy insolence and pride. On condition that you do these things and have, besides, rendered most amply and abundantly satisfaction to the Lord and His Christ whom I serve and to whom, in times of persecution just as in peace, I never cease to offer up sacrifices with pure and unstained lips, then and only then, these conditions fulfilled, will we be able to consider the question of being in communion with you, but still with the proviso, nevertheless, that we must continue, as always, to show respect for and stand in awe of God's strict censure. 9.2 And so I shall have to consult my Lord first to see whether He might give some sign and indication that He would give His permission for peace to be granted to you and for you to be admitted back into the communion of His Church.[33]

10.1 For I am mindful of the revelation which has already been made to me, or rather, to phrase it better, what the Lord God in His authority has enjoined upon an obedient and God-fearing servant. Among other things which He vouchsafed to reveal and disclose, He imparted this warning: "And so, whoever does not believe in Christ when He appoints a bishop shall begin to believe hereafter in Christ when He avenges that bishop."

10.2 I am very well aware that dreams and visions are thought by some people to be silly and absurd, but it is by precisely those very people who instead of believing in their bishops would rather believe anything against them. Yet it does not surprise me, when even Joseph's own brothers said of him: *Look, here comes that dreamer. Come now, let us kill him.*[34] But the dreamer afterwards saw accomplished what he had dreamed, to the confusion of those who would sell and slay him: though they had earlier refused to believe his words, they were later forced to believe them now verified as deeds.

10.3 But as for what actions you have done whether in time of peace or of persecution, it would indeed be foolish for me to want to sit in judgment upon you since, instead, you have already set yourself up as judge over us.

This reply I have written as my own clear conscience and my reliance upon my Lord and God have suggested. You have my letter and I have yours. On the day of judgment both of them will be read out before the judgment seat of Christ.[35]

NOTES

LIST OF ABBREVIATIONS

ACW	Ancient Christian Writers
AE	L'année épigraphique
AJP	American Journal of Philology
ANRW	*Aufstieg und Niedergang der römischen Welt*, ed. H. Temporini
CAH	Cambridge Ancient History
CCL	Corpus christianorum, series latina
CR	Classical Review
CSEL	Corpus scriptorum ecclesiasticorum latinorum
DACL	Dictionnaire d'archéologie chrétienne et de liturgie
DHGE	Dictionnaire d'histoire et de géographie chrétienne
Dig	Digesta
DTC	Dictionnaire de théologie catholique
ET	English translation
GCS	Die griechischen christlichen Schriftsteller der ersten drei Jahrhunderte
GRBS	Greek, Roman, and Byzantine Studies
Hartel	S. Thasci Caecili Cypriani opera omnia, ed. G. Hartel
HA	Historia Augusta
H.E.	Historia ecclesiastica
ILAf	*Inscriptions latines d'Afrique*, ed. R. Cagnat et A. Merlin
ILAlg	*Inscriptions latines de l'Algérie*, ed. S. Gsell
ILCV	*Inscriptiones latinae christianae veteres*, ed. E. Diehl
ILS	*Inscriptiones latinae selectae*, ed. H. Dessau
JAC	Jahrbuch für Antike und Christentum
JEH	Journal of Ecclesiastical History
JRS	Journal of Roman Studies
JTS	Journal of Theological Studies

MEFR   Mélanges d'archéologie et d'histoire de l'école française
            de Rome
MG   Patrologia graeca, ed. J. P. Migne
MGH   Monumenta Germaniae historica
ML   Patrologia latina, ed. J. P. Migne
Musurillo   H. Musurillo, *The Acts of the Christian Martyrs*
PIR²   Prosopographia imperii romani (2nd ed.)
PLRE   The Prosopography of the Later Roman Empire, vol. 1
PW   Pauly-Wissowa-Kroll, *Realencyclopädie der classischen Al-
            tertumswissenschaft*
RAC   Reallexikon für Antike und Christentum
REAug   Revue des études augustiniennes
RechAug   Recherches augustiniennes
REL   Revue des études latines
RIC   H. Mattingly, E. A. Sydenham, and C. H. V. Suther-
            land, *Roman Imperial Coinage*
SC   Sources chrétiennes
SVF   *Stoicorum veterum fragmenta*, ed. I. von Arnim
TLL   Thesaurus linguae latinae
TU   Texte und Untersuchungen zur Geschichte der
            altchristlichen Literatur
VC   Vigiliae christianae
ZfKG   Zeitschrift für Kirchengeschichte
ZfKT   Zeitschrift für katholische Theologie
ZPE   Zeitschrift für Papyrologie und Epigrafik

BIBLIOGRAPHY

This is not a systematic bibliography but merely gives fuller bibliographical details of works cited in this volume.

Achelis, H., *Die ältesten Quellen des orientalischen Kirchenrechtes*, TU 6.4
    (1891).
Adam, K., "Cyprians Commentar zu Mt. 16, 18 in dogmenge-

schichtlicher Beleuchtung," *Theologische Quartalschrift* 94 (1912) 99 ff., 203 ff.

Alföldi, A., "Zu den Christenverfolgungen in der Mitte des 3. Jahrhunderts," *Klio* 31 (1938) 323 ff.

Alföldi, A., *Studien zur Geschichte der Weltkrise des 3. Jahrhunderts nach Christus* (Darmstadt 1967).

Alföldy, G., "Herodians Person," *Ancient Society* 2 (1971) 204 ff.

Alföldy, G., "Der heilige Cyprian und die Krise des römischen Reiches," *Historia* 22 (1973) 479 ff.

Alföldy, G., "The Crisis of the Third Century as Seen by Contemporaries," *Greek, Roman and Byzantine Studies* 15 (1974) 89 ff.

Allard, P., *Les dernières persécutions du troisième siècle* (2nd ed., Paris 1898).

Andresen, C., " 'Siegreiche Kirche' im Aufstieg des Christentums: Untersuchungen zu Eusebius von Caesarea und Dionysius von Alexandrien," *Aufstieg und Niedergang der römischen Welt* 2.23.1 (1979) 387 ff.

Arbesmann, R., "The Concept of 'Christus Medicus' in St. Augustine," *Traditio* 10 (1954) 1 ff.

Aubé, B., *L'église et l'état dans la seconde moitié du IIIe siècle (249–284)* (Paris 1886).

Audollent, A., *Carthage romaine (146 av. J.-Ch.—698 ap. J.-Ch.)* (Paris 1901).

Augar, F., *Die Frau in römischen Christenprocess*, TU n.f. 13.4 (1905).

Bacchiochi, S., *From Sabbath to Sunday: A Historical Investigation of the Rise of Sunday Observance in Early Christianity* (Rome 1977).

Bakhuizen van den Brink, J. N., "Traditio im theologischen Sinne," *Vigiliae christianae* 13 (1959) 65 ff.

Baldus, H. R., *Uranius Antoninus: Münzpragung und Geschichte* (Bonn 1971).

Baldus, H. R., "Die 'reformierten' Tetradrachmen des Uranius Antoninus im Lichte eines neuen Fundes mit Nachträgen zur übrigen Münzpragung dieses 'Kaisers,' " *Chiron* 5 (1975) 443 ff.

Baldus, H. R., "Neue Münzen des Uranius Antoninus (Nachtrag II)," *Jahrbuch f. Numismatik und Geldgesch.* 27 (1977) 69 ff.

Ball, M. T., *Nature and the Vocabulary of Nature in the Works of St. Cyprian* (Washington D.C. 1946).

Barbieri, G., *L'albo senatorio da Settimio Severo a Carino (193–285)* (Rome 1952).

Bardy, G., "Melchisédech dans la tradition patristique," *Revue biblique* 35 (1926) 496 ff.; 36 (1927) 25 ff.

Barnard, L. W., *Justin Martyr: His Life and Thought* (Cambridge 1967).

Barnes, T. D., *Tertullian: A Historical and Literary Study* (Oxford 1971).

Bastiaensen, A. A. R., *Le cérémonial épistolaire des chrétiens latins* (Nijmegen 1964).

Bayard, L., *Le latin de saint Cyprian* (Paris 1902).

Beatrice, B. F., *Tradux peccati: Alle fonti della dottrina agostiniana del peccato originale* (Milan 1978).

Beatrice, B. F., "Due nuovi testimoni della lavandi dei piedi in età patristica: Cromazio di Aquileia e Severiano di Gabala," *Augustinianum* 20 (1980) = *Ecclesia orans: Mélanges . . . Hamman* 23 ff.

Bedard, W. M., *The Symbolism of the Baptismal Font in Early Christian Thought* (Washington D.C. 1951).

Bénabou, M., *La résistance africaine à la romanisation* (Paris 1975).

Benson, E. W., *Cyprian: His Life, His Times, His Work* (London 1897).

Bévenot, M., "A Bishop Is Responsible to God Alone (St. Cyprian)," *Recherches de science religieuse* 39/40 (1951/52) 397 ff.

Bévenot, M., "St. Cyprian and the Papacy: Musings on an Old Problem," *Dublin Review* 228 (1954) 161 ff., 307 ff.

Bévenot, M., " 'Primatus Petro datur': St. Cyprian on the Papacy," *Journal of Theological Studies* 5 (1954) 19 ff.

Bévenot, M., " 'Hi qui sacrificaverunt': A Significant Variant in St. Cyprian's De unitate," *Journal of Theological Studies* 5 (1954) 68 ff.

Bévenot, M., "The Sacrament of Penance and St. Cyprian's De lapsis," *Theological Studies* 16 (1955) 175 ff.

Bévenot, M., "Épiscopat et primauté chez s. Cyprien," *Ephemerides theologicae Lovanienses* 42 (1966) 176 ff.

Bévenot, M., review of Vogt, *Coetus sanctorum, Journal of Theological Studies* 20 (1969) 630 ff.

Bévenot, M., *Cyprian: De lapsis and De ecclesiae catholicae unitate* (Oxford 1971).

Bévenot, M., "Cyprian's Platform in the Rebaptism Controversy," *Heythrop Journal* 19 (1978) 123 ff.

Bévenot, M., " 'Sacerdos' as Understood by Cyprian," *Journal of Theological Studies* 30 (1979) 413 ff.

Bishop, W. C., "The African Rite," *Journal of Theological Studies* 13 (1911/12) 250 ff.

Blázquez, J. M., *Estructura económica y social de Hispania durante la anarquía militar y el bajo imperio* (Madrid 1964).

Blázquez, J. M., "La crisis del siglo III en Hispania y Mauretania Tingitana," *Hispania* 28 (1968) 5 ff.

Boppert, W., *Die frühchristlichen Inschriften des Mittelrheingebietes* (Mainz am Rhein 1971).

Botte, B. (ed.), *Hippolyte de Rome: La tradition apostolique* (Paris 1946) (= Sources chrétiennes 2).

Bradshaw, P. P., *Daily Prayer in the Early Church* (London 1981).

Brandenburg, H., "Das Grab des Papstes Cornelius und die Lucinaregion der Calixtus-Katakombe," *Jahrbuch für Antike und Christentum* 11/12 (1968/69) 42 ff.

Brightman, F. E., "Terms of Communion and the Ministration of the Sacraments in Early Times," in H. B. Swete (ed.), *Essays on the Early History of the Church and the Ministry* (London 1918) 315 ff.

Brind'Amour, L. and P., "La deuxième satire de Perse et le *dies lustricus*," *Latomus* 30 (1971) 999 ff.

Burton, G. P., "Proconsuls, Assizes and the Administration of Justice under the Empire," *Journal of Roman Studies* 65 (1975) 92 ff.

Butler, C., "Catholic and Roman: The Witness of St. Cyprian," *Downside Review* 56 (1938) 127 ff.

Cabié, R., *La pentecôte: L'évolution de la Cinquantaine pascal au cours des cinq premiers siècles* (Tournai 1965).

Cagnat, R., and Merlin, A., *Inscriptions latines d'Afrique* (Paris 1923).

Callu, J.-P., *La politique monétaire des empereurs romains de 238 à 311* (Paris 1969).

Campeau, L., "L'origine de la querelle baptismale," *Science et esprit* 21 (1969) 329 ff.

Campus, L., "Nuovi miliari della Sardegna," *Archeologia classica* 29 (1977) 411 ff.

Carcopino, J., "L'invocation de Timgad au Christ médecin," *Rendiconti della Pontificia Accademia Romana di Archeologia* 5 (1928) 79 ff.

Carey, H., *The Epistles of St. Cyprian, Bishop of Carthage and Martyr, with the Council of Carthage on the Baptism of Heretics* (Oxford 1844).

Casey, R. P., *The Excerpta ex Theodoto of Clement of Alexandria* (London 1934).

Caspar, E., *Geschichte des Papsttums* (2 vols., Tübingen 1930–33).

Cerfaux, L., "La multiplication des pains dans la Didachè," *Biblica* 40 (1959) 943 ff.

Chadwick, H., "Justification by Faith and Hospitality," *Studia patristica* 4 (1961) 281 ff.

Chapman, J., "Professor Hugo Koch on St. Cyprian," *Revue bénédictine* 27 (1910) 447 ff.

Chapman, J., *Studies on the Early Papacy* (London 1928).

Charles-Picard, G., *La civilisation de l'Afrique romaine* (Paris 1959).

Chartier, M.-C., "La discipline pénitentielle d'après les écrits de saint Cyprien," *Antonianum* 14 (1939) 17 ff., 135 ff.

Chastagnol, A., "Autour de la 'sobre ivresse' de Bonosus," in *Bonner Historia-Augusta Colloquium 1972/1974* (Bonn 1976) 91 ff.

Chaumont, M.-L., "Conquêtes sassanids et propagande mazdéene (IIIème siècle)," *Historia* 22 (1973) 664 ff.

Christol, M., "Les règnes de Valérien et de Gallien (253–268): Travaux d'ensemble, questions chronologiques," *Aufstieg und Niedergang der römischen Welt* 2.2 (1975) 803 ff.

Christol, M., "La prosopographie de la province de Numidie de 253 à 260 et la chronologie des révoltes africaines sous le règne de Valérien et de Gallien," *Antiquités africaines* 10 (1976) 69 ff.

Clarke, G. W., "Some Victims of the Persecution of Maximinus Thrax," *Historia* 15 (1966) 445 ff.

Clarke, G. W., "The Epistles of Cyprian," in *Auckland Classical Essays presented to E. M. Blaiklock* (Auckland 1970) 203 ff.

Clarke, G. W., "Barbarian Disturbances in North Africa in the Mid-third Century," *Antichthon* 4 (1970) 78 ff.

Clarke, G. W., "Cyprian's Epistle 64 and the Kissing of Feet in Baptism," *Harvard Theological Review* 66 (1973) 147 ff.

Clarke, G. W., "Double-Trials in the Persecution of Decius," *Historia* 22 (1973) 650 ff.

Clarke, G. W., *The Octavius of Marcus Minucius Felix* (ACW 39; New York 1974).

Clarke, G. W., "Persecution under Gallus: The Correspondence of

Cyprian during the Principate of Gallus," to appear in *Aufstieg und Niedergang der römischen Welt* 2.27.

Colin, J., "Les jours de supplices des martyrs chrétiens et les fêtes impériales," in *Mélanges d'archéologie et d'histoire offerts à André Piganiol* 3 (Paris 1966) 1565 ff.

Colson, J., *L'épiscopat catholique: Collégialité et primauté dans les trois premiers siècles de l'église* (Paris 1963).

Connolly, R. H., *Didascalia apostolorum* (Oxford 1929).

Conybeare, F. C., *Rituale Armenorum* (Oxford 1905).

Crawford, C. W., *The Eucharistic Symbolism of the Mixed Chalice: Some Historical and Theological Perspectives up to the Mid-third Century* (diss. Oxford 1983).

Crawford, M. H., and Reynolds, J., "The Publication of the Prices Edict: A New Inscription from Aezani," *Journal of Roman Studies* 65 (1975) 160 ff.

d'Alès, A., "La réconciliation des 'lapsi' au temps de Dèce," *Revue des questions historiques* 91 (1912) 337 ff.

d'Alès, A., *L'édit de Calliste: Étude sur les origines de la pénitence chrétienne* (Paris 1914).

d'Alès, A., "Le diacre Pontius," *Recherches de science religieuse* 8 (1918) 319 ff.

d'Alès, A., "(Ep. 59.14) Ecclesia principalis," *Recherches de science religieuse* 11 (1921) 374 ff.

d'Alès, A., *La théologie de saint Cyprien* (Paris 1922).

Daly, C. B., "Absolution and Satisfaction in St. Cyprian's Theology of Penance," *Studia patristica* 2.2 (1957) 202 ff.

Daly, C. B., "The 'Edict of Callistus,' " *Studia patristica* 3 (1961) 176 ff.

Daniélou, J., "La typologie millénariste de la semaine dans le christianisme primitif," *Vigiliae christianae* 2 (1948) 1 ff.

Daniélou, J., "La typologie de la semaine au IVᵉ siècle," *Recherches de science religieuse* 35 (1948) 382 ff.

Daniélou, J., "Le dimanche comme huitième jour," in *Le dimanche*, by D. Botte *et al.* (Paris 1965) 61 ff.

Daniélou, J., "Novatien et le De mundo d'Apulée," in *Romanitas et Christianitas*, ed. W. den Boer *et al.* (Amsterdam-London 1973) 71 ff.

Daniélou, J., *The Origins of Latin Christianity*, ET by D. Smith and

J. A. Baker (*History of Early Christian Doctrine before the Council of Nicaea* 3; London 1977).

Daremberg, C. V., and Saglio, E., *Dictionnaire des antiquités grecques et romaines* (5 vols. in 9, Paris 1877–1919).

Davies, J. G., *The Architectural Setting of Baptism* (London 1962).

de Ghellinck, J., de Backer, É., Poukens, J. B., Lebacqz, G., *Pour l'histoire du mot "sacramentum"* 1: *Les Anténicéens* (Louvain-Paris 1924).

Dekkers, E., "L'église ancienne a-t-elle connu la messe du soir?" in *Miscellanea liturgica in honorem L. Cuniberti Mohlberg* 1 (Rome 1948) 231 ff.

Dekkers, E., "Les traductions grecques des écrits patristiques latins," *Sacris erudiri* 5 (1953) 193 ff.

de Labriolle, P., *La crise montaniste* (Paris 1913).

de la Taille, M., "Les sens du mot *passio* dans la lettre 63 de s. Cyprien," *Recherches de science religieuse* 21 (1931) 576 ff.

Delattre, R. P., *Musée Lavigerie de Saint-Louis de Carthage* 3 (Paris 1899).

Delbrueck, R., "Uranius of Emesa," *Numismatic Chronicle* 8 (1948) 11 ff.

Deléani, S., " ' Gentiles viae' (Cyprien, *Lettre* 55, 17, 2): Contribution à l'étude du style de saint Cyprien," *Revue des études augustiniennes* 23 (1977) 221 ff.

Deléani, S., *Christum sequi: Étude d'un thème dans l'oeuvre de saint Cyprien* (Paris 1979).

Delehaye, H., *Les origines du culte des martyrs* (2nd ed., Brussels 1933).

Demoustier, A., "Épiscopat et union à Rome selon s. Cyprien," *Recherches de science religieuse* 52 (1964) 337 ff.

Demoustier, A., "L'ontologie de l'église selon s. Cyprien," *Recherches de science religieuse* 52 (1964) 555 ff.

de Rossi, G. B., *La Roma sotterranea cristiana descritta ed illustrata* 1 (Rome 1864).

de Ste. Croix, G. E. M., "Suffragium: From Vote to Patronage," *British Journal of Sociology* 5 (1954) 33 ff.

Didier, J.-C., "Le pédobaptisme au IVe siècle," *Mélanges de sciences religieuses* 6 (1946) 242 ff.

Didier, J.-C., "Un cas typique de développement du dogme: À propos du baptême des enfants," *Mélanges de sciences religieuses* 9 (1952) 191 ff.

Didier, J.-C., *Le baptême des enfants dans la tradition de l'église* (Tournai 1959).

Dodwell, H., *Dissertationes Cyprianicae* (Oxford 1684).

Doignon, J., " 'Refrigerium' et catéchèse à Vérone au IVe siècle," in *Hommages . . . Renard* 2 (1969) 220 ff.

Dölger, F. J., *Sphragis* (Paderborn 1911).

Dölger, F. J., *Sol Salutis* (1925, repr. Münster Westfalen 1972).

Dölger, F. J., "Der Kuss im Tauf- und Firmungsritual nach Cyprian von Carthago und Hippolyt von Rom," *Antike und Christentum* 1 (1929) 186 ff.

Dölger, F. J., "Die Kreuz-Tätowierung im christlichen Altertum," *Antike und Christentum* 1 (1929) 202 ff.

Dölger, F. J., "Der Rennfahrer Liber mit der Kreuztätowierung auf einem Goldglas aus der Kallistkatakombe," *Antike und Christentum* 1 (1929) 229 ff.

Dölger, F. J., "Tertullian über die Bluttaufe: Tertullian De baptismo 16," *Antike und Christentum* 2 (1930) 117 ff.

Dölger, F. J., "Die Heiligkeit des Altars und ihre Begründung im christlichen Altertum," *Antike und Christentum* 2 (1930) 161 ff.

Dölger, F. J., "Zwei neue Textheilungsversuche zu Tertullian De baptismo 16, 2," *Antike und Christentum* 3 (1932) 216 ff.

Dölger, F. J., "Zur Symbolik des altchristlichen Taufhauses," *Antike und Christentum* 4 (1934) 153 ff.

Dölger, F. J., "Die Eucharistie in den Händen der Laien," *Antike und Christentum* 5 (1936) 232 ff.

Dölger, F. J., "Beschwörungen bei 'Leib und Blut Christi' auf einem Bleitäfelchen und einem Papyrus-Amulett," *Antike und Christentum* 5 (1936) 255 ff.

Donna, Sister Rose Bernard, *St. Cyprian: Letters 1–81* (Washington D.C. 1964).

Downey, G., *A History of Antioch in Syria* (Princeton 1961).

Dubarle, A. M., "La pluralité des péchés héréditaires dans la tradition augustinienne," *Revue des études augustiniennes* 3 (1957) 113 ff.

Duchesne, L., *Le Liber pontificalis* (2 vols., Paris 1886–92).

Dudden, F. Homes, *The Life and Times of St. Ambrose* 1 (Oxford 1933).

Dugmore, C. W., "Lord's Day and Easter," in *Neotestamentica et Patristica: Eine Freundesgabe Herrn Professor Dr. Oscar Cullmann zu seinem 60. Geburtstag überreicht* (Leiden 1962) 272 ff.

Dugmore, C. W., "The Study of the Origins of the Eucharist: Retrospect and Revaluation," *Studies in Church History* 2 (1965) 1 ff.

Duncan-Jones, R., *The Economy of the Roman Empire* (Cambridge 1974).

Duquenne, L., *Chronologie des lettres de s. Cyprien: Le dossier de la persécution de Dèce* (Brussels 1972).

Duval, Y., *Loca sanctorum Africae: Le culte des martyrs en Afrique du IVe au VIIe siècle* (2 vols., Rome 1982).

Duval, Y.-M., and Pietri, Ch., "*Membra Christi:* Culte des martyrs ou théologie de l'Eucharistie? (A propos du vase de Belezma en Algérie)," *Revue des études augustiniennes* 21 (1975) 289 ff.

Edsman, C.-M., *Le baptême de feu* (Upsala 1940).

Ellspermann, G. L., *The Attitude of the Early Christian Latin Writers towards Pagan Literature and Learning* (Washington D.C. 1949).

Ennabli, A., *Lampes chrétiennes de Tunisie: Musées du Bardo et de Carthage* (Paris 1976).

Epstein, I. (ed.), *The Babylonian Talmud*, pt. 2, vol. 1, (London 1938; repr. 1961: Shabbath VIII, Seder Mo'ed, tr. H. Freedman).

Ernout, A., and Meillet, A., *Dictionnaire étymologique de la langue latine* (3rd ed., Paris 1951).

Evans, R. F., *One and Holy: The Church in Latin Patristic Thought* (London 1972).

Fahey, M. A., *Cyprian and the Bible: A Study in Third-Century Exegesis* (Tübingen 1971).

Feltoe, C. L., *ΔΙΟΝΥΣΙΟΥ ΛΕΙΨΑΝΑ: The Letters and Other Remains of Dionysius of Alexandria* (Cambridge 1904).

Fentress, E. W. B., *Numidia and the Roman Army: Social, Military and Economic Aspects of the Frontier Zone* (Oxford 1979).

Ferguson, E., "Origen and the Election of Bishops," *Church History* 43 (1974) 26 ff.

Ferguson, E., "Inscriptions and the Origin of Infant Baptism," *Journal of Theological Studies* 30 (1979) 37 ff.

Fernández, A., "La escatología de san Cipriano," *Burgense. collectanea scientifica* 22 (1981) 93 ff.

Février, P. A., "Inscriptions chrétiennes d'Algérie," *Rivista di archeologia cristiana* 48 (1972) 143 ff.

Février, P. A., "À propos des troubles de Maurétanie (villes et conflicts du IIIe s.)," *Zeitschrift für Papyrologie und Epigraphik* 43 (1981) 143 ff.

Fiebiger, O., "Ein Frankeneinfall in Nordafrika," *Germania* 24 (1940) 145 f.

Finley, M. I., "Private Farm Tenancy in Italy before Diocletian," in *Studies in Roman Property*, ed. M. I. Finley (Cambridge 1976) 103 ff.

Fischer, J. A., "Die ersten Konzilien im römischen Nordwest-Afrika," in *Pietas: Festschrift für Bernhard Kötting*, ed. E. Dassmann and K. S. Frank (Münster Westf. 1980) 217 ff.   •

Fischer, J. A., "Das Konzil zu Karthago im Mai 252," *Annuarium historiae conciliorum* 13 (1981) 1 ff.

Fischer, J. A., "Das Konzil zu Karthago im Frühjahr 253," *Annuarium historiae conciliorum* 13 (1981) 12 ff.

Flam-Zuckermann, L., "À propos d'une inscription de Suisse (*CIL*, XIII, 5010): Étude du phénomène du brigandage dans l'Empire romain," *Latomus* 29 (1970) 451 ff.

Fontaine, J., *Sulpice Sévère: Vie de saint Martin* (3 vols.; SC 133–35; Paris 1967–69.

Ford, J. M., "The Heavenly Jerusalem and Orthodox Judaism," *Donum Gentilicium. New Testament Studies in Honour of David Daube*, ed. Bammel, E., Barrett, C. K., Davies, W. D. (Oxford 1978) 215 ff.

Formigé, J., "Remarques diverses sur les baptistères de Provence," in *Mélanges en hommage à la mémoire de Fr. Martroye* (Paris 1941) 167 ff.

Fortin, B., "Problèmes de succession épiscopale au milieu de IIIe siècle," *Laval théologique et philosophique* 19 (1963) 49 ff.

Frank, Tenney (ed.), *An Economic Survey of Ancient Rome* 4/1: *Roman Africa*, by R. M. Haywood (Paterson N.J. 1959).

Franke, P., "Bemerkungen zur frühchristlichen Noe-Ikonographie," *Rivista di archeologia cristiana* 49 (1973) 171 ff.

Freis, H., "Das römische Nordafrika—ein unterentwickeltes Land?" *Chiron* 10 (1980) 357 ff.

Frend, W. H. C. "The *Seniores laici* and the Origins of the Church in North Africa," *Journal of Theological Studies* 12 (1961) 280 ff.

Frend, W. H. C., *Martyrdom and Persecution in the Early Church* (Oxford 1965).

Frend, W. H. C., "A Note on Tertullian and the Jews," *Studia patristica* 10 (1970) 291 ff.

Frend, W. H. C., "A Note on Jew and Christian in Third-Century North Africa," *Journal of Theological Studies* 21 (1970) 92 ff.

Frend, W. H. C., "The Christian Period in Mediterranean Africa, *c.* AD 200 to 700," in *The Cambridge History of Africa* 2 (Cambridge 1978) 410 ff.

Frend, W. H. C., "Jews and Christians in Third-Century Carthage," in *Paganisme, judaïsme, christianisme: Influences et affrontements dans le monde antique. Mélanges offerts à Marcel Simon* (Paris 1978) 185 ff.

Freppel, L'abbé, *Saint Cyprien et l'église africaine au IIIe siècle* (Paris 1865).

Frier, B. W., *Landlords and Tenants in Imperial Rome* (Princeton 1980).

Fronza, L., "Studi sull'imperatore Decio I: L' 'adventus Augusti,' " *Annali Triestini* ser. 1, 21 (1951) 227 ff.

Frye, R. N., review article of W. Ensslin, *Zu den Kriegen des Sassaniden Schapur* 1, in *Bibliotheca orientalis* 8 (1951) 103 ff.

Funk, F. X., *Didascaliae et Constitutiones apostolorum* (Paderborn 1905; repr. Turin 1959).

Gagé, J., *Apollon Romain* (Paris 1955).

Galtier, P., *L'église et la rémission des péchés aux premiers siècles* (Paris 1932).

Galtier, P., *Aux origines du sacrement de pénitence* (Rome 1951).

Garnsey, P., "Why Penalities Become Harsher: The Roman Case, Late Republic to Fourth-Century Empire," *Natural Law Forum* 13 (1968) 141 ff.

Gascou, J., *La politique municipale de l'Empire romain en Afrique proconsulaire, de Trajan à Septime-Sévère* (Rome 1972).

Gibbon, E., *Decline and Fall of the Roman Empire* (London 1910; repr. 1960).

Gilliam, J. F., "Trebonianus Gallus and the Decii: III et I cos," in *Studi in onore di Aristide Calderini e Roberto Paribeni* (Milan 1956) 305 ff.

Gilliam, J. F., "The Plague under Marcus Aurelius," *American Journal of Philosophy* 82 (1961) 225 ff.

Girardet, K. M., "Appellatio: Ein Kapitel kirchlicher Rechtesgeschichte in den Kanones des vierten Jahrhunderts," *Historia* 23 (1974) 98 ff.

Goulon, A., "Le malheur de l'homme à sa naissance: Un thème antique chez quelques Pères de l'église," *Revue des études augustiniennes* 18 (1972) 3 ff.

Grant, M., *The Climax of Rome* (London 1968).

Gregg, J. A. F., *The Decian Persecution* (Edinburgh and London 1897).

Grégoire, H., Orgels, P., Moreau, J., Maricq, A., *Les persécutions dans l'Empire romain* (Brussels 1950).

Gryson, R., *Les origines du célibat ecclésiastique: Du premier au septième siècle* (Gembloux 1970).

Gryson, R., "Les élections ecclésiastiques au IIIᵉ siècle," *Revue d'histoire ecclésiastique* 68 (1973) 353 ff.

Gryson, R., review of Vilela, *Condition collégiale*, in *Revue d'histoire ecclésiastique* 69 (1974) 108 ff.

Gülzow, H., *Christentum und Sklaverei in den ersten drei Jahrhunderten* (Bonn 1969).

Häussler, R. (ed.), *Nachträge zu A. Otto, Sprichwörter und sprichwörtliche Redensarten der Römer* (Hildesheim 1968).

Hamman, A., *Vie liturgique et vie sociale: Repas des pauvres, diaconie et diaconat, agape et repas de charité, offrande, dans l'antiquité chrétienne* (Paris 1968).

Hammerich, H., "Der tägliche Empfang der Eucharistie im 3. Jahrhundert," *Zeitschrift für Kirchengeschichte* 84 (1973) 93 ff.

Hannan, M. L., *Thasci Caecili Cypriani De mortalitate: A Commentary, with an Introduction and Translation* (Washington D.C. 1936).

Hanson, R. P. C., *Tradition in the Early Church* (Philadelphia 1962).

Harnack, A. von, *Brod und Wasser: Die eucharistischen Elemente bei Justin* (TU 7.2, 1891).

Harnack, A. von, *Geschichte der altchristlichen Literatur bis Eusebius* (2 vols., Leipzig 1893–1904; repr. 1958). Vol. 2 = *Chronologie*.

Harnack, A. von, *Eine bisher nicht erkannte Schrift Novatian's vom Jahr 249/50 ["Cyprian" de laude martyrii]* (TU 13.4, 1895).

Harnack, A. von, *Über verlorene Briefe und Aktenstücke, die sich aus der cyprianischen Briefsammlung ermitteln lassen* (TU 23.2a, 1902).

Harnack, A. von, "Porphyrius Gegen die Christen 15 Bücher: Zeugnisse, Fragmente, und Referate," *Abhandlungen der königlich preussischen Akademie der Wissenschaften, phil-hist. Klasse*, Berlin, 1 (1916).

Hefele, C. J., and Leclercq, H., *Histoire des conciles* 1 and 2 (Paris 1907–8).

Held, W., "Das Ende der progressiven Entwicklung des Kolonates am Ende des 2. und der ersten Hälfte des 3 Jahrhunderts im römischen Imperium," *Klio* 53 (1971) 239 ff.

Hertling, L., "La figura umana e religiosa di san Cipriano," *Civiltà cattolica* 3 (1958) 449 ff.

Hinchliff, P., *Cyprian of Carthage* (London 1974).

Hirschberg, H. Z., *A History of the Jews in North Africa* 1: *From Antiquity to the Sixteenth Century* (Leiden 1974).

Hofmann, K. M., *Philema Hagion* (diss. Erlangen, Gütersloh 1938).

Homo, L., "Les privilèges administratifs du sénat romain sous l'empire et leur disparition graduelle au cours du IIIᵉ siècle," *Revue historique* 137 (1921) 161 ff., 138 (1921) 1 ff.

Honigmann, E., and Maricq, A., "Recherches sur les *Res gestae divi Saporis*," *Mémoires de l'Acad. royale de Belgique (Lettres)* 47, fasc. 4 (1953).

Hopkins, K., "Models, Ships and Staples," in *Trade and Famine in Classical Antiquity*, ed. Garnsey, P., and Whittaker, C. R. (Cambridge 1983) 84 ff.

Hoppenbrouwers, H. A. M., *Recherches sur la terminologie du martyre de Tertullien à Lactance* (Nijmegen 1961).

Hopper, V. F., *Mediaeval Number Symbolism* (New York 1938).

Horton, F. L., *The Melchizedek Tradition* (Cambridge 1976).

Howe, Q., Jr., *St. Cyprian and the Christian Experience* (diss. Princeton 1970).

Hübner, S., "Kirchenbusse und Exkommunikation bei Cyprian," *Zeitschrift für katholische Theologie* 84 (1962) 49 ff., 171 ff.

Hummel, E. L., *The Concept of Martyrdom according to St. Cyprian of Carthage* (Washington D.C. 1946).

James, M. R., *The Apocryphal New Testament* (Oxford 1924; repr. 1963).

Janssen, H. H., *Kultur und Sprache: Zur Geschichte der alten Kirche im*

Spiegel der Sprachentwicklung von Tertullian bis Cyprian (Nijmegen 1938).

Jarrett, M. G., *A Study of the Municipal Aristocracies of the Roman Empire in the West, with Special Reference to North Africa* (diss. Durham 1958).

Jay, P., "Saint Cyprien et la doctrine du purgatoire," *Recherches de théologie ancienne et médiévale* 27 (1960) 133 ff.

Jeremias, J., *Infant Baptism in the First Four Centuries*, ET by D. Cairns (London 1960).

Johanny, R., *et al.*, *L'eucharistie des premiers chrétiens* (Paris 1976).

Jones, A. H. M., *The Later Roman Empire 284–602* (4 vols., Oxford 1964).

Joyce, G. H., "Private Penance in the Early Church," *Journal of Theological Studies* 42 (1941–42) 18 ff.

Jülicher, H., "Zur Geschichte der Abendmalsfeier in der ältesten Kirche," *Theologische Abhandlungen: Carl von Weizsäcker zu seinem siebzigsten Geburtstage* (Freiburg 1892) 217 ff.

Jungmann, J. A., *Missarum sollemnia* (2 vols., Wien 1948), ET by F. A. Brunner, *The Mass of the Roman Rite* (New York 1959).

Jungmann, J. A., "Oblatio und Sacrificium in der Geschichte des Eucharistieverständnisses," *Zeitschrift für katholische Theologie* 92 (1970) 342 ff.

Kajanto, I., *Supernomina: A Study in Latin Epigraphy* (Helsinki 1967).

Kelly, J. N. D., *Early Christian Doctrines* (2nd. ed., London 1960).

Keresztes, P., "The Decian *Libelli* and Contemporary Literature," *Latomus* 34 (1975) 761 ff.

Keresztes, P., "Two Edicts of the Emperor Valerian," *Vigiliae christianae* 29 (1975) 81 ff.

Kettenhofen, E., *Die römisch-persischen Kriege des 3. Jahrhunderts n. Chr. nach der Inschrift Šāhpuhrs. 1. an der Ka'be-ye Zartošt (ŠKZ)* (Wiesbaden 1982).

Klauser, T., "Bischöfe als staatliche Prokuratoren im dritten Jahrhundert?" *Jahrbuch für Antike und Christentum* 14 (1971) 140 ff.

Klijn, A. F. J., and Reinink, G. J., *Patristic Evidence for Jewish-Christian Sects* (London 1973).

Knipfing, J. R., "The *Libelli* of the Decian Persecution," *Harvard Theological Review* 16 (1923) 345 ff.

Knopf, R., and Krüger, G., *Ausgewählte Märtyrerakten* (Tübingen 1929; rev. ed. by G. Ruhbach, Tübingen 1965).

Koch, H., *Virgines Christi* (TU 3.1.2, 1907).

Koch, H., *Cyprian und der römische Primat* (TU 3.5.1, 1910).

Koch, H., *Cyprianische Untersuchungen* (Bonn 1926).

Koch, H., "I rapporti di Cipriano con Ireneo ed altri scrittori greci," *Ricerche religiose* 5 (1929) 137 ff.

Koch, H., *Theol. Literaturzeitung* 59 (1934) 10 ff.

Koch, H., "Pascha in der ältesten Kirche," *Zeitschrift für wiss. Theol.* 55 (1914) 289 ff.

Kottje, B., "Das Aufkommen der täglichen Eucharistiefeier in der Westkirche und die Zölibatsforderung," *Zeitschrift für Kirchengeschichte* 82 (1971) 218 ff.

Kraft, H., *Texte zur Geschichte der Taufe, besonders der Kindertaufe in der alten Kirche* (Berlin 1969).

Krautheimer, R., "Introduction to an 'Iconography of Mediaeval Architecture,' " *Warburg Journal* 5 (1942) 1 ff.

Lacey, T. A., *Selected Epistles of St. Cyprian, Treating of the Episcopate. After the translation of Nathaniel Marshall* (London 1922).

Langstadt, E., "Tertullian's Doctrine of Sin and the Power of Absolution in 'De pudicitia,' " *Studia patristica* 2.2 (1957) 251 ff.

Lawlor, H. J., and Oulton, J. E. L., *Eusebius, Bishop of Caesarea: The Ecclesiastical History and the Martyrs of Palestine* 2 (1928; repr. London 1954).

Lawlor, H. J., *Eusebiana* (Oxford 1912).

Lebreton, J., "Le désaccord de la foi populaire et de la théologie savante dans l'église chrétienne du IIIe siècle," *Revue d'histoire ecclésiastique* 19 (1923) 481 ff., 20 (1924) 5 ff.

Lebreton, J., "St. Cyprien et Origène," *Recherches de science religieuse* 20 (1930) 160 ff.

Lebreton, J., "Les origines de la primauté romaine," *Recherches de science religieuse* 21 (1931) 601 ff.

Leipoldt, J., *Der soziale Gedanke in der altchristlichen Kirche* (Leipzig 1952).

Leipoldt, J., *Die Frau in der antiken Welt und im Urchristentum* (Leipzig 1955).

Le Moyne, J., "St. Cyprien est-il bien l'auteur de la rédaction brève du 'De unitate' chapitre 4?" *Revue bénédictine* 63 (1953) 70 ff.

Lepelley, C., *Les cités de l'Afrique romaine au Bas-Empire* (2 vols., Paris 1979, 1981).

Le Saint, W. P., *Tertullian: Treatises on Penance* (ACW 28; New York 1959).

Leschi, L., *Études d'épigraphie, d'archéologie et d'histoire africaines* (Paris 1957).

Leveau, P., "Un nouveau témoinage sur la résistance maure en Maurétanie Césarienne centrale," *Antiquités africaines* 8 (1974) 103 ff.

Lewis, J. P., *A Study of the Interpretation of Noah and the Flood in Jewish and Christian Literature* (Leiden 1968).

Lewy, H., *Sobria ebrietas* (Giessen 1929).

Liesering, E., *Untersuchungen zur Christenverfolgung des Kaisers Decius* (diss. Würzburg 1933).

Lietzmann, H., *Mass and Lord's Supper*, ET by D. H. G. Reeve (Leiden 1953–64).

Lietzmann, H., *A History of the Early Church*, ET by B. L. Woolf (London 1967).

Littman, R. J. and M. L., "Galen and the Antonine Plague," *American Journal of Philology* 94 (1973) 243 ff.

Lomiento, G., "Cypriano per la preparazione al martirio dei Tibaritani (Epist. 58)," *Annali della Facoltà di Magisterio dell'Università di Bari* 3 (1962) 7 ff.

Loriot, X., "Chronologie du règne de Philippe l'Arabe (244–249 après J.C.)," *Aufstieg und Niedergang der römischen Welt* 2.2 (1975) 788 ff.

Lukken, G. M., *Original Sin in the Roman Liturgy: Research into the Theology of Original Sin in the Roman Sacramentaria and the Early Baptismal Liturgy* (Leiden 1973).

MacMullen, R., *Enemies of the Roman Order: Treason, Unrest and Alienation in the Empire* (Cambridge, Mass. 1967).

MacMullen, R., *Christianizing the Roman Empire (A.D. 100–400)* (New Haven and London 1984).

Magie, D., *Roman Rule in Asia Minor to the End of the Third Century after Christ* (2 vols., Princeton 1950).

Maier, J.-L., *L'épiscopat de l'afrique romaine, vandale et byzantine* (Neuchâtel 1973).

Mansi, J. D., *Sacrorum conciliorum nova et amplissima collectio* 1 and 2 (Florence 1759).

Mara, M. G., "Note sulla cristologia Ciprianea: L'interpretazione di Prov. 9, 1–6," *Augustinianum* 20 (1980) = *Ecclesia orans: Mélanges . . . Hamman* 243 ff.

Marcillet-Jaubert, J., "C. Iulius Sallustius Saturninus Fortunatianus légat de Numidie," *Bulletin d'archéologie algérienne* 4 (1970) 313 ff.

Maricq, A. "Res gestae Divi Saporis," *Syria* 35 (1958) 295 ff.

Marion, J., "Les trésors monétaires de Volubilis et de Banasa," *Antiquités africaines* 12 (1978) 179 ff.

Marquardt, J., *Das Privatleben der Römer* (Leipzig 1879).

Mattingly, H., "The Reigns of Trebonianus Gallus and Volusian and of Aemilian," *Numismatic Chronicle* 6 (1946) 36 ff.

Mattingly, H., Sydenham, E. A., Sutherland, C. H. V., *Roman Imperial Coinage* 4 (London 1949).

Melin, B., *Studia in corpus Cyprianeum* (Upsala 1946).

Merlin, A., and Poinssot, L., *Les inscriptions d'Uchi Maius* (Paris 1908).

Mersch, E., *Le corps mystique du Christ* (3rd. ed., Paris/Brussels 1951).

Meslin, M., "Vases sacrés et boissons d'éternité dans les visions des martyrs africains," in *Epektasis: Mélanges patristiques offerts au cardinal Jean Daniélou* (Paris 1972) 139 ff.

Metcalf, W. E., "The Antioch Hoard of Antoniniani and the Eastern Coinage of Trebonianus Gallus and Volusian," *Amer. Num. Soc. Museum Notes* 22 (1977) 71 ff.

Metcalf, W. E., and Walker, P. M., "The Antioch Hoard: A Supplement," *Amer. Num. Soc. Museum Notes* 23 (1978) 129 ff.

Millar, F., *The Emperor in the Roman World (31 B.C.—A.D. 337)* (London 1977).

Mohrmann, C., "Les origines de la latinité chrétienne à Rome," *Vigiliae christianae* 3 (1949) 67 ff., 163 ff.

Mohrmann, C., *Études sur le latin des chrétiens* (4 vols., Rome 1961–1977).

Molager, J., *Cyprien de Carthage: À Donat et La vertu de patience* (SC 291; Paris 1982).

Molland, E., "Encore une fois 'Omnis ecclesia Petri propinqua': Édit de Calliste ou édit d'Agrippinus?" in *Mélanges d'histoire des religions offerts à Henri-Charles Puech* (Paris 1974) 215 ff.

Mommsen, Th., "Zur lateinischen Stichometrie," *Hermes* 21 (1886) 142 ff., 25 (1890) 636 ff.

Monat, P. (ed.), *Lactance: Institutions divines livre V* (2 vols.; SC 204–5; Paris 1973).

Monceaux, P., "Chronologie des oeuvres de st. Cyprien et des conciles africains du temps," *Revue de philologie, de littérature et d'histoire anciennes* 24 (1900) 333 ff.

Monceaux, P., *Histoire littéraire de l'Afrique chrétienne depuis les origines jusqu'à l'invasion arabe* 2 (Paris 1902).

Moreau, J., *Lactance: De la mort des persécuteurs* (2 vols.; SC 39; Paris 1954).

Mortimer, R. C., *The Origins of Private Penance in the Western Church* (Oxford 1939).

Mortley, R., *Womanhood: The Feminine in Ancient Hellenism, Gnosticism, Christianity, and Islam* (Sydney 1981).

Musurillo, H. A., *The Acts of the Christian Martyrs* (Oxford 1972).

Nagel, E., *Kindertaufe und Taufaufschub: Die Praxis vom 3.–5. Jahrhundert in Nordafrika und ihre theologische Einordnung bei Tertullian, Cyprian und Augustinus* (Frankfurt/M, Bern, Cirencester 1980).

Narbey, C., *Supplément aux Acta sanctorum pour des vies de saints de l'époque mérovingienne* 2 (Paris 1900).

Nautin, P., *Homélies pascales* 1 and 2 (SC 27, 36; Paris 1950, 1953).

Navickas, J. C., *The Doctrine of St. Cyprian on the Sacraments* (diss. Würzburg 1924).

Nelke, L., *Die Chronologie der Korrespondenz Cyprians und der pseudocyprianischen Schriften ad Novatianum und Liber de rebaptismate* (diss. Thorn 1902).

Niemer, G., "Cyprian als Kritiker der spätrömischen Kultur und Bildner des Christentums" *Deutsche evang. Erziehung* 49 (1939) 96 ff., 146 ff.

Odom, R. L., *Sabbath and Sunday in Early Christianity* (Washington D.C. 1977).

Olmstead, A. T., "The Mid-third Century of the Christian Era," *Classical Philology* 37 (1942) 241 ff, 398 ff.

Opelt, I., *Die Polemik in der christlichen lateinischen Literatur von Tertullian bis Augustin* (Heidelberg 1980).

Orbán, Á. P., *Les dénominations du monde chez les premiers auteurs chrétiens* (Nijmegen 1970).

Osiek, C., "The Ransom of Captives: Evolution of a Tradition," *Harvard Theological Review* 74 (1981) 365 ff.

Otto, A., *Die Sprichwörter der Römer* (Leipzig 1890; repr. Hildesheim 1965).

Parássoglou, G. M., *The Archive of Aurelius Sakaon: Papers of an Egyptian Farmer in the Last Century of Theadelphia* (Bonn 1978).

Pearson, J., and Fell, J. (eds.), *Sancti Caecilii Cypriani opera* (Bremen 1690), containing also *Annales Cyprianici* by J. Pearson and *Dissertationes Cyprianicae* by H. Dodwell (original ed., Oxford 1682).

Pelikan, J., *Development of Christian Doctrine: Some Historical Prolegomena* (New Haven 1969).

Pellegrino, M., "Eucaristia e martirio in San Cipriano," in *Convivium Dominicum: Studi sull'Eucaristia nei Padri della Chiesa antica e Miscellanea patristica* (Catania 1959) 133 ff.

Pelletier, A., "Les sénateurs d'Afrique proconsulaire d'Auguste à Gallien," *Latomus* 23 (1964) 511 ff.

Pétré, H., *Caritas: Étude sur le vocabulaire latin de la charité chrétienne* (Louvain 1948).

Pflaum, H. G., *Les procurateurs équestres sous le Haut-Empire romain* (Paris 1950).

Pflaum, H. G., *Les carrières procuratoriennes équestres sous le Haut-Empire romain* (4 vols., Paris 1960).

Pflaum, H. G., "La romanisation de l'ancien territoire de la Carthage punique à la lumière des découvertes épigraphiques récentes," *Antiquités africaines* 4 (1970) 75 ff.

Pietri, C., *Roma christiana* (2 vols., Rome 1976).

Plumpe, J. C., *Mater ecclesia: An Inquiry into the Concept of the Church as Mother in Early Christianity* (Washington D.C. 1943).

Poschmann, B., "Zur Bussfrage in der cyprianischen Zeit," *Zeitschrift für katholische Theologie* 37 (1913) 25 ff., 244 ff.

Poschmann, B., *Ecclesia principalis: Ein kritischer Beitrag zur Frage des Primats bei Cyprian* (Breslau 1933).

Poschmann, B., *Paenitentia secunda: Die kirchliche Busse im ältesten Christentum bis Cyprian und Origenes* (Bonn 1940).

Poschmann, B., *Penance and the Anointing of the Sick*, ET and rev. by F. Courtney (London 1964).

Préaux, C., "Trébonian Galle et Hostilianus," *Aegyptus* 32 (1952) 152 ff.

Price, S. R. F., *Rituals and Power: The Roman Imperial Cult in Asia Minor* (Cambridge 1984).

Princeton Encyclopedia of Classical Sites, ed. Stillwell, R., MacDonald, W. L., McAllister, M. H. (Princeton N.J. 1976).

Quacquarelli, A., "L'ogdoade patristica e suoi riflessi nella liturgia e nei monumenti," *Rivista di archeologia cristiana* 49 (1973) 211 ff.

Quasten, J., " 'Sobria ebrietas' in Ambrosius De sacramentis," in *Miscellanea liturgica in honorem L. Cuniberti Mohlberg* 1 (Rome 1948) 117 ff.

Quasten, J., "Der Kuss des Neugetauften in altchristlicher Tauftliturgie," in *Liturgie, Gestalt und Vollzug: Festschrift J. Pascher* (Munich 1963) 267 ff.

Quasten, J., *Patrology* 1 and 2 (Utrecht 1950, 1953).

Quispel, G., "The Discussion of Judaic Christianity," *Vigiliae christianae* 22 (1968) 81 ff.

Rachet, M., *Rome et les Berbères: Un problème militaire d'Auguste à Dioclétian* (Brussels 1970).

Rahner, H., "Flumina de ventre Christi: Die patristische Auslegung von Joh. 7, 37.38," *Biblica* 22 (1941) 269 ff., 367 ff.

Rahner, H., "Navicula Petri," *Zeitschrift für katholische Theologie* 69 (1947) 1 ff.

Rahner, H., *Symbole der Kirche* (Salzburg 1964).

Ratcliff, E. C., "The Institution Narrative of the Roman *Canon Missae:* Its Beginnings and Early Background," *Studia patristica* 2.2 (1957) 64 ff.

Rebuffat, R., "Une zone militaire et sa vie économique: Le limes de Tripolitaine," in *Armées et fiscalité dans le monde antique* (Paris 1977) 395 ff.

Reekmans, L., *La tombe du pape Corneille et sa région cémétériale* (Vatican City 1964).

Renaud, B., *Eucharistie et culte eucharistique selon saint Cyprien* (diss. Louvain 1967).

Réveillaud, M., "Note pour une pneumatologie cyprienne," *Studia patristica* 6 (1962) 181 ff.

Ritschl, O., *De epistulis Cyprianicis* (diss. Halle 1885).

Ritschl, O., *Cyprian von Karthago und die Verfassung der Kirche* (Göttingen 1885).

Robertson, A. S., *Roman Imperial Coins in the Hunter Coin Cabinet, University of Glasgow* 3 (Oxford 1977).

Robinson, J. M. (ed.), *The Nag Hammadi Library in English* (Leiden 1977).

Romanelli, P., *Storia delle province romane dell'Africa* (Rome 1959).

Rondet, H., "La croix sur le front," *Recherches de science religieuse* 42 (1954) 388 ff.

Rordorf, W. A., *Der Sonntag: Geschichte des Ruhe- und Gottesdiensttages im ältesten Christentum* (Zurich 1962).

Rordorf, W. A., *Sabbat et dimanche dans l'église ancienne*, French tr. by E. Visinand and W. Nussbaum (Neuchâtel 1972).

Rosenfeld, H.-F., *Kindesfoot: Ursprung und Verbreitung einer Hansisch-niederdeutschen Brauchtumsbezeichnung. Zugleich ein Beitrag zur Benennung der Kindelfeiern* (Helsinki 1964).

Rostovtzeff, M., *The Social and Economic History of the Roman Empire* (2nd ed. rev. P. M. Frazer; 2 vols, Oxford 1957).

Routh, M. J., *Reliquiae sacrae* (2nd ed., 4 vols., Oxford 1846).

Roxan, M., "The *auxilia* of Mauretania Tingitana," *Latomus* 32 (1973) 838 ff.

Ruysschaert, J., "Le commémoration de Cyprien et de Corneille *in Callisti*," *Revue d'histoire ecclésiastique* 61 (1966) 455 ff.

Sage, M. M., *Cyprian* (Cambridge, Mass. 1975).

Salama, P., "La trouvaille de sesterces de *Rusguniae:* Histoire d'une découverte," *Revue africaine* 101 (1957) 205 ff.

Salaville, S., "L'épiclèse africaine," *Échos d'orient* 39 (1941–42) 268 ff.

Sauer, J., *Symbolik des Kirchengebäudes und seiner Ausstattung in der Auffassung des Mittelalters* (Freiburg 1902).

Saumagne, C., *Saint Cyprien, évêque de Carthage: "Pape" d'Afrique (248–258)* (Paris 1975).

Saxer, V., *Vie liturgique et quotidienne à Carthage vers le milieu du IIIe siècle* (Vatican City 1969).

Scheiwiler, A., *Die Elemente der Eucharistie in den ersten drei Jahrhunderten* (Mainz 1903).

Schrijnen, J., and Mohrmann, C., *Studien zur Syntax der Briefe des hl. Cyprian* (2 vols., Nijmegen 1936–37).

Schwartz, J., "Chronologie du IIIe s. p.C.," *Zeitschrift für Papyrologie und Epigraphik* 24 (1977) 167 ff.

Schweitzer, E., "Fragen der Liturgie in Nordafrika zur Zeit Cyprians," *Archiv für Liturgiewiss.* 12 (1970) 69 ff.

Seeck, O., *Geschichte des Untergangs der antiken Welt* (2nd. ed., vol. 3, Stuttgart 1921; 1st ed., Berlin 1909).

Shaw, B. D., "Fear and Loathing: The Nomad Menace and Roman Africa," in Wells, C. M. (ed.), *L'Afrique romaine, University of Ottawa Review* 52.1 (1982) 25 ff.

Shaw, B. D., "Bandits in the Roman Empire," *Past and Present* 105 (1984) 3 ff.

Simon, M., *Verus Israel: Étude sur les relations entre chrétiens et juifs dans l'empire romain* (Paris 1948).

Sordi, M., *Il cristianesimo e Roma* (Bologna 1965).

Sotgiu, G., "Treboniano Gallo Ostiliano Volusiano Emiliano (1960–1971)," *Aufstieg und Niedergang der römischen Welt* 2.2 (1975) 798 ff.

Spanneut, M., *Le stoïcisme des Pères de l'église de Clément de Rome à Clément d'Alexandrie* (2nd ed., Paris 1957).

Spanneut, M., *Tertullien et les premiers moralistes africains* (Paris 1969).

Speigl, J., "Zum Problem der Teilnahme von Laien an den Konzilien im kirchlichen Altertum," *Annuarium historiae conciliorum* 10 (1978) 241 ff.

Speyer, W., and Opelt, I., "Barbar" (Nachträge zum Reallexikon für Antike und Christentum), *Jahrbuch für Antike und Christentum* 10 (1967) 251 ff.

Srawley, J. H., *The Early History of the Liturgy* (Cambridge 1913).

Staats, R., "Ogdoas als ein Symbol für die Auferstehung," *Vigiliae christianae* 26 (1972) 29 ff.

Stadlhuber, J., "Das Stundengebet des Laien im christlichen Altertum," *Zeitschrift für katholische Theologie* 71 (1949) 129 ff.

Stam, J. E., *Episcopacy in the Apostolic Tradition of Hippolytus* (Basel 1969).

Stommel, E., "Die bischöfliche Kathedra in christlichen Altertum," *Münchener theologische Zeitschrift* 3 (1952) 17 ff.

Struckmann, A., *Die Gegenwart Christi in der hl. Eucharistie nach den schriftlichen Quellen der vornizänischen Zeit* (Vienna 1905).

Studer, B., "Die Soteriologie Cyprians von Karthago," *Augustinianum* 16 (1976) 427 ff.

Sullivan, D. D., *The Life of the North Africans as Revealed in the Works of St. Cyprian* (Washington D.C. 1933).

Swann, W. S., *The Relationship between Penance, Reconciliation with the Church and Admission to the Eucharist in the Letters and the De lapsis of Cyprian of Carthage* (diss. Catholic University, Washington D.C. 1980).

Tarradell, M., "La crisis del siglo III de J. C. en Marruecos," *Tamuda*, 1955, 75 ff.

Taylor, R. E., "Attitudes of the Fathers towards Practices of Jewish Christians," *Studia patristica* 4 (1961) 504 ff.

Telfer, W., *The Forgiveness of Sins* (London 1959).

Telfer, W., *The Office of a Bishop* (London 1962).

Testini, P., *Le catacombe e gli antichi cimiteri cristiani in Roma* (Bologna 1966).

Thébert, Y., "La romanisation d'une cité indigène d'Afrique: Bulla Regia," *Mélanges d'archéologie et d'histoire de l'école française de Rome* 85 (1973) 247 ff.

Thomas, J. D., "A Petition to the Prefect of Egypt and Related Imperial Edicts," *Journal of Egyptian Archaeology* 61 (1975) 201 ff.

Thomasson, B. E., *Die Statthalter der römischen Provinzen Nordafrikas von Augustus bis Diocletianus* (2 vols., Lund 1960).

Thouvenot, R., "Une inscription latine de Maroc," *Revue des études latines* 16 (1938) 266 ff.

Thraede, K., "Ursprünge und Formen des 'Heiligen Kusses' im frühen Christentum," *Jahrbuch für Antike und Christentum* 11/12 (1968/69) 124 ff.

Toulotte, A., *Géographie de l'Afrique chrétienne* (4 vols., Rennes/Montreuil-sur-mer 1894).

Trousset, P., *Recherches sur le Limes Tripolitanus au Chott el-Djerid à la frontière Tuniso-Libyenne* (Paris 1974).

Trousset, P., "Signification d'une frontière; Nomades et sédentaires dans la zone du limes d'Afrique," in Hanson, W. S., and Keppie, L. J. F. (eds.), *Roman Frontier Studies 1979* (Oxford 1980 = British Archaeological Reports 71) 3.931 ff.

Turcan, R., *Le trésor de Guelma: Étude historique et monétaire* (Paris 1963).

Turner, C. H., "Notes on the Old Latin Version of the Bible," *Journal of Theological Studies* 2 (1900/1901) 600 ff.

Turner, C. H., *Studies in Early Church History* (Oxford 1912).

Turner, C. H., "Papal Chronology of the Third Century," *Journal of Theological Studies* 17 (1915/16) 338 ff.

Turner, H. E. W., *The Patristic Doctrine of Redemption* (London 1952).

Turner, H. E. W., *The Pattern of Christian Truth* (London 1954).

Underwood, P. A., "The Fountain of Life in Manuscripts of the Gospels," *Dumbarton Oaks Papers* 5 (1950) 41 ff.

van Beneden, P., *Aux origines d'une terminologie sacramentelle: Ordo, ordinare, ordinatio dans la littérature chrétienne avant 313* (Louvain 1974).

van Dam, R., "Hagiography and History: The Life of Gregory Thaumaturgus," *Classical Antiquity* 1 (1982) = *California Studies in Classical Antiquity* 13 (1982) 272 ff.

van den Eynde, D., *Les normes de l'enseignement chrétien dans le littérature patristique des trois premiers siècles* (Paris 1933).

Vermeulen, A. J., *The Semantic Development of Gloria in Early-Christian Latin* (Nijmegen 1956).

Vilela, A., *La condition collégiale des prêtres au IIIᵉ siècle* (Paris 1971).

Vogt, H. J., *Coetus sanctorum* (Bonn 1968).

von Arnim, I., *Stoicorum veterum fragmenta* 3 (Stuttgart 1964).

von Campenhausen, H. F., *Die Idee des Martyriums in der alten Kirche* (Göttingen 1936).

von Soden, H., *Die cyprianische Briefsammlung: Geschichte ihrer Entstehung und Überlieferung* (TU 25.3, 1904).

von Soden, H., "Die Prosopographie des afrikanischen Episkopats zur Zeit Cyprians," *Königl. Preuss. Histor. Institut in Rom* 12 (1909) 247 ff.

Walker, G. S. M., *The Churchmanship of St. Cyprian* (London 1968).

Walser, G., "The Crisis of the Third Century A.D.: A Reinterpretation," *Bucknell Review* 13 (1965) 1 ff.

Waszink, J. H., *Tertullian De anima* (Amsterdam 1947).

Watkins, O. D., *A History of Penance: Being a Study of the Authorities* (2 vols., New York 1961; repr. of London ed. 1920).

Watson, E. W., "Cyprian in Greece," *Classical Review* 7 (1893) 248.

Watson, E. W., "The Style and Language of St. Cyprian," *Studia biblica* 4 (1896) 189 ff.

Weaver, P. R. C., "Vicarius and Vicarianus in the Familia Caesaris," *Journal of Roman Studies* 54 (1964) 117 ff.

Whittaker, E. C., *Documents of the Baptismal Liturgy* (London 1960).

Wickert, U., *Sacramentum unitatis: Ein Beitrag zum Verständnis der Kirche bei Cyprian* (Berlin 1971).

Wiles, M. F., "The Theological Legacy of St. Cyprian," *Journal of Ecclesiastical History* 14 (1963) 139 ff.

Willis, G. G., "St. Cyprian and the Mixed Chalice," *Downside Review* 339 (1982) 110 ff.

Wilmart, A., "La Lettre 58 de Cyprien parmi les lectures non bibliques du Lectionnaire de Luxeuil," *Revue bénédictine* 28 (1911) 228 ff.

Windisch, H., *Taufe und Sünde im ältesten Christentum bis auf Origenes: Ein Beitrag zur altchristlichen Dogmengeschichte* (Tübingen 1908).

Wölfflin, E., "Lupana (Cyp. epist. 62, 3)," *Archiv. für lat. Lexikog. und Grammatik* 8 (1893) 145.

Wuttke, G., *Melchisedech der Priesterkönig von Salem* (Giessen 1927).

York, J. M., "The Image of Philip the Arab," *Historia* 21 (1972) 320 ff.

Younge, R. G., *Cyprian of Carthage: Conversion and Influence* (diss. Berkeley 1979).

Zaccaria, C., "Il cesarato di Gallieno e i 'Caesares Augusti' del III sec. D.C.," *Labeo* 22 (1976) 343 ff.

Zapelena, T., "Petrus origo unitatis apud s. Cyprianum," *Gregorianum* 15 (1934) 500 ff.; 16 (1935) 196 ff.

Zernov, N., "Saint Stephen and the Roman Community at the Time of the Baptismal Controversy," *Church Quarterly* 117 (1934) 304 ff.

Zmire, P., "Recherches sur la collégialité épiscopale dans l'église d'Afrique," *Recherches augustiniennes* 7 (1971) 3 ff.

INTRODUCTION

1. At nearly every turn, the reconstruction in this section must be considered tentative; we do not have the sources for composing even a confident outline of events, let alone a detailed narrative. For bibliography on Decius see *Letters of Cyprian* 1 (ACW 43) intro. n. 109.

2. For treachery Zos. 1.23.2 ff. (cf. Aurel. Vict. *De Caes.* 29.4 *Decii . . . fraude cecidere*), for settlement with the Goths Zos. 1.24.2. For a general survey of the more recent bibliography on Gallus (1960–1971), see Sotgiu, ANRW 2.2 (1975) 798 ff. and note the bibliography also in Robertson, *Hunter Coin Cabinet* 3.xxxv f.

3. For the death of Hostilian by plague, Aurel. Vict. *De Caes.* 30.2 (cf. *Epit. de Caes.* 30.2), by treachery Zos. 1.25.1 f. and see further Préaux, *Aegyptus* 32 (1952) 152 ff. For the quick turnabout in official attitudes towards the Decii, see Gilliam, *Studi . . . Calderini e Paribeni* 1.305 ff., and on the changing status of Hostilian and Volusianus (mirrored in the coinage) see Mattingly, Sydenham, and Sutherland, RIC 4.3, 149 ff., and cf. Mattingly, *Num. chron.* 6 (1946) 36 ff.; Campus, *Arch. class.* 29 (1977) 411 ff. (milestone recording Volusian as Caesar but not yet Augustus).

4. For the residence in Italy, Aurel. Vict. *De Caes.* 31.1, Zos. 1.25.1; for the sea-borne raids, Zos. 1.28.1; for the incursion into northern Greece, Zon. 12.21.

5. On this Persian invasion see among others Olmstead, *Class. Phil.* 37 (1942) 401 ff.; Frye, *Bibl. orient.* 8 (1951) 103 ff.; Honigmann and Maricq, *Mém. Acad. roy. Belg.* 47.4 (1953) 150 ff.; Maricq, *Syria* 35 (1958) 309 f., 340 f.; Chaumont, *Historia* 22 (1973) 664 ff.; Metcalf, *Amer. Num. Soc. Mus. Notes* 22 (1977) 71 ff. and 23 (1978) 129 ff.; Kettenhofen, *Die römisch-persischen Kriege* (1982). On Uranius Antoninus see *Ep.* 55 n. 40.

6. For the *testimonia* on Aemilian see PIR² A. 330; Barbieri, *L'Albo*, no. 1417; and for bibliography see Sotgiu, ANRW 2.2 (1975) 798 ff. For *testimonia* on Valerian and Gallienus see PIR² L. 258 and 197; Barbieri, *L'Albo*, nos. 1634 and 1630. Zaccaria, *Labeo* 22 (1976) 343 ff., deals most recently with these opening stages of the princi-

pates of Valerian and Gallienus; and for a more general bibliographical survey, Christol, ANRW 2.2 (1975) 803 ff.

7. A version of this section is to appear in ANRW 27.

8. The date is given specifically as before Easter in the course of the ninth year of Gallienus' reign (Diony. Alex. *ap.* Euseb. *H.E.* 7.23.4). For discussion see the commentary of H. J. Lawlor and J. E. L. Oulton, vol. 2, 251 ff., and Andresen, ANRW 2.23.1 (1979) 387 ff., esp. 414 ff. (with coverage of preceding opinions). On the panegyrical character of Dionysius' remarks about Gallienus, cf. A. Alföldi, *Klio* 31 (1938) 338 ff. = *Studien* 301 ff.

9. See Lawlor and Oulton *loc. cit.* for discussion, and see Andresen *loc. cit.* facing p. 416 and p. 427 for tabulation of major views (all in early 260s).

10. Thus J. A. F. Gregg, *The Decian Persecution* 270, 274, dates the outbreak of the plague in Egypt to March 252. The *testimonia* on the plague are conveniently assembled by M. L. Hannan, *Thasci Caecili Cypriani De mortalitate* 13 ff., to which should be added *Orac. Sibyl.* 12.103 ff. (where Gk. *g' allos* = Gallus ?); (?) P. Oxy. 1666.20 f.; (?) P. Mert. 26.8; Porphyry *fr.* 80 (Harnack) = Euseb. *Praep. ev.* 5.1.9 f.; (?) Dionys. Alex. *ap.* Euseb. *H.E.* 7.11.24. In fact, the plague would seem to have—or could be said to have—carried off Hostilian (in Rome) by autumn 251 (Vict. *De Caes.* 30.2): see, for discussion, C. Préaux, *Aegyptus* 32 (1952) 152 ff.; J. F. Gilliam, *Studi in onore di Aristide Calderini e Roberto Paribeni* 305 ff.

11. For a typical sample see RAC 2 *s.v.* "Christenverfolgung I (historisch)" 1187 (J. Vogt).

12. Against the deduction of P. Allard, *Les dernières persécutions du III⁰ siècle* 23: "L'énergie avec laquelle saint Denys d'Alexandrie reproche à Gallus d'avoir persécuté les saints qui priaient pour l'empire, fait voir que l'Égypte ne fut pas épargnée."

13. Though 252 is confidently claimed as the date for the Synod of Antioch, Euseb. *H.E.* 6.46.3, 7.4 f. (e.g., Hefele-Leclercq, *Histoire* 1.1.169; Downey, *History of Antioch* 309), the claim appears to rest on guesswork. It would indeed be significant for our purposes if such a broadly based synod—with bishops freely coming in from Palestine, Cilicia, the Syrias, Cappadocia, Arabia, Mesopotamia, Pontus and Bithynia, and Egypt—was able to be held that year. (In

DHGE 3 [1924] *s.v.* "Antioche" 565 [C. Karalevskij] the death of Fabius, which occurred before the Synod, is not put until 253, but without supporting argument.) On the rhetorical nature of Gregory of Nyssa's composition, see van Dam, *Classical Antiquity* 1 (1982) 272 ff.; for an earlier (Syriac) version, Ryssel 228 ff.

14. For references to the persecuted Church consult *De mort.* 15, 19, 25; *Ad Demet.* 12 f., 17 ff., 21, 24, 25. Much is traditional apologetic material.

15. Opinions differ on the date of the martyrdom protreptic *Ad Fortunatum*, with 250/51 as the favoured date; at all events, it cannot properly be used to *establish* anything about the period 252/53. For lengthy discussion see Koch, *Cyp. Unter.* 149 ff.; also G. Alföldy, *Historia* 22 (1973) 486 f. n. 39.

16. Note especially *Ad Demet.* 3, 5, 23; *De mort.* 15; there is a clear enunciation of the logic in *Ep.* 58.2.2, and on the theme in Cyprian generally D'Alès, *La théologie de s. Cyprien* 77 ff. (with a full collection of texts); Alföldy, *Historia* 22 (1973) 485 ff., and more generally RAC 1 (1950) *s.v.* "Antichrist" 450 ff. (E. Lohmeyer).

17. The pseudo-Cyprianic tractate *Ad Novatianum* (CCL 4.137 ff.) is unfortunately of dubious date and provenance. Note especially the study of Koch, *Cyp. Unter.* 358 ff. The chapters of importance are 5 and 6 referring to a *secundum proelium;* they are discussed below in intro. n. 29.

18. Bibliography conveniently assembled in CCL 3.xii ff., esp. xxii ff.

19. A casual clause in *Ep.* 56.2.2 demonstrates that it was not [*puto*] *si acies etiam denuo venerit, gloriam suam posse reparare.*

20. For details and bibliography see introduction to *Ep.* 60.

21. *Ep.* 57.5.1: *quod credimus vobis quoque paternae misericordiae contemplatione placiturum; Ep.* 68.5.1 shows that the Roman pontiffs adopted such a policy in fact only after they had been driven out of Rome (*in glorioso martyrio constituti*).

22. E.g. §§1.2, 2.2, 7.1.

23. For details see *Ep.* 59 intro.

24. Cyprian was convinced that suffering was a mark of divine predilection, e.g. *Test.* 3.6 (CCL 3.94 ff.) on the theme *bonos quosque et iustos plus laborare . . . quia probantur.*

25. For reference to some views see *Ep.* 59 n. 31.

26. For texts which show that Christians were popularly blamed by contemporaries for the plague (*inter alia*) see *Ep.* 57 intro., *Ep.* 59 n. 31.

27. Cf. *Ep.* 7.1.1 (early 250). This was incurred not for the first time (*totiens ad leonem petitus, ad leonem denuo postulatus, Ep.* 59.6.1), echoed by Pontius *Vita Cyp.* 7.2 H.xcvii (*suffragiis saepe repetitis ad leonem postularetur*).

28. Note especially §13.2: *Miserorum paenitentiam mendaciorum suorum fraude corrumpunt ne Deo indignanti satisfiat. . . . Datur opera ne satisfactionibus et lamentationibus iustis delicta redimantur, ne vulnera lacrimis abluantur.* There is not a hint of any recent (and unprecedentedly) generous policy of reconciliation for penitent *lapsi*.

29. The *Ad Novatianum* 5.2 refers to *Cataclysmus ergo ille, qui sub Noe factus est, figuram persecutionis quae per totum orbem nunc nuper supereffusa est ostendit* (does this refer to Decius, Gallus, Valerian?— each has been canvassed); 6.4 f. reads: *duplex ergo illa emissio duplicem nobis persecutionis temptationem ostendit: prima in qua qui lapsi sunt victi ceciderunt, secunda in qua hi ipsi qui ceciderunt victores extiterunt. Nulli enim nostrum dubium vel incertum est, fratres dilectissimi, illos qui prima acie, id est Deciana persecutione, vulnerati fuerunt, hos postea id est secundo proelio ita fortiter perseverasse, ut contemnentes edicta saecularium principum hoc invictum haberent, quod et meruerunt exemplo boni pastoris animam suam tradere, sanguinem fundere et nullam insanae mentis tyranni saevitiam recusare* (CCL 4.141 f.). If the reference to the *secundum proelium* alludes to the time of Gallus (which seems feasible), it would be helpful to ascertain how rhetorical were the *edicta saecularium principum*. On the face of it, more than somewhat for the only blood (to our knowledge) which could be said, by any strain of language, to have been shed was that of Cornelius (who died a natural death after being removed from Rome). The language of Cyp. *Ep.* 55.9.1 f. is ominously close (with reference to Decius): *cum tyrannus infestus sacerdotibus Dei fanda atque infanda comminaretur . . . tyranni ferocientis ultores qui Cornelium adversus edicta feralia resistentem. . . .* (Koch even suggests the tractate is an exercise in ersatz Cyprianese "gar eine Stilübung," *Cyp. Unter.* 419.) With the date, status, and provenance (Rome? Africa?) so uncertain, it is difficult to do other than merely leave this evidence to be borne in mind.

30. For details see *Ep.* 60 intro.

31. For the calculation see, e.g., Turner, JTS 17 (1915/16) 345 ff.

32. I do not know on what source J. Moreau (*Lactance: De la mort des persécuteurs* 2.217) bases his remark concerning "des mouvements populaires qui sous son règne [of Gallus] aboutirent à l'exil des papes Corneille et Lucius." Does he envisage antiplague/anti-Christian rioting, with the officials removing the obvious scapegoats to enforced safety?

33. On some calculations of the events of 253 Gallus is even dead before these episodes occur which concern the Christians in Rome!

34. In *Ep.* 60.2.5 the phrase *quot illic lapsi gloriosa confessione sunt restituti* might be valuable, but the context rather suggests preparedness to face battle, not actual confession and its legal consequences. Similarly, Cyprian's declaration in *Ep.* 60.1.2 *ecclesia omnis Romana confessa est* seems a rhetorical way of describing the church's steadfast loyalty behind its leader, now *confessor*.

35. See *Ep.* 61 intro.

36. The (contemporary) writings of Novatian in Rome are without any reference to persecution difficulties under Gallus.

37. The most balanced treatment of these events is to be found in Grégoire *et al.*, *Les persécutions* 149 ff. (Note complémentaire 10).

38. For a convenient survey of the evidence for Councils in the late second century on Montanism and the paschal computation (our earliest known samples), Hefele-Leclercq, *Histoire* 1.1.127 ff.; for such meetings in the first half of the third century, *ibid.* 154 ff.

39. Arguments in favour of a second sitting in 251 are advanced, e.g., by Monceaux, *Rev. de phil., de litt. et d'hist. anc.* 24 (1900) 336; cf. *idem, Histoire* 2.43 f.; DHGE 1 (1912) *s.v.* "Afrique" 747 (Audollent); against, Koch, *Cyp. Unter.* 126 ff.; Harnack, *Chronologie* 2.353; cf. DHGE 11 (1949) *s.v.* "Carthage" 1221 (Ferron and Lapeyre). On this question see further below *Ep.* 64 intro., *Ep.* 59 n. 58.

40. Some conjecture an autumn meeting of African bishops as well in 253, based on the fact that Cyprian writes *Ep.* 61 *cum collegis*. But that is not a necessary deduction: see *Ep.* 61 intro. and n. 1.

41. For Syriac fragments that may belong to this letter (it was originally very lengthy, Euseb. *H.E.* 7.4) see Feltoe, ΛΕΙΨΑΝΑ 45 ff.

LETTER 55

Contents: Cyprian has received two letters from Antonianus, one adhering to the college of bishops and recognising Cornelius, the second and later one expressing indecision over Novatian, doubts about Cornelius, and concern over Cyprian's apparent shift in policy (§§1–3).

Cyprian's own policy change was simply dictated by the changes in circumstances and, as had been planned beforehand (and that plan was also agreed to by the Roman church), it was the assembly of bishops who determined the peacetime regulations over penitence after lengthy debate (and the Italian Council has also agreed upon those same regulations), §§4–7.

As for Cornelius, he has won universal approbation from the world's bishops: he has been well trained for his office by long clerical service; he displays the appropriate virtues of modesty, chastity, and reluctance to hold office; he is a popular choice; and his courage in taking up that office in the time of Decius the persecutor merits for him the rank of confessor and martyr (§§8–9). He is not stained with any certificate of sacrifice nor is he in communion with bishops who did sacrifice (as is rumoured); the case of Trofimus and his flock (apostates, now reconciled) was a special one, a concession made in the interests of reuniting large numbers of the brethren—and besides, Trofimus is no longer a bishop (§§10–11).

It is also rumored that Cornelius is reconciling indiscriminately those who have sacrificed. That simply misconstrues the fact that some who have been (properly) granted reconciliation on their deathbed, by God's goodness have subsequently recovered their health (§§12–13.1). Indeed, those who sacrificed (many of whom have very extenuating circumstances) should not be confused with those who obtained certificates (who may have acted in simple error, out of desire to avoid the evil of offering sacrifice). If the bishops cast these out, they will be answerable for driving them into heresy and schism (§§13.2–15).

Stoic philosophers may make no such distinctions and scorn pity and compassion, but that is not Christianity. Their harsh intransigence will only force the fallen either back to paganism or into the ranks of heretics, where there is no salvation. Therefore, it was resolved that those who obtained certificates, upon examination, should be reconciled, whilst those who sacrificed should be reconciled at the last, the Lord being the final Judge on all these matters (§§16–18). Mercy and compassion are Gospel precepts; offering hope to the penitent will not reduce the spirit of martyrdom in the Church, just as, in the past, allowing penitence to adulterers has not reduced virginity and chastity in the Church (§§19–20). Even on that question of adultery, some bishops obstinately refused to allow penitence—but *they* still did not go so far as to break the bonds of charity in the Church (§21). There are indeed many texts which enjoin penitence upon the sinner and offer to them hopes of deliverance from our loving Father; but (it was resolved) those who do no penance at all will not receive any reconciliation at the last (§§22–23).

As for Novatian, he has lost any claim to be heard, for he is now outside; he is a counterfeit bishop seeking to establish a man-made church and in his arrogance he lays claim to powers of judgment which belong only to the Lord (§§24–25). If he is honest, he must drive out from his own following adulterers and robbers who have committed far worse sins than *libellatici* and whose slavery to the devil is but a form of idolatry (§§26–27.2).

In accordance with Gospel precepts, therefore, sinners are invited back to the Church to do penance through the bishops, and the fruits of that penance are not cruelly denied to them. The Lord will come to pass judgment on all those whom He finds within the Church, but those who are outside cannot be granted the peace of the Church (§§27.3–29).

Date and circumstances: The date cannot be fixed with precision, but we can say what the letter must come after and what it must be placed before. It must be written after both the African Council of 251 (started meeting in late April 251?, see *Ep.* 44 intro.) and the Italian Council (which met sometime in the course of 251, after that African

Council—see *Ep*. 49 intro.), for the sessions of these two Councils are reported in §§6.1 f. And Novatian must have had time to circulate a letter which criticised resolutions of that Italian Council, §2.1 with n. 6 below. This *Ep*. 55 must also occur after the reconciliation of the Roman confessors (early July 251?, see *Ep*. 49 intro.), mentioned in §5.1, as well as after the death of Emperor Decius (an event which can be spoken of in the past), which occurred about early June 251, §9.2 with nn. 41 and 45 below. That begins to sound like a *terminus post* of (say) August 251 or thereabouts. And we can say what the letter must come before. It must be placed before the *next* African Council meeting, that of 252, which convened that year on May 15, *Ep*. 59.10.1—that meeting is not yet in prospect (and Cyprian cannot count on seeing Antonianus in the immediate future, §30.2). And it must also come before any danger threatened Christians under Gallus—such peril is not feared in §17.3 (it is certainly reported by summer 252, *Ep*. 59.6.1, if not earlier—see *Epp*. 57, 59 intro.). That results in the vague termini of last quarter of 251/first quarter of 252, with the likelihood (it is no more than that) that this was written earlier rather than later within that period. Further discussion in Nelke, *Chronologie* 73 ff.; Duquenne, *Chronologie* 32 ff.

There is one problem, however, with such a conclusion. Cyprian can report in §8.1 that Cornelius has been accorded universal approbation by the bishops of the world (*coepiscoporum testimonio quorum numerus universus per totum mundum concordi unanimitate consensit*). But we do know from Euseb. *H.E.* 7.4 f. (cf. 6.46.3) that it is in a letter to Cornelius' successor, Stephen (May 254+), that Dionysius of Alexandria can report that the churches everywhere, having rejected the innovation of Novatian, have now resumed peace among themselves, that "all the churches of the East and still further away, which were formerly divided, have been united and all their presidents everywhere are of like mind . . . and, in a word, all everywhere rejoice exceedingly in their concord and brotherly love." That must mean that before this Synod of Antioch assembled (not before 252—to allow Demetrian time to replace Fabian in Antioch and Heliodorus to replace Thelymidres in Syrian Laodicea—and more likely in 253) the eastern bishops could not universally have given Cornelius their approbation as Cyprian here asserts. We shall have to conclude that Cyprian either was ill-informed in making his claim or (more probably) that he was being propagandistic in his efforts to win allegiance from hesitant bishops like Antonianus (cf. n. 31 below).

This letter is a major document not only for our understanding of the persecution of Decius itself (note the details in §§13.2 ff. on *sacrificati*, *libellatici*, and *profugi*) but especially for our knowledge of the long-postponed settlement reached during 251 on the vital question of the *lapsi*, those who were considered to have apostatised in the course of that persecution. But there is one thing about this version of that settlement which stands out immediately. This is a letter from a bishop to a bishop urging him to maintain concord within the college of his fellow bishops and, therefore, to abide by the decisions already reached by the assemblies of bishops. The focus of the letter is on concord, collegiality, and consensus between the members of the body episcopal (cf. n. 2 below); confessors, lower clergy, and faithful laity who had all been promised, many times, roles in the Councils that were to regulate these disciplinary questions are lost sight of before this overriding vision (though, e.g., the presence of numerous presbyters and deacons is attested elsewhere, e.g. *Ep.* 59.15.1 [Carthage], Euseb. *H.E.* 6.43.2 [Rome]). The arguments presented are designed to appeal to episcopal ears. And within that overall framework Cyprian is seeking to put the record straight both about himself and about his leading colleague, Cornelius, as well as to defend—against Novatianist criticisms—the disciplinary regulations that had been drawn up by those episcopal Councils. The selection of information and argument in the letter has been dictated by the attacks to which this is a riposte.

Still, the broad lines on which the decisions were reached can be discerned:

(1) The basic premise was that the lapsed, as a category of sinner, should be conceded a *locus paenitentiae*, an opportunity to do penitence, and that hope of reconciliation should not be denied to those who did such penance (the Novatianists refused it, §28.1; their proud claim can be reported, *se . . . idolatris non communicare*, §27.1). Hence Cyprian's basic assertion in §27.3 *neminem putamus a fructu satisfactionis et spe pacis arcendum*.

(2) That a category distinction should be drawn between *libellatici* (who had polluted only their consciences, §14.2) and *sacrificati*: *nec tu existimes . . . sicut quibusdam videtur* [= Novatianists], *libellaticos*

cum sacrificatis aequare oportere, §13.2. Hence, Novatianists can be charged with being Stoics and not Christians in that, in making no such distinction, they are acting according to the Stoic adage *omnia peccata paria*, §16.1.

(3) That in the case of the *libellatici*, after individual examination, they are to be restored to communion, §17.2.

(4) That in the case of *sacrificati*, they are to be reconciled *in exitu*, §§13.1, 17.2.

(5) That in the case of *lapsi* who do no penance, they cannot be reconciled *in exitu*, §23.4.

(6) That the proper authority to judge each case should be the bishop in the place where the offence was alleged to have been committed (*Ep.* 59.14.2, where see n. 72).

(7) That in all these dealings it is the Lord who is the ultimate Judge, who shall determine if in fact a sinner's *paenitentia* is *plena et iusta* (§18.1). But at least the Lord when He comes to judge will find the sinner kept safe inside the Church (§19.2 *hunc curatum Deo iudici reservamus*, §29.2), not outside, among pagans (§§6.1, 17.2) or damned heretics (§§15.1, 17.2, 29.3).

Idolatry (with which the lapsed of whatever category had been polluted) was a sin against God; as such, there was a considerable tradition, of which Cyprian, and no doubt colleagues like Antonianus, were heirs, which regarded this delict, therefore, as irremissible. That is to say, it could not be remitted by the Church but was reserved for God alone to judge. As Cyprian put it baldly in *Test.* 3.28 (CCL 3.122) *non posse in ecclesia remitti ei qui in deum deliquerit*. It was only with caution, diffidence, and considerable unease that he moved away from that position of unyielding rigour, as is reflected in *Ad Fort.* 4 (CCL 3.190 f.) on the significantly-worded topic *non facile ignoscere deum idolatris*, and as is also observable in the *ad hoc* disciplinary *concessions* granted under the stress of the persecution conditions (e.g. for the lapsed who were dying, *Epp.* 18.1.2, 19.2.1). But pastoral concerns and realities even then had made it clear to him that idolatry, however grievous a fault, could not be regarded as absolutely irremissible, e.g. *Ep.* 16.2.3. All the same, Cyprian is painfully aware that he is now making concessions (*laxandam pacem putaverim*, §3.2, cf. §20.1), he is yielding to the needs of the present circumstances (*necessitate temporum succubuisse*, §7.2) at a time when apostates can no longer cancel their sin by resorting to confession and martyrdom, §4.1, cf. 16.3. And he is careful to register that such a shift has not been made without long and serious forethought (*non sine librata diu et ponderata ratione*, §3.2).

And he is clear-eyed as to why those concessions ought now to be made. It was in the interest of the salvation of the many (*saluti multorum providendum*, §7.2); it would help to gather the brethren together (*conligendae fraternitatis . . . utilitas*, §7.2): Cornelius is defended similarly, §11.1 (*conligendis fratribus nostris . . . necessitate succubuit*). For Cyprian and his colleagues were drawing up their decisions against a background in which the great mass of their congregations had fallen (cf. *Ep.* 14.1.1). To revert to the strict rigour of the past would be to drive the bulk of their numbers *outside*, whether to despair and paganism or to join a schismatic church (already visibly there in Carthage). The imperatives of church *unitas* and pastoral *salus* had also to be answered. The outcome was a *salubris moderatio*, an undisguised *temperamentum* (see §6.1). The major concession to reconcile the *libellatici* (not foreshadowed, e.g., in the *De lapsis*) would go some way to satisfy those who favoured the laxists, whereas the restrictions imposed on the reconciliation of the *sacrificati* would go some way to satisfy those who favoured the rigorists. Needless to say, for some it went too far (Novatianists), for others it did not go far enough (e.g. party of Felicissimus).

The bishops had been called upon to formulate rules and procedures on circumstances that were unprecedented. Tradition could not provide the particular answers; its general aid was, however, invoked. Cyprian makes a rare allusion to the past by drawing a significant analogy with penitential concessions granted in the case of the once irremissible sin of adultery (§§20.2, 21.1), and Cornelius is defended for making concessions in the interests of pastoral unity, *sicut et antecessores nostri saepe fecerunt*, §11.1. But that could not get them very far. It was to their Bible that they therefore must go. The *biblical* level at which the case is argued in this letter is remarkable; there are nearly thirty direct biblical quotations and some twenty more biblical allusions. And the *Ad Novatianum* shows clearly that it was on grounds of biblical interpretation that the battle continued to be fought with the Novatianists (e.g. . . . *Novatiani, apud quos scripturae caelestes leguntur potius quam intelleguntur, parum si non et interpo-*

liantur, Ad Novat. 2.8 (CCL 4.139). The only descriptive touch we are given in this letter of the sessions of this African Council of 251 is revealing: there was a lengthy debate in which scriptural passages on both sides of the issue were produced (*Scripturis diu ex utraque parte prolatis*, §6.1). And, as this letter shows, those scriptural passages which prescribed charity and compassion were now shifting the vision of the Church away from the Novatianists' assembly of saints more towards a sanctuary for sinners (§§18.1, 19.2, 29.2). Significantly perhaps, it is in this letter that there occurs the only passage in Cyprian which makes God Himself (as opposed to the Holy Spirit) the author of Scripture (*iuxta scripturarum divinarum fidem auctore et hortatore Deo ipso*, §29.3, cf. Fahey 44 f.). One element of the past could be, however, openly discarded. The traditionally sanctioned *libelli martyrum* (*Ep.* 15.3.1 *quae et qualia in praeteritum antecessores vestri martyres concesserint*) go unmentioned as a factor in the decision-making; the market had been so flooded with them as to render their currency valueless.

There is abundant literature: see *Ep.* 8 n. 25, *Ep.* 15 n. 12 where relevant studies are cited (and where there is further discussion), and see *Ep.* 30 intro. for material on Novatian. There is an excellent translation of much of this epistle by M. Bévenot in his *De lapsis and De ecclesiae catholicae unitate* (1971) 101 ff., to which I am much indebted, and there is recent discussion of the context of the letter by Deléani, REAug 23 (1977) 221 ff., esp. 232 ff., and Vogt, *Coetus sanctorum* 140 ff. ("Cyprians Polemik"). And on the agenda of the Council of 251, see further the introduction to this volume.

1. *Cyprianus Antoniano fratri s.* Antonianus must be a bishop. That is clear from the body of the letter; he is a member of the *collegium* of bishops, e.g. §30.1. And he was absent from the Council of 251 (§6.1), although travel to Carthage is not entirely out of the question for him (*si . . . opportunitas et facultas fuerit*, §30.2). He is, therefore, an *African* bishop, and it is a reasonable assumption—but no more than that—that, being unable to attend the Council in 251, he should be located at least somewhere farther distant than Africa Proconsularis. But attempts to place him as far west as Mauretania (involving the hazardous step of identifying the presbyter Quintus of §2.1 with the later bishop Quintus from Mauretania of *Epp.* 71,

72.1.3, 73.1.1) must remain highly speculative, especially when a bishop Antonianus occurs among the addressees of *Ep.* 70 and they are all firmly identified as Numidian by Cyprian himself, *Ep.* 72.1.3 (*ad coepiscopos in Numidia praesidentes*). By economy of effort, the see of Antonianus should be located somewhere within Numidia. For discussion, Turner, *Studies* 124 n. 1; von Soden, *Prosopographie* 261; Maier, *L'épiscopat* 255.

The Numidian church has, therefore, not only bishops inclined towards a laxist position (at least four of them gave their support to Privatus, *Ep.* 50.10.2 ff.) but also colleagues, like Antonianus, inclined (it emerges) towards a more rigorist and Novatianist position (note the open nature of the letter, §3.1). This fairly reflects the dilemma being faced by all the churches in 251. See *Letters of Cyprian* 2 (ACW 44) intro. pp. 5 ff.

2. *primas litteras . . . concordiam collegii sacerdotalis firmiter obtinentes et catholicae ecclesiae cohaerentes.* This letter must have been written after the question of the legitimacy of Cornelius had been settled for the African church. That settlement was reached only after the African Council of 251 had itself dispersed (*Ep.* 45.1.3 makes that clear). Antonianus and his fellow bishops would have been written to, therefore, when Cyprian and the colleagues who were advising him in Carthage (*Ep.* 44.1.2 and n. 6) had reached their decision on the issue (c. end of June 251 or thereabouts?). This letter from Antonianus would be in response to such a communication sent from Carthage *per provinciam nostram . . . collegis singulis, Ep.* 45.1.3. We get some notion of the delays involved before *Cornelius* could receive such letters of recognition, if, first, letters had to get from Carthage out to remote dioceses (such as Antonianus'), then the local incumbent had to come to his own decision and send an appropriate letter back to Carthage ("we have instructed that they should send back brethren with letters," *fratres [nostros] cum litteris redigendos esse, Ep.* 45.1.3, cf. *Ep.* 48.3.2) before, eventually, the communications received were forwarded from Carthage over to Rome. Cornelius had understandable reasons for suspecting treachery in such delays. See also Harnack, *Über verlorene Briefe* 33 f.

Note the phrasing, so characteristic of Cyprian's thought and especially appropriate for an episcopal correspondent: where there is *concordia* between bishops, there is to be identified the *ecclesia catholica*.

Cyprian is aiming to convince Antonianus, and others like him, of the overriding importance of maintaining that *concordia* in the body episcopal; they must, therefore, uphold the decisions harmoniously reached by the episcopal *collegium* at the Councils of Africa and Italy (§§6.1 f.). Cyprian's concluding words pointedly echo these opening sentiments, §§30.1 f.: *te . . . collegii et corporis nostri societate coniungerem . . . quae in salutarem concordiam faciant.* A wordcount alone on this theme in this letter is impressive, *consacerdos, coepiscopus,* and *collega* (used exclusively of bishops) occurring altogether 15 times, *collegium* and *corpus* (when used of bishops only) 9 times, *consensus, consensio,* and *concordia* 10 times.

3. *sequi consilium nostrum:* most translate "my counsel." That is misleading. Cyprian is writing as a *collega,* insisting throughout on the collective authority of the *collegium* of bishops. It is *"our* counsel," therefore, "the council of us bishops."

4. *te secum hoc est cum catholica ecclesia communicare.* The Antonianus of *Ep.* 70 appears to be a relatively junior bishop—several years later, he figures in 16th place in a list of 18 bishops—but he here shows some administrative prudence in making his reply to Cyprian also serve as his letter of recognition to Cornelius. Any potential misunderstandings could thereby be eliminated. The stress on the *catholica ecclesia* echoes the argument of Cornelius: *his* church was the *catholica ecclesia* in Rome. See *Ep.* 49.2.4 and n. 16; Cornelius *ap.* Euseb. *H.E.* 6.43.11 ff.

5. *per Quintum conpresbyterum.* Sr. R. B. Donna 134 n. 5 calls this man "Quintus of Mauretania . . . the African bishop." But Cyprian's language here makes it plain that this Quintus is not an episcopal colleague. In Cyprianic usage a bishop and a presbyter may be termed *conpresbyteri,* but one bishop is not termed *conpresbyter* in relation to another bishop (rather *collega, consacerdos, coepiscopus,* etc.); see Vilela 279 ff. for an analysis, also Watson 258 f. n. As likely as not, the Quintus here was a Numidian presbyter who was travelling down to Carthage; for the unlikelihood of his being Mauretanian see n. 1 above.

6. *Novatiani litteris postmodum te esse commotum.* Antonianus appears to have received this document of Novatian's only after he had sent off his letter of communion in favour of Cornelius (cf. §3.1), i.e. after early July 251 or thereabouts. Indeed, to judge by the con-

tents of Novatian's letter (case of Trofimus [see n. 51 below], Novatian condemned as a heretic, great stress on the question of penitence, §§11 f., 20 ff., 24 ff.), we can reasonably deduce that this particular letter from Novatian was sent out by him in riposte to actions and decisions taken by the Roman Council of 251 (cf. Euseb. *H.E.* 6.43.2 ff.). It apparently contained also fair abuse of Cornelius personally (hence §§8 ff.). It is, therefore, to be distinguished from earlier correspondence of Novatian's composed *before* that Council met (*Epp.* 44.1.1, 45.2.1 f.), contra Harnack, *Über verlorene Briefe* 12 f.

7. *et consilium et consensum tuum firmiter ante fixisses.* Cyprian carefully repeats words he has used to characterise favourably Antonianus' first letter in §1.1 (*firmiter . . . sequi consilium nostrum . . . unum tenere consensum*).

8. *quam haeresim . . . qua ratione Trofimo et turificatis communicet.* The charge of heresy is confronted below in §§24 ff., that of communion with Trofimus and the *turificati* in §§11 f. (where see nn. 49 ff.). The word *turificatus* occurs only here (save several times in the Erasmian pastiche *De duplici mart.* H. 3.220 ff.), apparently quoted from Antonianus' own letter. Was it perhaps coined during the process of discerning special mitigating factors that distinguished Trofimus and his flock (§§11.1 ff.): they had scattered but a few grains of incense on some brazier, not actually tasted the abominable sacrificial meats on the pagan altars themselves as had full *sacrificati*, and they, therefore, formed a separate, less offending subcategory of lapsed? (It has been suggested that *turificati* were too poor to be able to provide their own sacrificial victims, DACL 4.1 [1916] *s.v.* "Dèce" 312 n. 13 [H. Leclercq]—but that would have applied to the bulk of the Roman population in all likelihood. On the significance of incense offering—it need not be inferior to animal sacrifice in terms of veneration—see Price, *Rituals and Power* 228 f.)

Along with *turificatus*, the neologism *libellaticus* occurs also only in this letter (§§13.2, 14.1, 17.3, 26.1), *sacrificatus* only here (§§12.1, 17.3) and in *Ep.* 59 (§§10.3, 11.1, 11.3). These were terms presumably devised during the technical debates of the Councils of 251. On all three words Hoppenbrouwers 142 f.

9. *pro sollicitudine fidei . . . sollicitus . . . animi sollicitudo.* Such heavy-handed repetition is suggestive of irony. Cyprian appears to

harbour some suspicion that he may possibly be being baited by Antonianus' inquiry.

10. *graves viros et semel super petram solida stabilitate fundatos.* The allusion is to Matt. 7.24 f. cf. Lk. 6.48 (omitted by Fahey 289). Cyprian has used the phrase *graves viri* previously in *Ep.* 41.2.1 (of reliable informants); he reuses it in §7.3 (of bishops), and in §16.1 *vir gravis* figures as a variant for *vir sapiens*, the ideal philosophic character. In *Ep.* 59.9.1 the bishops in the Council of 251 have advanced to become *gravissimi viri*.

11. *ne apud te vel apud quemquam.* . . . A clear indicator that Cyprian has composed this lengthy document not only for Antonianus' benefit. Copies would be made for those expressing similar sympathies or misgivings. No doubt Cornelius received a copy; the handsome vindication of him in §§8 ff. could do nothing but good.

12. *quod utrumque non sine librata diu et ponderata ratione a me factum est.* Cyprian has to defend himself against the accusation of *levitas* (a charge with which he has, in defensive anticipation, already threatened Antonianus in §3.1): he was strictly unyielding towards the lapsed during the persecution but he has become unprincipledly lax in dealing with them after the persecution. Hence, in retaliation, he weighs heavy stress on the long and ponderous argumentation that preceded his (undeniable) shift in position.

13. Cyprian is quoting from his *Ep.* 19.2.3 (where see n. 17 for discussion). The Council of Ancyra in the early fourth century codified for the first time regulations on such rehabilitative confession. Canon 1, *inter alia*, excludes from rehabilitation fallen presbyters who seek for reinstatement by means of contrived and bogus tortures; in other words, the canon is correcting abuse of the discipline which Cyprian here (somewhat brutally) recommended to his flock under persecution; Hefele-Leclercq, *Histoire* 1.1.301 ff.

14. *ipse a communicatione abstineretur.* Cyprian eventually reached the point (via his presbyters and deacons) of so excluding Gaius Didensis and his deacon and of threatening similar treatment to other clerical offenders in *Ep.* 34 (§§1, 3.2), where see nn. 2 and 15. Suspension of clerical faculties (*ut interim prohibeantur offerre*) was an earlier warning, *Ep.* 16.4.2.

15. Cyprian is referring to his *Epp.* 27 and 28. The phrasing gives emphatic pride of place to the honourable confessors (who en-

dorsed his policy) and stresses the significance of the union of such dignitaries with Cornelius (where the holy *ecclesia catholica* is to be found). This remark dates *Ep.* 55 firmly after *Epp.* 49–54, which record the reconciliation between the Roman confessors and Cornelius.

16. *Ep.* 30.5.3 (where see nn. 31 and 32).

17. *Novatiano tunc scribente et quod scripserat sua voce recitante et presbytero Moyse tunc adhuc confessore nunc iam martyre subscribente.* What is Cyprian's purpose in inserting this parenthesis (referring in particular to remarks made in *Ep.* 30.8)? (1) Even Novatian wrote out a letter which approved of the plan enunciated by Cyprian. It is, therefore, rather Novatian who has shown *levitas* in deviating himself from that plan. And that plan already included the provision of *pax* for the penitent dying (even that now denied by Novatian). (2) The honoured martyr Moyses gave to that policy the seal of his signature. It can have been, therefore, no frivolous programme; in fact, it is a sacred duty to execute such wishes evinced by the martyred dead. And that policy already included, as an interim measure, the granting of *pax* to the lapsed in emergency situations.

Cyprian may well have derived most of his information from *subscriptiones* appended to his copy of *Ep.* 30 (e.g. *Novatianus scripsi et mea voce recitavi, Moyses subscripsi* etc.); see further *Ep.* 30 intro. And see *Ep.* 49.1.4 (and n. 9 there) on the value given to a confessor's signature; a martyr's signature would be even more persuasive. Cf. *Ep.* 67.6.3: Cyprian invokes the testimony of the now martyred Cornelius as irrefutable support for a policy which he has long maintained himself.—On Moyses see *Ep.* 28 n. 1.

18. *quae litterae per totum mundum missae sunt* etc. It remains unclear who was responsible for the dissemination of copies of *Ep.* 30—Cyprian, or Rome, or both? Cyprian at least encouraged copy-taking and distribution, *Ep.* 32.1.2; Sicily received a similar message from Rome (*Ep.* 30.5.2), but not apparently a copy of this personal letter directed to Cyprian (*Ep.* 30). It would certainly be in character for Cyprian to wish to clear his international standing, and to forward his policy by gaining for it international agreement and support through the spread of copies of *Ep.* 30. One thing at least we can say: in Cyprian's perception, affairs in the Mediterranean were not so dislocated as to disrupt unduly the flow of communications between all the Christian churches. Cf. *Antichthon* 4 (1970) 78 f.

19. *persecutione sopita cum data esset facultas in unum conveniendi*. Observe that there was no abrupt abatement to the dangers of persecution. Dionysius of Alexandria appears to have used a similar expression (*tou diōgmou lelōphēkotos*), Euseb. *H.E.* 7.4. For the historical implications see *Letters of Cyprian* 1 (ACW 43) intro. pp. 30 f., and cf. n. 39 below.

20. *copiosus episcoporum numerus . . . integros et incolumes*. We have no precise statistics on the number of bishops who attended the African Council of 251. Cyprian appears somewhat defensive here in stressing its size (*copiosus numerus;* elsewhere they are merely *multi*, *Ep.* 59.9.1, *plurimi* in *Ep.* 59.1.1, *plures* in *Ep.* 59.10.2, cf. *concilio frequenter acto*, *Ep.* 59.13.1), and the remark in §6.2 (*si minus sufficiens episcoporum in Africa numerus videbatur*) is also a touch suggestive that there may have been some noises about unrepresentative attendance at this Council meeting. Antonianus may not have been alone in failing to attend; vital though the decisions to be taken were, circumstances may well have not been easy for many bishops at the time, or they may have offended already against Cyprian's interim policy (*Ep.* 27.3.1). Such absentees were sent copies of the Council's resolutions, §6.1 *ad fin*.

The Anonymous *Libellus synodicus* (published by J. Pappas, Strasburg 1601) does record (§22) the fact that a synod was convened in Carthage by Cyprian and that it denounced Novatus (*sic*) for shutting off penitence for the fallen; it was attended by 84 other bishops. This is quoted by, *inter alios*, Mansi 1 (Florence 1759) 871, and by Routh, *Reliquiae sacrae*[2] 3.134 (3.109 f. in 1815 edition). That statistic would indeed be invaluable for this meeting of 251, but unfortunately the compilation of the *Libellus synodicus* is late and totally unreliable. No confidence ought to be placed in its testimony (85 bishops being the number actually in attendance at the meeting of Sept. 1, 256). See Harnack, *Geschichte* 1.801 f. (who opines the work to have been concocted "mit einer unverschämten Fälschung"); Hefele-Leclercq, *Histoire* 1.1.128 ff.

Observe the characterisation of these attending bishops: they have all managed to emerge from the perils of the persecution uncompromised and unscathed (*integros et incolumes*—on the word *incolumis* see *Epp.* 5 n. 3, 81 n. 13, 82 n. 2); their findings must, therefore, be respected. There have been, in fact, no episcopal deaths in the persecution; the honour of becoming the protoepiscopal martyr of Africa is to be reserved for Cyprian himself (Pontius, *Vit. Cyp.* 19 H.CIX).

As bishop writing to bishop, Cyprian fails to allude here to the presence at the Council of the lower clergy and the laity (see *Epp.* 45.2.1 f., 59.15.1 for their attestation); the concord between *bishops* is the essential link in Cyprian's ecclesiology.

21. *scripturis [diu] ex utraque parte prolatis.* So Hartel's text, in which is excluded by editorial fiat the satisfactorily attested *diu* (see Bayard's *app. crit.*). It ought to be reinstated. It echoes §3.2 (*non sine librata diu . . . ratione*) and reinforces Cyprian's defensive message there that the changed policy in penitential discipline was reached only after lengthy and massive cogitation. Compare, too, *Ep.* 54.3.3 *diu multumque tractatu inter nos habito,* alluding to the same Council.

22. *temperamentum salubri moderatione libravimus.* The epithet *salubris* is not otiose: they struck a moderation which was needful in order to be able to restore spiritual health (*salus*) to men (*saluti multorum providendum* is his rephrasing in §7.2). Pontius, *Vit. Cyp.* 8.4 H.XCVIII f., pays tribute to Cyprian, the man of pre-eminent spiritual temperance (*vir ingenii praeter cetera etiam spiritaliter temperati*) who skilfully steered the Church on a middle course (*iter medium librato limite gubernaret*): he is referring to the present schisms over the question of penitence. Cyprian's need to defend himself here demonstrates that such a *via media* is always exposed to attack.

23. *quod sibi ecclesia cluderetur.* There is a literal element here: penitents were locked out from the congregation. See *Ep.* 30 n. 39 for references.

24. *examinarentur causae et voluntates et necessitates singulorum.* Cyprian describes further in §§13.2 ff. the various grades of extenuation that may be discerned, given the differences in *voluntates* and *necessitates* among the lapsed.

25. *libello . . . ubi singula placitorum capita conscripta sunt.* Contra Carey and Lacey in their translations *ad loc.*, this is not a reference to Cyprian's tractate *De lapsis,* which was composed in advance of the Council's decisions (see *Ep.* 54 n. 15). Rather, it is a summary of the decisions reached at that Council meeting; see Harnack, *Über verlorene Briefe* 22 f. Absentee bishops would have to be sent such a document for promulgation and implementation.

26. *etiam Romam super hac re scripsimus ad Cornelium collegam nostrum.* This document is lost but Eusebius appears to have seen a copy which was sent by Cornelius over to Fabius of Antioch, *H.E.* 6.43.3. Observe that Cyprian addressed the communication to Cornelius, that is to say after the question of the legitimacy of Cornelius had been resolved for the African church. Hence Cyprian was able to add to it the remark that "in the reason of things it was fitting that the leader of the heresy should be excommunicated from the catholic Church, and likewise all those who were led away with him" (Euseb. *loc. cit.*, trans. Oulton). The document presumably contained reason and argument, as well as the bare list of regulations enacted (the *libellus* of n. 25 above). For a separate document also emanating from the Council and sent over to Rome (a fully detailed account on the excommunication of the rebel Felicissimus and company) see *Ep.* 45.4.1 and n. 32 *ad loc.*

27. *ipse cum plurimis coepiscopis . . . in eandem nobiscum sententiam pari gravitate et salubri moderatione consensit.* It is clear (contrary to the impression of Eusebius) that the African Council met in advance of the Italian Council (Euseb. *H.E.* 6.43.2 f. with Lawlor and Oulton's commentary *ad loc.*). The *plurimi coepiscopi* who convened in Rome were 60 in number (along with a still greater number of presbyters and deacons), Euseb. *loc. cit.* Once again Cyprian emphasises the weighty care devoted to the deliberations and repeats for good measure the apologetic phrase *salubri moderatione* (on which see n. 22 above): if all the many bishops of Italy are not guilty of *levitas*, neither can Cyprian be, whose policy they are following. The remarks here imply a lost communication from Italy to Cyprian after the Roman Council had reached its decisions.

28. *ut scias me nihil leviter egisse.* Cyprian is winding up to the conclusion of his apologia, rebutting the allegation of *levitas* and insisting that he is abiding by the all-important *concordia* of the collective bishops.

29. *collegii concordia.* On this significant phrase cf. n. 2 above. Nowhere is there any hint of dissentient minority views on the conclusions of this Council of 251, controversial though its decisions clearly were (as indeed this letter shows).

30. *sed quid collegae tui modesti et graves viri faciant de vitae et disciplinae nostrae exploratione perpendere.* Once again *nostrae* is collective

(cf. n. 3 above), referring to the college of bishops. For literature on the word *disciplina* see *Ep.* 11 n. 9; on *graves viri* see n. 10 above.

31. *coepiscoporum testimonio quorum numerus universus per totum mundum concordi unanimitate consensit.* Observe Cyprian's emphasis on the harmony between the world's bishops in acknowledging the legitimacy of Cornelius. It is extremely doubtful, however, if they were as harmoniously agreed as Cyprian here so liberally claims in order to impress the hesitant Antonianus. For Eusebius provides circumstantial evidence of protracted and widespread indecision and dispute in the eastern churches (*H.E.* 6.46.3, 7.4 f.) that is most unlikely to have been resolved by the date of this letter (see intro. to this letter, and *Letters of Cyprian* 2 [ACW 44] intro. pp. 11 ff.). This discrepancy alerts us, with a salutary reminder, to the propaganda element in Cyprian's rhetoric, especially in a letter intended to be circulated widely (cf. n. 11 above).

32. *ad sacerdotii sublime fastigium cunctis religionis gradibus ascendit.* An arresting passage, bearing remarkable testimony how well established the regular steps within the clerical *cursus* had now become ([doorkeeper], lector, exorcist, acolyte, subdeacon, deacon, presbyter). For Cyprian to be able to produce this as Cornelius' outstanding qualification for office, Cornelius must have been a long-established figure within the Roman clergy, the senior presbyter perhaps; he is to die (of natural causes) not long hence, in exile in early June 253 (see *Ep.* 60 intro.). Of course, Cyprian is wanting to imply a contrast between this ideal cleric, Cornelius, and Novatian's clerical career (of the irregular nature of which Cornelius gives a biased account *ap.* Euseb. *H.E.* 6.43.14 f., 17). It is not without irony that Cyprian himself would have been but poorly qualified for office on the criterion he here provides in Cornelius' eulogy (see vol. 1 [ACW 43] intro. pp. 14 ff.) as would Cornelius' predecessor, Fabian, Euseb. *H.E.* 6.29.2 f. It strikes us as very Roman to stress as paramount the virtues of such a well-regulated career in administrative service, rather than spiritual integrity (to follow), theological acumen, intellectual capacity, leadership qualities, pastoral devotion, or even administrative skills (all absent). For a parallel, note the commendation by Gregory of Nazianzus of Basil for the office of bishop, *Or.* 43.26 f. (*In laud. Basil.*) MG 36.532 f. (invoking the analogy of the apprenticeship needed for ship captains, generals, doctors, and painters). By the course of the

fourth century it was even felt necessary to put Ambrose, as episcopal candidate, hastily through all the ecclesiastical offices after his
baptism, so that on the eighth day he could be formally consecrated
bishop—*baptizatus itaque fertur omnia ecclesiastica officia implesse atque
octava die episcopus ordinatus est*, Paulinus, *Vit. Ambros.* 9 ML 14.32. Cf.
Counc. Nicaea can. 2, Hefele-Leclercq, *Histoire* 1.1.532 ff. (with
commentary including exceptional cases); Counc. Sardica can. 10,
Hefele-Leclercq, *op. cit.* 1.2.790 f. And see further "The Letters of
Cyprian" in *Auckland Classical Essays* (Festschrift E. M. Blaiklock)
207 ff.

   33. *ipse vim passus est ut episcopatum coactus exciperet.* That reluctance to take office is the best indicator of suitability for office is a
common motif. It is a principle clearly enunciated by Cyprian's own
biographer Pontius, *Vit. Cyp.* 5.2 H.XCV *humiliter ille secessit . . . ut
dignus magis fieret. magis enim dignus efficitur qui quod meretur excusat.*
For parallels, Palladius, *Dial. de vita J. Chrys.* 10.35 MG 47.35 (the
one most unwilling to submit to episcopal election is to be chosen as
John Chrysostom's successor); Greg. Naz., *Or.* 43.26 MG 36.533 (he
who takes a lowly stand is worthy of high office); Jerome, *Ep.* 60.10.4
CSEL 54.559 (on Nepotian's ordination as presbyter) *sed quanto plus
repugnabat, tanto magis . . . merebatur negando, quod esse nolebat, eoque
dignior erat, quod se clamabat indignum.*

   Throughout this paragraph implicit contrast is intended with
Novatian's bid for the bishopric (the antithetical displays of *arrogantia*
and *superbia*, eagerness for office, open canvassing for it, even the employment of *vis* and forcible seizure of it are all to be attributed to
Novatian). This being so, we need not take too literally the claim that
Cornelius had in fact to be put under constraint (*vis*) in order to get
him to take on his office—though such cases of compulsion are not
unknown, e.g. Greg. Naz., *Or.* 18.33 MG 35.1028 f. (Eusebius in
Caesarea); Sulpic. Severus, *Vit. Mart.* 9.1 ff. (SC 133 ed. J. Fontaine
270); and other examples collected by Homes Dudden, *Ambrose*
1.71 f.

   Among Cornelius' varieties of humility here (*quietus, modestus,
humilitas, verecundia*) figures *pudor virginalis continentiae.* That ought
to imply celibacy. This has been doubted by Gryson, *Les origines du
célibat ecclésiastique* 36: "*continentiae* n'a pas nécessairement une connotation sexuelle: ce mot peut vouloir dire, en un sens général, 'maî-

trise de soi, modération, retenue,' " but the presence of the epithet *virginalis* here can hardly make the interpretation otherwise. On the question of clerical celibacy, see further *Ep*. 1 nn. 6 and 15. (The claims of the MS variant *conscientiae*, for *continentiae*, are not strong.)

34. *litteras honorificas et laudabiles et testimonio suae praedicationis inlustres*. These are the affidavits which Cyprian and his African colleagues secured via Caldonius and Fortunatus from the bishops present for Cornelius' consecration (they were in fact 16 in number, §24.2: they are termed here, with impressive vagueness, *plurimi*). See *Epp*. 44.1.2, 45.1.2, and 48.4.1 (with nn. *ad loca*).

35. *de clericorum paene omnium testimonio, de plebis quae tunc adfuit suffragio, de sacerdotum antiquorum et bonorum virorum collegio*. A succinct account of the processes of episcopal election in which the openness and the solidarity of the support for Cornelius are stressed (as opposed to the clandestine ceremony at night, with three hoodwinked rustic bishops, for Novatian, Cornelius *ap*. Euseb. *H.E.* 6.43.8 f. Photius, *Biblioth*. 280 p. 544b *et sqq*., cf. 182 p. 127b, purports to give the actual names of Novatian's consecrators, relying on Eulogius of Alexandria; no credence need be given to this testimony). The clergy provided character evidence and recommendations (*testimonio*), whereas the laity merely joined in at the final stage of voting approval (*suffragio*). Observe that Cyprian is constrained to qualify the support given by the Roman clergy (*paene omnium*): at least Novatian himself and five presbyters (Cornelius *ap*. Euseb. *H.E.* 6.43.20) and quite probably the confessor-presbyter Maximus and the deacons Rufinus and Nicostratus (see *Ep*. 46 intro.) were all in open dissent—an influential and not insignificant group. On the processes of election see further *Ep*. 29 n. 13, *Ep*. 38 n.1.

Cyprian has already invoked the witness of the 16 bishops who were physically present (see previous n.). The *collegium* of bishops here should, therefore, represent the world-wide corpus of bishops who (Cyprian avers) have universally supported Cornelius' election (see n. 31 above), which they will have done by sending to him letters of communion (see *Epp*. 44 n. 12, 45 n. 12, 48 n. 18). Their description (*antiquorum . . . virorum*) would include Cyprian himself; we should probably deduce that he cannot be unusually young for his episcopal office; cf. n. 112 below. Observe that the *Didascalia* 2.1 (Connolly 29 f.) laid down an age minimum of 60 for bishops (but with exceptions tolerated); and cf. Pope Siricius, *Ep.* 1.13 f. ML 13.1142 f. (385 A.D.), laying down a minimum age of 45 for bishops.

This last phrase (*de sacerdotum . . . collegio*) has occasioned needless misgivings. Ritschl, *Cyprian von Karthago* 175 interpreted it to mean "das Presbytercollegium von Rom," followed by Gryson, *Rev. d'hist. ecclés.* 68 (1973) 371 n. 1. That is most unlikely, not least as the presbyters would naturally be included already in the previously mentioned *clericorum paene omnium*, and on Cyprian's use of *sacerdos* = "bishop," see *Epp.* 40 n. 6, 43 n. 10. The word *collegium* itself (in parallel with *testimonium* and *suffragium*) has also caused hesitation. Hartel (followed by Bayard) was inclined to emend to *consensu* (citing the closely parallel *Ep.* 59.5.2, where the general support of fellow bishops is described as *coepiscoporum consensus*), and Gryson, *Rev. d'hist. ecclés.* 69 (1974) 114 has even claimed: "*collegium* ne signifie pas ici 'collège' mais 'soutien' 'appui'; ce sens est rare, mais néanmoins parfaitement attesté; il s'agit d'ailleurs, étymologiquement, de deux mots différents." For all that, the TLL *s.v.* "collegium" (Schwering) does not recognise the claimed difference in sense, neither do Ernout and Meillet, *Dictionnaire étymologique de la langue latine*[3], *s.v.* "lex" (vol. 1, 630), recognise the claimed difference in etymology. Given the sustained motif of this letter (see nn. 2 and 31 above), *collegium* ought to remain, and with its natural significance.

36. *cum Fabiani locus id est cum locus Petri et gradus cathedrae sacerdotalis vacaret.* Once again this is aimed at Novatian: Cornelius' election was the prior in time (cf. *Ep.* 44.3.2) and linked to the chain of successive bishops, whereas Novatian was *nemini succedens a se ipso ortus*, *Ep.* 69.3.2. On Fabian see *Ep.* 9 n. 4, *Ep.* 28 n. 5, and note that Peter is identified as a bishop (on which see *Ep.* 3 n. 16, *Ep.* 33 nn. 2 and 3). On the *cathedra* of a bishop see *Ep.* 3 n. 4: it was probably raised (hence *gradus cathedrae*) as was the fourth-century practice, e.g. Counc. Carth. 398 can. 35: *ut episcopus in ecclesia et in consessu presbyterorum sublimior sedeat*, cf. Hefele-Leclercq, *Histoire* 2.1.116. One could overdo the elevation, however: Paul of Samosata is criticised for the worldly and ostentatious "tribunal and lofty throne that he has prepared for himself, not befitting a disciple of Christ," *ap.* Euseb. *H.E.* 7.30.9. For other evidence Stommel, *Münch. theol. Zeit.* 3 (1952) 28 ff.

37. *omnium nostrum consensione firmato.* A reference to the con-

firmatory letters of communion which the bishops of the world (*omnium nostrum*) have written. See nn. 31 and 35 above.

38. *post episcopatum nec exambitum nec extortum sed de Dei . . . voluntate susceptum.* Once more Cyprian is describing Cornelius' episcopate with Novatian as foil; Novatian, by implication, did resort to violence and corruption in order to contrive his "episcopate." Compare *Ad Novat.* 2.6 CCL 4.139 (on Novatian): *illic impudenter et sine ulla ordinationis lege episcopatus appetitur.* To judge from the sequence of thought here (Cornelius' sufferings in the face of threatening dangers follow immediately), God's will is to be further indicated (after His choice has been made manifest through clergy, laity, and bishops) precisely by those sufferings to which the new bishop is to be subjected and by those fearless virtues with which he responds to them; for the devil bothers to attack only the *genuine* bishop. Cyprian has a similar line of argument (about himself) in *Ep.* 59.7.1 f. and in §24.2 below (see n. 112). Compare *Test.* 3.6 CCL 3.94 ff. illustrating Cyprian's conviction that suffering is a mark of divine predilection (*bonos quosque et iustos plus laborare . . .*).

39. *eo tempore cum tyrannus infestus sacerdotibus Dei fanda atque infanda comminaretur.* Insofar as we can compute it, Cornelius was elected bishop in early March 251 (see *Ep.* 44 intro. for references). It should, therefore, follow that at the time of his election all danger had not yet passed, even though about that period prisoners were being released (*Ep.* 46 intro.) and Cyprian was planning to return to Carthage and to hold there a Council (*Ep.* 43). Indeed, Cyprian's whole argument in the next section (§9.2) requires a continuing sense of danger for Cornelius *after* that election, in which Cornelius could display his confessor's nerve and his martyr's *voluntas.* The persecution had merely died down (*sopita*, n. 19 above), it was not extinguished.

Emperor Decius (*tyrannus*) is designated as *infestus sacerdotibus Dei.* Individual bishops had certainly been singled out for attack (Cyprian among them), not least because they were the visible leaders of their local Christian communities and might be induced to guide their flocks in compliance (see *Ep.* 5 n. 2 for evidence, and note Trofimus below in §11), but we cannot securely deduce from this passage that there had been any special orders issued against bishops as a specific class by Decius. The reaction in Alexandria on receipt of Decius' orders was promptly to search for the local bishop, Dionysius (*ap.* Euseb. *H.E.* 6.40.2): that is to say, prominent bishops (Cornelius now among them) were especially vulnerable in the execution of Decius' general orders. See also n. 112 below. Cyprian's *episcopal* focus on affairs (when the whole Church was suffering) is remarkable.

For the collocation *fanda atque infanda* see Otto, *Sprichwörter* no. 642 (*s.v.* "fari").

40. *[eo tempore] cum multo patientius et tolerabilius audiret levari adversus se aemulum principem quam constitui Romae Dei sacerdotem.* Many deductions (not always compatible) have been drawn from this remark. Its context should not be overlooked. Cornelius had survived the persecution in Rome totally unscathed—there is no word of prudent withdrawal before angry crowds or even of the daily perils of detection. In tacit contrast, Cyprian is contriving to make his fearless act of assuming the prominent bishopric of Rome as tantamount to a gesture of public confession—which could well have entailed the fulfillment of martyrdom (given Decius' documented savagery towards bishops).

(1) We cannot, therefore, be sure (as many commentators are) that we have here historically valid information about Decius' personal animosity towards Christianity and not rather a rhetorical contrivance devised on the part of Cyprian to achieve his desired portrait for Cornelius. After all, Cyprian had been a rhetor. Given the unlikelihood of accurate stories reaching Cyprian from Decius' court—at the time of Cornelius' appointment the emperor was away in the Danube area, never to return (see *Letters of Cyprian* 2 [ACW 44] intro. pp. 4 f.)—prudence suggests we should incline towards the latter (rhetorical) explanation. Note that this whole passage is closely imitated by Lucifer of Calaris, *Moriundum* 9 CCL 8.284 and there he can rhetorically taunt Constantius as follows: *multo tolerabilius audire semper desiderans fueris ac sis, adversum te aemulos surgere principes quam Christum dei filium confitentes existere victores.* (But for a contrary view see e.g. M. Grant, *The Climax of Rome* 229: ". . . Decius saw with even greater clarity the organized nature of the institution he opposed. For after executing their Roman leader St. Fabian, he is said to have remarked 'I would far rather receive news of a rival to the throne than of another bishop of Rome.' " Cf. Frend, *Martyrdom* 405). Even more improbably, J. M. York, *Historia* 21 (1972) 328 suggests that Decius'

(genuine) apprehensions were due to the fact that his predecessor, (the Christian) Philip, had been made by a bishop (Babylas of Antioch ?) to do public penance; cf. *idem*, diss. Univ. of Southern California (1964) 92, 97 ff. Gibbon, *Decline and Fall* (ed. J. B. Bury) 2.113 f., has a characteristic period drawn from this passage: "Were it possible to suppose that the penetration of Decius had discovered pride under the guise of humility, or that he could foresee the temporal dominion which might insensibly arise from the claims of spiritual authority, we might be less surprised that he should consider the successors of St. Peter as the most formidable rivals to those of Augustus."

(2) It has been further deduced that Decius was referring to a revolt that occurred in Rome and that revolt must have happened at the time of Cornelius' appointment (March 251). So Seeck, *Geschichte des Untergangs der antiken Welt*[2] 3.501; PW 15.1 (1931) *s.v.* "Messius (9)" 1271 f. (Wittig); cf. Liesering, *Untersuchungen* 11; RAC 3 (1957) *s.v.* "Decius" 614 (K. Gross); G. Alföldy, *Historia* 22 (1973) 492 n. 68 (cf. *idem*, *Ancient Society* 2 [1971] 217); L. Fronza, *Studi sull'imperatore Decio:* 2 (1953) 25 f. With a variant A. Alföldi, CAH 12.167 concluded that the pretender was soon crushed "certainly before the election of the Pope Cornelius, March 251." None of these deductions seems to be at all necessary. The imperfect tense of the verb (*audiret*) strongly suggests a generalising statement rather than any reference to a specific incident.

There was indeed a very short-lived (*mox caesus*) uprising with a popular backing (*cupientissimo vulgo*) led by one Julius Valens Licinianus, Vict., *De Caes.* 29.3 cf. *Epit. de Caes.* 29.5. Polemius Silvius (ed. Mommsen, MGH 9.521) locates the revolt in Rome (*Priscus in Macedonia et Valens Romae tyranni fuerunt*). PIR[2] J.610, Barbieri, *L'Albo*, *App.* no. 19, 406 f. There are no coins (hence we should deduce a very brief rebellion, rather than attempt to dissolve away the incident altogether as does Mattingly, *Num. Chron.* 6 [1946] 45). Mommsen had suggested that Valens' Roman revolt was the cause of Decius' name occurring *in rasura* in Italian inscriptions and for the curious inscriptional formula *tertium et semel cos:* however, the *rasura* and the formula have been found subsequently in Germany, Dacia, Caria, and Syria, and Mommsen's explanation can no longer stand (see J. F. Gilliam in *Studi in onore . . . Calderini e . . . Paribeni* 307 ff.). Valens' revolt could well have occurred in the course of 250, any time after Decius' departure for the frontier, Vict., *De Caes*. 29.2 f., cf. *Letters of Cyprian* 2 (ACW 44) intro. pp. 4 f. He is sometimes confused with the later usurper Valens under Gallienus, on whom see Homo, *Rev. hist*. 137 (1921) 193 ff. (PLRE 1.929 f.).

(3) It has been otherwise deduced that the emphatic sentence structure requires that the (specific) revolt referred to occurred elsewhere than Rome (so e.g. Gregg, *Decian Persecution* 97). In which (unlikely) case the candidate would be T. Julius Priscus (mistakenly called Lucius Priscus by Aurelius Victor, *De Caes*. 29.2), on whom see PIR² J.489, Barbieri, *L'Albo* 1610, for collected references to his revolt in the Balkans. For a succinct account of his attempted usurpation, Walser, *Bucknell Review* 13.2 (1965) 5 f. There was also a (perhaps) longer-lasting revolt continuing at Emesa in Syria (Uranius Antoninus), Magie, *Asia Minor* 1.704, 2.1566 (nn.); Barbieri, *L'Albo*, *App*. no. 18, 405 f.; PIR² J.195; RIC 4.3.203 ff.; A. S. Robertson, *Hunter Coin Cabinet* 3.CIX f. (with literature there cited, especially Delbrueck, *Num. Chron*. 8 [1948] 11 ff.); Baldus, *Uranius Antoninus*, especially 229 ff.; *idem*, *Chiron* 5 (1975) 443 ff. (?not until late 253/ early 254); and *idem*, *Jahr. f. Numismatik und Geldgesch*. 27 (1977) 69 ff.

41. *nonne inter gloriosos confessores et martyras deputandus qui tantum temporis sedit expectans corporis sui carnifices et tyranni ferocientis ultores*. Cyprian is arguing that after his election (first half March 251, as likely as not Sunday, March 6 or 13, cf. C. H. Turner, JTS 17 [1915/16] 345 ff.; Reekmans, *La tombe du pape Corneille* 110 f.), Cornelius sat with all a martyr's courage on his *cathedra*, calmly awaiting the worst from the savage tyrant, and that he did so over a lengthy period of time (*tantum temporis*). Decius, that enraged tyrant, must, therefore, have remained in office himself for a similarly lengthy period of time after Cornelius' election, in order so to imperil the bishop of Rome. This contemporary observation must demolish the suggestion put forward by Schwartz, ZPE 24 (1977) 173 that Decius' principate should have terminated as early as March 24, 251 (a calculation based on the—summarily emended—evidence of the Chronographer of 354). The 8–15 days (or thereabouts) thus allowed between Cornelius' election and Decius' presumed death—even granted Cyprian's habits of rhetorical hyperbole—cannot accommodate the *tantum tem-*

poris in a letter written (at the broadest) within 12 months of the events alluded to. Decius must be restored to a principate that lasted several more months, until about mid-year 251 (but which must have terminated before June 24, 251, CIL 6.36760 cf. 31130 [Rome], when Decius is *divus*). For the first half of 251 apprehension of danger clearly continued for Christians, even though the persecution had visibly eased (cf. nn. 19 and 39 above); what had happened once could readily happen again.

It is perhaps a trifle ironical that Cyprian here echoes words used by that archenemy of his, the confessor Lucianus (*Ep.* 22.1.2 *iam inter martyres deputande*).

The attempt by Nelke, *Chronologie* 63 ff., to associate *Ep.* 60 with this period of courageous defiance by Cornelius under Decius (and not under Gallus) meets insuperable difficulties: see von Soden, *Briefsammlung* 28 f., for an adequate rejoinder.

For a close parallel to this passage, see Lucifer of Calaris, *Moriundum* 1 CCL 8. 265 f.

42. *adversus edicta feralia resistentem.* No great reliance should be placed on the plural *edicta* here (more than one edict issued, therefore, concluded A. Alföldi, *Klio* 31 [1938] 324 n. 4). In such a rhetorical context the plural imparts an impressive amplitude. In the *De lapsis* Cyprian can employ just as easily (referring to a Decian *libellaticus*) the singular *edictum: servivit saeculari domino, obtemperavit eius edicto, magis obaudivit humano imperio quam Deo, De laps.* 27 CCL 3.236, whereas a generalising plural occurs in *Epp.* 30.3.1 (Novatian), 58.9.2, cf. *Ad Novat.* 6.5 CCL 4.142. On Decius' edict see *Letters of Cyprian* 1 (ACW 43) intro. pp. 22 ff.

43. *quantum ad eius devotionem pertinet.* On the technical military connotations of *devotio* (a general's vowed death in return for victory and the safety of his men) see *Ep.* 10 n. 7.

44. *passus est quidquid pati potuit.* See *Ep.* 12.1.2 for an outstanding formulation of the principle "they have endured . . . whatever they were prepared and ready to endure": a martyr's *voluntas* is the essential ingredient for true martyrdom. Cyprian echoes here his own argument there (*passus est quidquid pati voluit*). For commentary see *Ep.* 12 n. 8.

45. *tyrannum armis et bello postmodum victum prior sacerdotio suo vicit.* For the death of Decius and his son in battle at Abrittus in the

Dobrudja (c. June 251) see *Letters of Cyprian* 2 (ACW 44) intro. pp. 4 f. There may be further allusions to this event in *De laps.* 1 CCL 3.221 (*ope adque ultione divina securitas nostra reparata est*), on which see *Ep.* 49 intro., and in *Ad Demet.* 17 CCL 3A.45 (*documentum recentis rei satis est quod sic celeriter quodque in tanta celeritate sic granditer nuper secuta defensio [divina] est ruinis rerum, iacturis opum, dispendio militum, deminutione castrorum*), on which see Koch, *Cyp. Unter.* 140 ff. The theme of Lactantius' *De mort. pers.* has a lengthy tradition. Again the wording (*postmodum*) implies a reasonable interval between the beginning of Cornelius' *sacerdotium* and Decius' disastrous defeat (cf. n. 41 above).

46. *ut qui conscientiae suae luce clarescunt alienis rumoribus sordidentur.* On *conscientia* in Cyprian see Watson 283 n. 2 (though I remain unconvinced by his interpretation of this passage: "*conscientia sua* seems to mean the general knowledge of Cornelius' merit, not his own conscious innocence"). On *alienus* see *Ep.* 54 n. 4: the word carries overtones of "unholy," "profane," "scandalous," etc.

47. *explorasse autem collegas nostros scias.* That is, the expedition to Italy of Caldonius and Fortunatus (see *Epp.* 44, 45, 48). Cyprian is now prepared to be specific (as he was not in those letters) about some of their inquiries (Cornelius charged with being an idolatrous *libellaticus* himself and joined in sacrilegious communion with *sacrificati* bishops). At the delicate time of those letters, even to have entertained the charge would have been to insult. Such robust eulogy has now preceded this information (*nonne inter gloriosos confessores et martyras deputandus* §9.2) that insult could no longer be registered. See further *Ep.* 44 intro.

48. *eos demum quorum causa audita et innocentia conprobata sit coniunxisse nobiscum.* Note the sense of communion implied (*coniunxisse nobiscum*): the whole Church would be infected by the pollution of anyone illegitimately reconciled *sacrificatus*, especially if he were a member of the corpus of the episcopate (the reference is to *bishops* charged with idolatry). See n. 127 below. We also catch here something of the disputatious atmosphere that followed in the wake of the persecution—a spate of accusations over conduct under persecution, inquiries, trials, and judgments (cf. the charges, countercharges, and investigations concerning *traditores* that ensued in the West in the aftermath of the persecution of Diocletian). The disputes continued for years; see e.g. *Epp.* 65, 67.

49. *conligendis fratribus nostris . . . necessitate succubuit.* Cyprian has prepared carefully for this defence: he has already cleared himself of charges by employing similar language (*conligendae fraternitatis . . . utilitas, necessitati temporum succubuisse,* §7.2)—but that referred to *policy* regulated by the full African Council of 251 (and endorsed by the Roman Council §6.2). The vague invocation of *antecessores,* with its undefined appeal to tradition (cf. *Ep.* 1 n. 22), is suggestive that Cyprian has here a difficult case for which specific precedents are indeed hard to seek.

50. Trofimus was an Italian bishop; that much is clear. And he had led his flock into *error.* Cyprian, however, leaves it totally vague what that *error* was. His words are evasively neutral in tone (*pars maxima plebis abscesserat . . . errorem pristinum confitente . . . fraternitatem quam nuper abstraxerat*). That must be Cyprian studiously eschewing (in the interests of persuasion) the odium of any words to do with idolatry and sacrifice, reeking altars and the smoke of incense; there are no *ruinae,* no *lapsi,* no verbs like *deicere, cadere.* For, despite impressions to the contrary, it is clear from the run of thought that Trofimus' is a particular instance in the defensive argument being presented by Cyprian that Cornelius has not joined in communion with *sacrificati* bishops. In §2.1, Cyprian had reported that he has been asked to explain specifically: *Cornelius qua ratione Trofimo et turificatis communicet.* It would be natural to equate these *turificati* (on whom see n. 8) with the *plebs* of Trofimus. The *error* was some form of lapse in time of persecution. This makes it doubly unlikely that Trofimus was one of the three consecrators of Novatian (the one who repented, Cornelius *ap.* Euseb. *H.E.* 6.43.10), as has been often suggested e.g. d'Alès, *Réconciliation* 365 n. 1. For the complaint about the improper reconciliation of Trofimus comes precisely from Novatian's own letter (*secundum quod ad te malignorum litterae pertulerunt* §11.3, and see n. 6 above). Cf. *Ep.* 50 n. 7; Vogt, *Coetus sanctorum* 48 f.

Cyprian has also been at pains to register that all the normal conditions for granting exomologesis to Trofimus have been fulfilled: acknowledgement of guilt (*errorem . . . confitente*), proper disposition (*paenitentia deprecationis; cum plena humilitate*), and adequate amends (*satisfaciente; cum plena . . . satisfactione*).

51. *tractatu ergo illic cum collegis plurimis habito.* Cornelius would

have been wise to secure the backing of as many bishops as possible before making such a controversial reconciliation. We cannot tell whether this gathering was an *ad hoc* group convened for the issue or (in all probability) the Italian Council of 251, with 60 bishops in attendance (cf. the language where that Council is described in §6.2: *ipse cum plurimis coepiscopis habito concilio*). Cyprian carefully reserves the authority of these *collegae plurimi* as the culminating defence: they provide in themselves sufficient guarantee that the return of Trofimus' congregation was indeed adequate *satisfactio* for the reconciliation effected.

Cyprian was asked to explain: *Cornelius qua ratione Trofimo et turificatis communicet*. He has now provided that explanation. A natural reading of this passage would conclude that Trofimus' *plebs* (although *turificati*) have been restored to communion just as Trofimus has. They will have been reconciled (like penitent *libellatici*) without prolonged penitence. Their guilt (it was doubtless argued) did not involve the personal infection of touching the sacrificial meats, the personal pollution of tasting the abominable victims; they could be treated, therefore, on a par with *libellatici*, they were not true *sacrificati* (hence the claim in §12.1 *init.*—Cornelius has no communion with *sacrificati*).

Cyprian's skilful rhetoric cannot altogether disguise the fact, however, that major concessions have been made in the interests of mass reunion. Cornelius' conciliatory outlook (again in evidence in *Ep.* 49) no doubt made him an attractive episcopal candidate to many in this troubled period. Discussion in Mortimer, *Origins* 39 ff.; Galtier, *L'église et la rémission des péchés* 355 ff.

52. *Trofimus ut laicus communicet*. Note the rule of laicisation for offending clergy, on which see *Ep.* 49 n. 18 for assembled contemporary evidence. Cyprian can later refer to a general regulation on this issue universally agreed upon by the world's bishops at this time: *cum iam pridem nobiscum et cum omnibus omnino episcopis in toto mundo constitutis etiam Cornelius collega noster . . . decreverit eiusmodi homines . . . ab ordinatione . . . cleri adque sacerdotali honore prohiberi, Ep.* 67.6.3. The question no doubt figured as an item on the conciliar agenda of 251. For an early-fourth-century restatement, Peter of Alexandria, *Ep. can.* 10 MG 18.488 f.

53. *quod passim communicare sacrificatis Cornelius tibi nuntiatus est,*

hoc quoque de apostatarum fictis rumoribus nascitur. This appears to have been a further claim contained in the letter of Novatian (see n. 6 above)—hence *apostatarum* (which word refers to *heretics* on the few occasions Cyprian employs it: Watson 293). Cyprian is going to proceed to defend Cornelius against the charge of indiscriminate (*passim*) reconciliation of *sacrificati:* he has in fact reconciled only those who appeared to be dying. It is irrelevant to the charge that some recovered their health after that reconciliation.

54. *ut placeamus illis qui nobis displicentes.* . . . There is probably an echo of 2 Tim. 3.2, on which see *Ep.* 11 n. 7a.

55. *si qui enim infirmitatibus occupantur, illis sicut placuit in periculo subvenitur.* This was part of the interim *forma* both in Africa (*Ep.* 18.1.2, *Ep.* 20.3.1 f.) and in Rome (*Ep.* 30.8; cf. *Ep.* 8.3.1), a regulation clearly endorsed (*sicut placuit*) by the subsequent Councils. On the technical use of the verb *subvenio*, see *Ep.* 8 n. 25 and the discussion on this topic there.

56. *qui pignus vitae in data pace percipiunt hic quoque ad vitam percepta pace teneantur.* There is (as often) play on the word *vita*, difficult to render in English. For the argument that once a penitent has been absolved he should not be required to resume penance cf. *Ep.* 64.1.2 (*pacem* . . . *quomodocumque a sacerdote Dei semel datam non putavimus auferendam*); Dionys. Alex., *Ep. to Conon* (ed. Feltoe, *Letters and Other Remains* 60 ff.) is on precisely the same topic of recovery after deathbed reconciliation and draws conclusions parallel to Cyprian's. Council of Nicaea can. 13 laid down more stringent regulations for those penitents who survived a near-fatal illness, Hefele-Leclerq, *Histoire* 1.1.593 ff. Cyprian now proceeds in §§13.2 ff. to whittle down even further the charge of *indiscriminate* reconciliation of *sacrificati* by drawing a categorical distinction between *libellatici* and *sacrificati:* the former cannot be lumped with the latter and they merit, therefore, quite different treatment.

57. *qui reluctatus et congressus diu ad hoc funestum opus necessitate pervenit.* Cyprian had already suggested some such variations in lapse as he here enumerates in *De lapsis* 8 f. CCL 3.225. For cases of *necessitas* see e.g. *Ep.* 24.1.1 (Bona—physical coercion) with n. 8 *ad loc.*, or *Ep.* 56.1.1 (Ninus, Clementianus, and Florus—physical tortures: *gravem lapsum non voluntate sed necessitate susceptum*). But in §26.1 below, Cyprian can speak of *libellatici* generally as having acted *necessitate:* that

must yield the very attenuated sense "by force of circumstances." See further n. 121.

58. *uxorem et liberos et domum totam periculi sui pactione protexit.* We have one Decian *libellus* in which sacrifice is made on behalf of wife, two sons, and a daughter (Knipfing no. 33); cf. *Oxy. Pap.* 2601 for a later case of a Christian using a proxy for performing a (forbidden) sacrificial act. Would *domus tota* include slaves (therefore included in Decius' orders)? See *Ep.* 15.4 with n. 33 *ad loc.*, and *Letters of Cyprian* 1 (ACW 43) intro. pp. 27 f.

59. *ille qui inquilinos vel amicos suos ad facinus conpulit et qui inquilinis et colonis pepercit. Inquilini* were, characteristically, lessees of a house; they would form the class of cottagers on an estate (as craftsmen, labourers, etc.). In distinction, *coloni* were lessees of a farm, tenant farmers who characteristically paid the owner part of the produce of their land and were also obliged to give him some days of their own and their cattle's labour; they often lived in villages on or near the main estate. For the distinction, *Dig.* 19.2.24.1 f.; landlords were obliged to declare *inquilini* as well as *coloni* in their census returns, *Dig.* 50.15.4.8. For some literature on the topic, A. H. M. Jones, *Past and Present* 13 (1958) 1 ff.; M. I. Finley in *Studies in Roman Property* 103 ff.; W. Held, *Klio* 53 (1971) 239 ff.; B. W. Frier, *Landlords and Tenants* (1980); and on the complexities of the labour forces and agricultural patterns of North Africa, see especially C. R. Whittaker, *Klio* 60 (1978) 331 ff.

Cyprian implies here that there were Christian *patroni* who were wealthy enough to command landed estates (as he no doubt had done himself). They could put pressure on their own *inquilini* and *coloni* to conform to their own religious behaviour (to which Tertullian alludes in *De idol.* 17.1 CCL 2.1117 f. *quid facient servi vel liberti fideles, item officiales sacrificantibus dominis vel patronis vel praesidibus suis adhaerentes?*)—or they could protect them by acting in their stead as proxies. In either case we appear to have significant social units that were predominantly Christian: further discussed in *Ep.* 15 n. 33 and cf. Dölger, *Ant. und Christ.* 6 (1950) 297 ff. ("Christliche Grundbesitzer"), and other examples of Christian households in MacMullen, *Christianizing the Roman Empire* 65 f. See Livy 34.55.3 for a *supplicatio* to be made in household groups together (*omnes . . . ex una familia . . .*

pariter); similar arrangements could have obtained also in the time of Decius.

60. *fratres . . . plurimos qui extorres et profugi recedebant.* To provide *hospitium* to travellers was a fundamental work of mercy; Celerinus' sisters had engaged in similar work in mitigation of their lapse (see *Ep.* 21.2.2, 4.1 with n. 19 there). On this topic H. Chadwick, "Justification by Faith and Hospitality," *Stud. patr.* 4 (1961) 281 ff. Observe the further evidence for refugee movements (*profugi*) set in train by the persecution (on which see e.g. *Epp.* 5 n. 8, 8 n. 27, 12 n. 19, etc.). *Extorres* can be either legal or voluntary exiles: see *Ep.* 10 n. 5 for assembled evidence.

61. *is cui libellus acceptus est.* The phrase is equivalent to "he who acknowledged a certificate to be his own," for *libellatici* (as we learn from what follows) need not have obtained their *libellus* in person. Compare *Ep.* 30.3.1 (*illos qui accepta fecissent*) and see further *Letters of Cyprian* 1 (ACW 43) intro. n. 176.

62. *episcopo tractante:* a relatively rare direct allusion in Cyprian to the role of bishop as *teacher* (he habitually stresses more his functions as guide, ruler, intercessor, etc.). For the use of the verb *tracto* (soon to become the verb par excellence for biblical exegesis) see Mohrmann, *Études* 2.70 f.

63. *nisi ostensa fuisset occasio.* Cyprian is thinking of such openings as a sympathetic or bribable official, a helpful friend who volunteers to negotiate on one's behalf, etc.

64. *conscientiam tamen eius esse pollutam.* For a clear enunciation of this principle *De laps.* 27 CCL 3.236. Cyprian approved of exomologesis for those who even *thought* of obtaining a *libellus* but who nevertheless did not do so; their consciences were still contaminated, *De laps.* 28 CCL 3.236 f. (*quamvis nullo . . . libelli facinore constricti . . .; non est tamen immunis a crimine*).

65. *in haeresim vel schisma diabolo invitante rapiuntur.* In this case they would be taking refuge not with the rigorous Novatianists but with *laxist* groups, who have disappeared largely from our view since *Ep.* 43; Novatianism has posed the more menacing threat. On "heresy" and "schism" in Cyprian see *Ep.* 3 n. 18, *Ep.* 43 n. 38, *Ep.* 49 n. 10.

66. *nos non tantum non quaeramus lassos.* For *lassos* there is the

(commonly adopted) variant reading *lapsos*. Cyprian here slips from using the feminine (of sheep) to the masculine, in order to register a change in reference.

67. *quos persecutio infesta non perdidit eos nos duritia nostra et inhumanitate perdamus.* Cyprian exploits easily the ambiguities of *perdo*, which can mean "lose" as well as "destroy." The main source for this passage would be Luke 15.4 f. (Fahey 353), plus Ezek. 34.4 (the wounded sheep, Fahey 231 f.).

68. A triplet of citations from First Corinthians: 10.33 + 11.1, 9.22, and 12.26 (Fahey 453 f.).

69. *Alia est philosophorum et Stoicorum ratio.* One of the few direct references in Cyprian to pagan philosophy. There is another outburst in *Ep.* 60.3.1 (aimed *nominatim* at Novatian): *magis durus saecularis philosophiae pravitate quam sophiae dominicae lenitate pacificus*, and compare §24.1 below: *Iactet [Novatianus] se licet et philosophiam vel eloquentiam suam superbis vocibus praedicet.* This makes it clear that Novatian is the target here. Cornelius' sneers at Novatian *ap.* Euseb. *H.E.* 6.43.8, 16 (*houtos gar toi ho dogmatistēs; heteras . . . philosophias erastēs*) are similarly directed; cf. Pacian *Ep.* 2.4 ML 13.1060 *Novatiani philosophiam per quam ille in naufragium religionis incurrit.* Of the philosophic schools Novatian was associated most closely with the Stoic; its influence has been traced in his thought and writings. See e.g. Daniélou, "Novatien et le De mundo d'Apulée," in *Romanitas et Christianitas* 71 ff.; Lebreton, *Rev. d'hist. ecclés.* 19 (1923) 481 ff., 20 (1924) 5 ff.; Vogt, *Coetus sanctorum* 136 ff.; Spanneut, *Le stoïcisme des Pères*[2] 340 f., 375 f., 412 f., etc.; Koch, *Cyp. Unter.* 272 ff.; and for collected *testimonia* on Novatian's philosophy and eloquence, Harnack, TU 13.4 (1895) 37 f. Novatian's overall view of Christianity (an assembly of saints) has a distinctly Stoic ring: there is no place for sinful and erratic Christians within the *secta* of the virtuous and constant Christian sages (cf. Bévenot, JTS 20 [1969] 630 ff.).

70. *qui dicunt omnia peccata paria esse et virum gravem non facile flecti oportere.* (1) For *testimonia* on the notorious and much publicised Stoic paradox that all sins are equal, see von Arnim, SVF 3, nos. 524–543. Cicero devotes *Paradoxon iii* of the *Paradoxa Stoicorum* to the proposition *aequalia esse peccata et recte facta.* Novatianists would not draw, accordingly, the vital distinction between *libellatici* and *sacrificati.* Ambrose in *De poenit.* 1.2 (391) ML 16.487 attacks the Nova-

tianists for their denial of forgiveness to lapsed and refers similarly to the influence on them of this Stoic doctrine (*cum omnia peccata Stoicorum quodam modo paribus putent aestimanda mensuris*).

(2) For *testimonia* on the imperturbability and constancy (*non facile flecti*) characteristic of the Stoic *sapiens* (= *vir gravis*; see n. 10 above), see von Arnim, SVF 3, nos. 567–581, 638–640. There is a good description in Lactantius, *Div. inst.* 5.13.15 (ed. P. Monat, SC 204) *haec est vera virtus, quam philosophi . . . iactant, disserentes nihil esse tam congruens viri sapientis gravitati atque constantiae quam nullis terroribus de sententia et proposito posse depelli.* This Stoic ideal (which opponents would term intransigence) was an obstacle to the flexibility demanded by the times (*necessitas temporum* §7.2); it prevented them from being responsive, through gentleness and compassion (virtues enjoined on Christians in the texts of §16.2 below), to the plight of the fallen. Hence, in the context, *flecti* means something like "to be swayed by pity" (and therefore to relax one's *sententia et propositum*). By contrast Cicero could say of the Stoic sage, *Pro Murena* 29.61, *sapientem . . . numquam cuiusquam delicto ignoscere, neminem misericordem esse nisi stultum et levem . . . sapientem sententiam mutare numquam.*

71. *inter Christianos . . . et philosophos plurimum distat.* The quotation is from Col. 2.8, Fahey 500 (used again in *De pat.* 2 CCL 3A.118 f. attacking the false *patientia* of the Stoic *sapiens*). Cyprian's general attitude towards secular philosophy (seldom voiced) is further exemplified in *capitula* of his *Testimonia*, e.g. *Test.* 3.53 CCL 3.140: *Dei arcana perspici non posse, et ideo fidem nostram simplicem esse debere; Test.* 3.69 *op. cit.* 157: *non in sapientia mundi nec in eloquentia esse regnum Dei sed in fide crucis et virtute conversationis.* But this variety of anti-intellectualism (sophisticated reasoning only disguises the simple Truth) was itself also a hardy *topos* of the intellectual classical tradition: see ACW 39.248 f. on Min. Fel., *Oct.* 16.5 f., for references. Cyprian was, of course, sharing a tradition with Tertullian (e.g. *De praescr. haer.* 7.9 ff. CCL 1.193: *quid ergo Athenis et Hierosolymis? quid academiae et ecclesiae? quid haereticis et christianis? . . . nobis curiositate opus non est post Christum Iesum nec inquisitione post evangelium*). And for further study on Cyprian and pagan philosophy, see Ellspermann, *Attitude of Early Christian Latin Writers towards Pagan Learning* 46 ff.; and for other early Christians' attacks on philosophy, Spanneut, *Le stoïcisme des Pères*[2] 101 ff.

72. Num. 12.3 (Fahey 84 and 572 ff. for the figure of Moses in Cyprian), Luke 6.36 (Fahey 342), and Matt. 9.12 (Fahey 292 f.).

73. *ego solos sanos curo, quibus medicus necessarius non est.* This is normally printed as being entirely the direct speech of the false doctor, but it makes better sense if the first clause only reports his *ipsissima verba* while the second clause remains authorial comment. I have translated accordingly (so, too, Bévenot, *Cyprian: De lapsis and De ecclesiae catholicae unitate* [1971] 107). On Cyprian's extension of the *Christus medicus* theme to include bishops as physicians of the Church (which follows), see Arbesmann, *Traditio* 10 (1954) 7; and for parallel use made of medical analogy in early Christian writings, Spanneut, *Le stoïcisme*[2] 198.

74. *numquam de isdem postmodum et confessores et martyres fierent.* Cyprian's argument is that the *lapsi* cannot be entirely dead, for before they were restored to full life by any reconciliation from the Church, some were able to stand up again by themselves, confront the enemy, and redeem their fall by a courageous confession or even martyrdom. For instances of such recoveries see *Ep.* 24.1.1 (Felix, Victoria, and Lucius) for confessors, *De laps.* 13 CCL 3.228 (Castus and Aemilius) for martyrs. And for further discussion consult *Ep.* 19 n. 17 and *Historia* 22 (1973) 655 ff. Dionysius of Alexandria seems to allude to a similar notion concerning the fallen *ap.* Euseb. *H.E.* 7.8 ". . . he [Novatian] entirely banishes the Holy Spirit from them, even though there was some hope of His remaining with or even returning to them"; and see Feltoe's n. in ed. *ad loc.* (*Letters and Other Remains of Dionysius of Alexandria* 56).

75. *ad gentiles se vias et saecularia opera convertat.* The language here is discussed at length by Deléani, *REAug* 23 (1977) 221 ff. (especially on the "biblisme" *gentiles vias*).

76. *extra ecclesiam constitutus et ab unitate adque a caritate divisus coronari in morte non poterit.* This theme is picked up again in §29.3, and for parallels elsewhere in Cyprian to the argument that there can be no true martyrdom outside the Church see *Epp.* 60.4, 73.21.1 (no baptism, therefore no baptism of blood either); *De unit.* 14, 19 CCL 3.259, 263; *De dom. or.* 24 CCL 3A.105 f.; and cf. *De rebap.* 11 H.3.83: *neque nomen Christi sine ipso Christo ad confessionem cuiquam possit patrocinari,* Hummel 119 ff., 178. To maintain the integrity of the argument, it was essential to deny the claims made

by those outside the Church to have confessors and martyrs within their number: on that theme see *Ep.* 52 n. 7. That argument was, of course, commonly voiced during the Donatist controversy (for many examples, von Campenhausen, *Die Idee* 171 ff.) leading to the coining of many choice phrases in the heat of the debate, such as *martyrium satanae, martyr daemonum.* Hence Lucilla's dubious but favourite relic can be described as a bone *nescio cuius hominis mortui et si martyris sed necdum vindicati,* Opt. Milev. 1.16 CSEL 26.18 (Ziwsa). Augustine is heir to the Cyprianic tradition, e.g. *Ep.* 173.6 CSEL 44.644: *foris autem ab ecclesia constitutus et separatus a compage unitatis et vinculo caritatis aeterno supplicio punireris, etiamsi pro Christi nomine vivus incendereris.*

The toughness of the argument here may shock; it is outstanding testimony to the horror in which schism was held.

77. *placuit . . . examinatis causis singulorum libellaticos interim admitti.* This is one of the resolutions of the Council of 251 (*placuit*), and, to our knowledge, its most outstanding one. *Libellatici,* after examination (for *voluntates et necessitates* §6.1, penitence since fall, etc.), are to be readmitted to communion without further penance. As a class, *libellatici* cease to cause trouble. See further intro. to this letter.

Much debate has centered around the precise meaning of *interim* here. It has been maintained that in the context it can only mean "forthwith," "immediately," "at once" (e.g. Watson 313 n. 3; d'Alès, *Réconciliation* 366; Galtier, *L'église et la rémission* 293 n.; Koch, *Cyp. Unter.* 213 ff., 264 ff.). It is equally possible, however, that the significance should be, and much more naturally, "for a start," "as a first measure" (= "we should begin by"), the question of the duration of the penitence of the second class of *lapsi,* viz. the *sacrificati,* being left for the time being unresolved (save in the case of the dying: see next n.). That issue was to be settled at a subsequent Council (*Ep.* 57). For further discussion of this passage, see Joyce, JTS 42 (1941–42) 36 ff.; Hübner, ZfKT 84 (1962) 210 ff.; J. Grotz, *Die Entwicklung* 147 f.; Mortimer, *Origins* 31 ff.; Bévenot, JTS 5 (1954) 71 and n.; and cf. *Ep.* 4 n. 30.

78. *sacrificatis in exitu subveniri.* For this further conciliar resolution cf. n. 55 above. When Cyprian next reports this resolution (*Ep.* 56.2.2) his wording is *cum in concilio placuerit paenitentiam agentes in*

infirmitatis periculo subveniri et pacem dari. He has been asked to have considered the very special case of three *sacrificati*, but there is no word that any specific time limit but the deathbed had been put on the penitence required of this category of lapsed. In the subsequent conciliar letter to Cornelius (*Ep.* 57), however, the resolution is referred to in more expanded terms: *statueramus . . . pridem . . . ut qui . . . sacrificiis se inlicitis maculassent, agerent diu paenitentiam plenam et si periculum infirmitatis urgeret, pacem sub ictu mortis acciperent* (*Ep.* 57.1.1). We cannot tell whether the additional clause, vague and indefinite as it is (*agerent diu paenitentiam plenam*, on which see *Ep.* 4 nn. 33 and 34), formed part of the original conciliar resolution, but we would still have to conclude, on this evidence, that little in the way of specific relief (other than deathbed reconciliation after continuous penitence) had been proposed for *sacrificati* in the African and Roman Councils of 251. The original intention may well have been to determine subsequently the *iustum tempus* judged appropriate for each particular case; hence it was possible to lodge the petition of *Ep.* 56 (*consulendum putatis an eos ad communicationem iam fas esset admittere* §1.1), and Cyprian, in response, was prepared to express his personal inclination to be lenient (*aestimamus ad deprecandam clementiam Domini posse sufficere . . .* §2.1). But prospects of reconciliation for the general *sacrificatus* cannot have been in any way immediate if, even after a *triennium* of penitence, these exceptional cases (succumbed under prolonged tortures) are approached with such grave caution, *res tanta exigit maius et pensius de multorum conlatione consilium, Ep.* 56.3. (After much more experience and greater leniency in these matters, 14 years of penitence were still required by the Council of Nicaea for those who had lapsed, under little pressure, in the time of Licinius: Counc. Nicaea can. 11, Hefele-Leclercq, *Histoire* 1.1.590; and see Brightman in Swete's *Essays* 369 ff. on the length of penances imposed by early Church Councils.) Even so Cyprian is prepared to claim (in §20.1 below) that now *paenitentibus spes pacis oblata:* no formal embargo at least had been placed on pre-deathbed reconciliation. This process of petition and cautious review seems also implied by *Ep.* 64.1.1 (on an illicit reconciliation): *recessum esse a decreti nostri auctoritate ut ante legitimum et plenum tempus satisfactionis et sine petitu et conscientia plebis, nulla infirmitate urgente ac necessitate cogente, pax ei concederetur.* Further discussion in Poschmann, ZfKT 37 (1913) 44 ff.; *idem, Penance and the Anointing of the Sick* 53 ff.

79. *quia exomologesis apud inferos non est.* At first sight a strangely worded explanation; it is repeated and expanded somewhat in §29.2 *quia apud inferos confessio non est nec exomologesis illic fieri potest.* The Church cannot (physically) perform the rites of reconciliation (*exomologesis*) after death; therefore, they are to be performed over the sincerely repentant *sacrificatus* just before death, with the final verdict on the sinner reserved for the Judge to come. The strangeness of the wording is due to an allusion to Ps. 6.6 *apud inferos autem quis confitebitur tibi?* This is quoted in *Test.* 3.114 CCL 3.176 on the relevant theme *dum in carne est quis, exhomologesin facere debere.* In Cyprian's text of Ps. 6.6 *confitebitur* translates the LXX *exomologēsetai*, which provides the *verbal* link germane to Cyprian's present argument. The allusions are omitted by Fahey 127. On the word *exomologesis* see *Ep.* 4 n. 35.

80. This generally worded observation places *Ep.* 55 firmly *before* any threatened persecution under Gallus (contrast *Ep.* 57). There is no sense of any immediate or impending danger.

81. *si paenitentiam plenam et iustam peccatoris invenerit, tunc ratum faciat quod a nobis fuerit hic statutum.* Observe the firm reservation of final judgment for Christ: man proposes but God disposes. For close parallel note *Ep.* 30.8 *Deo ipso sciente quid de talibus faciat,* where see n. 50, and there is further discussion in *Ep.* 49 n. 19, J. Grotz, *Die Entwicklung* 77 f. The notion of cancelling out sin by countervailing *paenitentia* is given clear expression here (cf. *Ep.* 4 nn. 33 and 34): see Telfer, *Forgiveness* 67 ff.; W. P. Le Saint in ACW 28.155 f., 158 f.

82. *Deus qui non deridetur et qui cor hominis intuetur.* There are allusions to Galat. 6.7 (*Deus non deridetur*), Fahey 478 f., and to 1 Sam. 16.7 (*homo videt in faciem, Deus autem in cor*), omitted by Fahey 104.

83. This catena of texts on charity and mercy towards sinners (contra Fahey 526, it is not designed "to prove that God later judges what the Church only imperfectly judges," rather to prepare for the argument to follow in §19.1 f.) is drawn, in order, from Prov. 18.19 (Fahey 165), Gal. 6.1 f. (Fahey 478), 1 Cor. 10.12 (Fahey 453), Rom. 14.4 (Fahey 424), 1 John 2.1 f. (Fahey 526), Rom. 5.8 f. (Fahey 428 f.).

84. Allusion to Rom. 12.15 (omitted by Fahey 435 f.).

85. *inmites et pertinaces*. On this unusual use of *pertinax*, Watson 305.

86. *sicut in evangelio sacerdos et levites*. The allusion is to Luke 10.29 ff. For Cyprian, the new dispensation equivalent of *sacerdos* is the bishop, and he thus proceeds to read off applications of Luke's parable accordingly (*ut sacerdotes Dei et Christi*). In the next section there is also allusion to Matt. 22.37 (cf. Mk. 12.30), Fahey 319 f. (*diligentes corde toto Deum*).

87. *nec quia adultero paenitentia et venia laxatur, continentiae vigor frangitur*. Cyprian employs an interesting analogy drawn from the effects of relaxing penitential discipline for sins of adultery in the time of his predecessors (*apud antecessores nostros*, §21.1). Adultery had been classed among the *aeterna peccata* (cf. *Ep*. 73.19.1 on blasphemy), irremissible sins entailing *ipso facto* no hope of reconciliation even *in articulo mortis*. The debate to relent and to allow adulterers to be admitted to penitence had been a heated one: Cyprian refers to African bishops who refused to yield (§21.1) and Tertullian doubtless reflects the intensity of the African dispute, especially in the *De pudicitia* (e.g. his famous remark in 1.6 CCL 2.1281 f. *Audio etiam edictum esse propositum, et quidem peremptorium. Pontifex scilicet maximus, quod est episcopus episcoporum, edicit: "Ego et moechiae et fornicationis delicta paenitentia functis dimitto."*). The *De pudic.*, on available evidence, dates the African dispute to which Cyprian refers in §21.1 to early in the second decade of the third century (see Barnes, *Tertullian* 45 ff., 247; W. P. Le Saint in ACW 28.47 ff., 284 ff.). A similarly bitter and intense debate is reflected somewhat later in Rome (c. 220) between Callistus and Hippolytus (Hippol., *Philos*. 9.12.20 ff., GCS Hippolytus Werke 3.249 ff.), and Origen in a number of passages (e.g. *De orat.* 28.9 f. GCS Origenes Werke 2.380 f.) shows that the eastern Church was equally agitated. For how long and where adultery had figured as an irremissible sin is a question open to debate. There is evidence to suggest that in the later second century there had been a move towards rigorism generally as church discipline itself became more formalised (there is a parallel and contemporaneous movement towards more rigorous *poenae* within the Roman legal system; see Garnsey, *Natural Law Forum* 13 [1968] 141 ff.).

Many date the Council which regulated the issue in Africa to the time of Bishop Agrippinus (under whom a Council is attested on the question of rebaptism). But there is nothing known to me which in fact associates Agrippinus with this particular matter.

The literature on the topic is voluminous. Among others, Brightman in Swete's *Essays* 374 ff.; de Labriolle, *Crise montaniste* 425 ff.; Galtier, *L'église et la rémission* 184 ff.; Koch, *Cyp. Unter.* 233 ff.; Joyce, JTS 42 (1941–42) 19 ff.; d'Alès, *Édit de Calliste;* Mortimer, *Origins* 6 ff.; Kelly, *Early Christian Doctrines*[2] 217 ff.; Molland, *Mélanges . . . Puech* 215 ff.; Langstadt, *Stud. patr.* 2.2 (1957) 251 ff.; J. A. Fischer in *Pietas* (= Festschrift . . . Kötting) 1980, 223 ff.

On virginity in the early Church see *Ep.* 4 n. 5.

88. *aliud est ad veniam stare.* For the turn of phrase cf. *Ep.* 60.2.5 *nec iam stare ad criminis veniam. Stare ad* can be used of slaves waiting on their master's pleasure (e.g. Suet., *J. Caes.* 49: *ad cyathum et vinum . . . stetisse*), a usage which may provide the overtone here.

89. The allusion is to Matt. 5.25 f. (Fahey 275 f.). Cyprian is thinking of the long *paenitentia* required to pay off the reparation incurred by a sinner's *delicta*, cf. n. 81 above.

90. *aliud statim fidei et virtutis accipere mercedem.* The second contrasting clause (as throughout this section) refers to the ideal Christian, the martyr. In Cyprian *fides et virtus* is standardly used of a martyr's essential qualities (see *Ep.* 10 n. 3); and in Cyprian's somewhat vague celestial chronology a martyr receives his reward *statim,* directly after death (repeated for good measure at the end of this section, *aliud statim a Domino coronari*). Compare *Ad Fort.* 13 CCL 3.214 ff., where the key notion (*statim*) also occurs twice (*ut cum Christo statim gaudeat; aperire eosdem [oculos] statim ut Deus videatur*). Discussion, with other examples, in *Ep.* 6 n. 14, adding Bévenot, *Theol. Stud.* 16 (1955) 194 f. What exactly was the contrasting timetable for the non-martyr, Cyprian fails to say.

91. *pro peccatis longo dolore cruciatum emundari et purgari diu igne.* This whole passage has been exploited for testimony that Cyprian subscribed to a doctrine of purgatory, e.g. DTC 13.1 (1936) *s.v.* "Purgatoire" 1214 (A. Michel): "Cette souffrance purificatrice, ce feu d'outre-tombe, ne peuvent être que le purgatoire"; cf. d'Alès, *Théologie . . . Cyprien* 35 n. 1: "le feu dont il est question dans ce texte, ne peut être que le feu du purgatoire"; Hummel 160: "apostates reinstated in this manner, upon dying will not go directly to heaven, but

will have to make additional satisfaction in the next world." Cf. also
A. Fernández, *Burg. Collect. Scient.* 22 (1981) 163 ff. That conclusion
is highly doubtful. Cyprian is talking about the cleansing works of
penance in metaphorical language; *diu igne* (sc. *paenitentiae* or the like)
is merely parallel to the equally metaphorical *longo dolore cruciatum*.
Fire provided an image that was at once suitably painful yet purifying
(*aurum ignitum* is "purified gold" in Cyprian, exploited in a relevant
passage of *De op. et eleemos.* 14 CCL 3A.63 f.: *eme tibi a Christo aurum
ignitum ut sordibus tuis tamquam igne decoctis esse aurum mundum possis,*
alluding to Apoc. 3.18). The purifying fire of divine judgment (on
which see Edsman, *Le baptême de feu* 76 ff.) is a less likely explanation.
For discussion Jay, *Rech. théol. anc. méd.* 27 (1960) 133 ff.; Fahey 276;
Bévenot, *Theol. Stud.* 16 (1955) 194 f. n. 74; Vogt, *Coetus sanctorum*
135; and see in more general terms Waszink's nn. on Tert. *De an.*
58.8. (The text *diu igne*—an unusually bald expression for Cyprian—
is itself not above suspicion; the variant reading *divine* has led to the
plausible conjecture *diutine*.)

92. *peccata omnia passione purgasse.* The Christian use of *passio* as
a technical term (of a martyr's sufferings) makes it clear that, as before, this contrasting clause concerns the martyr whose death acted
as an immediately purging "second baptism" (*aliud . . . baptisma quod
nos de mundo recedentes statim Deo copulat, Ad Fort. praef.* 4 CCL 3.185).
On the word *passio* see de la Taille, *Rech. de sc. relig.* 21 (1931) 576 ff.;
Hoppenbrouwers 116 ff.

93. *istic in provincia nostra.* For the meaning of *provincia* in Cyprian see *Ep.* 27 n. 14, *Ep.* 48 n. 15. For a debate on such a major issue
as reconciliation for adulterers (see n. 87 above), it is most unlikely
that the bishops who gathered were *confined* to the proconsular province only—if at the time of meeting bishoprics were established elsewhere in North Africa (on the spread of Christianity see Barnes,
Tertullian 70 f.): Agrippinus' Council on rebaptism included the bishops of Numidia as well, *Ep.* 71.4.1. Therefore, *provincia* may possibly
be used here in its more extended sense (contra Chartier, *Antonianum*
14 [1939] 22).

94. *perseverante catholicae ecclesiae individuo sacramento.* On the
use of *sacramentum* here (close to "sacred bond"?) see de Ghellinck,
de Backer, Poukens, *et al.* 202 ff.

95. *episcopus rationem propositi sui Domino redditurus.* Cyprian's

celebrated formulation for preserving unity in episcopal diversity is repeated in *Epp*. 59.14.2 (*rationem sui actus Domino redditurus*), 69.17 (*unusquisque praepositus actus sui rationem Domino redditurus*), and 72.3.2; cf. *Ep*. 57.5.2 (*reddet ille rationem in die iudicii Domino . . .*). Augustine reformulated it as *salvo iure communionis diversa sentire, De bapt. contr. Donat*. 6.7.10 CSEL 51.305 f. Bévenot, *Rech. sc. relig*. 39 (1951) 397 ff. analyses the concept and its origins, drawing attention to *Ep*. 30.1.1 *animus . . . soleat se solo Deo iudice esse contentus . . . cum conscientiam sciant Deo soli debere se iudici*, where see n. 3 for further discussion. Novatian's sin was above all a failure in charity. But Cyprian, despite the formulation here, was not prepared just to sit back all the same and leave to *laissez faire* the question of penitential discipline. That at least could be argued about (and colleagues who deviated censured, *Ep*. 64.1.1 f.); but *schism* left no common ground for discussion, on the principle *nulla societas fidei et perfidiae potest esse* (*Ep*. 59.20.2). Cyprian's language here may allude to Rom. 14.12 (*unusquisque nostrum pro se rationem dabit*), which he quotes verbatim in a similar context in *Ep*. 69.17.

96. Apoc. 2.5, Fahey 537 f.

97. Tob. 4.10, Fahey 112 f.

98. *morte . . . a qua [aqua] nos salutaris baptismi et redemptoris nostri gratia liberavit*. Hartel ingeniously conjectures a lost *aqua* after *a qua;* I am not convinced that it is necessary and have translated accordingly. Observe Cyprian's view here of the redemption as liberation from sin and death: further analysis in e.g. Kelly, *Doctrines*[3] 178; H. E. W. Turner, *Patristic Doctrine of Redemption* 104; and see *Ep*. 63.13.1 (with n. 31 *ad loc*.) for what is more a "substitution" view of the redemption.

99. *ab ea [morte] quae per delicta postmodum serpit*. The verb *serpit* is doubtless chosen for its close association with Satan.

100. Apoc. 2.20 ff., Fahey 537 f. The manuscripts leave the strong impression that Cyprian's text read, at the very end of the quotation, *gesserit* rather than *gesserint* ("unless she does penitence for her deeds").

101. Luke 15.7, Fahey 353 f.

102. Wis. 1.13, Fahey 172.

103. Joel 2.12 f., Fahey 245 f.

104. Ps. 88.33 f., Fahey 147 f.

105. Matt. 7.9 ff., Fahey 286 f. Cyprian proceeds to comment rather on the parable of the Prodigal Son (Luke 15.11 ff.) than on the text he here cites.

106. An allusion to Matt. 5.4, Fahey 269. Cyprian implausibly restricts the interpretation here of *plangentes* from "those who mourn (= suffer tribulations)" to "those who mourn (= lament for sins)."

107. *paenitentiam non agentes . . . prohibendos omnino censuimus a spe communicationis et pacis.* The wording suggests a further conciliar regulation, and implies indeed an atmosphere in which concessions were yielded to the lapsed only with much reluctance; cf. *Ep.* 59.13.1 (*decrevimus*). Characteristically, Dionysius of Alexandria appears to have imposed no such restriction, *Epist. to Conon* (*frag.* 6, ed. Feltoe, *Letters and Other Remains* 60): "As to those who are nearing the end of life, if they desire and beg to obtain absolution . . . these, too, it is part of the Divine mercy to send on their way free" (trans. Feltoe); *idem, Epist.* to Fabius of Antioch, *ap.* Euseb. *H.E.* 6.44.4: "I had given an order that those who were departing this life, if they besought it, and especially if they chanced to have had made supplication even before, should be absolved, that they might depart in hope." The Council of Arles endorsed (in the case of dying apostates) this restrictive African position, can. 22 (Hefele-Leclercq, *Histoire* 1.1.294), while the Council of Nicaea can. 13 (*op. cit.* 593 ff.) opened out the possibility of receiving deathbed viaticum to all sinners if they should ask for it.

108. *iactet se licet et philosophiam vel eloquentiam suam . . . praedicet.* On Novatian and philosophy see n. 69 above; on Novatian's *eloquentia* see *Ep.* 30 intro. (enemies could call it *perfidia et loquacitas captiosa*, *Ep.* 49.2.4), the *testimonia* collected by Harnack in TU 13.4 (1895) 37 f., and the analysis of Novatian's *facundia* in the *De Trin.*, Mohrmann VC 3 (1949) 163 ff.

109. *etiam quod prius fuerat amisit.* From the run of the paragraph, what Novatian has lost is not so much his rank of presbyter (as some translate) but rather his status as Christian and, therefore, his role as teacher. By definition he can no longer say anything worth hearing; as Cyprian baldly ruled in the *Test.*, *cum hereticis non loquendum*, *Test.* 3.78 CCL 3.161.

110. *adulter atque extraneus episcopus fieri a desertoribus per ambitum*

nititur. Cyprian has no doubt received a version of Novatian's consecration similar to that sent by Cornelius to Fabius of Antioch (*ap. H.E.* 6.43.8 ff.). On the *desertores* see *Ep.* 50 n. 7, and n. 50 above; on Novatian's *ambitus* cf. n. 38 above; and on the word *adulter*, *Ep.* 45 n. 7.

111. *novos apostolos suos mittat ut quaedam recentia institutionis suae fundamenta constituat*. The repetition of *suos . . . suae* is deliberately emphatic: this is Novatian's own (not God's) work. Likewise *novos . . . recentia* (cf. *Ep.* 52 n. 2), exploiting the Roman horror of novelty and corresponding respect for antiquity (especially in religious matters)—on that theme see e.g. Min. Fel., *Oct.* 6.3 and n. 83 *ad loc.* in ACW 39. The Church of Christ, in comparison with Novatian's, can be regarded as of honoured and venerable antiquity.

112. *episcopi in aetate antiqui, in fide integri, in pressura probati, in persecutione proscripti*. This general characterisation of the world's bishops requires explanation. In §8.4 Cyprian has already described the *collegium* of bishops as consisting of *sacerdotes antiqui* (see n. 35). The repetition leads one to suspect that Novatian may himself have been considered unsuitably immature and youthful (date of birth quite unknown). In §9.1, after reporting Cornelius' election, Cyprian promptly proceeded to illustrate the integrity of Cornelius' faith and his suitability for office by the persecuting pressure to which he was then subjected (see n. 38). The genuine bishops (unlike the new *pseudoepiscopi*) have been similarly tried and tested. In §9.1 also, bishops were being threatened in time of persecution with *fanda atque infanda;* here they have been (more specifically and alliteratively) proscribed. Given the character of this present passage (Cyprian is making a rhetorical generalisation), it would be unsafe to deduce that *all* bishops had been *ipso facto* proscribed. But bishops who had fled and were sought, certainly had been so liable—as were others of the faithful (see *Ep.* 10 n. 5 for evidence of sequestration of property belonging to *extorres*, clerical and lay, and cf. *De laps.* 10 CCL 3.1.226 *patrimonii facienda iactura*). Cyprian could speak out on his own record here— he was himself *in tempestate proscriptus*, *Ep.* 59.6.1, cf. *Ep.* 66.4.1: *persecutio . . . me . . . proscriptionis onere depressit* (referring to himself in the context as *homo dignatione Dei honoratus:* persecuting sufferings are evidence of divine favour), and he elsewhere talks in general terms of

bishops under the persecution, but with an additional, explanatory clause: *vel cum de medio recederent proscripti sunt*, *Ep.* 66.7.2 (and see further *Ep.* 66 n. 15).

113. *super eos creare alios pseudoepiscopos audeat*. Cyprian could well be speaking from bitter personal experience—Maximus was appointed Novatianist bishop for Carthage before the African Council meeting of 252 (Ides of May, *Ep.* 59.10.1); Cyprian was in a position to have included that information in the (lost) letter written to Cornelius after that meeting, *Ep.* 59.9.2 f. Cyprian writes of Novatian creating bishops for other communities, just as Cornelius does of himself when he replaced Novatian's consecrators (*ap.* Euseb. *H.E.* 6.43.10: "And as for the remaining bishops, to these we have appointed [*cheirotonēsantes*] successors whom we have sent into the places where they were," and cf. *Ep.* 50.1.2), and just as Cyprian can appear to demand of Stephen (*dirigantur . . . litterae quibus abstento Marciano allius in locum eius substituatur*, *Ep.* 68.3.1, where see n. 13). Appearances may well be somewhat misleading, however, given Cyprian's firmly expressed comments elsewhere (e.g. in *Ep.* 67), on the generally accepted role of *plebs*, clergy, and comprovincial bishops in the process of approving an episcopal candidate (whatever the nominating source). In the case of Maximus e.g. may we assume at least formal acceptance by the local Novatianist community in Carthage (he had started the breakaway church there earlier, *Ep.* 44.1.1, where see n. 2)?

For discussion see Walker, *Churchmanship* 30 f., 41 f. (but note *Times Lit. Supp.* of 23.1.1969, p. 91); Chapman, *Studies on the Early Papacy* 43 f.; Gryson, *Rev. d'hist. ecclés.* 68 (1973) 383.

I have translated as Hartel punctuates, but G. F. Diercks suggests, *per epistulam*, that a full stop should come after *nititur* (and not after *amisit*). That elegantly leaves the following *conetur*, *mittat*, and *audeat* to function as the preceding *iactet* with the full taunting force of their subjunctive mood ("let him attempt . . . let him send out . . . let him have the effrontery . . ."). Diercks must be right.

114. Ephes. 4.2 f., Fahey 483 f.

115. Cyprian has already exploited these images of wheat, tares, winnowing fan, and threshing floor (drawn from Matt. 3.12 and 13.24 ff.) in *Ep.* 54.3.1 f., where see n. 8.

116. A quotation from 2 Tim. 2.20, Fahey 513 f., plus allusion

to Apoc. 2.27 f., Fahey 541 ("rod of iron," cf. Ps. 2.9), again occurring in *Ep.* 54.3.1 f., where see nn. 9 and 10 (Novatian may well have exploited these same images himself).

117. If i.e. he has arrogated to himself godlike powers of discernment and censure over others (alluding to Apoc. 2.23, Fahey 540 f.).

118. The argument is that Novatian excludes from his communion sinners such as *lapsi* (idolaters), even the *libellatici* among them. If he does so, to be consistent he ought to exclude even worse sinners (adulterers and robbers) who are to be found within his own communion; adultery and robbery, besides, are but kinds of idolatry.

119. John 5.14 (Fahey 379 f.) here apparently invoked—unusually—as a text for the avoidance of evil company (and therefore further sins) rather than by way of criticising Novatian "for his refusal to admit the principle of forgiveness of sin" (Fahey 380).

120. *fraudatores et moechos.* Nicostratus had been accused of *fraudes* (*Epp.* 50.1.2, 52.1.2), Novatus similarly (*Ep.* 52.2.1 f.)—if he was still associated with the Novatianists. But adultery does not figure in their catalogue of alleged crimes, as it had in the case of (the laxist) Felicissimus (*Ep.* 41.2.1 cf. *Ep.* 59.1.2, 12.2, 14.1). We need not, however, presume that Cyprian failed to distinguish the laxists from the Novatianists (laxist heretics are recognisable in §15.1, where see n. 65); rather, such charges are simply part of the religious abuse opponents freely cast at each other. Compare Bishop Purpurius of Liniata, accused early in the following century not only of theft of charitable funds and temple robbery (*Gesta apud Zenoph.* 23a CSEL 26.194 f.) but also of double murder (*dicitur te necasse filios sororis tuae duos,* Aug. *Contr. Cresc.* 3.27.30 CSEL 52.436). Watkins, *Penance* 1.214, interpreted this passage to mean that Novatian's following included some who had been reconciled (in the past) for adultery by virtue of the "edict of Callistus"; that is an unnecessary deduction.

121. *hic necessitate ille voluntate peccaverit.* The argument is pretty sophistic; on the logic here, the most minor, but deliberate, lie would be far more grave than all the acts of idolatry Christians, under compulsion, performed in the persecution of Decius. The sense of *necessitas,* the compulsion under which *libellatici* acted, is very attenuated (see n. 57 above); it is much less so in *De laps.* 14 CCL 3.228 *nec excusat oppressum necessitas criminis, ubi crimen est voluntatis,* where *necessitas* re-

fers to overwhelmingly painful tortures. In the *De unit.* 19 CCL 3.263 Cyprian makes a parallel contrast between a *lapsus* and a heretic: *hic potest necessitas fuisse, illic voluntas tenetur in scelere.* Firmilian exploits the same line of reasoning in *Ep.* 75.22.2: the heretic was far worse than a *sacrificatus.* The latter had acted *necessitate persecutionis coactus,* whereas the former was a rebel against the Church *sacrilega voluntate.*

After establishing here that adultery is worse than idolatry, Cyprian goes on, in traditional rhetorical style, to establish that, besides, adultery is nothing else than a form of idolatry! (Cyprian's argument here that sins of lust are worse than apostasy under threat of torture is traceable to Tertullian *De pudic.* 22.12 ff. CCL 2.1329 f., where it is argued *nemo volens negare compellitur, nemo nolens fornicator.*)

122. *vel lupanar ingressus ad cloacam et caenosam voraginem vulgi:* phrases carefully turned to arrest attention. *Vulgi* discloses a touch of Cyprian's unself-conscious upper-class outlook?

123. 1 Cor. 6.18, Fahey 449. Cyprian's text reads here *moechatur* whereas in *Test.* 3.63 CCL 3.154 the equivalent word is *fornicatur.* Fahey suggests the change is deliberate, for Cyprian is "applying the text to condemn Novatian of the specific sin of adultery." But Cyprian is attacking not Novatian but some of Novatian's *followers,* and in the quotations which follow he fails to change *fornicationibus* in 2 Cor. 12.21, *fornicator* in Ephes. 5.5, and *fornicationem* in Col. 3.5. Besides, the trip to the brothel (presumably, therefore, allowing fornication) is given as an alternative to adultery (*matrimonii expugnator alieni*). If the change in the text was deliberate, Cyprian chose a more emotively charged word rather than sought to discriminate between adultery and fornication. On these variations see von Soden, *Das lateinische N.T. in Africa* 73 f.

124. 2 Cor. 12.20 f., Fahey 470 f. (omitting verse 20b).

125. Ephes. 5.5 (Fahey 489) and Col. 3.5 f. (Fahey 501 f.). The purely verbal level at which Cyprian is content to let his argument operate is well exemplified here.

126. There is allusion to 1 Cor. 6.15, Fahey 449 (our bodies are members of Christ), and 1 Cor. 3.16, Fahey 444 f. (temple of God). The logical conclusion of Cyprian's (not very powerful) argument would be that all sinners are guilty of idolatry, as they are all being slaves to the devil.

127. *si peccato alterius inquinari alterum dicunt et idolatriam delin-*

quentis ad non delinquentem transire . . . contendunt etc. There is reference back to Ephes. 5.5 quoted above. Cyprian could be reporting another claim (*si . . . dicunt et . . . contendunt*) to be found in Novatian's letter (n. 6 above). We have here a clear enunciation of the pollution argument advanced by the Novatianists (the reverse of the "communion of saints")—the contamination of deadly sin infected the whole community. There are indeed many passages in the *De lapsis* which suggest similar thinking (hence the horrors of premature reconciliation, e.g. *De laps.* 15), as does the attitude towards penitence as a necessary process of *expiation* from pollution (e.g. *De laps.* 16, 35). Compare §10.2 and n. 48 above, and discussion in Vogt, *Coetus sanctorum* 148 f.

128. *secundum fidem nostram et divinae praedicationis datam formam.* This has been taken as a variation for the *regula fidei* (the rule of faith), e.g. van den Eynde, *Les normes de l'enseignement chrétien* 244 ff.; cf. Bakhuizen van den Brink, VC 13 (1959) 65 ff. (interpreting *forma* as the approximate equivalent of "guide of revelation," "purpose of revelation"). That is not so likely. Cyprian has fought out this issue very noticeably from his *biblical* sources; they have provided on inquiry the basis for his conclusions and his policy (cf. *diu scripturis ex utraque parte prolatis*, §6.1). He is, therefore, appealing here more specifically (and less generally) to their conformity to all the biblical precepts he has cited (*divinae praedicationis . . . formam*). For further discussion Hanson, *Tradition* 79 ff., 140 ff.

129. Ezek. 18.20 (Fahey 230), plus Deut. 24.16 (Fahey 94 f.).

130. *nullam vindemiam premes.* This clause is square-bracketed by Hartel (as an interpolation); it does not appear in a number of manuscripts. It does fit in here rhetorically, however, obeying the rule, in such cases of *anaphora* and *amplificatio*, that each clause should be longer than its predecessor ("increasing members"); but Cyprian's habit of adhering to the rhetorical trio for illustration should mean that the clause has in fact crept in as an explanatory gloss on the preceding *nullam messem metes.* This whole chapter is a touch sarcastic, furnishing as it does a collection of three citations (as biblical citations are so often given) as if they were sayings taken from the gospel according to Novatian (cf. Fahey 55 f.).

131. *quia apud inferos confessio non est nec exomologesis illic fieri potest.* For explication see n. 79 above.

132. *in ecclesiam debent interim suscipi et in ipsa Domino reservari.* Cyprian, in this recapitulation, is referring back to the processes of reconciliation as now regulated for the repentant. He is insisting, as he did before in §18.1, where see n. 81, and in §19.2 (*hunc curatum Deo iudici reservamus*), that such reconciliation this side of the grave is provisional only—hence *interim* (on which word see also n. 77 above).

133. The allusion is to Ephes. 4.2 f., on which Cyprian dilated in §24.4.

LETTER 56

Contents: Five bishops have jointly written requesting that a special penitential case should be considered. It concerns three apostates who bravely withstood intimidation by magistrate and mob but succumbed afterwards under torture before the proconsul himself. Their penitence has now lasted three years. Cyprian is convinced the Lord will be merciful to them: the merits they have earned by their confession help to compensate for the weakness of their flesh, and they have proven that they would be courageous should fighting come again. They clearly deserve to take precedence over the dying in receiving reconciliation. But the question is a serious one and demands wide consultation. When the bishops convene after Easter, Cyprian will be able to reply after soliciting views and debating the issue.

Date and circumstances: This letter is written in the season of Easter with a meeting of bishops scheduled to follow (§3). It must be written before *Ep.* 57 (a conciliar letter which reports a decision to reconcile, upon examination, all the penitent lapsed §§1.2, 5.1—*ipso facto* the three apostates here concerned would have been included).

The apostates have now been doing penitence *per hoc triennium* (§1.1). That could make the year 252 or 253, depending on the particular time in the year 250 when their tortures and lapse occurred in the presence of the proconsul. Easter Sunday (about the time of writing) fell on April 11 in 252, April 3 in 253 (see on the dates of Easter, *Letters of Cyprian* 1 [ACW 43] intro. pp. 45 f. with n. 247). The likelihood, on the evidence available to us, is that 253 should be our choice, for tortures are reported in April 250 as a recent innovation, with the subsequent death of Mappalicus (*Ep.* 10), the proconsul being present in Carthage (earlier part of April 250)—whereas these three apostates hail from somewhere away in the south, in the vicinity of Capsa (n. 4 below). Any computation cannot, however, be compelling (could the prisoners have been referred up to Carthage for trial there in early April? could *triennium*, besides, be overgenerously calculated?), but a provisional date of spring 253 seems to be warranted. See further n. 8 below.

The clinching factor will be the date of *Ep.* 57. If that letter *must* be dated to 252, then this letter has to precede it. However, it is argued in *Ep.* 57 intro. that the Council meeting there reported is not consistent in tone or detail with the Council of 252 as reported in *Ep.* 59 (datable to summer 252); in *Ep.* 59.13 ff. there is no sign of the general moratorium for those doing penitence which *Ep.* 57 records. Therefore, *Ep.* 57 must report a subsequent Council, the meeting of spring 253, and this reckoning consequently allows this epistle to find its most natural place about Eastertide 253.

For discussion Nelke, *Chronologie* 75; Ritschl, *De epist.* 26 f.; Monceaux, *Rev. de phil., de litt. et d'hist. anc.* 24 (1900) 336 f.; Duquenne, *Chronologie* 38 ff.; Turner, *Studies* 126 f.; Fischer, *Ann. hist. concil.* 13 (1981) 12 ff.

There are several consequences:

(1) There is no sense yet of any major threat from Gallus, §2.2 (see n. 12 below). That becomes overwhelmingly urgent by the time the Council of 253 does in fact meet: see *Epp.* 57 and 58 passim. Neither is there any suggestion in this letter that a major amnesty for penitents is yet being contemplated (as granted by that Council). The threatening storm of persecution, we must conclude, blew up very suddenly. See further "Persecution under Gallus," ANRW 2.27.

(2) Though the year is 253, the case of these penitents who fell after confession and tortures is a novelty. No disciplinary provision has yet been made for any parallel case which Cyprian can cite as precedent. The clause to admit dying penitents to communion is the only one he can invoke for contrast (§2.2). That is a little startling. Should we conclude that there had been few similar cases? Certainly,

none had come, so far, to the attention of Cyprian at least, to judge from his reaction to the problem.

(3) *Ep.* 64 can now be comfortably placed as reporting Council affairs of spring 252. There the case of a premature reconciliation carried out before deathbed (*nulla infirmitate urgente*), without special circumstances (*nulla . . . necessitate cogente*), had been dealt with (§1.1 f.). It was not until 12 months later that the question of reducing the terms for some penitents had been raised by these present, and unusual, cases of *Ep.* 56—and by the menace of violent persecution that suddenly appeared imminent in North Africa.

1. *Cyprianus Fortunato Ahymmo Optato Privatiano Donatulo et Felici fratribus s.* This is clearly a group of bishops (they had gathered at Capsa *propter ordinationem episcopi*, §1) and as likely as not they should hail from areas not too far distant from that town (in Byzacium).

(1) *Fortunatus.* There are at least two orthodox bishops so named (*Ep.* 57) and one *pseudoepiscopus* (*Ep.* 59.9.1). The one known see of a bishop Fortunatus is at Thuccabor, some 65 km west of Carthage; quite some distance, therefore, from Capsa (270 km SW of Carthage). See *Ep.* 44 n. 7 and further discussion in Maier, *L'épiscopat* 323; von Soden, *Prosopographie* 258 ff.

(2) *Ahymmus.* There is a bishop Ahymmus in *Sent. episc.* 50 H.453 *ab Ausuaga.* The site remains unidentified but appears to have been proconsular: Maier, *L'épiscopat* 107, 253; von Soden, *Prosopographie* 259; PW 2.2 (1896) *s.v.* "Auzuagga" 2624 (Dessau); DHGE 5 (1931) *s.v.* "Ausuaga" 799 f. (Audollent); DACL 9 (1930) *s.vv.* "listes épiscopales" 1289 (Leclercq).

(3) *Optatus.* Occurs in no other episcopal list of this period. Diocese unknown, Maier, *L'épiscopat* 371.

(4) *Privatianus.* No doubt the bishop Privatianus who occurs in *Sent. episc.* 19 H.444 *a Sufetula*, i.e. not far from Capsa, some 212 km SW of Carthage (near modern Sbeïtla); Maier, *L'épiscopat* 204, 389; PW 4 A.1 (1931) *s.v.* "Sufetula" 651 f. (Dessau); Gascou, *Politique municipale* 30 f.; DACL 9 (1930) *s.vv.* "listes épiscopales" 1282 (Leclercq); Lepelley, *Les cités* 2.308 ff. A bishop Privatianus appears in 39th place (out of 42) in *Ep.* 57.

(5) *Donatulus.* *Sent. episc.* 69 H.457 records a bishop Donatulus *a*

Capse. He ought to be identified with the Donatulus here. Observe his relatively junior ranking in 256; it will have been for his consecration that the other bishops have convened at Capsa: Maier, *L'épiscopat* 122, 293; von Soden, *Prosopographie* 253, 259; DACL 9 (1930) *s.vv.* "listes épiscopales" 1269 (Leclercq).

(6) *Felix.* There are at least seven bishops so named (*Sent. episc.* 12, 26, 33, 46, 63, 74) as well as one heretical bishop (*Ep.* 59.10.2). The most likely candidate here is Felix *a Marazana: Sent. episc.* 46 H.452 (Marazana being located in Byzacium, precise site unidentified); Maier, *L'épiscopat* 166, 310; DACL 9 (1930) *s.vv.* "listes épiscopales" 1295 (Leclercq); PW 14.2 (1930) *s.v.* "Marazana" 1436 (Schwabe).

The bishops' names cannot be in strict descending order of seniority (Donatulus would have to be the most junior). Cyprian will reflect the order of names in the original letter to which he now replies; was the name of Felix placed last as *scriptor* of that letter? Presumably Cyprian replies sending a copy of the letter to each of the six bishops (and one for Superius, n. 4 below): the bishops will have all dispersed in time to be with their own people for Easter (cf. §3 below).

2. *in Capsensi civitate.* That is, Capsa (modern Gafsa), 270 km SW of Carthage: Toulotte, *Géographie de l'Afrique chrétienne (Byz. et Trip.)* 70 ff.; Gascou, *Politique municipale* 89 ff.; PW 3.2 (1899) *s.v.* "Capsa" 1553 (Dessau); DHGE 11 (1949) *s.v.* "Capsa" 965 ff. (Audollent); Lepelley, *Les cités* 2.281 f.

3. *propter ordinationem episcopi.* The bishops gathered from the surrounding locality, giving final approval to the episcopal candidate and performing the consecration ceremonies (already in Hippoly. *Apost. trad.* 2, ed. Botte[2] 40, *qui praesentes fuerint episcopi;* compare Euseb. *H.E.* 6.11.2, Alexander appointed bishop of Jerusalem in the early third century "with the common consent of the bishops who were administering the churches round about"). Cyp., *Ep.* 67.5.1 f., generously refers to this traditional arrangement as a *traditio divina et apostolica observatio;* neighbouring bishops gather (*episcopi eiusdem provinciae proximi quique conveniant*) and pass final judgment on the candidate (*de episcoporum qui in praesentia convenerant . . . iudicio*) before the rites of *ordinatio* are carried out; cf. *Ep.* 59.5.2: *post populi suffragium, post coepiscoporum consensum; Ep.* 55.8.4:

factus est episcopus [Cornelius] a plurimis collegis nostris qui tunc in urbe Roma aderant. The fourth-century Councils sought to regulate the minimum number of such episcopal witnesses, e.g. Counc. Arles can. 20 (7 preferred, with an absolute minimum of three—*si tamen non potuerit septem, infra tres non audeat ordinare*, Hefele-Leclercq, *Histoire* 1.1.294); Counc. Nic. can. 4 (minimum of three compro-vincial bishops—cf. Novatian's three consecrators, Corn. *ap.* Eu-seb. *H.E.* 6.43.8: Cornelius questions their sobriety, but not their sufficiency); Hefele-Leclercq, *op. cit.* 539 ff. (with lengthy com-mentary). In the present case there appear to have been five bishops gathered to consecrate the sixth (Donatulus) addressee of this letter. Further discussion on episcopal elections in de Ste. Croix, *Brit. Journ. Soc.* 5 (1954) 33 ff.; Zmire, *Rech. aug.* 7 (1971) 15 ff.; Fortin, *Laval théol. et philos.* 19 (1963) 49 ff.; Ferguson, *Ch. Hist.* 43 (1974) 26 ff. (evidence of Origen); van Beneden, *Aux origines d'une termi-nologie sacramentelle* passim, esp. 66 ff., 94 ff.

The bishops receive Cyprian's reply written *inter Paschae prima sollemnia* (§3). No doubt there would be some concern to have a bishop installed for the vacancy at Capsa in time for the Easter cer-emonies there.

4. *pertulerit ad vos Superius . . . Ninum Clementianum Florum.* *Perferre* is an ambiguous verb: does Superius send word or bring it himself? As he is not among the addressees of this letter, the simplest interpretation is that he *wrote* a letter for the attention of the assem-bling bishops. Superius' see is unknown (he occurs nowhere else) but it is in all likelihood to be located somewhere in the vicinity of Capsa. For it was a standard procedure (included by Cyprian under the ru-bric of his *divina et apostolica observatio* quoted in n. 3 above) that if a local bishop could not attend an episcopal *ordinatio* in person, he should write giving his *sententia;* hence *Ep.* 67.5.2: *de episcoporum qui in praesentia convenerant quique de eo ad vos litteras fecerant iudicio.* Counc. Nic. can. 4 formalised this customary procedure (if there is any dif-ficulty either through urgent necessity or the length of the journey, those who are absent should cast their votes and convey them by let-ter and then the minimum of three who have gathered together should proceed to hold the election): Hefele-Leclercq, *Histoire* 1.1.539 ff. (with commentary); cf. *Const. apost.* 8.27 (ed. Funk 530). We might plausibly conjecture, therefore, that Superius may well

have taken the opportunity to attach to his letter (in which he recorded his *sententia*) a request put to the bishops present by which he sought their collective guidance on the special case of Ninus, Clementianus, and Florus.

I do not know by what warrant Keresztes, *Latomus* 34 (1975) 773 n. 104, can refer to *Bishop* Ninus. Saumagne, *Cyprien, évêque de Carthage* 84, incredibly describes these three unfortunate apostates as "un couple . . . mari et femme." On his reading "ils n'avaient pas apostasié et on ne leur avait pas demandé de le faire"; and he deduces that Cyprian's missionaries sent to the south have encountered this case of unnecessary penance and the bishops have, therefore, written to Cyprian to confirm for them "une rémission que nos Gafsiens n'ont peut-être pas eu l'idée de réclamer avant la visite des missionaires de Cyprien." That is fantasy, and perverse fantasy at that.

5. *violentiam magistratus et populi frementis inpetum vicerant.* This occurred presumably in their home town (in the diocese of Superius) when they refused to comply with Decius' orders for general sacrifice. The singular *magistratus* could conceivably be collective (= "the magistrates") but it more probably refers to the one official who presided over the sacrificial ceremonies in the local town; see further *Letters of Cyprian* 1 (ACW 43) intro. pp. 30 ff. In §2.1 below Cyprian dilates on these facts, using the plural (*violentiam magistratuum*). Observe the popular hostility which public failure to sacrifice to the gods aroused—Carthaginian parallels collected at *Ep.* 6 n. 32.

6. *cum apud proconsulem poenis gravibus excruciarentur.* The three prisoners will have been referred by the local magistracy to the tribunal of the proconsul, who alone possessed the *ius gladii*, the power to deal with capital crimes. (See *Ep.* 38 n. 9 and *Letters of Cyprian* 1 [ACW 43] intro. pp. 35 f.) They may well have been sent on to a neighbouring town like Capsa, there to await in prison (*passos esse carcerem* §2.1) the proconsul on his assize round; that Capsa itself was on the *conventus* (assize list) is, however, pure conjecture (but note CIL 8.98 [c. 127/28] recording the presence there of a proconsul). On activities of this proconsul in 250, see *Ep.* 10 n. 20, *Ep.* 38 n. 9, and see also on this incident *Historia* 22 (1973) 651 f. On the proconsul's *conventus*, note Burton, JRS 65 (1975) 92 ff.; Thomasson, *Die Statthalter* 1.58 ff.

7. *lapsum non voluntate sed necessitate susceptum.* Cyprian dis-

closes his sympathy for these three penitents by couching his explanation in language which helped to win *libellatici* their restoration to communion. See *Ep.* 55.26.1 and n. 121 *ad loc.* For a contemporary parallel note Dionys. Alex. *ap.* Euseb. *H.E.* 6.41.13: "some were captured, and of these some went as far as bonds and imprisonment, and certain, when they had been shut up for many days, then forswore themselves even before coming into court, while others, who remained firm for a certain time under tortures, subsequently gave in" (trans. Oulton).

8. *per hoc triennium.* By Roman reckoning this can indicate any time over 24 months and up to 36 months; it need not cover the full three-year period. It can be argued that the proconsul did not introduce tortures until the course of April 250 (*Ep.* 10.1.1 f., with nn. 5 and 6 there, where the innovation is noted: Mappalicus, Cyprian insists, was one of the first so to suffer, and he died under torture in mid-April, *Ep.* 10 n. 20). That was in Carthage. Capsa, away in the south, would come later on the proconsul's itinerary (if at Capsa these recusants were tried). The bishops will have used *triennium* of their penitence, writing some time *before* Easter (April 11 if this is 252, April 3 if this is 253), in time for Cyprian now to reply *inter Paschae prima sollemnia.* Therefore, in order to accommodate *triennium* here, this letter must belong not to 252 but rather to 253: so argues Ritschl, *De epist.* 26 f. Though strong, this is a not altogether cogent argument: it involves too many assumptions (tortures occurred first at Carthage?) and unknowns (where were these three tried?). Besides, the bishops in using *triennium* could well have erred a little on the side of generosity in urging their case. But the argument does at least make altogether feasible that this letter could well date to 253; and on this reckoning, 252 does cause something of a squeeze. See further intro. to this letter; Nelke, *Chronologie* 75 (arbitrarily dating the proconsul's visit to this area to January/February 250, thereby keeping *Ep.* 57 to 252!).

9. *de quibus consulendum putastis an eos ad communicationem iam fas esset admittere.* Observe Cyprian's role, qua "metropolitan" (see *Ep.* 48 n. 15), as arbiter and interpreter of conciliar decrees. *Epp.* 1, 3, 4 provide examples where the procedure by which Cyprian calls in a number of colleagues (episcopal and minor clerical) for guiding coun-

sel and proffers subsequent advice is well illustrated. The bishops had asked that their problem should be aired similarly, *cum pluribus collegis*, §3. See further *Ep.* 1 nn. 2 and 3.

In *Ep.* 55.6.1 Cyprian had indicated that, by conciliar resolution, each man's particular *voluntates et necessitates* should be scrutinised before granting reconciliation. These extenuating factors have now been carefully registered. There is no suggestion anywhere that anything specific had been decreed for such exceptional cases. In fact, this provides our only indication of what was considered a *legitimum et plenum tempus satisfactionis* (*Ep.* 64.1.1), and for a highly untypical sample. The majority of *sacrificati* were plainly expected to wait until the approach of death: *Ep.* 57.2.1 *merito . . . trahebatur dolentium paenitentia tempore longiore ut infirmis in exitu subveniretur* (cf. n. 13 below). But the fact that the bishops can now put their inquiry implies that the possibility of an earlier settlement had not been formally ruled out. Cf. *Ep.* 55 n. 78.

10. *quod ad mei animi sententiam pertinet, puto.* Cyprian is at pains to indicate a private and individual reaction in all that follows. It is a prima-facie and preliminary assessment; the ultimate decision will be jointly made at the forthcoming Council of bishops, *multorum sacerdotum consilio* §3.

11. *quibus aestimamus ad deprecandam clementiam Domini posse sufficere quod triennium . . . planxerunt.* Though weighting his argument heavily in favour of leniency, Cyprian is cautious enough still to couch it in potential terms (*posse sufficere*); he has avoided irretrievable commitment in the event that the Council might incline otherwise.

12. *si acies etiam denuo venerit, gloriam suam posse reparare.* As in *Ep.* 55.17.3 (*si proelium prius venerit . . .*), there is no persecution of Gallus yet in sight. The argument presented in *Ep.* 55 was that, as confession and martyrdom were no longer possible for cancelling a fall, *paenitentia* for the lapsed had to be introduced as a second, but necessary, best (§§3.2 ff.). The same attitude continues still; they are being measured by the yardstick of such a (potential) cancellation through confession and martyrdom. The argument in *Ep.* 57 (e.g. §4) is startlingly different.

13. *paenitentiam agentibus in infirmitatis periculo subveniri et pacem dari.* For this particular resolution see *Ep.* 55 n. 78. Had there been

specific clauses about reconciliation earlier than deathbed, we could reasonably expect Cyprian to have referred to them here. Instead, he has to argue out the case *ab initio*.

14. *carnem quae infirma est fatigarent.* Cyprian strengthens the case for sympathetic treatment by alluding to Matt. 26.41 (*caro autem infirma*), Fahey 327.

15. *res tanta exigit maius et pensius de multorum conlatione consilium.* It remains indeterminate whether the adverbs here are merely intensive or are truly comparative (more mature and serious deliberation sc. than I can now give by myself).

16. *inter Paschae prima sollemnia.* For the meaning of *Pascha* in Cyprian, see *Ep.* 29 n. 10; Renaud, *Eucharistie* 39 ff. The date of this letter must be close to Easter Sunday. Koch interprets the present expression to mean "das Osterfest und seine Oktav," *Z. f. wiss. Theol.* 55 (1914) 297 f. (adducing, *inter alia*, Commod., *Instr.* 2.34.1 ff. CSEL 15.105 f.: *congruit in Pascha, die felicissimo nostro, / laetentur et illi, qui postulant sumpta diurna: / erogetur eis quod sufficit, vinum et esca*).

17. *rescribatur vobis firma sententia multorum sacerdotum consilio ponderata.* It seems implied that (1) these bishops to whom Cyprian replies would have been content and satisfied with an *ad hoc* decision reached by Cyprian advised (as usual) by a number of other bishops. It was Cyprian himself who chose to put the question, as a *res tanta*, on the Council agenda. He writes as one in charge of its affairs (*tractabo cum singulis plenius*). (2) As a group these bishops did not anticipate being present at the conciliar meeting themselves—but note that there is more than one Fortunatus and a Privatianus present for *Ep.* 57. The relative remoteness of their sees will have made it unlikely that all would be attending as a matter of course. (3) The post-Easter Council meeting seems to occur routinely and not to have been specially invoked.

LETTER 57

Contents: It had been previously agreed to admit to communion on their deathbed those who had been doing penitence, but divine signs have warned Cyprian and his colleagues of a further outbreak of persecution to come. They have, accordingly, granted to all those who have been doing continuous penitence admittance to communion so that they can be thus strengthened for the coming battle. To have conceded them reconciliation can only bring glory to the bishops if these penitents, now reconciled, prove themselves martyrs; but if they have hypocritically asked for reconciliation, they deceive only themselves, not their Judge who sees all. The Eucharist now given to the penitent prepares them for confessing the Name at their trial— or for death should they perish in flight; it is their bishops' duty, as good shepherds, in this way to provide the proper protection for their flocks. But any colleague who refuses so to grant reconciliation will have to answer to God for his unnatural harshness.

Date and circumstances: A conciliar meeting, attended by 42 African bishops, has been held; acute fear of a coming persecution has induced those bishops to decree a major change in penitential discipline, profoundly modifying that established by the Council of 251 (spoken of in the past, *pridem,* §1.1). The year of this meeting can only be 252 or 253 (Cornelius, the addressee, dying in the course of June 253). The persecution that is feared (but not actual) must be, therefore, that of Gallus (on which see Introduction to this volume). In which of the two possible years, 252 and 253, should this Council meeting be placed?

We have seen that *Ep.* 56 (which preceded the general amnesty granted to penitent lapsed, here announced) fits most easily but not inevitably at Eastertide 253: see intro. to *Ep.* 56. That certainly pushes this epistle towards the post-Easter meeting of bishops (announced in *Ep.* 56.3) in 253, but it does not fix it there beyond question.

Ep. 59 (datable, roughly, to summer 252) rehearses to Cornelius events and activities over 251/252, including the recent period, during and after the Council meeting of mid-May 252. Does this letter fit with the description there given (and thus record the actual meeting of May 252)?

The tone and atmosphere of *Ep.* 59 is remarkably at variance. Whereas here persecution is a dreaded apprehension of the immediate future (as it is again in *Ep.* 58, written after *Ep.* 57, in which Cyprian cancels a projected trip to Thibaris in view of the coming dangers), in *Ep.* 59 Cyprian can regard the time of writing basically as a period of peace: *ipsam pacem persecutione peiorem fratribus [sc. haeretici] faciunt* §18.2 ("the heretics are making peace itself worse for the brethren than the persecution ever was"); indeed, the word *persecutio* in *Ep.* 59 refers throughout to the *past* (e.g. §§10.3, 12.2, 13.1—all referring to the period of Decius; expressions like *in ipso persecutionis tempore*, §13.1, do not require any qualification). There is one reference (§6.1) to a local outcry in the circus for Bishop Cyprian (an edict had been posted demanding popular sacrifice), but there is none of the atmosphere of impending disaster as is present in this letter (nor is Cornelius in any way so threatened either; note esp. §19.1). It begins to look as if this letter cannot belong to May of 252.

In *Ep.* 59.13 ff. there is lengthy talk about penitence and about the terms on which Cyprian is endeavouring, in the interests of church unity, to admit schismatics back into the Church. Throughout, there is no suggestion anywhere that a general moratorium has been declared for the *paenitentiam facientes* in view of the threatening hostilities, even though it would have helped Cyprian's case at several points to have referred to it (esp. §16.3 *ad fin.*). Rather, it is full of talk of making satisfaction to God, appeasing the Lord by penitence, compensating for sin by sorrow, curing faults by repentance, knocking on the church door begging for readmittance, etc. (see esp. §§13 and 16). The conclusion seems inescapable: there has been no relaxing of penitential regulations in order to prepare penitents for persecution and martyrdom. *Ep.* 57 must be referring to a meeting that took place later than *Ep.* 59, and, therefore, cannot be identified with the Council meeting of May 252. In the light of *Ep.* 56, it should be placed, accordingly, about a month after Easter 253, i.e. in early May (there was an interval of 34 days between Easter and the Council meeting in 252). Discussion in Ritschl, *De epist.* 26 ff.; Nelke, *Chronologie* 75; Turner, *Studies* 126 ff.; Duquenne, *Chronologie* 38 ff.; Fischer, *Ann hist. concil.* 13 (1981) 12 ff.

There are several corollaries:

(1) The admonitions and warnings that signalled the oncoming of persecution should be placed in that month's interval between *Ep.* 56 (where there is no hint of such fears) and this *Ep.* 57 (where such apprehensions are rampant). The bishops give Cornelius no indication of sources of knowledge on which they have been prepared to

make such a startling modification in penitential discipline other than divine *ostensiones* and *visiones;* there is no word of informants, no hint of rumours—nor is there yet any actual persecution.

(2) There is no sense at all that Cornelius in Rome is similarly endangered (see n. 32 below). But when Cyprian next writes to Cornelius (*Ep.* 60), Cornelius has been under attack himself (*unum primo adgressus, Ep.* 60.2.2) but is not yet apparently in exile at Centumcellae; there he died before late June 253 (when Lucius, his successor, took office). Cornelius' exile can have lasted at the very longest five or six weeks. Events will have moved swiftly, and *Ep.* 60 will have been written not too long after this letter. See further *Ep.* 60 intro.

(3) We can only surmise the atmosphere which induced the African bishops to make their surprising decision and to modify so dramatically their previous counsel to the repentant fallen (they could always, it had been said to them, redeem their fault by confronting confession and martyrdom; but it was certainly not entertained that they should be readmitted first to communion, as an essential preliminary to that action; see n. 11 below). The disastrous plague will have come to the North African cities by the summer of 252 (it could be said to have claimed a Roman victim, the coemperor Hostilian himself, by autumn of 251: Aurel. Vict., *De Caes.* 30.2; Préaux, *Aegyptus* 32 [1952] 152 ff.). During that summer of 252, as the plague ravaged unabated (see the lurid descriptions in Pont., *Vit. Cyp.* 9 H. xcix f.; *De mort.* 14 CCL 3A.24), there had been heard, once again, popular outcry against Christians (noticeably absenting themselves from the religious observances that protected the community? see *Ep.* 59.6.1). Now, in 253, another summer is about to come upon them, bringing with it further deaths by plague and the attendant strains and apprehensions of Christians. With this devastating disease and a run of other public disasters (note *De mort.* 2, 25; *Ad Demet.* 2, 5, 10, 17) there has already been talk of the coming of Antichrist (e.g. *Ep.* 59.7.1, 13.4, 18.2, 18.3). Persecution was only to be expected as one of the signs of those cataclysmic times. That logic is enunciated clearly in *Ep.* 58.2.2: *nec quisquam miretur persecutionibus nos adsiduis fatigari et pressuris angentibus frequenter urgeri, quando haec futura in novissimis temporibus Dominus ante praedixerit.* This all adds up to a highly tense mood of eschatological forebodings and millenarian apprehensions (seen clearly in the contemporary treatises *De mortalitate* and *Ad*

Demetrianum). Everything possible should, therefore, be done to help prepare all those who have demonstrated the capacity to face with fortitude the coming End, in the last days of the dying world (see *Ep.* 58.1.2 ff.). We have a remarkable document in which such apocalyptic fears have been translated into conciliar action. After examination (§5.1), all those *sacrificati* who have been doing continuous penitence since their fall (§1.2) are now to be readmitted to communion. But there is no evidence that those fears ever became a reality in North Africa.

For the connection between persecution and the Second Coming which the African bishops have now drawn, compare half a century earlier in the days of Septimius Severus: "At this time Judas also, another writer, composed a written discourse on the seventy weeks in the book of Daniel; he stops his record of time at the tenth year of the reign of Severus. He also was of the opinion that the much-talked-of coming of the antichrist was already near. So strongly did the persecution which was stirred up against us disturb the minds of the many" (Euseb. *H.E.* 6.7, trans. Oulton). And for stories of bishops stirred to action by similar convictions, see Hippol., *In Dan.* 4.18 (a Syriac bishop), 4.19 (a Pontic bishop), SC 14.296 ff.

1. Analysis and identification of episcopal names is rendered difficult by the frequency of homonyms: e.g., there appear within this list two bishops named Donatus, two named Fortunatus, and four named Saturninus. And for the period of Cyprian's correspondence there are demonstrably multiple bishops named Felix (at least six), Aurelius (2), Honoratus (2), Quintus (2), Rogatianus (2), Secundinus (2), and Victor (3); one each of these appears in this list. Despite this handicap, we are, however, assisted in analysis by (i) the *Sent. episc.* lxxxvii, where the names and sees of 87 bishops are listed, and (ii) *Ep.* 70, where there is a group of 32 bishops from the proconsular area who address 18 bishops from the Numidian district. Of those 32 proconsular bishops, some 26 of the names reoccur in this present list of 42 bishops (if Herculaneus = Herculanus); of the remainder of the present list, the *Sent. episc.* can provide a proconsular diocese for all but nine names—if one can safely assume identity where the same name occurs in the two lists (an assumption not without hazard). The nine names thus unaccounted for are, in order, Faustinus,

Eutyches, Ampius, the fourth Saturninus, Priscus, Manthaneus, Verianus, the second Fortunatus, and Rogatus. It certainly looks as if we have here a predominantly proconsular gathering of bishops, and locally proconsular at that—the sees, where identifiable, are "surtout des villes de la côte, de la banlieue de Carthage, de la vallée du Bagrades ou de ses affluents" (Monceaux, *Histoire* 2.50). The most distant bishops would have come from places like Girba (Djerba) in Tripolitania, the see of Monnullus (on Tripolitanian bishops see Romanelli, *Le Sedi* 157 ff., and Ward Perkins & Goodchild, *Arch.* 95 [1953] 1 ff.), Lares (Henchir Lorbeus), and Thabraca (Tabarka), the sees of Hortensianus and Victoricus, over to the southwest and west of Carthage, or Sufetula (Sbeïtla), the see of Privatianus (see *Ep.* 56 n. 1), down in Byzacium. But only a couple will have had to travel more than 200 km in order to get to the meeting in Carthage, and most well under 150 km. Further on these bishops in von Soden, *Prosopographie* 257 f.; Fischer, *Ann. hist. concil.* 13 (1981) 15 ff.

 2. *statueramus quidem pridem.* Cyprian's time span for *pridem* is vague and imprecise: see *Ep.* 1 n. 7. The bishops are referring back to the Council of 251, in all probability now two years ago (see intro. to this letter)—on which see *Ep.* 55 intro. (There is strong mss warrant for reading *iam* before *pridem*.)

 3. *participato invicem nobiscum consilio.* A description of the debates at the Council of 251; cf. *Ep.* 54.3.3: *diu multumque tractatu inter nos habito.* For the turn of phrase *invicem nobiscum*, see the discussion by Dölger, *Sol Salutis* 128 f. n. 2.

 4. *agerent diu paenitentiam plenam.* On the vague and indeterminate expression here, see *Ep.* 55 n. 78 and compare *Ep.* 56 nn. 9 and 13. *Diu* (cf. below *tempore longiore*, §2.1) has occurred already in Cyprian's various formulations of the terms of penitence for the fallen (*Ep.* 55.6.1: *traheretur diu paenitentia*); it admits the general possibility of some termination of penitence *before* deathbed—which is about to be announced.

 5. *pacem sub ictu mortis acciperent.* For this conciliar resolution of 251, see *Ep.* 55.17.3 (with n. 78).

 6. *ecclesiam pulsantibus cludi.* For the practical origins of this metaphor (penitents being shut out, literally, from the assembled congregation of the faithful), see *Ep.* 30 n. 39 and compare below in §3.1: *ab ecclesiae limine non recedentes.* There may be here a passing al-

lusion to Matt. 7.7 ("knock and it shall be opened to you"), to which Cyprian refers in *Ep.* 11.2.2 with the words *pulsemus quia et pulsanti aperitur.*

7. *sine communicatione . . . ad Dominum dimitterentur.* On the custom of giving the *viaticum* to dying penitents, see *Ep.* 8 n. 25.

8. *solvi autem possent illic quae hic prius in ecclesia solverentur.* The allusion is to Matt. 16.19, cf. 18.18, Fahey 312. It is surprising that neither these texts nor John 20.23 are exploited elsewhere on the penitential issue—and the bishops make little of the one allusion here. Significance has been sought in the collocation *solvi . . . possent:* it appears to be a carefully potential expression ("might be loosed") rather than a dogmatic assertion. That appearance is deceptive. The turn of phrase is merely a Cyprianic way of achieving a future passive subjunctive. Bévenot, *Theol. Stud.* 16 (1955) 210 f., appositely compares *De zelo* 18 CCL 3A.85: *cogita quod filii Dei hi soli possint vocari qui sint pacifici,* where *possint vocari* = will be called; cf. Schrijnen and Mohrmann 2.45 ff.

9. *crebris adque adsiduis ostensionibus admoneamur.* Phrases elsewhere in the letter leave us in no doubt that direct divine monitions (via dreams, visions, etc.) are meant: §2.1: *ostensionibus adque admonitionibus iustis;* §5.1: *sancto spiritu suggerente et Domino per visiones multas et manifestas admonente;* §5.2: *hoc nobis divinitus frequenter ostendi, de hoc nos . . . saepius admoneri.* As this is a collective letter, the precise authority for these warnings cannot be divined. But *Epp.* 58 and 60, which repeat the forebodings, are by Cyprian alone and make it clear that Cyprian was one (if not the only one) recipient of such omens of danger (e.g. *Ep.* 58.1.2: *cum Domini instruentis dignatione instigemur saepius et admoneamur; Ep.* 60.5.1: *providentia Domini monentis instruimur et divinae misericordiae consiliis salubribus admonemur*). The reliance Cyprian is prepared to place on occult phenomena has already been encountered in *Epp.* 7.1, 40.1.1 f. (signs and revelations), *Epp.* 11.3 ff., 16.4.1 f. (visions and admonitions, cf. *Ep.* 39.1.2), *Ep.* 15.3.2 (visitations); for commentary see *Ep.* 16 nn. 27–30. It is not surprising that Cyprian is soon to come under attack over the issue of his *somnia* and *visiones* (*Ep.* 66.10.1 f.). The fourth dissertation of Dodwell is devoted to this topic also, pp. 10 ff. of *Dissertationes Cyprianicae* in 1682 edition of Pearson and Fell.

10. *necessitate cogente.* In *Ep.* 64.1.1 Cyprian and his colleagues

dealt with a case of reconciliation that had been effected prematurely, *nulla infirmitate urguente ac necessitate cogente* ("though there was no dangerous illness nor was it demanded by special circumstances"). Those required preconditions for a hastened reconciliation have now been met; *necessitas* here = inevitable persecution (bringing along with it, besides, danger of death).

11. *eos ad proelium quod imminet armari et instrui oportere.* The bishops elaborate their meaning in §2.2—the former penitents, thus granted reconciliation, may put on the protective armour (*tutela*) of the Eucharist. For the Eucharist regarded as a prophylactic (strongly emphasised in this letter), see Dölger, *Ant. und Christ.* 5 (1936) 258. It is nothing short of astonishing that this present argument can be stated without any apparent embarrassment, even though it was granted no validity earlier while the persecution of Decius continued (the lapsed were expected to confront confession and martyrdom without such strengthening weapons: *Ep.* 55.4.1 f. quoting *Ep.* 19.2.2, *Ep.* 55.7.1, 16.3). It could be argued that circumstances are now different: these are penitents who have been accumulating *satisfactio* for their sincerely regretted fall now for a triennium. But if this is so, the bishops fail to emphasise duly that essential difference; there is no word that their *satisfactio* is now nearing completion, as there had been, e.g., in *Ep.* 15.4 (*paenitentiam satisfactioni proximam*). Rather, it is emphasised that the divine revelation of danger to come, the new *necessitas*, warrants the mitigation of the established penitential discipline; the protection, and the powers of inspiration, provided by the Eucharist are essential for *all* (note especially §4.2). The difference lies in the fact that that penitential discipline had now been explicitly established by episcopal agreement in 251 (*Ep.* 55). That, in turn, now makes possible further changes in its rulings under the changing circumstances, likewise by episcopal agreement. All the same, the ruling is explicitly restricted: it is for the *paenitentiam facientes* only, for penitence has now strengthened them for the battle (cf. *Ep.* 60.2.5). See further n. 26 below.

12. *obtemperandum est namque ostensionibus adque admonitionibus iustis.* The bishops seem to talk here of the divine signs as if they were something akin to weather-alert warnings in the sky. The addition of the epithet *iustis* ("reliable") might perhaps appear a touch defensive—just as later in §5.1 the Lord is found warning through many

visions that are "explicit" (*manifestas*). But all the same, Cyprian (and his bishops) feel confident enough roundly to castigate with untimely *censura* and unnatural *duritia* any colleague (here = African bishop ?) who disagrees with their ruling—a ruling founded specifically upon the testimony of these very signs and visions (§5.2).

13. *quae differre diu plangentium lacrimas et subvenire sero morientibus in infirmitate pateretur.* As before (e.g. *Ep.* 55 n. 78, *Ep.* 56 n. 13), there is no mention of any clauses, formally agreed upon, which laid down the conditions for reconciliation *before* deathbed. It would have been timely to have quoted them here.

14. *quomodo ad martyrii poculum idoneos facimus si non eos ad bibendum in ecclesia poculum Domini . . . admittimus?* For the cup (*poculum*) as a symbol of martyrdom—linking it richly with Christ's cup of suffering, the cup of the Eucharist (as here), and the unfailing, heavenly cup of paradise (*Act. Perp.* 8.3: *fiala aurea plena aqua . . . quae fiala non deficiebat*, Musurillo 116; *Act. Marian.* 6.14, Musurillo 202)—see the study of Meslin in *Epektasis* 139 ff. Other examples of the symbol in the letters occur in *Epp.* 28.1.2, 37.2.2, 76.4.2; and cf. *Ep.* 63.15.1 f. for the close link in Cyprian's thinking between Eucharist and martyrdom (prominent also in *Ep.* 58.9.2), on which see Pellegrino, "Eucaristia e martirio in San Cipriano," in *Convivium Dominicum* 133 ff. (138 ff. on *Epp.* 57 and 58).

15. *ad saeculum cui renuntiaverant reversi.* That is to say, reneged on their baptismal vows, which included a renunciation of the world: see *Ep.* 11 intro. (*ad fin.*) and *Ep.* 11 n. 7. In what follows, the bishops lump together, as Cyprian did in *Ep.* 55.17.2, the unrepentant sinner and the heretic: that they are both *outside* is of far greater significance than any distinction that may exist between them. Cf. *Ep.* 59.11.3: *nec de sacrificatis nec de haereticis viginti quinque colligi possint.*

16. *hoc in tempore pacem nos non dormientibus sed vigilantibus damus.* There is play on the word *dormientibus*. By now the verb *dormio* was established as a "Christianism," meaning "to die" (= fall asleep in the Lord); cf. *Ep.* 73.23.1: *in ecclesia dormierunt*, *Ep.* 1 n. 25, *Ep.* 21 n. 22, and see ILCV Index XII *s.v.* "dormio." Hence *dormientibus* can be a metaphysical variant for *morientibus*, the category to whom reconciliation has previously been granted. The expression was already Pauline: Cyprian's text of 1 Thess. 4.13 f. had *nolumus ignorare vos, fratres, de dormientibus . . . eos qui dormierunt in Iesu*, Fahey 503. Com-

pare the later [Cyprian] *Ep.* 4. H.3. 279.3 f.: *nam si dormientes dicimus, dormientes utique credere debemus et non mortuos, sed requiescentes interim . . . ;* ILCV 3199: *inter dormientes Zone anno VIIII.*

17. *sacerdotes qui sacrificia Dei cotidie celebramus.* Note the *daily* liturgical sacrifice—this is in fact our earliest testimony for the practice (for the Eucharistic rite regarded regularly by Cyprian in sacrificial terms, see *Ep.* 1 n. 12); *Ep.* 63.15.1, 16.2 emphasises that these are now *morning* services. Distinction can be drawn between this daily liturgical celebration and the daily reception of the Eucharist, which could be partaken privately, out of the domestic *arca.* For such private communion already in Tertullian, see e.g. *De orat.* 6.2 (interpreting *panem quotianum* in a Eucharistic sense), 19.1 ff. CCL 1.261, 267 f.; and in the tractate *De centesima: qui corpus Christi sanctum sine intermissione diei suscipis,* ML Supp. 1.63; as well as elsewhere in Cyprian, *De dom. orat.* 18 CCL 3A.101: *eucharistiam eius cotidie ad cibum salutis accipimus; De laps.* 26 CCL 3.235; and cf. *Ep.* 58.1.2: *cotidie calicem sanguinis Christi bibere* (where see n. 7). For discussion Renaud, *Eucharistie* 2 ff.; Saxer, *Vie liturgique* 46 f.; Kottje, ZfKG 82 (1971) 218 ff., with addendum by Hammerich, ZfKG 84 (1973) 93 ff.; Achelis, TU 6.4 (1891) 183 ff.; DTC 3 (1923) *s.vv.* "Communion eucharistique (fréquente)" 515 ff., esp. 517 f. (Dublanchy); and see commentary on *Ep.* 63.15 f.

For a humble terra-cotta lidded pot (16 cm. high), found in a N. African church at Belezma (NW of Batna in Algiers), apparently used as a receptacle for the reserved Eucharist, see Y.-M. Duval and Ch. Pietri, RÉAug 21 (1975) 289 ff.

18. *occultorum scrutator et cognitor cito venturus et de arcanis cordis adque abditis iudicaturus.* There has been allusion to 1 Sam. 16.7: *homo videt in faciem, Deus autem in cor* (omitted by Fahey 104 on the text here, *faciem singulorum videmus, cor scrutari . . . non possumus*) as well as to Apoc. 2.23, Fahey 540 f. (*ego sum scrutator renis et cordis*) and possibly to Dan. 13.42 (*Deus aeterne qui absconditorum es cognitor,* Vulg.). There is a close parallel in the contemporary tractate *De mort.* 17 CCL 3A.26: *Deus scrutator est renis et cordis et occultorum contemplator et cognitor.* Note the adverb *cito:* it suggests a sense not just of impending persecution but even of the impending End, the coming of Antichrist in the last days, a note which becomes explicit and strident in the following letters, *Epp.* 58, 60, and 61.

19. *obesse autem mali bonis non debent, sed magis mali a bonis adiuvari*. The second clause neatly completes the aphorism but does not seem particularly germane to the run of the present argument.

20. *non ideo martyrium facturis pax neganda est quia sunt quidem negaturi*. The understood supplement to *negaturi* may be *martyrium* (= refuse martyrdom) or, more naturally, *Christum* (or *fidem*).

21. *ne per ignorantiam nostram ille incipiat praeteriri qui habet in proelio coronari*. *Incipiat* is normally translated with its inceptive force (e.g. "lest he be the first to be passed over" [Carey]) but the expression here is merely a standard Cyprianic periphrasis for achieving a future passive subjunctive; see Bayard, *Latin* 99 f.; Schrijnen and Mohrmann 2.21 ff.

22. *qui martyrium tollit sanguine suo baptizatur*. Martyrdom seems to be linguistically assimilated, by the choice of the verb *tollo*, to the Christian's cross (e.g. Mark 8.34, Luke 9.23) and hence to Christ's cross (cf. Dölger, *Ant. und Christ.* 3 [1932] 218). Observe the notion of baptism of blood, for which Cyprian provides justifying argument in *Ep.* 73.22 and on the special qualities of which he expatiates in *Ad Fort. praef.* 4 CCL 3.185 (*baptisma in gratia maius, in potestate sublimius, in honore praetiosius, baptisma in quo angeli baptizant* etc.). For a full account of the notion in the early Church, Dölger, *Ant. und Christ.* 2 (1930) 117 ff.; also H. Windisch, *Taufe und Sünde* 414 ff., 481 ff. (for a collection of the oldest texts); Hummel 108 ff.; Dodwell, *Diss. Cyp.* xiii, also provides a lengthy treatment of the theme *de secundo martyrii baptismo* (pp. 107 ff. in 1682 ed. of Pearson and Fell).

23. *accepturo maiorem de Domini dignatione mercedem*. That is, instead of merely *pax* and *communicatio* in the Church, he will receive immediate reception into paradise, a crown from Christ's own hand, a place on the judgment seat, etc., all the powers and prerogatives of the hallowed martyrs.

24. Matt. 10.19 f., Fahey 294 ff., one of Cyprian's most favoured texts. For discussion, *Ep.* 10 n. 19. Cyprian here links such promised inspiration to the reception of the Eucharist (*recepta eucharistia*), which will serve *verbally* to assist a Christian on trial before the magistrate's tribunal. There are closely parallel magical amulets and formulae designed to inspire their pagan users, similarly, before the

courts, e.g. Preisendanz, *Pap. Graec. Mag.*[2] 4.2162 (*en dikastēriō hōsau-tōs*).

25. *in confessione nominis constitutis*. There is an echo here of *Ep.* 21.1.1: *qui in confessione Christi sunt constituti* (Celerinus), where see n. 7 for discussion.

26. *ipse loquitur et confitetur in nobis*. For this theme of *Christus in martyre*, see *Ep.* 10 intro. and n. 31. Observe, again, that there is no mention of any previous *satisfactio* on the part of the penitents; their needs for facing successfully the coming trials are given over-whelming priority. See n. 11 above.

27. *in latrones forte incurrerit*. There are other references in Cyprian to brigandage in *Epp.* 58.4.2 (in similar context), 66.6, 68.3.3; *Ad Donat.* 6 CCL 3A.6; *Ad Demet.* 11 *op. cit.* 41. For a useful collection of evidence on this subject (an endemic plague in the Ro-man Empire), Rostovtzeff, *Social and Economic Hist.*[2] 738 f., and see further MacMullen, *Enemies* 255 ff.; Flam-Zuckermann, *Latomus* 29 (1970) 451 ff. (with extensive bibliography). The bishops can assume, without any hint of criticism, that Christians will take to flight before the onslaught of persecution: in *Ep.* 58.4.1 f., in a hortatory context, Cyprian can assume as natural a mass scattering of the flock, put to flight by oncoming persecution. That is a course of action about which Cyprian now no longer feels defensive: see e.g. *Epp.* 5 n. 2, 7 n. 3, 8 n. 4, etc. In what follows (abandoning home, family, and chil-dren) there is probably a passing allusion to Luke 18.29, which Cyp-rian cites verbatim in *Ep.* 58.2.3 and elsewhere in similar contexts, Fahey 360; cf. Matt. 19.27, Fahey 318 f.

28. *quod contribulatum est non consolati estis*. To judge from the evidence of the mss here and in *Ep.* 68.4.1 (where the citation is repeated), there is an outside chance that Cyprian's text may have had instead of *consolati estis* the reading *consolidastis* ("you have mended").

29. Ezek. 34.3–6, 10, 16, Fahey 231 f. (At Ezek. 34.5 Hartel's text reads *facta sunt in comestura; facta* appears to be a misprint for *factae*, which is the reading of the mss. I owe this information to the kindness of Dr. G. F. Diercks.)

30. *quo duritiam magis humanae crudelitatis quam divinae et pater-nae pietatis opponimus*. An abstract noun appears to have dropped out

after *pietatis*. Hartel suggests *lenitatem* (which I translate), comparing *Ep*. 68.1.1: *divinae pietatis et lenitatis paternae solacia;* to which add *Ep*. 60.3.1: *magis durus philosophiae pravitate quam sophiae dominicae lenitate pacificus*. There is one ms (Parisinus 1650) which does read *clementiam* after *pietatis*.

31. *placuit nobis sancto spiritu suggerente et Domino per visiones multas et manifestas admonente*. This is the only case where Cyprian (and his colleagues) seem to invoke the guidance of the Holy Spirit specifically in church Councils, a valued weapon here when a previous conciliar regulation is being profoundly modified. But even so, appearances are perhaps a little misleading: the words focus on the divinely-inspired nature of the prompting signs and warning visions that led to this particular conciliar decision rather than on the guiding presence of the Holy Spirit that brooded over the conciliar meeting as a whole. The first explicit reference to the latter notion seems to come early in the next century with the Council of Arles (Letter to Silvester: *praesente spiritu sancto et angelis eius*. See *Ep*. 1 n. 23 for further details). But Acts 15.28, *visum est Sancto Spiritui et nobis*, when linked specifically to the church hierarchy, is not too far distant from the present passage (cf. Fahey 417 f.). For the warning signs see n. 9 above.

32. *quod credimus vobis quoque paternae misericordiae contemplatione placiturum*. Cyprian and his colleagues, acutely convinced that a desperate trial is about to be staged for Christians, have moved quite unilaterally, even though they have decreed a major change in ecclesiastical discipline. They counsel their Roman brethren (*vobis* = Cornelius and his church ?) to follow suit, but the suggestion is a passing one and made but lightly; and the Romans are expected to be moved by compassion rather than compelled by necessity themselves. There is no sense that the Roman brethren, whom they address, are confronting the same overwhelmingly urgent crisis as they are themselves in Africa. We will have to conclude that at the time the impending *agon* was perceived to be a local, African one. But despite the independent status of the African Church, as exemplified by these procedures, the divine prescription for church unity also required that attempts be made to win consensus abroad for such decisions made at home. In this the African bishops were eventually successful: *Ep*. 68.5.1: *illi [Cornelius et Lucius] enim pleni spiritu Domini et in glorioso martyrio constituti dandam esse lapsis pacem censuerunt et paen-*

*itentia acta fructum communicationis et pacis negandum non esse litteris suis
signaverunt.* From this description, however (*in glorioso martyrio constitutis*), it looks as if the Roman bishops adopted this African policy
themselves only *after* the troubles in Rome had actually broken out
(there, an occurrence without forewarnings: *illic repentina persecutio
. . . saecularis potestas subito proruperit, Ep.* 61.3.1).

33. *si de collegis aliquis extiterit . . . reddet ille rationem in die iudicii
Domino vel importunae censurae vel inhumanae duritiae suae.* See *Ep.* 55
n. 95 for this Cyprianic outlet for episcopal disagreement within the
overall framework of church unity. Any dissentient *collega* will have
to be *African*, where their flocks are now endangered by the oncoming encounter (*urguente certamine*). These words can hardly be intended as a minatory remark to Cornelius (the addressee) and his
colleagues.

34. *nos quod fidei et caritati et sollicitudini congruebat, quae erant in
conscientia nostra protulimus.* There is a close parallel in *Ep.* 11.7.1 after
Cyprian has reported two visions and their messages: *dissimulare haec
singula et apud conscientiam meam solus occultare non debui, quibus unusquisque nostrum et instrui et regi possit.* Duty and charity have now been
similarly done by divulging the guiding instructions of these warning
visions. *Protulimus* seems to refer rather to the occasion of the African
Council (when the signs will have been reported more fully, cf. *Ep.*
11) than to the rather oblique presentation of them in this letter. (Pontius can report at length a Cyprianic vision in direct speech, with even
lengthier interpretative comment, in *Vit. Cyp.* 12 f. H.ciii ff.; no
doubt Pontius had heard the vision described in such detail by Cyprian himself.)

LETTER 58

Contents: Cyprian has had to cancel his projected trip to Thibaris
given the present critical state of affairs. God has warned that persecution, more savage than ever before, is coming. It is the persecution that was foretold as coming in the last days; it will put
Christians to the test, bringing to them by their deaths life everlasting, for Christ has promised to confess before His Father those who

confess Him. Even if a man dies alone in flight, Christ will still be with him and will still have witnessed his martyrdom. Models for the conduct now required of Christians are to be found in the Old Testament (Abel, Abraham, the three youths in the fiery furnace, Daniel, the Maccabees), as well as the Holy Innocents and Christ Himself in the New. God, who made them His sons, watches over the spectacle of their encounter; they must now put on their spiritual armour in readiness to win the resplendent glories and rewards He has promised to the victors.

Date and circumstances: This letter must be closely associated with *Ep.* 57: the divine signs of coming persecution mentioned there (§§2.1, 5.1, 5.2) are explicitly repeated here (§1.2). That places this letter, along with *Ep.* 57, in the vicinity of May 253 (see *Ep.* 57 intro.). It cannot be determined with certainty, however, whether this letter should be placed before or after the Council meeting which *Ep.* 57 reports and, thus, the decision of that Council to admit penitent lapsed to communion. In §8.2 Cyprian exhorts: *armentur et lapsi ut et lapsus recipiat quod amisit.* In view of *Ep.* 57.2.2 it is most probable that the arming which he here envisages for the lapsed is the *tutela* of the Eucharist: [sc. *lapsos] protectione sanguinis et corporis Christi muniamus . . . munimento dominicae saturitatis armemus (Ep.* 57.2.2). In all likelihood, therefore, *Ep.* 58 should be placed after the Council of 253 had passed its resolution to relax penitential discipline and to fortify the lapsed with the armour of the Eucharist. See further Duquenne, *Chronologie* 38 ff.; Nelke, *Chronologie* 81 f.

The letter allows us a rare glimpse of Cyprian's activities in communities outside Carthage. *Ep.* 48.1 lets us see, by chance, an actual visit, that time to the church at Hadrumetum. We can only speculate on the extent to which Cyprian was pressed with invitations to come and preach (as he here reports in §1.1) and how often in fact he accepted them and made such journeys over the African countryside. Many of Cyprian's "treatises" may indeed owe their origins and present form to such exhortatory missions and pulpit performances delivered around such towns of Proconsular Africa.

As with *Ep.* 57, though the coming persecution is acutely feared, it is still an apprehension of the immediate future and not yet an actuality (e.g. §§1.2, 2.2, 7.1). Nor is there any further evidence provided for the grounds of those fears and apprehensions besides the divine warnings §1.2 (see *Ep.* 57 intro.). What is additional, however, to *Ep.* 57 is the shrill note of millenarian prediction: the world is dying (*occasum saeculi* §1.2; *de saeculo iam moriente* §2.1), the Antichrist is coming on the rampage (§§1.2, 7.1) and, therefore, Christian deaths and tribulations must inevitably occur (§2.1 f.; *occidi necesse est* §4.1). The letter thus provides a valuable gloss on the thinking that lay behind the conciliar decisions reported in *Ep.* 57.

It is noticeable how frequently the biblical citations exploited in this letter reappear in the martyrdom protreptic, the *Ad Fortunatum*—12 out of the 15 direct quotations of this letter are repeated there. It is indeed quite probable that the *Ad Fortunatum* is a contemporary production (its talk of Antichrist in *praef.* 1 f. being far more characteristic of this period); cf. G. Alföldy, *Historia* 22 (1973) 486 f. n. 39; Koch, *Cyp. Unter.* 149 ff. (for lengthy discussion).

The section of the letter from §6.3 *ad fin.* to the end of §8.1 is found in the famous Merovingian Lectionary of Luxeuil: see Wilmart, *Rev. bénéd.* 28 (1911) 228 ff. G. Lomiento has devoted a lengthy study to this letter (*Annali della Facoltà . . . dell'Università di Bari* 3 [1962] 7–39).

Besides the usual run of renderings of this letter into English, there are two early versions, one by J. Scory, *Certein Workes of Blessed Cypriane the Martyr* (Zurich? 1556, no pagination), and the other by J. Copinger, *Mnemosynum; or Memoriall to the Afflicted Catholicks in Irelande . . . with an Epistle of S. Cyprian Written unto the Thibaritans* (Toulouse 1606) 313 ff.

1. *Cyprianus plebi Thibari consistenti s.* For this greeting cf. *Ep.* 1: *Cyprianus presbyteris et diaconibus et plebi Furnis consistentibus s.* Plebs, by Cyprianic usage, ought to refer to laity only (see *Ep.* 1 n. 1); we are left to speculate why the bishop and his clergy at Thibaris are not included in this address. As likely as not, a separate (lost) message was added for them; it could well have accompanied a copy of the minutes of the Council of 253 (cf. *Ep.* 57), sent at the same time. For there is, three years later, in September 256, a relatively senior bishop of Thibaris, Vincentius, who gave his *sententia* in 37th place (*Sent. episc.* LXXXVII H.450), but he was not present among those who signed *Ep.* 57, a document of the Council of 253. A Vincentius

also occurs in *Ep.* 67 (in 30th place, out of 37 present). See von Soden, *Prosopographie* 259 f. (suggesting the see may have been currently vacant); Maier, *L'épiscopat* 216.

Thibaris (modern Tunisian Henchir Thibar or Hammamet) is some 117 km WSW of Carthage (being some 17 km to the NW of Thugga and lying halfway between Carthage and Thagaste). See Gascou, *Politique municipale* 174; Lepelley, *Les cités* 2.189 f.

2. Cyprian long contemplated the scene in which he, as bishop, inspired with his martyr's dying words as the Gospel promised him (cf. §5.2 below), should go forth to his death witnessed by these *plebs* whom he has led and bringing glory upon them. *Ep.* 81.1.1 ff. eloquently records those aspirations five years later: *congruat episcopum in ea civitate in qua ecclesiae dominicae praeest illic Dominum confiteri et plebem universam praepositi praesentis confessione clarificare.* Cyprian's tone in this letter suggests he is now preparing himself for such a heroic role, such a *nobile letum.*

3. *has interim pro me ad vos vicarias litteras misi.* For this literary motif of *vicariae litterae,* cf. *Ep.* 6.1.2 (with n. 6 there).

4. *ad vestram quoque conscientiam admonitionis nostrae sollicitudinem perferre debemus.* See *Ep.* 57 n. 34 on Cyprian's concept of the duty to disseminate publicly divine monitions vouchsafed privately. The phrase *admonitionis nostrae sollicitudinem* is a little opaque: can it rather mean "the anxious concern which these warnings have caused us to feel"? Note what would appear here to be Cyprian's personal involvement as a recipient of these admonitions (cf. *Ep.* 57 n. 9).

5. *scire enim debetis et pro certo credere ac tenere pressurae diem super caput esse coepisse et occasum saeculi atque antichristi tempus adpropinquasse.* The triple set of verbs with which Cyprian announces his proposition is arrestingly emphatic: Cyprian is making it clear that his apocalyptic talk is not just emotive rhetoric—he is convinced of the *reality* of the decay and, therefore, of the coming end of the world. And that entails, in turn, persecution as one of the events foretold of the last days (§§2.1 below). Cyprian's contemporary treatises, the *Ad Demetrianum* and the *De mortalitate,* provide invaluable background to this viewpoint (note esp. *Ad Demet.* 3 f., 5, 23; *De mort.* 15, 25), which also finds expression in the (also contemporary?) *Ad Fortunatum praef.* 1 f., where he is even prepared to declare *sex milia annorum iam paene conplentur* (cf. Apoc. 17.9 ff.). See also *De unit.* 16 CCL 3.261, where

the increase in schism and heresy, quarrelling and discord is used to deduce that the forecast decline of the world is now more than ever approaching. The plague, wars, false prophets (Novatian etc.), and natural disasters have all helped to form this millenarian perception of the world, and the focus has been further sharpened by the visions and divine monitions which have warned of coming and ferocious persecution (cf. n. 6 below); that has served to fix Cyprian's developing view of the world about him, giving it the authority of divine warrant (cf. *Ep.* 57 intro.). Having formed that picture, he is now prepared to read off consequences of it, one of which is simply this cancellation of the projected trip to Thibaris.

For parallels to Cyprian's view of the senescence of the world (a commonplace in the classical tradition), see Spanneut, *Stoïcisme*[2] 413 f.; and for the evidence of Cyprian's contemporaries, Alföldy, GRBS 15 (1974) 89 ff., and *idem, Historia* 22 (1973) 479 ff.; and on the millenarian outlook see Daniélou, VC 2 (1948) 1 ff. There is a full collection of references to Antichrist in Cyprian assembled by d'Alès, *Théologie . . . Cyprien* 77 ff., and on the concept see more generally RAC 1 (1950) *s.v.* "Antichrist" 450 ff. (E. Lohmeyer).

6. *gravior nunc et ferocior pugna imminet.* A sentiment repeated in *Ep.* 57.5.2: *pugnam . . . graviorem multo et acriorem venire,* and there vouched for on divine authority (*hoc nobis divinitus frequenter ostendi*). Cf. *De mort.* 25 CCL 3A.30: *corruente iam mundo et malorum infestantium turbinibus obsesso, ut qui cernimus coepisse iam gravia et scimus imminere graviora. . . .*

7. *se cotidie calicem sanguinis Christi bibere.* See *Ep.* 7 n. 17 on daily Eucharistic services. The use of the *cup* here suggests that Cyprian is not thinking of the daily reception of Communion from the privately reserved sacrament; that is normally referred to in terms of *panis* or *corpus;* see e.g. Tert. *Ad uxor.* 2.5.2 CCL 1.389: *non sciet maritus, quid secreto ante omnem cibum gustes? Et si sciverit panem, non illum credet esse, qui dicitur?;* Tert. *De idol.* 7.3 CCL 2.1106: *isti quotidie corpus eius lacessunt;* and see further Saxer, *Vie liturgique* 47, and Renaud, *Eucharistie* 3 f.

8. *ut possint et ipsi propter Christum sanguinem fundere. Ep.* 63.15.2 is close in argument: *quomodo autem possumus propter Christum sanguinem fundere qui sanguinem Christi erubescimus bibere?;* and cf. *Ep.* 57.2.2 *ad fin.*

9. 1 John 2.6 (Fahey 527 f.) and Rom. 8.16 f. (Fahey 430).

10. John 16.2 ff., Fahey 397.

11. *iusto iustorum praecedentium exemplo*. Cyprian is thinking of the prophets and holy men of Old Testament times who were seen, in their sufferings, as prefiguring the Christian martyrs. This theme is elaborated in §§5.1 ff. below and has appeared already in *Ep.* 6.2.1 (*in origine statim prima Abel iustus occiditur et exinde iusti quique et prophetae et apostoli missi*), where see n. 16 for parallels and literature. (Only one ms in fact records the reading *iusto:* it ought in all likelihood to be excised, having arisen by dittography from the following *iustorum*.)

12. 1 Pet. 4.12 ff., Fahey 523.

13. Luke 18.29 f. (Fahey 360) followed by Luke 6.22 f. (Fahey 341 f.).

14. *martyribus patent caeli*. Can Cyprian be alluding to Acts 7.55, the dying words of Stephen, the Christian protomartyr (n. 29 below): *ecce video caelos apertos* (Vulg.)? And see *Ep.* 6 n. 14, *Ep.* 55 n. 90 for the immediate reception of the martyr into paradise, which is implied here.

15. An allusion to John 5.22, Fahey 381.

16. An allusion to Matt. 10.32 f., Fahey 300 f. (who, however, overlooks this instance).

17. *nec tractantes episcopos audiat*. See *Ep.* 55 n. 62 on the phrase *episcopo tractante*, and Saxer, *Vie liturgique* 222 f. (suggesting that sermons or homilies are being alluded to here). Observe Cyprian's assumption that there will be a mass scattering of the flock, in flight before the onset of persecution; cf. *Ep.* 57.4.3, where see n. 27.

18. *quibus occidere non licet sed occidi necesse est*. The first clause refers to the injunctions against homicide which Christians obey; it is not the statement of a pacifist (see *Ep.* 39 n. 15 on Cyprian's attitude to military service). The second clause refers to the inevitability of Christian deaths that will occur in the last days (which are perceived now to be coming), e.g. Matt. 24.9: *tunc tradent vos in pressuram et interficient vos* (quoted in *Ad Fort.* 11 CCL 3.202). For the present conceit cf. Lucifer Calar., *Moriundum esse pro dei filio* 5 CCL 8.277: *dei religionis . . . in qua non occidere, sed occidi propter dei filium docemur.*

19. Allusion to 1 Cor. 3.16, Fahey 444 f.

20. Allusion to Luke 14.14, Fahey 352 (who omits this passage). Cyprian appears to telescope particular and general judgments; cf. Bévenot, *Theol. Stud.* 16 (1955) 196.

21. *sufficit ad testimonium martyrii sui testis ille qui probat martyras.* . . . Note the elaborate verbal play on *testis/martyr, testimonium/ martyrium*, on which see *Ep.* 21 n. 29, *Ep.* 37 n. 18, adding Vermeulen, *Gloria* 65.

22. On *Abel iustus* as the martyr prototype in Cyprian, see *Ep.* 6 n. 16, and Fahey 559 ff. for the figure of Abel generally in Cyprian's writings.

23. Dan. 3.16 ff., Fahey 235 f.

24. Matt. 10.19 f., Fahey 294 ff.

25. *ipse in nobis et loquitur et coronatur.* See *Ep.* 10 intro. and n. 31 on this common motif of *Christus in martyre*.

26. Dan. 14.5(4), Fahey 239.

27. *nonne magnae virtutis et fidei documenta testantur.* There may be an allusion to 2 Macc. 6.31, on which see *Ep.* 10 n. 3 and note Fahey 598 ff. on Cyprian's extended commentary devoted to the sufferings of the Maccabees in *Ad Fort.* 11 CCL 3.205 ff.

28. *quid apostoli quos Dominus elegit.* See *Ep.* 6 n. 16 on the apostles as martyrs in Cyprian (again in §10.1 below).

29. Allusion to Matt. 2.16 ff., Fahey 263 f., 604 f. Cyprian, although he speaks of the Innocents as having endured martyrdom (*martyria fecerunt*), nevertheless seems to reserve the title of first *Christian* martyr for Stephen, who is designated *primum martyrem Christi* in *De pat.* 16 CCL 3A.127.

30. *nominis christiani servum pati nolle cum passus sit prior Dominus.* I translate Bayard's emendation of *nominis* for the *hominis* which most mss read (and which Hartel prints; there is one ms [Parisinus 1658] which does indeed present the reading *nomini christiano*). For Cyprian may be playing on the servile connotations of the =*ianus* ending of the word *christianus*, picked up by the *servus–Dominus* contrast which follows. On this *-ianus* termination, see P. R. C. Weaver, JRS 54 (1964) 123 ff., and note also *Ep.* 43 n. 29 on Cyprian's surprisingly infrequent use of the word *christianus*.

31. *Filius Dei passus ut nos filios Dei faceret.* Observe the view of

redemption here, with the stress on the divine filiation it acquired for mankind. See Mersch, *Le corps mystique*[3] 2.22 ff., and Turner, *Patristic Doctrine* 96 ff., on this viewpoint.

32. John 15.18 ff., Fahey 396 f. In *Ad Fort.* 11 CCL 3.201 the same text is also quoted but with the six instances of *saeculum* replaced by *mundus*. See Orbán 191 f. n. 1, 192 n. 4 for other examples of such interchange in Cyprian's biblical text (e.g. *Ep.* 63.18.3 *lumen saeculi*, but *lumen mundi* in *De zelo* 11 CCL 3A.81). On *saeculum/mundus* variations see also von Soden, *Das lateinische N.T. in Africa* 69 ff.

33. Matt. 10.28, Fahey 298 f., followed by John 12.25 (Fahey 391 f.) and Apoc. 14.9 ff. (Fahey 547 f.).

34. Ephes. 6.12 ff., Fahey 493 f. For the image which has preceded, of God as the divine spectator at the martyr's *agon*, see *Ep.* 10 n. 30.

35. *galeam spiritalem ut muniantur aures ne audiant edicta feralia.* As the persecution is feared but not actual, *edicta feralia* is best taken as a rhetorical generalisation. Cyprian has so used the phrase (of the preceding Decian persecution) in *Ep.* 55.9.2, where see n. 42. For the preceding image of crushing the serpent, see *Ep.* 39 n. 12.

36. *muniantur oculi ne videant detestanda simulacra.* Cyprian seems to have in mind one of those large Roman helmets (with movable vizor) which were especially used by gladiators in the arena; for illustration, Daremberg-Saglio 2.2 (1896) *s.v.* "galea" 1449 (S. Reinach). For Christians' avoidance of looking directly at pagan images (abodes of demons), see *Ep.* 31 n. 35 (on *oculi qui male simulacra conspexerunt*).

37. *muniatur frons, ut signum Dei incolume servetur.* For the sign of the cross traced on the forehead, see *Test.* 2.22 CCL 3.60 (*quod in hoc signo crucis salus sit omnibus qui in frontibus notentur*); *De laps.* 2 *op. cit.* 221 (*frons cum signo Dei pura*) and *De unit.* 18 *op. cit.* 263 (*in fronte maculatus est, ea parte corporis notatus . . . ubi signantur qui Dominum promerentur*). The *locus classicus* on this ritual gesture is Tert. *De cor. mil.* 3.4 CCL 2.1043 (*quacumque nos conversatio exercet, frontem signaculo terimus*), and see the study of Dölger, *Sphragis* 171 ff. The evidence for actual crosses painted or tattooed on the forehead comes considerably later: Dölger, *Ant. und Christ.* 1 (1929) 202 ff.; Rondet, *Rech. de sc. relig.* 42 (1954) 388 ff.

38. *dexteram . . ut eucharistiae memor quae Domini corpus accipit.*

. . . The Eucharistic bread was received in the hand. This is exemplified elsewhere in Cyprian, e.g. *De pat.* 14 CCL 3A.126: *nec post gestatam eucharistiam manus gladio et cruore maculatur; De laps.* 15 CCL 3.229: *ad sanctum Domini sordidis et infectis nidore manibus accedunt;* cf. *op. cit.* 16, 22, 26 CCL 3.229, 233, 235; *De dom. or.* 18 CCL 3A.101; also *Ep.* 75.21.3. *Act. Perp.* 4.9 Musurillo 112 probably envisages the same liturgical ceremony (*et ego accepi iunctis manibus et manducavi; et universi circumstantes dixerunt: Amen*), as likewise Inscription of Pectorios 1.6 *ichthun echōn palamais* (DACL 13 [1938] s.v. "Pectorios" 2884 ff. [H. Leclercq]), and ILCV 1825 1.13: *sacramento manus porrigere gaudens;* cf. Tert. *De idol.* 7.1 ff. CCL 2.1106. Note, too, the story in the apocryphal *Acta Thomae* 51 (hands of a young murderer, when he takes Communion, shrivel: he cannot bring the Eucharist to his mouth). See further Hummel 71 n. 50; Dölger, *Ant. und Christ.* 3 (1932) 235 f., 5 (1936) 232 ff.

39. 1 Cor. 2.9. One of the very rare instances when Cyprian actually quotes from his biblical text without providing some introductory formula of identification: Fahey 442.

40. Rom. 8.18, Fahey 430 f.

41. *inextinguibili igne torqueri.* An allusion to Matt. 3.12, Fahey 266 f.

LETTER 59

Contents: Cyprian has received two letters from Cornelius. One displays full episcopal vigour, telling how Felicissimus and his henchmen were thrown out of the church in Rome, as they deserve; the other, however, reveals how by their violent threats they forced Cornelius to accept the despatch they had brought. But a bishop has to live his life resolutely facing threats like these, whether they come from Jew, Gentile, or heretic (§§1-2).

The abusive tongue of such men reveals the evil in their hearts—and God has promised to avenge insults done to His high priests, men whom He appoints and honours. Such disrespect for the appointed leaders in the Church is indeed the source of heresy (§§3-5). And to abuse by their words (as they have done) a duly-appointed bishop

who has a well-established record of service, who has been and is
being honourably singled out for persecuting attack, who has been
preserved by divine providence, to abuse such a bishop of Christ is
manifestly to do the work of the Adversary of Christ. But that is only
to be expected in these last days. We must endeavour to cure such
diseased minds, but those who reject our treatment only condemn
themselves (§§6–8).

Cornelius had already been told of the condemnation the year
before of Fortunatus and Felicissimus. That explains why Cyprian
did not consider their more recent follies (the appointment of Fortunatus as pseudo bishop) an item of urgent news—just as he has not
mentioned the appointment of a Novatianist pseudo bishop in Carthage. Besides, Cornelius had for his guidance a compendium (recently sent) listing the names of all the African bishops who were
sound in faith. And in fact Felicianus was to deliver a despatch which
included information about Fortunatus, but he had been delayed.
The despatch outlined the character of the five excommunicated
bishops who supported Fortunatus (not 25, as they falsely claim),
§§9–11.

Cyprian cannot pass by in silence their offensive behaviour that
dates from the very first day of the persecution—to continue to be in
communion with apostates and to obstruct their repentance. And
they have persisted in this grievous error despite letters from Cyprian
during the persecution and despite the resolution and warnings of the
subsequent Council. In addition, they now heap abuse upon the bishops, confessors, and virgins of the Church—to their own utter ruin.
But even that has proved not enough for them: they have appointed
a pseudo bishop of their own, and this faithless crew has now even
sailed off with their cargo of lies to the very source of episcopal unity,
to the Roman Church whose faith was proclaimed by the apostle
Paul. But their case has already been heard in a full African Council,
where they were in fact outnumbered by the bishops, presbyters,
and deacons in attendance. And there they were solemnly condemned. It would be, therefore, improper to hear their case again
(§§12–15.1).

Since the appointment of that pseudo bishop, many of their followers have woken up to their deception and seek readmission to the
Church. Some of these are so grossly sinful that they would infect

the flock—and the brethren unyieldingly oppose their entry; in the case of other evildoers Cyprian has to wring concessions from his people to agree to their admission. But the enormities committed by the group now in Rome are beyond description. Nevertheless, so eager is Cyprian to reunite his brethren that he runs the risk himself of offending by not being overnice in his examination even of sins committed against God. Repentance and atonement can win such favours, but threats and menaces never. To yield to them is to surrender to the forces of paganism and to provide Novatian with rich material for his abusive attacks. May they return to sanity and repent, but if they persist, no bishop can be found so feeble and weak that he would not stoutly resist them (§§15.1–18).

Out of mutual charity Cornelius would ordinarily read this letter before his clergy and people as a matter of course, but even so, Cyprian specifically asks now that this be done so as to remove all stain of heretical calumny among the faithful there. And for the future the evil company of such heretics must be shunned, utterly (§§19–20).

Date and Circumstances: It is beyond doubt that this letter belongs to the year 252, for in §9.1 Cyprian refers to a letter written *priore anno,* which was in fact sent in 251 (cf. §§15.1, 10.2 for similar references). And within this year 252, the letter must be dated (considerably) later than May 15: the Council meeting (now over), which had been held *Idibus Mais quae proxime fuerunt,* is mentioned in §10.1. How much later in the year 252 can be conjectured from the following incidents which have occurred meantime:

(1) Privatus' request to have his case heard was rejected by the Council at its session, §10.1 (in mid-May).

(2) There followed a propaganda campaign which preceded the election of the rival Carthaginian bishop, the laxist Fortunatus (§11.1).

(3) After Fortunatus had been consecrated, the delegation headed by Felicissimus was despatched over to Rome to announce the news (§§1.1 ff., 14.2).

(4) Felicissimus' party was first thrown out by Cornelius but subsequently (it seems) they forced their way in before him with

noisy intimidation (§§1 and 2). They have been active in purveying their poisons in Rome (§§ 11.1, 19).

(5) Whereupon Cornelius sent to Cyprian his two letters on these two incidents (§§1.1, 2.1).

(6) Meantime, the reaction to the extreme step of appointing a *pseudoepiscopus* has been felt in Carthage. Many are returning, realising their deception (§15.1), and Cyprian has been holding public sessions, adjudicating the terms of readmission in the individual cases (§§15.2 ff.).

(7) And now Cyprian composes this lengthy reply to Cornelius' two letters.

We must be well on into the summer of 252 (but not before the sailing season is over, §9.4). The letter should thus, in all probability, come in sequence *after Epp.* 55, 65, and 64 (and *before Epp.* 56–58, 60–61). Further discussion in Nelke, *Chronologie* 78 ff.; Ritschl, *De epist.* 25, 28; Duquenne, *Chronologie* 20, 33 f.; Turner, *Studies* 126.

Given the fact that Cyprian (somewhat heatedly) rehearses events of the past, both recent and more remote in time, the letter becomes an invaluable document for our understanding of church life at this time. In particular, features of the landscape within the Christian communities of Carthage come much more clearly into focus. The laxist group, in the face of the condemnation of its leaders by the Council of 251 (*Ep.* 45.4.1 f.), has now hardened into a formally schismatic church with its own bishop, having (apparently) fused forces with the heretic Privatus, another bishop of Privatus' creation, and three excommunicated lapsed bishops (§§10 and 11). It sounds to be an ominous challenge, but Cyprian is scornful of the exaggerated numbers of their following (the events in Rome, however, showed, if nothing else, that the movement could not altogether be dismissed so summarily); and Cyprian emphasises (in Apologia see n. 80) the extent to which he is conciliatory towards and accommodating with their now disenchanted followers (though it clearly could be an intimidating ordeal to appear before Cyprian and his community as they considered their cases in public session, §§15.2 ff.). Two years later the movement is still stirring up irksome opposition against Cyprian (*Ep.* 66). But there is now not only a laxist *pseudoepiscopus:* there is a rigorist, Novatianist *pseudoepiscopus* as well in Carthage (§9.2). The presence of three rival bishops within the one city could give us no more powerful indication of the depths now reached in the cleavages over the penitential issue. It is no longer surprising that the African Council the following year was prepared to consider, and to agree upon, a major modification of its penitential regulations (*Ep.* 57).

When we are told of the large African Council which had condemned Privatus in the previous decade (§10.1), we also see (a rare view) previous close contacts between the sees of Carthage and Rome (*Fabiani et Donati litteris . . . notatum:* see n. 48 below), a tradition which Cyprian and Cornelius have obviously inherited. §9.4 discloses the presence of a bishop Perseus and an acolyte Felicianus whom Cornelius has sent on business over to Carthage; conversely, §9.3 discloses an address list of the sound African bishops which Cyprian has sent over to Rome and a (lost) despatch on items judged deserving of being drawn to Cornelius' attention (= some items considered at the Council meeting of 252?; cf. n. 45). It was only to be expected, therefore, that Fortunatus should promptly seek to win the approval of Cornelius after his election (§§1.1 ff., 14.2); Cornelius and Novatian had both made the same move in reverse, after their (disputed) elections (*Epp.* 44 f.).

In the past Cyprian had suffered from the contumely of having his character and actions grossly misrepresented before these brethren in Rome (see *Epp.* 8, 20, 27). Now, he feels, it is happening all over again. Felicissimus and his party have been allowed to sow their insidious poisons (the mixed metaphors are Cyprian's, §19) among the Roman congregation (cf. §11.1), and it is all because Cornelius has been deficient in episcopal *vigor, censura, auctoritas* (cf. n. 2 below and note especially §18.3). And he is alarmed at the possibility that their case (already solemnly condemned) may even be opened for further hearing elsewhere (§§14.2 f.). Cyprian is hotly indignant, and jealous for his authority, his status, and his reputation. But he has to hold that heat and indignation under some restraint, even though to have countenanced Fortunatus' envoys (whether from pusillanimity, if not treachery) is tantamount to impugning his own episcopal standing. While wishing to make his own feelings plainly and vigorously understood (e.g. §6), he cannot afford to offend Cornelius too deeply nor can he pen his remarks about Cornelius' part too sharply; for he wants Cornelius to give this letter a public reading in order to clear his name and standing before the assembled clergy and laity of Rome (§19). His imputations will have to be oblique. And he still has to meet the charge that he failed himself adequately to forewarn Cornelius in time of the delegation coming from Fortunatus (§§9.1 ff). The result is a diplomatic tour de force. We are introduced to some lengthy sermonising on the duties and *disciplina* expected of a bishop, on calumny, on the dignity and authority of a bishop, on the sources of heresy, on enduring insult and abuse, on avoiding evil company; these wrap up Cyprian's spirited apologia of his own episcopal record (a fine Roman outburst) and in particular of his humanitarian dealings with repentant schismatics, his vigorous attack on his opponents, Fortunatus' *factio*, and their poisonous teachings, and his own somewhat embarrassed defence for judging the affair of Fortunatus not to rank among *magna aut metuenda*. Cornelius is largely left to make his own conclusions from the sermonising about his own episcopal role, and the sting is somewhat drawn from those (pointed) conclusions by a passage of notable flattery on the great traditions of the see of Rome which Cornelius now occupies (§14.1). Above all, the bias of the letter shows that Cyprian is particularly perturbed by an impression he has received from Cornelius' behaviour and his letters, and from his informants. Cornelius had a reputation for being generously (some would say, overgenerously) conciliatory (witness the cases of Trofimus, *Ep.* 55.11.1 f., and the Novatianising confessors, *Ep.* 49, and compare the rumours reported in *Ep.* 55.10.2). To Cyprian there now appears to be a distinct risk that Cornelius *pacificus* (cf. *Ep.* 60 n. 5) may be tempted mistakenly to extend that same peacemaking spirit towards Fortunatus and Felicissimus. He needs, therefore, to establish in no uncertain terms the miserable and disreputable character of their followers and supporters (§§1.2, 9.3 ff., 12.2, 13.1, 14.1, 15.3, 16.1 f., etc.), the heretical nature of their erroneous teachings (§§13.1—15.4), and the solemn and weighty episcopal condemnation that has already come down so heavily against them (§§1.1, 9.1, 14.2, 15.1).

We do not know the sequel; the next communications we have between Cyprian and Cornelius belong to the following year (in all probability): *Ep.* 57 (a conciliar letter written in the face, it was feared, of coming persecution) and *Ep.* 60 (generously congratulating Cornelius on his courageous confession). We should conclude that

the suspicions and misunderstandings between Cyprian and Cornelius were successfully eased by this correspondence, but we are left
ourselves with the distinct suspicion that relations must nevertheless
have been still warily cautious, if not uncomfortably prickly, after
such an episode.

(The letter contains an important but incidental remark about
popular sacrifices ordered by an edict: see n. 31 below and Introduction to this volume on persecution under Gallus.)

1. There is a Carthaginian Saturus (variant reading, Satyrus)
who was appointed lector in 250 (*Epp.* 29.1.2, 32.1.2, 35.1.1; see *Ep.*
29 n. 10). If we are here dealing with the same young man (and we
may not be), then he has now been advanced, two years later, to the
next-but-one clerical grade of acolyte (if exorcist has been firmly established as a *regular* clerical post by this date: see *Ep.* 23 n. 6); he has
been over to Rome, from which he now returns (cf. his mission to
Rome in 250, *Ep.* 35.1.1). It is feasible that he may have accompanied
the Roman acolyte Felicianus, so that he might bring back a reply
from Rome (§9.4); as Felicianus brought over to Cornelius a letter
condemning the activities of Fortunatus and Felicissimus, so Saturus
now brings back a reply echoing that condemnation. Cyprian might
also use such a messenger as a source for general information on affairs abroad (cf. n. 80). On the duties of acolytes, see *Ep.* 7 n. 13.

2. *non tantum mea sed et plurimorum coepiscoporum sententia condemnatum*. For Cyprian's initial condemnation of Felicissimus (via his
"ecclesiastical commission"), see *Epp.* 41 and 42 with *Ep.* 41 nn. 4 and
11; for confirmation of that sentence by the subsequent African
Council of 251 (referred to here as occurring *iam pridem*), see *Ep.*
45.4.1 (with n. 30 *ad loc.*), and cf. §9.1 below. On the number of bishops involved (*plurimi*) cf. *Ep.* 55 n. 20.

Colson, *Épiscopat* 96, wishes to discover in Felicissimus' voyage
to Rome proof that in the churches of the third century it was possible
to lodge an appeal "à Rome, à l'évêque de Rome, après jugement
rendu par l'évêque local." But to plead for his own reinstatement does
appear to have been the prime object of Felicissimus' voyage (cf. n.
6 below).

Cyprian has lost no time before sounding one of the dominant
refrains of this epistle: the paramount importance of upholding *sacer-*

dotalis censura, episcopatus vigor, sacerdotalis auctoritas, ecclesiastica disciplina; cf. §§2.2, 3.1, 4.1 ff., 5.1, 9.2, 14.2, 18.1, 18.3, etc. There is a good discussion of *vigor* in Cyprian by Daniélou, *Origins of Latin Christianity* [Eng. trans.] 440 ff.

3. *schismatis et discidii auctor.* Whatever proliferation of divisions may have followed in Carthage, Felicissimus still retained the dubious title of the standard-bearer of rebellion there (*signifer seditionis*, §9.1). His (laxist) break was in clear advance of the Novatianists.

4. *pecuniae commissae sibi fraudator.* For the possibility that Felicissimus was a deacon of Cyprian's before he was made one of Novatus, see *Epp.* 52 n. 15, 41 n. 4; deacons were especially involved in handling church finances entrusted to their care. And on this particular charge of abusing monies held in sacred trust, see *Ep.* 50 nn. 5 and 6 (on Nicostratus). In §12.2 below, Cyprian generalises on the laxists' *fraudibus ecclesiae;* he is not thinking, therefore, of *commercial* embezzlement, and the phrase lends mild support to the notion that Felicissimus was alleged to have purloined *church* funds (qua deacon?).

5. *stuprator virginum . . . matrimoniorum multorum populator atque corruptor.* Splendidly polemical phrases, but how far they reflect unembroidered truth is quite another matter. In *Ep.* 41.2.1 Felicissimus was facing the (yet unheard) charge of adultery (*adulterii . . . crimen*). Compare the remarks in *Ep.* 52 n. 19 on Novatus' alleged enormities, and *Ep.* 55 n. 120 on the iniquities of Novatian's followers. There are further general remarks about the laxists' *adulteria* in §§12.2, 14.1, 15.3 below.

6. *si litteras quas adtulerant non accepisses, publice eas recitarent.* This despatch contained news of Fortunatus' appointment as (schismatic) bishop of Carthage (§§9 f., 14.2 below); no doubt it justified that appointment (Cyprian had forfeited his post by his grossly vicious behaviour; see next n.) and requested Cornelius' recognition of Fortunatus; see Harnack, *Über verlorene Briefe* 9 f. Recognition would, of course, entail repudiation of the condemnation passed by the African Council of 251; Cyprian argues strongly against any such review, above all at another court (§§14.2 f., cf. 2.5).

Cyprian had resisted (he had declared) such rough and rowdy stand-over tactics in dealing with Novatianist opponents of Cornelius in Carthage (*Ep.* 44.2.1) and he had refused to read out the defamatory letters they had brought (*Ep.* 45.2.1 f.). Apparently these delegates of Fortunatus had noisily forced their way in at some religious *statio* or *conventus* in Rome, as had the Novatianists at Carthage; hence they could threaten a *public* reading (*publice*) of their missive. In fact, however, like Cornelius here, Cyprian did not actually refuse to *receive* the Novatianists' letters (*Epp.* 44.1.1, 45.2.1 f.), but Cornelius' acceptance of Fortunatus' letter Cyprian is now prepared to construe as an act of episcopal pusillanimity, if not treachery.

Cornelius' lost *addendum*, which reported these events, contained the complaint that he had not been forewarned on such a matter of importance; hence Cyprian's rejoinder in §9: sufficient warning had already been given, as warranted by the matter, and more was in fact on its way. Cornelius may even have gone so far as to hint that it was Cyprian's unpopularity and unseasonable severity which had driven these men into rebellion; hence his defence in §15 on their exaggerated numbers and his own accommodating discipline (cf. n. 80 below).

7. *multa turpia ac probrosa et ore suo digna proferrent.* That is to say, slanderous charges against Cyprian himself. In *Ep.* 66.7.1, two years later, the smear campaign continued unabated, with calumnies in circulation which are characterised (by Cyprian) as being *incesta*, *impia*, and *nefanda*. It was essential so to blacken the reputation of Cyprian if the election of a replacement bishop was to win recognition as legitimate. For many, to make such a replacement had proved the last straw, inducing their return to Cyprian (§15.1 below).

8. *nam et gentiles et Iudaei minantur.* Cf. §2.4 below: *neque enim solas Gentilium vel Iudaeorum minas cogitare debemus;* Frend, JTS 21 (1970) 95; *Stud. patr.* 10 (1970) 296; and *Camb. Hist. Africa* 2 (1978) 460 dubiously concludes from these very standard and general remarks that Carthaginian Jews have actually been threatening violence against Cyprian and his community. ("The Jews of Carthage made common cause with the pagans against the Church.") There is no real evidence to corroborate that for contemporary Carthage, but note the role in which Jews are cast in the contemporary martyrdom of Pionius at Smyrna (3.6, 4, 13 f., Musurillo 138 ff., 152 ff.), and see *Ep.* 13 n. 9; Hirschberg, *A History of the Jews in North Africa* 1.71 ff. (for earlier evidence of Jewish-Christian relations in Carthage), and

Frend, "Jews and Christians in Third Century Carthage," *Mélanges
. . . Marcel Simon* 185 ff.

9. On this list of OT predecessors in persecution, cf. *Ep.*
58.5.1 and see *Ep.* 6 n. 16. And consult Fahey 559 f. (Abel), 568 f.
(Jacob), and 570 f. (Joseph) on Cyprian's treatment of these three particular figures, here cited as victims of *fraternal* violence.

10. *domesticos inimicos futuros.* There is allusion to Matt. 10.36
(Vulg.: *et inimici hominis domestici eius*), Fahey 301.

11. *cum nobis semel moriendum sit.* Can there be an allusion to
Hebr. 9.27 (Vulg.: *et quemadmodum statutum est hominibus semel mori*)?
But see Fahey 40 f. on Cyprian's failure to quote Hebrews explicitly.

12. This triplet of citations on the ultimate fate of the presumptuous is drawn from Habak. 2.5 (Fahey 249 f.), 1 Macc. 1.62 f.
(Fahey 115 f.), and Ps. 36.35 f. (Fahey 136 f.).

13. The quotations are taken from Isa. 14.13 f., 14.15 f., and
2.12 (Fahey 191 f.). Note the appearance of Antichrist, on which see
Ep. 57 intro., *Ep.* 58 n. 5, *Ep.* 22 n. 5.

14. Matt. 12.34 f. (Fahey 304) is quoted and there is then allusion to Luke 16.19 ff. (Dives and Lazarus), Fahey 356; there is good
reason to believe that Cyprian's text here read "Eleazarus" for "Lazarus": Turner JTS 2 (1901) 600 ff. This passage from Luke figures
frequently in discussions of the nature of the soul and its relation to
the body (see Waszink on Tert. *De an.* 7); Cyprian's own (incautious?)
wording here seems to leave him liable to some notion of the corpo-
reality of the soul. Cf. *Excerpta ex Theodoto* 14.4 (ed. Casey 52): "But
from the story of Lazarus and Dives, the soul is directly shown by
its possession of bodily limbs to be a body."

15. The three quotations are 1 Cor. 6.10 (Fahey 447 f.), Matt.
5.22 (Fahey 274), and Deut. 17.12 f. (Fahey 92 f.).

16. 1 Sam. 8.7 (Fahey 104), Luke 10.16 (Fahey 346 f.), Matt.
8.4 (Fahey 290), followed by John 18.22 f. (Fahey 401).

17. The quotations come from Acts 23.4 f. (Fahey 418 f.). Observe Cyprian's reuse of many of these quotations of §4 in *Ep.* 66.3.2
f.: they form a good example of the range, variety, and types of proof-
texts which Cyprian apparently found satisfying to amass and by
which he expected his correspondents to be equally impressed in response (cf. *Ep.* 3.2.1 f.). The medley relies for conviction, insofar as

its contents may be of any relevance, on the direct link between OT *pontifex*, *iudex*, and *sacerdos*, and the NT bishop.

18. *unus in ecclesia ad tempus sacerdos et ad tempus iudex vice Christi.* This same conclusion on the sources of schism is drawn in both *Ep.* 3.3.2 and *Ep.* 66.5.1. Observe the bishop regarded as *iudex:* already the powers he exercised in excommunication (cf. *Ep.* 3 n. 4) as well as his role in penitential discipline (where he sat in judgment on alleged delicts) had been couched in the judicial terminology of *cognitio, causa, iudicium,* and *sententia.* Compare *Ep.* 72.3.2 (*arbitrium liberum*), *Sent. episc.* LXXXVII *init.* H.436 (*arbitrium proprium*), *Ep.* 66.3.2. It was an attitude which contributed to the formal judicial powers that bishops came to exercise in the next century; see Girardet, *Historia* 23 (1974) 98 ff.

19. Note the stages in the appointment of the legitimate bishop: God makes the choice (*iudicium*) which is revealed in the election by clergy and people (*populi suffragium*—on this meaning of *populus* see *Ep.* 49 n. 22 and cf. §6.1 below, *populi universi suffragium*), and which is ratified in turn by the acceptance of fellow bishops (*coepiscoporum consensum*). Cf. *Ep.* 55.8.4 for a close parallel, where see n. 35 for discussion, and see further *Epp.* 29 n. 13 and 38 n. 1 on the processes of clerical election.

20. *nemo sibi placens ac tumens.* There is probably an allusion to 2 Tim. 3.2: *erunt homines sibi placentes*, on which see *Ep.* 3 n. 18.

21. Matt. 10.29, Fahey 299 f.

22. *fidem . . . qua vivimus.* There is probably biblical allusion here, whether to Habak. 2.4 (Fahey 249), *iustus autem ex fide mea vivit*, or to a Pauline exploitation of that passage (e.g. Rom. 1.17, *iustum fide vivere*, Fahey 422 f.; cf. Gal. 3.11, Hebr. 10.38).

23. Hos. 8.4 and 9.4 (Fahey 243) plus Isa. 30.1 (Fahey 202).

24. *quando episcopus in locum defuncti substituitur, quando populi universi suffragio in pace deligitur.* After the lengthy introductory skirmishes of protest (§2), and protestation on the principle of episcopal *dignitas* and *auctoritas* (§§3 ff.), Cyprian is only now ready to come out in self-defence, but referring to himself, with somewhat heated hauteur, in the third person singular and speaking in consciously Pauline mode (2 Cor. 11.23 ff.). His first line of counterattack is to establish his credentials as the legitimate bishop of Carthage.

Cyprian was appointed to replace the deceased Donatus (§10.1 below) *in locum defuncti*. As in the case of Cornelius, it was of prime importance to establish that he had been elected *cum nemo ante se factus esset, cum . . . gradus cathedrae sacerdotalis vacaret* (*Ep.* 55.8.4, where see n. 36); that cleared the first requirement for episcopal legality. And then that appointment had been made by the congregation of Carthage electing in full participation (*populi universi*), as was possible in time of peace (*in pace*). Cyprian, of course, finds no need to refer to the divisions and disputes which accompanied that election (Pont., *Vit. Cyp.* 5 H.xcv f.), and of which the present division and dispute is a legacy (*Ep.* 43). On the date of Cyprian's appointment *in pace*, see Intro. to *Letters of Cyprian* 1 (ACW 43) 16 f. and n. 78, and cf. n. 27 below; and on the use of *populus* here, Schrijnen and Mohrmann 1.57 ff., and cf. *Ep.* 49 n. 22.

25. *quando Dei auxilio in persecutione protegitur.* Cyprian now turns to his record since his election as bishop and, with a clearly defensive touch, starts by asserting his survival under persecution as providential, highlighting it as a mark of special grace. See *Ep.* 5 n. 2 for the attacks made on Cyprian's flight under persecution; we can see them continuing to rankle Cyprian two years later, *Ep.* 66.4.1 and n. 14 *ad loc.*; and Pontius, even after Cyprian's martyrdom, still felt the need to defend this record, *Vit. Cyp.* 7 H. xcvii f. (*Domino latebram tunc iubenti paruisset*).

26. *collegis omnibus fideliter iunctus.* A characteristic touch of Cyprian's ecclesiology: the true bishop will be recognised by his fellow bishops in the harmonious college of bishops. This very letter discloses the tensions between such high-minded theory and practical reality.

27. *plebi suae in episcopatu quadriennio iam probatus.* Cyprian prudently fails to mention what loyalty and respect he has won from his *clergy. Quadriennium:* that is, for over three to four years; cf. *Ep.* 43 n. 18 (on *biennium*), *Ep.* 56 n. 8 (on *triennium*). With a composition date for this letter of summer 252 (see intro. to this letter), that still leaves Cyprian's episcopal appointment dated to the range 248/249. His highly defensive mode here, however, should at the least prevent positing his election too early on in 248; in this context Cyprian is unlikely to have chosen *quadriennium* when the more impressive *quinquennium* would have been legitimate. See further *Ep.* 66 n. 20.

28. *in quiete serviens disciplinae.* It is appropriate for the theme of this letter (see n. 2 above) that Cyprian should single out *disciplina* as the virtue characteristic of his prepersecution episcopate (if this is what he intends by *quies*). The tractate *De hab. virg.* and the contents of *Epp.* 1–4 (*if* they belong to that period) would illustrate what he is meaning. If *quies* is larger in reference (= days without active persecution), then the postpersecution period has seen his dedication to church discipline (*De unitate*) and in particular penitential discipline (*De lapsis*).

29. *in tempestate proscriptus, adplicito et adiuncto episcopatus sui nomine.* The somewhat elliptical phrasing here is fortunately explicated fully by *Ep.* 66.4.1: the notice posted up proscribing Cyprian's possessions referred to him specifically as *episcopus christianorum.* That is to say, even the devil (the source of persecution) recognized his sacred authority as bishop; for the Adversary does not waste his efforts attacking bogus bishops (see *Ep.* 60.3.2 on this reasoning). Note the parallel in Pont., *Vit. Cyp.* 7 H. xcvii: Cyprian gained the *gloria* of proscription *ut . . . etiam publice celebrata gentilium fama titularet.* For proscription of Christians under Decius, see *Ep.* 10 n. 5, *Ep.* 55 n. 112, and (on Cyprian specifically) *Ep.* 66 n. 15.

30. *dominicae dignationis testimonio honoratus.* For popular hostility against Cyprian under Decius, see *Epp.* 5 n. 11, 6 n. 32, 7 n. 3. Cyprian's implicit argument here is that such imperilling hostilities are a mark of divine predilection (*dominica dignatio*), a source of the much-coveted *tituli gloriae;* they indicate the continuing and special favour of God on his episcopate: see *Ep.* 55 nn. 38 and 112, 66 n. 15 for further explication of this theme, and Hummel 44 f. In *Ep.* 66.5.1, after a similar context of proscription and persecution, Cyprian refers to himself similarly as *homo dignatione Dei honoratus.* Pontius likewise expatiates on Cyprian's providential preservation from such perils, echoing Cyprian's wording here (*maxime cum et suffragiis saepe repetitis ad leonem postularetur*), *Vit. Cyp.* 7 H. xcvii. For parallels on "Christians to the beasts," see DACL 1 (1924) *s.vv.* "Ad Bestias" 449 ff. (H. Leclercq), Colin in *Mélanges . . . Piganiol* 3.1565 ff.

31. *his ipsis etiam diebus . . . ob sacrificia quae edicto proposito celebrare populus iubebatur clamore popularium ad leonem denuo postulatus in circo.* Very recently (*his ipsis etiam diebus*), i.e. in the summer of 252, Cyprian has been subject to renewed (*denuo*) public outcry in the Car-

thaginian circus. The occasion for this outburst of hostility (the first was under Decius in 250, see previous n.) is explained. It was because of sacrifices ordered by edict upon the populace. That must mean that Cyprian failed to be present at the ceremonies concerned and the absence of such a prominent local figure was noted with popular rage and indignation, *clamore popularium* (cf. the imperial remarks in *Act. Cyp.* 1.1 Musurillo 168: *qui Romanam religionem non colunt, debere Romanas caeremonias recogoscere;* Christians were exposed to attack when they did not participate in pagan festivals, *Apost. const.* 2.8 ed. Funk 42 ff. = Connolly 39 *[suspicamur autem et blasphemari nos a gentilibus eo quod iam non eis miscemur nec compopulamur cum eis];* the people of Lycia and Pamphylia petition Maximinus in 311–12 that "the Christians . . . be made to stop and not by any foolish new worship to transgress that which is due to the gods," ILCV 1b [Arycanda]).

We are left with two main questions: (1) what was the reason for the proclamation of the edict and (2) was the edict local or imperial in application? We can only speculate on (1), but the best, and standard, guess (it is only that) is that in this season of high summer expiatory sacrifices were called for to avert the disastrous plague which had reached the west in the previous year (Vict., *De Caes.* 30.2 [Rome]). It was a standard procedure to resort to such apotropaic religious ceremonies and sacrifices (e.g., in the face of similar epidemics, Suet., *Titus* 8.4, HA Marcus 21.6; cf. HA Gallienus 5.5; and for further evidence, Gilliam, AJP 82 [1961] 225 ff., and R. J. and M. L. Littman, AJP 94 [1973] 243 ff.). Ire against the absent Christian leader, Cyprian, would readily be fired, for the Christians were blamed by contemporary pagans for this plague (see e.g. *Ad Demet.* 2, 5 CCL 3A.35, 37). A mass gathering in the circus, with special *ludi, lectisternium, sacrificia,* etc., may have been the occasion; for such traditional ceremonies against plague, Gagé, *Apollon Romain* 69 ff., 148. (The dialogue in *Acta Acacii* 2.1 f. Knopf-Krüger 58 is relevant for this mentality: "Marcianus said: . . . Despise invisible things and acknowledge instead the gods whom you can see. Acacius replied: Who are those gods to whom you bid me offer sacrifice? Marcianus said: Apollo our Saviour, the averter of famine and pestilence, through whom the whole world is saved and ruled.")

As for the second question, though many deduce from this passage that there had been issued a universal, *imperial* edict (e.g. Monceaux, *Histoire* 2.223; Lietzmann, *History* 2.170; Grégoire *et al.*, *Les persécutions* 151 f.; Sordi, *Il cristianesimo* 284), the evidence of this letter itself is decidedly against such a deduction. There is no suggestion here or elsewhere in this epistle that Cyprian understands that the *Roman* Christians (whom he addresses) are currently being troubled in a similar way. There is no word to them of fraternal sympathy and unity in suffering; the Roman Church is considered to be flourishing (see n. 90 below) and able to adhere to its normal procedures; this very letter, Cyprian confidently anticipates, is to be read out before the clergy and laity of Rome gathered in full assembly (§19). They are not under persecuting siege. So far as these hints go, Roman Christians, from Cyprian's perception, appear to be free of trouble. And Cyprian himself in Africa shows no sense of an urgent, general persecution deflecting his concentration away from his own ecclesiastical troubles; indeed, he can talk in §18.2 of the heretics making the peace worse than a persecution (see further n. 87 *ad loc.* and cf. n. 55 below). In other words, he does not consider the present time to constitute a period of persecution. That entails that the edict Cyprian here refers to was local only, and the perils it brought were neither great nor long-lasting. But that is not to say that further troubles were not in store (*Epp.* 60, 61) and further dangers were not to be feared (*Epp.* 57 and 58) at a later date under this principate of Gallus. See further on persecution under Gallus, intro. to this volume; and on the posting up of edicts by provincial governors (*edicto proposito*), Crawford and Reynolds, JRS 65 (1975) 161; Millar, *Emperor* 582.

There is a close, contemporary parallel to this section in Dionysius of Alexandria, where he lists concerning himself (against criticisms from Germanus) "sentences, confiscations, proscriptions, spoiling of possessions, losses of dignities, despising of worldly glory, disdaining of commendations and the reverse from prefect and council, endurance of threats, outcries, perils, persecutions, wanderings, anguish and divers tribulations, such as happened to me under Decius and Sabinus, up to the present time under Aemilianus" (tr. Oulton), *ap.* Euseb. *H.E.* 7.11.18.

32. *gubernatore sublato . . . ecclesiae naufragia.* For the nautical imagery cf. *Ep.* 17 n. 13, *Ep.* 21 n. 17, and on this particular passage Rahner, ZfKT 69 (1947) 23 f.

33. Cyprian is referring to such passages as John 16.2 ff. and 2 Tim. 3.1 ff., both of which texts he exploits elsewhere to illustrate the signs of the coming Antichrist (Fahey 397, 515).

34. John 6.68, Fahey 385.

35. *legem qua homo libertati suae relictus . . . sibimet ipse vel mortem adpetit vel salutem.* That man is endowed with freedom of will and choice is vigorously and relentlessly asserted by most Christian writers of the later second and third centuries (in opposition to widespread notions of fatalism, especially astral determinism). For many parallels see ACW 39 nn. 582, 603 ff., on Min. Fel. *Oct.* 34.12, 36.1 f.

36. The last three biblical quotations are drawn from John 6.69 f. (Fahey 385), 1 John 2.19 (Fahey 530 f.), and Rom. 3.3 f. (Fahey 426 f.), and there has been allusion as well to Matt. 15.13 (Fahey 308 f.), the seedbed planted by the Father (*plantationem . . . plantatam a Deo patre*), and Matt. 16.18 (Fahey 309 ff.), the Church built upon Peter.

37. Gal. 1.10, Fahey 473 f.

38. *quod autem tibi de Fortunato . . . a paucis et inveteratis haereticis constituto non statim scripsi.* Cyprian now turns to meet the reproachful complaint which Cornelius' appended letter had contained (§2.1 with n. 6 above). He prepares the ground by establishing from the start the miserable and despicable nature of Fortunatus' supporters—not a large number of bishops of integrity, but a few backers only (*paucis*) and those already matured in heresy from the distant past (*inveteratis haereticis*), points he then effectively holds in reserve for later deployment (§§10.1 f.). It was, therefore, no momentous affair which called for urgent warning (*statim*).

Cyprian's remarkable string of elaborated apologies which follows does, however, disclose a certain embarrassment, for the affair has manifestly proved to be potentially of far greater moment than he had calculated. There had been an obvious misjudgment when his own status and reputation could stand in serious danger of being publicly impugned in Rome (§2.1); it was, in the outcome, a *res sollicita* (*Ep.* 36.4.1). But he nonetheless still continues spiritedly to hint that the miscalculation lay partly in Cornelius' own (imperfectly sustained) *disciplina* (§9.2) and episcopal *vigor* (cf. §1.2); cf. n. 2 above. See further on this passage Bévenot, *Dublin Review* 228 (1954) 313 f.

39. *sententia coepiscoporum nostrorum multorum et gravissimorum virorum.* For other references to this condemnation by the bishops at the Council of 251, see n. 2 above. To emphasise the responsible nature of their inquiry, Cyprian characterises the bishops as *gravissimi viri* (cf. *Ep.* 55.7.3, where the bishops figure as *collegae tui modesti et graves viri,* and see *Ep.* 55 n. 10), and he further suggests the gravity of their proceedings by the solemn, five-times-repeated *-orum* termination.

40. *abs te illic nuper de ecclesia pulsus est.* In this section, Cyprian has elegantly used, in turn, as time indicators *iam pridem . . . nuper . . . pridem . . . nuper.* The first three all refer to the previous year (251) whereas the last here (*nuper*) refers to comparatively recent events in Rome as just reported by Cornelius to Cyprian (§§1.1 f). On *pridem* and *nuper* in Cyprian, see further *Ep.* 1 nn. 7 and 27.

41. *Maximum presbyterum nuper ad nos . . . missum adque a nostra communicatione reiectum.* Cyprian slips in a quietly scoring contrast: a heretic comes *nuper* in reverse, from Rome to Carthage, and there he is also ejected, but unequivocally and without further fuss. On this Maximus and his expulsion (in 251)—which occurred, in fact, not without delays—see *Epp.* 44.1.1 (and n. 2), 50.1.1 (and n. 2); he has now come back to Carthage as Novatianist bishop. I do not know how Sr. R. B. Donna 180 n. 33 finds grounds to designate him "African lapsed schismatic with Felicissimus" (unless he is being somehow confused with the *sacrificatus* bishop, also called Maximus, of §10.2).

Nicostratus is the only other known contemporary Novatianist bishop in North Africa (see unrecorded); see *Epp.* 28 n. 1, 50 n. 4. The former orthodox bishop Evaristus may also have been coming to North Africa to occupy such a chair, or to assist in appointing others to them (*Epp.* 50.1.2, 52.1.2). The lively issue of the validity of Novatianist baptisms, soon to come onto the scene (*Epp.* 69 ff.), indicates that these schismatic communities established themselves fully and promptly; see DTC 11 (1931) *s.vv.* "Novatien et Novatianisme" 841 ff. ("L'église novatienne": É. Amann).

42. *miserim tibi proxime nomina . . . de omnium nostrorum consilio placuit tibi scribere.* This conciliar resolution was acted upon *proxime.* That should make it a decision of the meeting held in May of this year, 252 (*in concilio quod habuimus Idibus Mais quae proxime fuerunt,*

§10.1). Many would equate this register with the list of 42 bishops who send the conciliar letter *Ep*. 57; but see *Ep*. 57 intro. against a date of 252 for *Ep*. 57, and, besides, 42 bishops (those actually in attendance at that Council) would be far too too few (one hopes) to constitute the full tally of *integri et sani* bishops in Africa (*istic*). The episcopal check list is, therefore, regrettably unrecoverable, but the need for its existence provides remarkable testimony of the confusion and splintering divisions within the African Church at this time. (*Ep*. 64, written by 66 bishops, is in fact a more likely candidate for a document from the Council of 252; see *Ep*. 64 intro.). Monceaux, *Histoire*, 2.49 f., rightly describes the lost list as "un document qui serait infiniment précieux pour l'histoire du christianisme africain à cette époque." See Harnack, *Über verlorene Briefe* 20 f.

43. *ut . . . scires tu et collegae nostri . . . quibus scribere et litteras mutuo a quibus vos accipere oporteret*. A neatly calculated rejoinder (it was rather Cornelius who had erred, therefore; for he had accepted those letters from Fortunatus, §2.1). We are given an incidental and fascinating glimpse of a ramifying network of communications between the Italian and the African churches (cf. *Ep*. 48.1, Hadrumetum, as a single sample). Cornelius was apparently expected to inform the Italian bishops in his turn (*tu et collegae nostri*) of the contents of the catalogue.

44. *nanctus . . . occasionem familiarissimi hominis et clerici per Felicianum acolythum qui cum Perseo collega nostro miseras*. Observe Cyprian's insistence on sending letters by a trusted, *clerical* carrier; see *Ep*. 29 n. 4, and for this sort of incident cf. *Ep*. 49.3.1 and n. 21 *ad loc*. Perseus and Felicianus both appear to be Italian; we do not know the occasion for their visit to Carthage. The timing seems to rule out any possibility that they may have been sent by Cornelius discreetly to seek information on the spot about Fortunatus' claims to be now the bishop of Carthage. On Perseus see also Maier, *L'épiscopat* 380.

45. *inter cetera quae in notitiam tuam perferenda hinc fuerant etiam de Fortunato isto tibi scripsi*. By his careful wording Cyprian avoids conceding that news of Fortunatus' election as a pseudo bishop was a *perferendum*. Cyprian's communication to Cornelius is lost and its other subject matter unknown apart from what is divulged in §10.1 (it may have contained a résumé of the contents of *Ep*. 64); Harnack, *Über verlorene Briefe* 21 f.

46. *vel in accipiendis aliis epistulis a nobis detinetur*. Further (lost) messages for Cornelius, or was Cyprian seizing the opportunity (as was customary) to send letters to others? There were many Africans in Rome (see *Ep.* 21 intro.) and we have to remember that the more private side of Cyprian's correspondence goes almost unrepresented in our collection (but note the new fragment ML Supp. 1.41 ff. = *Ep.* 82).

Observe *Ep.* 36.4.2, where Privatus' agent similarly arrived in Rome in advance of Cyprian's (lost) note of warning, and *Ep.* 52.1.2, where the Novatianist party arrived in Carthage a day ahead of Cornelius' note of warning (*Ep.* 50).

47. *Privatum veterem haereticum in Lambesitana colonia ante multos fere annos ob multa et gravia delicta nonaginta episcoporum sententia condemnatum*. Privatus Lambesitanus has been encountered already in *Ep.* 36.4.1 f. (where see n. 18). The date of his condemnation can merely be fixed within the period when Fabian and Donatus were both bishops (see next n.), i.e. between (roughly) 236 (accession of Fabian) and 248 (death of Donatus; see n. 24 above). It is to Cyprian's present purpose to emphasise that Privatus is a character hard-grained in heresy; hence the condemnation is described as occurring *ante multos fere annos*, whereas it is not likely to have occurred much more than a decade or so ago. Privatus had clearly been a bishop, and, as likely as not, bishop of Lambaesis, the city with which he is firmly identified; that city was the legionary headquarters and provincial capital of Numidia and hence at this time the leading see of that province—see *Ep.* 62 n. 1. (On the status of Lambaesis as a *colonia*, see e.g. Gascou, *Politique municipale* 194 f.; Lepelley, *Les cités* 2.416 f.; this passage in fact provides the first attestation of its promotion in status from a *municipium*. It is still a *municipium* in e.g. CIL 8.18256 [Lambaesis], dated to 197 A.D., and possibly still in CIL 8.2611 [Lambaesis], now datable to 246/47 and reading in its last line *[mun]icipii*; see Thomasson, *Statthalter* 2.216 ff.) It must have been a *cause célèbre* to put on trial and depose such a leading bishop; the unprecedentedly high number of bishops mustered for the occasion (90) supports that conclusion. (Cyprian managed to line up only 87 *sententiae* for his great meeting of Sept. 1, 256.) We do not know the *gravamen* of the charges against Privatus, but Cyprian's language here (*multa et gravia delicta*) suggests (it is no more than that) that it may have concerned

rather moral misdemeanours than dogmatic errors; but in any case, by refusing to accept his condemnation and by persisting in his claims to be bishop he would have turned himself *ipso facto* into a *haereticus*. (It is clear, at any rate, that the *laxist* cause was not uncongenial to his sympathies.) Though it is often supposed that the Council meeting was held at Lambaesis (and Cyprian's language is quite ambiguous on the point), the probabilities that such a gathering of 90 bishops would be convened at a spot 400 km. down to the SW from Carthage are slender (unless the principle of §14.2 applied: *uniuscuiusque causa illic audiatur ubi est crimen admissum*); so e.g. Hefele-Leclercq, *Histoire des conciles* 1.162 n. 2; Monceaux, *Histoire* 2.5; DACL 8 (1928) *s.v.* "Lambèse" 1068 (Leclercq) against Benson 227; Lietzmann, *History* 2.225; Klauser, JAC 14 (1971) 144; Quasten, *Patrology* 2.236; Barnes, *Tertullian* 71 n. 6; Frend, *ap. Camb. Hist. Africa* 2 (1978) 458 f.; Campeau, *Science et esprit* 21 (1969) 348 f. (unconvincing in his argument that the 90 were all *Numidian* bishops). See also on the incident DHGE 1 (1912) *s.v.* "Afrique" 730 f. (Audollent), and J. A. Fischer in *Pietas* (= Festscrift . . . Kötting) 225 ff.

48. *Fabiani et Donati litteris severissime notatum.* This sounds like a joint letter, rather than two independent documents (though that is a possible interpretation). Privatus clearly persisted in fighting for recognition and rehabilitation (see his mission to Rome, after Fabian's death, *Ep.* 36.4.1 f., and his recent request for a review of his case in Carthage, below). Fabian (it appears) had responded to such overtures by roundly condemning Privatus; perhaps he issued (with Donatus) a joint circular letter to be distributed widely among the churches in order to trounce, by means of such an authoritative document, all possibility of his drumming up further sympathy and support for his cause. (Fabian may have, in fact, simply endorsed with his *subscriptio* a document already drawn up by Donatus.) By remarking on this detail, Cyprian has pertinently drawn attention to the cooperative partnership exercised in the past by their two immediate predecessors in vigorously imposing and upholding strict episcopal *censura*. The contrasting parallel with the present mission sent by Fortunatus and its reception in Rome (§2.1) is apposite. See Harnack, *Über verlorene Briefe* 6.

There is no need to conclude that Fabian was himself *present* at the Council meeting in Africa (contra Maier, *L'épiscopat* 18).

49. *in concilio quod habuimus Idibus Mais quae proxime fuerunt.* This fixes the Council meeting of 252 to May 15, Easter Sunday falling that year on April 11; this allowed the African bishops, therefore, after celebrating Easter at home (*Ep.* 56.3), about a month in which to make the journey to Carthage. (As it happens, the Council of Elvira also opened its session *die Iduum Majarum;* Mansi, *Concilia* [Florence, 1759] 2.5.) There were, in all probability, 66 bishops in attendance; see *Ep.* 64 intro. Cyprian here makes it clear that it was only after Privatus had failed to gain access to this Council meeting that Fortunatus was appointed *pseudoepiscopus,* an event which must have occurred, therefore, some time after mid-May 252.

50. *sententia novem collegarum nostrorum condemnati et iterato quoque a pluribus nobis anno priore in concilio abstenti.* A further item on the agenda of the Council of 251 (*anno priore*) is disclosed: excommunication of two unrepentant *sacrificati* bishops. On the *plures* (sc. *episcopi*) who were there present, cf. n. 2 above. Observe that the Council endorses a preceding condemnation issued jointly by nine bishops. The fact that the *sacrificati* bishops have been already *condemned* suggests that the nine bishops were not merely an investigative committee set up to prepare the case for the decision of the full Council meeting. The parallel with Felicissimus may be instructive: he was condemned by Cyprian along with three other bishops assisting him (*Ep.* 42 with n. 2 above), and, subsequently, the Council of 251 confirmed that excommunication (§1.1 above and *Ep.* 45.4.1). In this particular case nine bishops appear to have banded together (presumably from the locality of Maximus and Jovinus—Numidia perhaps, cf. §11.1) to issue similarly a joint, initial condemnation which the full Council of bishops afterwards endorsed. The nine bishops may have felt it imperative to alert as hastily as possible the flocks of these two *sacrificati* bishops to the perils of sacrilegious contagion by making such a preliminary but public condemnation (cf. *Ep.* 65.3.3 ff.). Or they may have actually gathered for the *ordinatio* of successors to Maximus and Jovinus (cf. *Ep.* 56.1.1 with n. 3).

Maier, *L'épiscopat* 361, hopelessly confuses the *sacrificatus* bishop Maximus here with the Novatianist *pseudoepiscopus* of Carthage in §9.2 ("un Maximus novatien de Carthage s'allia à Privatus de Lambaesis").

51. *Repostus Sutunurcensis.* Repostus had been bishop at Sutunurca (= Henchir Aïn el Askeur), a *civitas* some 50 km to the SW of

Carthage. See Maier, *L'épiscopat* 206; DACL 9 (1930) *s.v.* "Listes épiscopales" 1261 (Leclercq); PW 4A (1931) *s.v.* "Sutunurca" 996 (Dessau); but, contra Dessau, this lapsed bishop can have nothing to do
with the Repostus *de extorribus* of *Ep.* 42: cf. *Ep.* 42 n. 3. Many mss
have Repostus' locality in garbled form, but for inscriptional evidence of the words "Sutunurca" and "Sutunurcensis" see CIL 8.
24003 f. and Cagnat and Merlin, *Insc. lat. d'Afr.* nos. 300 ff.
(superseding, therefore, Benson 80 n. 5, "No trace remains of any
place answering to Hartel's Sutunurcensis"). For a lapsed bishop similarly dragging down his flock, cf. Trofimus, *Ep.* 55.11.2. Repostus,
like his fellow consecrators, had also been excommunicated (§11.2).
Cyprian has contrived to paint a grim portrait gallery of Fortunatus'
five consecrators, laying strong emphasis on the chasm separating
them from the college of *sani et integri* bishops. We are left in no doubt
that such outlaws are quite without power to consecrate a fellow
bishop. Cyprian may well have expatiated further on their criminal
traits (after the lurid style of *Ep.* 52) in Felicianus' letter, of which he
is now presenting a brief synopsis.

    52. *Hi quinque cum paucis vel sacrificatis vel male sibi consciis.* . . .
As there were but five bishops present at the consecration (§11.1),
these *pauci* who joined them at the ceremony must be the congregation (clergy and laity) who constituted Fortunatus' following. They
are described in §14.2 as *pauci desperati et perditi*, and there are further
remarks on the insignificant numbers of this Carthaginian breakaway
group in §§11.3 and 15.1, where see n. 76 (its formation was, therefore, no *res sollicita* calling for the prompt alerting of Rome). There
may conceivably be an allusion to these few followers (with execrable
punning) in *Ad Novat.* 2.5 CCL 4. 138 f: *quid ad ista respondeant* . . .
vel nunc infelicissimi pauci?

    53. *dicentes viginti quinque episcopos de Numidia esse venturos.* It
would be reasonable to deduce from this claim alone that there must
have been established a good few more than 25 bishoprics in Numidia
by this date (there are 18 Numidian bishops together in the *salutatio*
of *Ep.* 70, and in fact 25 identifiable Numidian bishops are present
at the Council of 256; see Sage, *Cyprian* 6; Benson 572; von Soden,
Prosopographie 257, 260 f.).

    54. *nec me oportet* . . . *paria nunc cum illis facere.* The metaphor
here could be gladiatorial (*paria* = a matched pair in combat) or it

could be derived, less bellicosely, from accountancy procedures (*paria facere* = to square accounts).

55. *a primo statim persecutionis die*. This is a startling revelation, even allowing for polemical hyperbole. It means that the dispute with this laxist group had been openly festering all the time from the early months of 250 right up to the period when the Council of 251 could hold its deliberations and legislate on the issue. It is not surprising that such a sharp and public disagreement over this emotionally-charged question, when left without authoritative resolution for so long, should have polarised into irreconcilable divisions. For the first evidence of the disagreement in the correspondence, see *Ep*. 14.4 with nn. 32 and 34 *ad loc*. Note Cyprian's unqualified use of the word *persecutio* here: it refers to the past (Decius), not to the present (cf. n. 31 above).

56. Exod. 22.20 (Fahey 76 f.), Matt. 10.33 (Fahey 300 f., a fairly free citation) followed by Isa. 57.6 (Fahey 211), the first and third texts reappearing in the roughly contemporary *Ep*. 65 (§1.2). Cyprian has apparently used deliberately the turn of phrase *diaboli altaria* (instead of the expected *diaboli arae*) in order to heighten the sense of sacrilege of which these lapsed are guilty (so, too, in *De laps*. 8 CCL 3.225; and on the usual distinction between *ara* and *altare*, cf. n. 86 below).

57. This could well refer to *Ep*. 14.4 with specific allusion to (apparently) the presbyters who led the rebellious movement, as well as to subsequent letters both to clergy (*Ep*. 16, 18, 19) and to confessors, some of whom supported the dissident clergy (*Ep*. 15).

58. *concilio frequenter acto . . . decrevimus . . . ut paenitentiam non agentibus nemo temere pacem daret*. For this resolution of the Council of 251, see *Ep*. 55 intro. and *Ep*. 55.23.4: *paenitentiam non agentes . . . prohibendos omnino censuimus a spe communicationis et pacis* (with n. 107 *ad loc*.). Observe the stress on the high attendance at the Council: the resolution was backed by the authority of the collective *collegium* of bishops. See *Ep*. 55 n. 20 on the number of bishops involved. (The turn of phrase *frequenter acto* has sometimes been misunderstood; e.g. Aubé, *Seconde moitié* 263 glosses it with the words "Le concile de Carthage . . . se prolongea vraisemblement pendant plusieurs mois," but it is merely a variant for the *copiosus episcoporum numerus* of *Ep*. 55.6.1.)

59. It is difficult to believe that Cyprian would have so com-

posed this paragraph *after Ep.* 57, which reports that all *paenitentiam facientes* upon scrutiny are being admitted back into communion. We would surely have expected here the additional observation to the effect that if the laxists had not so hindered their penitence, the lapsed they have deceived would now be enjoying full rights of communion again within the Church. And Cyprian has no echo of the arguments of that *Ep.* 57, justifying penitential leniency in the face of threatening persecution; they would have been very much to the point here. *Ep.* 57 must be reporting, therefore, a Council meeting *later* than that of May 252; see *Ep.* 57 intro.

60. *conpelluntur adhuc insuper lapsi ut linguis adque ore quo in Capitolio ante deliquerant sacerdotibus convicium faciant.* For the Capitol as the characteristic venue in Roman towns for the Decian sacrifices, see *Ep.* 8 n. 20; *Ep.* 21 n. 26; *De laps.* 8 CCL 3.225; intro. to *Letters of Cyprian* 1 (ACW 43) 31 f. By the verb *conpelluntur* can Cyprian be implying anything akin to the oath and curse (against Cornelius) which Novatian is alleged to have demanded of his followers before they received communion, *ap.* Euseb. *H.E.* 6.43.18 f.? The verb, at any rate, helps to keep the blame on the leaders (already excommunicated) rather than on the followers (with whom Cyprian is striving to reach accommodation).

61. *sensus alienus est.* On the nuances of the epithet *alienus,* see *Ep.* 54 n. 4. Cyprian has contrived to compose a sentence suitably ugly with repulsive sibilants (*illis percussa mens et hebes animus et sensus alienus est*).

62. Isa. 29.10 (Fahey 200) followed by 2 Thess. 2.10 ff. (Fahey 504), both passages found in a very similar context and argument in *De laps.* 33 CCL 3.239 f.

63. *et non subsit paenitentia per quam culpa curatur.* So Hartel, which I translate; there is much uncertainty, however, over the reading *subsit* (*sumpta sit, subveniat* are also attested possibilities), but the sense of the passage is not unduly impaired by the uncertainty.

64. *dum tollitur vigor et timor Christi.* Vigor (*Christi*) is often interpreted here more narrowly as signifying the (penitential) *discipline* of Christ (cf. *episcopatus vigor* §2.2), but in the present military context it seems preferable to take *vigor et timor* together as a hendiadys ("the bracing fear of Christ").

65. Mal. 2.1 f., Fahey 256.

66. *ne pulsetur ad ecclesiam Christi*. For this image, prevalent in penitential contexts, compare §15.1 below, *ad ecclesiam pulsant*, and see *Ep.* 30 n. 39 on the basis for the imagery.

67. *pax a presbyteris verbis fallacibus praedicetur et . . . communicatio non communicantibus offeratur*. Can the first clause possibly mean "presbyters fraudulently pronounce reconciliation upon them"? Cf. §13.2: *falsae pacis mendacio*. Cornelius, as bishop, is expected to register indignation that *presbyteri* should be so acting when the bishop is now available to regulate *pax*. We do not know how many of the four other Carthaginian *presbyteri* continued to support Fortunatus (presumably no longer Novatus, *Ep.* 52.2). In the second clause there is some ms warrant and the close parallel of *De laps.* 33 CCL 3.240 *[lapsi] communicationem non communicantium ratam ducunt* to suggest that the correct reading here ought to be < *a* > *non communicantibus*, which I translate (cf. Bévenot, *Theol. Stud.* 16 [1955] 190).

68. *fraudibus involutos vel adulteriis commaculatos vel sacrificiorum funesta contagione pollutos*. Generous religious abuse to discredit the character of Fortunatus' following; see nn. 4 and 5 above. For the appearance of *fraus* among the most repellent of deadly sins, cf. *Ep.* 50 n. 5.

69. *conventiculum perditae factionis*. The word *conventiculum* is so used of heretics' gathering-places in *De unit.* 12 CCL 3. 258, but it is soon to be found referring to the church buildings of the orthodox: e.g. Arnob. 4.36 CSEL 4.171; Lact. *De mort persec.* 15.7, 36.3, CSEL 27.189, 215; *Div. inst.* 5.11.10 CSEL 19.435 (and see Millar, *Emperor* 579). For Cyprian's derogatory connotation see TLL *s.v.* "conventiculum" [Burger] §1 (*saepe cum contemptu dictum, apud ecclesiasticos praecipue de haereticis*).

70. *ad Petri cathedram adque ad ecclesiam principalem unde unitas sacerdotalis exorta est*. Cyprian is arguing that there cannot conceivably be any *societas* between the emissaries of this *conventiculum* (a veritable cesspool of sin, as he has described it) and the hallowed Church of Rome, to which those emissaries have gone, between the *pseudoepiscopus* Fortunatus and Cornelius who has been elevated to the pre-eminent episcopal Chair of Rome. He, therefore, highlights the special qualities, the sacred status, and the venerable dignity which distinguishes that Chair which Cornelius occupies. In the first place, it is not merely apostolic, it is impressively so, it is the seat of Peter him-

self (a fact of which the contemporary Roman Church was deeply proud: *Ep.* 8 n. 14); i.e. the seat of the leading apostle who was himself the first bishop (on this point see *Ep.* 3 n. 16). For Cyprian had no doubt that to Peter had first been given episcopal authority (cf. Matt. 16.18 f. and among many passages note §7.3 above: *Petrus . . . super quem aedificata . . . fuerat ecclesia, unus pro omnibus loquens et ecclesiae voce respondens* and, of course, *De unit.* 4 [both versions] CCL 3, 251 f.; see Benson 197 ff. for a full collection of such passages, as well as Fahey 309 ff.) before it was conferred upon others. This bestowed upon the Church of Rome a special dignity and a unique place of honour; it was the *ecclesia principalis*—the primordial or foundation church—and it is accordingly the ultimate source of episcopal unity and concord. Such a see can, therefore, have no business dealings with the emissaries of episcopal disunity and discord, with the henchmen of a *pseudoepiscopus*. In all this it is worth reminding ourselves that Cyprian is here not phrasing some dogmatic theory, much less thinking of Rome's jurisdictional authority; he is writing a skilful blend of indignant expostulation and knowing flattery. This is talk which at once expresses Cyprian's genuine respect for the great traditions of the great See of Rome—and which Cornelius of Rome would much like to hear.

Much ink has flowed to make the text say more (or less) than it intends, and I do not propose to add to the flood. For some studies, Caspar, *Geschichte* 1.72 ff.; Poschmann, *Ecclesia principalis* (1933); Koch, *Cyp. u. der röm. Primat* (1910); Zapelena, *Gregorianum* 15 (1934) 500 ff., 16 (1935) 196 ff.; Chapman, *Rev. bénéd.* 27 (1910) 447 ff.; K. Adam, *Theol. Quartal.* 94 (1912) 99 ff., 203 ff.; Koch, *Theol. Zeit.* 59 (1934) 10 ff.; Lebreton, *Rech. sc. rel.* 21 (1931) 601 ff.; Le Moyne, *Rev. bénéd.* 63 (1953) 111 ff.; Demoustier, *Rech. sc. rel.* 52 (1964) 337 ff.; 555 ff.; Colson, *Épiscopat* 97 ff.; d'Alès, *Rech. sc. rel.* 11 (1921) 374 ff., Hanson, *Tradition* 153 f.; Kelly, *Doctrines*[3] 203 ff.; Butler, *Downside Rev.* 56 (1938) 134 ff.; Wickert, *Sacramentum unitatis* 108 ff.; Bévenot, *Dublin Review* 228 (1954) ii.307 ff.; Bévenot, JTS 5 (1954) 19 ff.; Bévenot, *Ephem. theol. Lovan.* 42 (1966) 176 ff.; Pietri, *Roma christiana* 301 ff. (last two authors especially recommended).

71. *Romanos quorum fides apostolo praedicante laudata est.* Cyprian continues his skilful and calculated flattery of the Roman Church as the seat of unity and faith (against which the forces of disunity and

faithlessness *[perfidia]*, represented by Fortunatus' men, cannot therefore prevail); he refers to that other great pillar of the Roman foundation, St. Paul, and the praise he gives to the faith of the Romans in Rom. 1.8, a text with which contemporary Roman Christians could flatter themselves (*Ep.* 30.2.2, where see n. 9) and which Cyprian is to exploit again in *Ep.* 60.2.1. Cyprian concludes this letter (§20.2) sharply demanding absolute severance between *fides* and *perfidia*: *nulla societas fidei et perfidiae potest esse.* Tertullian in *De praesc. haer.* 36.3 CCL 1.216 f. uniquely adds the apostle John as a source for the *auctoritas* and *doctrina* of the "happy Church" of Rome: *ista quam felix ecclesia cui totam doctrinam apostoli cum sanguine suo profuderunt ubi Petrus . . . ubi Paulus . . . ubi apostolus Johannes. . . .*

72. *cum statutum sit ab omnibus nobis . . . ut uniuscuiusque causa illic audiatur ubi est crimen admissum.* This sounds like a resolution of the African Council of 251; there would be obvious need to regulate which was the proper authority to adjudicate the many investigations of *crimina* that followed the Decian persecution. As the *placita* of that African Council met with the general approval of the Italian Council of 251 (*Ep.* 55.6.1 f.), Cyprian could be intending by *omnibus nobis* pointed inclusion of Cornelius himself in the agreement.

73. *portio gregis . . . quam regat unusquisque et gubernet rationem sui actus Domino redditurus.* For this principle (to which Cyprian clearly anticipates Cornelius wholeheartedly subscribes), see *Ep.* 55.21.2 with n. 95 *ad loc.* and see also *Ep.* 30 n. 3.

74. *iudicii sui nuper gravitate damnarunt.* A reference, once again, to the trial and condemnation of Felicissimus and his presbyters at the Council of 251, *Ep.* 45.4.1 f. (cf. nn. 2 and 39 above). Cyprian is plainly agitated that to suffer Felicissimus to stay around Rome may be taken to imply that the African excommunication of 251 is not being given its full gravity and solemnity. The apprehensions which the African bishops revealed in sending over to Rome a full dossier on that trial (*Ep.* 45.4.1 f.) were well enough grounded. By the early fourth century it was indeed found necessary to legislate that one bishop should not receive those ejected by another bishop: e.g. Counc. Elvira can. 53; Counc. Arles can. 16; Counc. Nic. can. 5; Hefele-Leclercq, *Histoire* 1.1.250, 292, 548 ff.

75. Matt. 5.37, Fahey 277.

76. *si eorum qui de illis priore anno iudicaverunt numerus cum pres-*

byteris et diaconis conputetur. For presbyters and deacons present at Council meetings (but clearly with a lesser role than bishops), see *Ep.* 1 n. 3. We simply do not know in what proportion to bishops the presbyters and deacons attended; all we can say is that at the equivalent Italian Council of 251 the presbyters and deacons well outnumbered the bishops (60), Euseb. *H.E.* 6.43.2. (And to attend the Council of Arles Constantine provided transport for Chrestus, bishop of Syracuse, along with *two* attendant presbyters, *ap.* Euseb. *H.E.* 10.5.23; in fact, the bishops at this Council of Arles were standardly accompanied by one to two clerics, but five attendants altogether came from Arles itself, the host diocese. See the subscriptions [which have variant mss traditions] recorded in CCL 148.14 ff., and consult Hefele-Leclercq, *Histoire* 1.2.1177 ff., for other parallels.) Neither do we have precise figures for the bishops present at the African Council of 251 to which Cyprian is here referring (see *Ep.* 55 n. 20). The number of bishops in attendance at the *next* Council meeting in May of 252 appears to have been 66 (see *Ep.* 64 intro.). At the crudest of guesses, therefore, and assuming conservatively, on average, but one attendant cleric per bishop, Cyprian is talking about a number somewhere in excess of 120 or 130 people. (Cyprian has already claimed in §11.3 that Fortunatus' party cannot even muster 25 supporters, but he seems there to be referring to supporters from *outside* Carthage.)

77. *posteaquam viderunt illic pseudoepiscopum factum*. *Illic* seems here to be used as a variant of *foris* (= outside the Church) in opposition to *istic* (= here inside the Church). In this hierarchically-minded Church the creation of a *pseudoepiscopus* was, for many, fatal; it took resistance to Cyprian's policies too far.

78. *nobis . . . anxie ponderantibus et solicite examinantibus qui recipi et admitti ad ecclesiam debeant*. From what follows (note esp. §§15.3 f.) it is clear that Cyprian is referring to the reception of these *schismatici* into the Church *on penitential terms:* they are not being admitted back immediately to communion. He is dealing with sinners who have come from heresy, and from a heresy which was itself characterised as a sink of iniquity (§14.1).

79. For the dangers of pollution from grievous sinners (who have not been legitimately shriven), which both Cyprian and his *fratres* feared alike, see *Letters of Cyprian* 2 (ACW 44) intro. pp. 7 f.

and *Ep.* 55 nn. 48 and 127. At this point the best mss omit a manifestly interpolated—or, at least, certainly misplaced—passage which reads: "And pay no attention to their numbers; one man who fears God is worth more than a thousand sons who are ungodly. As the Lord has spoken through the prophet: *My son, take no joy in having sons that are ungodly, however numerous they may be; for the fear of God has not been in them*" (Sir. 16.1 f.).

80. Cyprian has been representing himself as being lenient to the point of error in his efforts to conciliate these renegades. His protestations here, along with those in §16.3 (*nec ecclesia istic cuiquam cluditur nec episcopus alicui denegatur*), strongly suggest that he is aware that he is being criticised by his opponents in Rome for exacerbating and perpetuating the schismatic division through rigorist intransigence on his part. That charge certainly continued to be levelled against him by the laxists (see *Ep.* 66.8.1 ff.). Cyprian would know only too well what propaganda line Felicissimus and his band would be peddling in Rome (cf. n. 1).

Observe the popular congregational court at which the cases of these apostates were considered: the bishop certainly presided over the hearing as the magistrate with authority, but the *fratres* (§§15.2 and 3—the word could include clergy, cf. *Ep.* 45 n. 15) and *plebs* (i.e. laity, §§15.3 and 4) could play a significant role in noisily voicing their opinions and hence effectively modifying the magistrate's determinations (§15.2). It was no different for a Roman magistrate sitting on his public tribunal at a *cognitio* and conscious of the cheers or jeers from the *corona* of bystanders crowding around his dais. So in §16.2 Cyprian anticipates that the *fratres* will shout accusations (*crimina*) against Felicissimus and his group should they ever appear before him (*nec episcopus alicui denegatur* §16.3). Penitence, though firmly in the bishop's hands (the people's resistance might be overridden, therefore, as here), was ultimately a community concern; they were normally present as praying witnesses at the actual ceremony of reconciliation. For other evidence of the presence of the *plebs* at similar inquiries, see *Ep.* 34.4.1: *cognitio . . . cum plebe ipsa universa* (with n. 18), *Ep.* 44.2.1 (*statio*, with n. 11), *Ep.* 49.2.3 and 5 (*voluntas* of Roman *populus* ascertained and reconciliation of Novatianist sympathisers effected *cum ingenti populi suffragio*—see n. 19 *ad loc.*), *Ep.* 64.1.1 (*sine petitu et conscientia plebis*, where see n. 4 for further discussion); and see Vilela 296 f.; Galtier, *Aux origines* 168 ff. ("Manière dont se faisait et s'administrait la pénitence"); Speigl, *Annuarium hist. conciliorum* 10 (1978) 241 ff.

81. *per provinciam circumveniendis fratribus et spoliandis pererrant.* For the variable reference which *provincia* may have in Cyprian (the local district of Africa Proconsularis or the wider area over which he was in effect "metropolitan"), see *Epp.* 27 n. 14, 48 n. 15, 55 n. 93. As Fortunatus could invoke the aid of *Numidian* supporters (§§10.1 ff.), *provincia* may here perhaps be used in a broader sense.

82. *etiam quae in Deum commissa sunt non pleno iudicio religionis examino.* To illustrate the full extent of his leniency, the keenness of his anxiety to reunite the brethren, Cyprian represents his concessive dealings with the blackest of all sins in the calendar, the *in Deum delicta* (such as idolatry or blasphemy). Even over these sins (which, as a class, he once regarded as absolutely irremissible, *Test.* 3.28 CCL 3.122: *non posse in ecclesia remitti ei qui in deum deliquerit*) he is now prepared to exercise pastoral *facilitas et humanitas,* to show a laxity of which the laxists could not reasonably complain. On these "sins against God" see further *Ep.* 8 n. 25, *Ep.* 15 n. 12, *Ep.* 55 intro., *Ep.* 67 n. 22.

83. *Zacharias antistes Dei.* On the use of *antistes* see *Ep.* 21 n. 24, and for the figure of Zechariah in Cyprian, Fahey 588.

84. 2 Chron. 24.20, Fahey 109. The symbolic site for the slaying of Zechariah is probably drawn from Matt. 23.35, Fahey 321; there was often conflation made with the father of John the Baptist, who was slain as martyr in the forecourt of the temple of the Lord according to the *Protoevangelium* 23 f., James 48 f.; and cf. Origen on this legend, discussed in *Homélies sur s. Luc* SC 87.31. Cyprian, in his extant writings, happens nowhere else to quote this text, though he does adduce the example of Zechariah in *Ad Fort.* 11 CCL 3.204 to illustrate persecution of the *boni* and *iusti* from the beginning of time.

85. *ut iudicare velle se dicant de ecclesiae praeposito extra ecclesiam constituti [haeretici].* Hartel places *haeretici* in square brackets, for there is much ms confusion over the precise form of the word here. That excision improves the concinnity, but the word ought probably to be retained (as I have translated). The ms confusion may have indeed been occasioned by a phrase falling out before *haeretici,* such as *de episcopo* (which happens to be attested).

86. *sacerdotibus . . . Domini altare removentibus in cleri nostri sacrum venerandumque congestum simulacra adque idola cum aris suis transeant.* Note the distinction drawn between (Christian) *altare* and (pagan) *ara;* there is here the further suggestion (but no more than that) that the Christian *altare* was a temporary and removable object (*altare removentibus*). On both these points see ACW 39.225 and cf. *Ep.* 1 n. 12, *Ep.* 45 n. 18 (*altari posito*), *Ep.* 65 n. 5, n. 56 above; also Watson 271 and Renaud, *Eucharistie* 69 ff. The word *congestus* should rightly mean "assembly" (see TLL *s.v.* "congestus" [Probst]), but it seems here to be used of the "place of assembly," perhaps more specifically (like *suggestus*) of the raised dais on which the assembled presbyters sat; for evidence of this *consessus* see *Ep.* 39 n. 26; Watson 263, 271; Dölger, *Ant. und Christ.* 2 (1930) 161 f.; and cf. *clero tecum praesidenti* in §19 below. Does Cyprian's wording suggest some *permanent* place of assembly?

87. *dum ipsam pacem persecutione peiorem fratribus faciunt.* Cyprian is meaning that the present assaults on the faithful by these enemies within are only serving to train and prepare them all the better to confront any attacks that may one day come from enemies without. It is clear from his (carefully turned) phrasing here that he does not consider the present time to be a period of persecution (*persecutio* in this letter refers to the *past*, in §§6.1, 10.3, 12.2, 13.1), and see n. 31 above. For a confirmatory parallel see *Ep.* 66 n. 14. For the oxymoron that peace has been turned by heretics into a time of persecution, see *Ep.* 43 n. 11 for parallels.

88. These stirring words in fact conceal a stinging rebuke for Cornelius by implicitly contrasting Cyprian's own readiness to resist to the death the plots and menaces of Fortunatus and his friends with Cornelius' pusillanimous performance before their *minae ac terrores* in §2.1. But that incident and these comments are diplomatically kept far apart. We are left to wonder, however, how far the threat to pour out Cyprian's lifeblood (with which they are accredited) may be anything more than sheer rhetoric on Cyprian's part (but see *Ep.* 43.4.2 and n. 19 *ad loc.* for genuine fears of physical danger originating from this group).

89. *antichristi iam propinquantis adventum conentur imitari.* That is to say, they are the occasion for tribulation and persecution for the elect, signs heralding the advent of Antichrist; see for this

thinking *Ep.* 58.2.2, Matt. 24.9, intro. to *Epp.* 57 and 58, and cf. n. 33 above.

90. *quamquam sciam . . . florentissimo illic clero tecum praesidenti et sanctissimae adque amplissimae plebi legere te semper litteras nostras.* A veritable arabesque of politesse to ensure that this letter will be given a public reading before the assembled Roman congregation. Despite the *semper* here, not all letters which Cyprian had forwarded in the past to Cornelius had in fact been so read out as a matter of course (see the gently modulated reminder in *Ep.* 45.4.2: *melius . . . facies si . . . exempla litterarum quae . . . proxime miseram . . . legi illic fratribus iubeas*, where see nn. 32 and 33). Cyprian would hardly have selected these honorific and flattering epithets for the Roman clergy (*florentissimus*) and laity (*amplissimus*) were he aware that the Roman Church was currently suffering from a "persecution of Gallus" (cf. n. 31 above). Cornelius (*ap.* Euseb. *H.E.* 6.43.11 f.) took pride in his flourishing clergy (he could list by categories all 154 of them and refer to them as a "multiplying number") and in his multitudinous laity (which he describes as "vast and countless"). Cyprian shows the skill of the practised flatterer in providing Cornelius with what he would most wish to hear. Cyprian describes Cornelius' clerical *ordo* in terms which might be used for honoring a secular town-council, e.g. AE 1975.877 [Municipium Vruensium]: *splendidissimus et flo[re]ntissimus ordo.* On the epithet *sanctissimus* see *Ep.* 49 n. 16; on *praesidenti* see n. 86 above, and on Cyprian's use of *clerus* here, Vilela 260 f. (is he referring to *presbyters* only?), Watson 263.

91. A congeries of texts drawn from 2 Tim. 2.17 (Fahey 512 f.), 1 Cor. 15.33 (Fahey 462), Tit. 3.10 f. (Fahey 518 f.), Prov. 16.27 (Fahey 165), Eccles. 28.24 (Fahey 180 f.), and Prov. 17.4 (Fahey 165).

92. Matt. 18.17 (Fahey 313) followed by 2 Thess. 3.6 (Fahey 504 f.). *Test.* 3.78 CCL 3.161 f. is devoted to the bald proposition *cum hereticis non loquendum.*

93. *si cum precibus et satisfactionibus veniunt, audiantur, si maledicta et minas ingerunt, respuantur.* A highly effective conclusion, and a spirited contrast with the audience Cornelius had conceded to *maledicta et minas* at the opening of the letter (§2.1).

LETTER 60

Contents: Cyprian congratulates Cornelius on his joyous confession and on the model which he has set for his congregation. They, in their turn, have responded by demonstrating their own readiness to become confessors themselves also. The devil was no match for such a united front of fighting faith, and those who had previously fallen in terror before the unexpected attacks of the past have now been restored by their glorious and courageous confession. By contrast with this display of unanimity and charity, Novatian and his followers continue their divisions and quarrels; the Adversary does not bother to attack them, for they are already his, and, besides being outside the Church, they cannot win any crown of faith even if they should happen to be put to death. The Lord has warned that the day of combat is now approaching; all should watch and pray that they may be found in readiness for the encounter, and the charity of their mutual prayers should continue even if some may go on ahead, blessed with an early death.

Date and circumstances: If we rely on the Papal Calendars, Cornelius' pontificate lasted two years, three months, and a few days, i.e. in all likelihood from early in March 251 until the course of June 253 (with the pontificate of his successor, Lucius, commencing in late June 253). In this letter Cyprian has no word of Cornelius' actual trial or sentence (Monceaux, *Histoire* 2.223, reports, therefore, inaccurately: "Il félicitait Cornelius à l'occasion de son exil"); he has heard early news only of his arrest and detention, awaiting formal trial.

When Cornelius was last written to in *Ep.* 57, in about early May 253 (see *Ep.* 57 intro), Cornelius was not yet in difficulties. This letter must be placed, therefore, not too long after that *Ep.* 57 and belongs accordingly to the course of May 253. After this letter Cornelius was promptly to be tried and banished to nearby Centumcellae, a little to the north of Rome on the west Italian coast, where he died about a month later, apparently of natural causes (*ibi cum gloria dormitionem accepit*, Chronog. 354 ed. Mommsen, MGH 9.75). Cf. Turner, *Studies* 128. (Swann, *Relationship* 138, erroneously asserts that Cornelius "was forced to go into hiding.")

This letter is referred to in the *Liber pontificalis* xxii (ed. Duchesne 150): *Cornelius episcopus Centumcellis pulsus est et ibidem scriptam epistolam de sua confirmatione missam accepit a Cypriano, quam Cyprianus in carcerem scripsit:* i.e., by the time this letter, directed to Cornelius in prison, in fact reaches him, Cornelius is already away at Centumcellae in exile. (It is imaginatively made the basis of a verbal exchange between the angry persecutor Decius [*sic*] and the persecuted Cornelius, *Lib. pontif., loc. cit.*) Some make Cornelius accompanied to his exile by many companions (e.g., "avec tout le corps presbytéral et diaconal de l'Église de Rome," DACL 3 [1914] *s.v.* "Civita-Vecchia" 1842 [H. Leclercq]), but any authority for that is hard to uphold (drawn from the *Passio Cornelii* Narbey 2.315: *cum universo clero suo, tam presbiteris quam diaconibus*, perhaps based on an incautious reading of the rhetoric of this letter along with *Ad Novat.* 6.5, which in fact refers to erstwhile lapsed who have redeemed themselves by confession; see n. 8 below).

Notoriously, Cornelius was later regarded as having been martyred (e.g. *Liber pontificalis, loc. cit.*, reflecting the worthless *Passio Cornelii*); he is already given the honorific title of martyr by Cyprian in *Epp.* 61.3.1, 67.6.3, 68.5.1, 69.3.2, but without any hint of the violent death which those *Acta* record (*os . . . cum plumbatis caedi . . . capite truncari*, *Lib. pontif.* xxii, ed. Duchesne 150 f.); cf. *Ep.* 12.1 for the argument that those who die in prison are to be included among the blessed martyrs. In fact, the title of martyr appears to be a later addition to his epitaph placed by Callistus' crypt (part of anti-Novatianist propaganda? cf. §§3.2 f. below). And his feast day was subsequently made coincident with Cyprian's own *natale* (Sept. 14), cf. Jerome *De viris illust.* 67 ML 23.714: *passus est [Cyprianus] . . . eodem die quo Romae Cornelius sed non eodem anno;* and for the pair in the Canon of the Mass, Jungmann, *Missa* 2.217 ff.

For studies of Cornelius' celebrated tomb and epitaph (in fact the first of the papal tombs to be inscribed in Latin), see de Rossi, *Roma sotterranea* 1.274 ff.; DACL 3 (1914) *s.v.* "Corneille" 2968 ff. (H. Leclercq); DACL 5 (1922) *s.v.* "évêque" 943 f. (H. Leclercq); Duchesne, *Liber pontificalis* 1.150 ff. (with xc, xciii, xcvi); Ruysschaert, *Rev. d'hist. ecclés.* 61 (1966) 455 ff.; and, for lengthy study, Reekmans, 109 ff., 144 ff. (along with the review article by Brandenberg, JAC 11/12 [1968/69] 42 ff.).

This letter makes it plain (§5.1) that Cyprian does not regard the forecast persecution as having yet arrived. Cornelius' arrest was still a relatively isolated incident, representing a danger to which prominent church leaders were constantly liable. (Under early-summer plague conditions it might be well to remove a source of popular trouble should there be the possibility of anti-Christian demonstrations; cf. *Ep.* 59.6.1, popular outcry in the Carthaginian circus against Cyprian in the summer of the preceding year. For Christians popularly blamed for the plague, *Ad Demet.* 2, 5 CCL 3A. 35, 37 [Carthage]; Porphyry *fr.* 80 Harnack [Rome] = Theodoret, *De cura. graec. affect.* 12 MG 83.1152, etc.) It is also clear that persecution has not yet come to Carthage—if it ever did at this period. Cyprian himself can even be described at this period as mustering his entire flock together and organising them in open action to help in what way they could with the public disaster; see Pont., *Vit. Cyp.* 9 f. H. xcix f. For further study see my article "Persecution under Gallus," to appear in ANRW, and Introduction to this volume.

    1. *ut in meritis ac laudibus vestris nos quoque participes et socios conputemus.* For this turn of thought—the communion of martyrdom— compare *Ep.* 28.2.4: *honoris vestri participes et nos sumus, gloriam vestram nostram gloriam conputamus* (to the Roman confessors of 250).

    2. *ducem te illic confessionis . . . dum praecedis ad gloriam . . . confessorem populum suaseris fieri, dum primus paratus es . . . confiteri.* Note the stress on the leadership role of Cornelius; it was regarded as a special honour to have such precedence in confession. Emphasis has already been placed on this distinction in *Ep.* 28.1.1 f. (Roman confessors), *Ep.* 39.2.1 (Celerinus), *Ep.* 40.1.1 (Numidicus), and see further *Ep.* 6 n. 33. By using the singular *confessorem*, qualifying *populum*, Cyprian neatly underscores the unanimity under Cornelius' leadership; it is an adroit compliment, given the fact that the Roman Church has been so rent by disunity these past two years. On Cyprian's use of the word *populus*, see *Ep.* 49 n. 22.

    3. *dum apud vos unus animus et una vox est, ecclesia omnis Romana confessa est.* The effective aphorism cannot disguise the fact that Cornelius alone has been attacked (cf. §2.2: *unum primo adgressus*). Though his language is rhetorical and vague, what Cyprian seems to have in mind is a scene where news of Cornelius' arrest travels around

the Christian community in Rome; all who hear word of it come rushing up (§2.4), crying out indignantly and demonstrating their own
readiness to die by this public protestation of their faith. They courageously escort him as he leads the way off to his place of detention
(Cyprian has no word of trial or sentence of exile for Cornelius). Cyprian is to enact a similar scene himself in 258: on September 13 *universus populus fratrum* gather about him while he is under arrest; next
day, at his trial, after sentence has been passed, they shout "Let us
be beheaded with him," and after the execution, to which they had
escorted him in a *multa turba*, they publicly accompany his body, in
torchlight procession, to its grave (*Act. Cyp.* 2.5 ff., Musurillo 170
ff.). It is some such public appearance in Rome in the role of sympathetic fellow believers—with all the attendant risks and perils—
that constitutes the "confession" of Cornelius' united *ecclesia*. But by
this aphorism *ecclesia omnis Romana confessa est*, Cyprian the rhetorician
is cleverly preparing for the cutting contrast about to be drawn with
the church of Novatian in §§3.1 ff.

4. An allusion to Rom. 1.8, which Cyprian has already exploited in *Ep.* 59.14.1 and to which reference was made in *Ep.* 30.2.2,
where see n. 9.

5. *quicquid simul petitur a cunctis Deum pacis pacificis exhibere.* By
reporting the vision in *Ep.* 11.3.1 f., Cyprian had stressed the im-
potence of disunited prayer and the efficacy of united prayer (*quod si
secundum pacem quam Dominus nobis dedit universis fratribus conveniret,
iam pridem de divina misericordia inpetrassemus quod petimus*). Note the
epithet *pacificus:* it occurs three times in this letter (again in §§3.1 and
4, contrasted, specifically, with Novatian). Cornelius' role as peace-
maker (with the Roman confessors, with Trofimus and his flock, in
his penitential regulations, etc.) is being acknowledged (sc. as opposed to that arch warmonger, the quarrelsome and contentious Novatian).

6. *subplantare se iterum posse crediderat Dei servos.* The previous
downfall (*iterum*) occurred, of course, in the Decian persecution. The
verb *subplantare* ("trip up") is appropriate for a serpentine adversary
(cf. *Ep.* 58.9.1: *serpens . . . mordere et subplantare non possit*).

7. *cum occidere innocentibus nec nocentem liceat.* For comment see
Ep. 58 n. 18 (on *quibus occidere non licet*).

8. *quot illic lapsi gloriosa confessione sunt restituti.* On the can-

cellation of lapse by subsequent confession, see *Ep.* 19 n. 17. Cornelius will not, as yet, have readmitted to communion the penitent lapsed as the African bishops had recommended (see *Ep.* 57 n. 32). The context suggests that the lapsed now openly displayed preparedness to face battle by their defiant presence in the crowd of bystanders rather than made an actual confession themselves (in the sense of undergoing arrest and a legal trial as Christians); cf. n. 3 above.

Ad Novat. 6.5 CCL 4.142 refers also to those who in the Decian persecution were wounded but who so bravely persevered in this second battle: *ut contemnentes edicta saecularium principum hoc invictum haberent, quod et meruerunt exemplo boni pastoris animam suam tradere, sanguinem fundere et nullam insanae mentis tyranni saevitiam recusare.* Despite the generalising rhetoric, the author appears ambiguously to indicate that such Christians were now deserving of a martyr's death (*meruerunt . . . tradere*) rather than that they actually suffered such a fate (for *meruerunt* editors frequently read *non metuerunt*). Reekmans 113 unpersuasively identifies the "good shepherd" of this passage with Cornelius ("il est indiqué de reconnaître le pape Corneille dans ce bon pasteur"); he is following Monceaux, *Histoire* 2.88 ("le 'bon pasteur' qui donne l'exemple ne peut être que le pape Corneille, mort en exil").

9. *nuper subitatos esse et novae adque insuetae rei pavore trepidasse.* Cyprian attributed, along similar lines, in *De lapsis* 5 f. CCL 3.223 f., the devastation caused by the persecution of Decius to the long years of peace (*pax longa*) which had preceded it and which had left faith languid and unprepared. In the case of the Roman community the last attested arrests occurred during the principate of Maximinus Thrax: the deportation of the pope, Pontian, and the presbyter Hippolytus to Sardinia in 235 (see e.g. *Historia* 15 [1966] 451 f. for evidence and discussion). On the rare verb *subito* ("take by surprise") see Watson 310.

10. *lingua sua perstrepens et facundiae venenata iacula contorquens.* On Novatian's *facundia*, which Cyprian, with equal *facundia*, is prepared to argue was Novatian's undoing, see *Ep.* 55 n. 108, *Ep.* 30 intro.

11. *magis durus saecularis philosophiae pravitate quam sophiae dominicae lenitate pacificus.* On Novatian's (stoically-inclined—hence *durus*)

philosophy, see *Ep.* 55 nn. 69 and 70; on the contrasting epithet *pacificus*, cf. n. 5 above. And on Cyprian's general attitude towards "philosophy," see *Ep.* 55 n. 71. Cyprian's play on the words *philosophiae . . . sophiae* implies some awareness of their (Greek) etymology; this is similarly exemplified in *Ep.* 63.5.1 (where see n. 13 on *apostoli*), *Ep.* 69.16.2 (*utrumne clinici an peripatetici*), and *Ep.* 70.2.2 (*chrismate . . . gratiam Christi*), but no particularly deep knowledge of Greek need thereby be implied. See Bayard, *Le latin* xv (concluding—a little too baldly—"Saint Cyprien a appris le grec"), Watson 296 f. Unlike Tertullian, Cyprian reveals little awareness of the *Greek* text of his Latin Bible (but note *Ep.* 55 n. 79).

12. This argument—persecution is an indicator of hell's hostility and heaven's favour—has already been implied in *Ep.* 55.9.1 f. (where see n. 38 and cf. *Ep.* 55.24.2 and n. 112), and it is used more directly in *Ep.* 59.7.1 ff. as well as *Epp.* 61.3.1 f., 66.4.1. The opposite conclusion—persecution is an indicator of divine disfavour—could also be drawn (e.g. *Ep.* 11, *De lapsis* 5 f.) via different premises.

13. For this argument—there can be no martyrs outside the Church—see *Ep.* 52 n. 7 and *Ep.* 55 n. 76. Cyprian's present line of reasoning is exploited by Pacian, *Ep.* 2.7 ML 13.1062. There is a passing allusion here (*in domo Dei inter unianimes habitaturos*) to Ps. 67.7: *Deus qui inhabitare facit unianimes in domo* (omitted by Fahey 143 ff.).

14. *providentia Domini monentis instruimur . . . adpropinquare iam certaminis et agonis nostri diem.* On these divine warnings and auditions, see *Ep.* 57 n. 9, *Ep.* 58 n. 4. Cyprian's remark makes it clear that the anticipated persecution cannot yet be regarded as having arrived, nor can there be at this time any equivalent troubles in Carthage—words about sharing in the preliminaries of the sufferings would have been forthcoming (cf. *Ep.* 28 *init.*). It might appear as less than tactful so to address Cornelius, qua confessor, with hortatory advice to watch and pray, but Cyprian is rather thinking of the wider audience whom he could expect to hear this letter; copies would no doubt be read out to gatherings of Cornelius' flock for their flattering encouragement in the face of coming perils (cf. *Ep.* 59.19). Cyprian could well read it out to his own people also (cf. *Ep.* 28, addressed to the Roman confessors, but distributed also to his own congregation; see *Ep.* 28 intro.).

15. *si quis . . . nostrum prior . . . praecesserit, perseveret apud Dominum nostra dilectio, pro fratribus et sororibus nostris apud misericordiam patris non cesset oratio.* This passage has caused needless difficulties in interpretation. Cyprian is referring to the special efficacy attached to the intercessory prayers before God of the confessors and the martyrs (those who have "gone on ahead"). See *Ep.* 6 n. 14, *Ep.* 15 n. 1, and *Ep.* 21 n. 16; Celerinus alludes in very similar terms to this invocation of the saints in *Ep.* 21.3.2 (*quicumque prior vestrum coronatus fuerit . . . tale peccatum remittant*), and cf. *De hab. virg.* 24 H.205: *tantum mementote tunc nostri cum incipiet in vobis virginitas honorari*, and *Ep.* 82 n. 7. Euseb. *H.E.* 6.5.6 provides an early example (the now martyred Potamiaena appears to Basilides by night "wreathing his head with a crown and saying that she had called upon the Lord's favour for him and had obtained what she requested and that before long she would take him to herself"), and see Delehaye, *Les origines*[2] 108 ff., for other contemporary and many later parallels, and Hummel 156 ff. for similar passages in the Cyprianic corpus.

LETTER 61

Contents: Not long ago Lucius was doubly felicitated, on his elevation to the Roman episcopate as well as on his confession. Now he and his companions are equally to be felicitated on their return from their banishment, coming back as they do with their shining honours quite undimmed. They have forerunners in the three youths and in Daniel himself: like them, they demonstrated their readiness for death but were preserved by a protecting God to live on in glory. The bishop, thus preserved, now with enhanced effectiveness trains his army for martyrdom, not by mere words but by his deeds. And by these recent and sudden attacks God has disclosed where the true Church—bishop, presbyters, and laity—is to be found in Rome; for the devil has passed by the heretics as being already his captives. The rejoicing that greets their arrival is a foretaste of the joy there will be at Christ's own coming (which draws near). The prayers of Cyprian and his colleagues are unceasing that one day Christ will perfect their confession in martyrdom.

Date and circumstances: The dating can be fixed within reasonable limits, for Lucius' pontificate, during which this letter is written, lasted for some eight months only (see n. 2 below), from about late June 253 until very early March 254. Lucius and his companions are now in the process of making their way back to Rome (*regredientibus vobis* §2.3; *vobis regredientibus, episcopo . . . redeunte* §4.1) from their place of banishment to which they had been sent promptly upon Lucius' *ordinatio* (§1.1). That had occurred *nuper* (recently)—but unfortunately the word is of unhelpful elasticity in Cyprian (see *Ep.* 1 nn. 7 and 27) for establishing the timing of that return within the period of (say) July 253 to March 254 more precisely. All we can say is that Cyprian gives no sense at all of any protracted period of long-suffering and languishing exile for Lucius; there is no lengthy separation from his people, no long-unsatisfied yearning: there is only preparedness to face *supplicium* and *poena*, §2.2. There is left the distinct impression that the banishment has been of relatively brief duration. Many have suggested (e.g. Monceaux, *Histoire* 2.44 f., 53) that this letter is in fact to be placed in the autumn of 253 (which could indeed be the correct season), but on the grounds that, as Cyprian is writing *cum collegis*, this indicates an autumn Council meeting (on the model of the meeting on Sept. 1, 256). That is not a compelling postulate: that Council of 256 is our only attested meeting at such a time of the year and it was convened for extraordinary reasons. No such pressing business is known for the year 253. Cyprian is more likely to be writing, as was his frequent habit, simply "entouré peut-être de quelques collègues voisins ou de passage" (Duquenne, *Chronologie* 37, and cf. n. 1 below). Nevertheless, Lucius and his companions could indeed be now making their way back to Rome as Valerian and Gallienus establish themselves in power (securely there by about September-October 253), helping thereby, perhaps, to win for them in Christian circles the reputation they enjoyed for initial friendliness towards the brethren (Diony. Alex. *ap.* Euseb. *H.E.* 7.10.3: "at the beginning he [Valerian] openly welcomed them in the most intimate and friendly manner"). It is not beyond reasonable speculation that as a general opening bid for popularity and clemency, the new emperors may have cancelled banishments imposed under their now dead and defeated predecessors (Gallus and the short-lived emperor Aemilian), as is specifically attested in the case of a recent emperor, Philip (*Cod.*

Just. 9.51.7: *generalis indulgentia nostra reditum exsulibus seu deportatis tribuit*), emperors being the arbiters of such recisions, *Dig.* 48.19.4. But we cannot tell for certain whether they had to wait even that long for their recall. Dating, therefore, to be fixed (very roughly) within about the last four or five months of 253.

The letter is an interesting, elaborate, and eloquent consolation to Lucius for failing to achieve the hoped-for goal of martyrdom, seeking to provide a number of explanations (other than, of course, the unworthiness of the confessor) and a variety of heavenly purposes for such a bitter spiritual disappointment. It reveals incidentally the suddenness of the outbreak of persecution in Rome (§3.1) and that there has still been none of the so confidently predicted disasters in Carthage (see n. 11 below). The shrill note of apocalyptic forebodings that characterised the closely preceding letters (*Epp.* 57, 58, 60) is noticeably reduced in tone, as all signs of immediate danger apparently recede.

1. *Cyprianus cum collegis Lucio fratri s.* For the phrase *cum collegis*, compare later §4.2; *ego et collegae et fraternitas omnis has . . . litteras mittimus*. Many deduce from this phrasing that this must be a "conciliar" letter, i.e., written by Cyprian and his episcopal colleagues convened in Council. As the letter must occur before the post-Easter Council of 254 (Lucius dying on March 4 or 5, according to the Papal Calendars, and Easter falling not until April 23 in 254) and as the letter cannot be referred to the post-Easter gathering of 253 (when Cornelius was still alive: see intro. to *Epp.* 56 and 57), such scholars propose that there must have been an (otherwise unattested) autumnal meeting in 253, to which date this letter must, therefore, belong. Such a deduction is, however, by no means conclusive. Cyprian conferred frequently *cum collegis* and such *ad hoc* meetings could produce letters that are demonstrably nonconciliar; *Ep.* 4 provides a clear example of this. For all we know, this could well be the case here, Cyprian writing while he has visiting or neighbouring bishops about him and citing their concurrence to lend his message enhanced official status and authority. (Observe that Cyprian and his colleagues proceed to claim that they had written jointly congratulating Lucius on his election, which occurred in late June 253; that lost letter could not have been "conciliar" at all events.)

2. *confessorem pariter et sacerdotem constituit divina dignatio.* With Lucius' death fixed by the Papal Calendars to March 5 (minor variant, March 4) in 254 and with the length of his pontificate being a matter of some eight months and a few days (lopping off the *ann. 11* which goes with the *m. viii d.x.* for the duration of his pontificate in the Liberian Catalogue, ed. Mommsen MGH 9.75; cf. Euseb. *H.E.* 7.2: "exercised his ministry for less than eight full months"), the conclusion is that Lucius' *ordinatio* as bishop of Rome occurred in late June 253. Lucius' arrest and deportation must have followed almost immediately afterwards. The (lost) letter of felicitation from Cyprian and his colleagues should, therefore, be placed within the first half of July 253. We are left to speculate—as we were in the case of his predecessor, Cornelius, also—what may have been the precise causes for such a banishment (cf. *Ep.* 60 intro.), as indeed for its subsequent cancellation (see intro. to this letter). It is a reasonable presumption that the circumstances that led to Cornelius' *relegatio* still prevailed a couple of months later, leading to Lucius' exile also. The *Liber pontificalis* 23 (ed. Duchesne 153) records of Lucius: *hic potestatem dedit omni ecclesiae Stephano archidiacono suo, dum ad passionem pergeret.* As Lucius died a natural death, this might just conceivably preserve a garbled memory of Lucius' having left Stephen as administrator of the Roman Church as he went off to what in the event proved to be a brief period of exile.

3. *nunc non minus tibi et comitibus tuis.* In the body of the letter Cyprian uses the second person plural of Lucius and these companions in exile. We simply do not know how numerous they may have been. In §3.1 there is a hint that clergy as well as laity were included: the devil attacked both loyal *presbyteri* and the *verus Christi populus,* thereby disclosing where the genuine Christians (versus heretical Novatianists) were to be located.

4. *cum eadem gloria et laudibus vestris reduces.* This sounds the dominant note of the letter: there is no dishonour in failing to consummate their confession in martyrdom; rather, it is all part of the divine design that they should now return to their own. It is an interesting glimpse into current Christian mentality to observe that Cyprian should feel obliged so to argue and to console. And besides, to forestall counterattack from the Novatianists, Lucius and his companions must emphatically be cleared of any hint of cowardice or dis-

grace. Compare Eusebius' defence of Origen's escape from youthful martyrdom in *H.E.* 6.2.4: "it were but a very little step and the end of his life was at hand, had not the divine and heavenly Providence acting for the general good . . . stood in the way of his zeal."

5. *non ut episcopus relegatus et pulsus ecclesiae deesset.* Cyprian is careless of technical terms but presumably Lucius *et al.* were indeed officially sentenced to some form of *relegatio* at a locality not too far distant from Rome (place unrecorded): there is no word of lengthy journeying for them into distant parts. The present argument is partly echoed in the Liberian Catalogue (ed. Mommsen, MGH 9.75): *hic exul fuit et postea nutu dei incolumis ad ecclesiam reversus est* (repeated almost verbatim in the *Liber pontificalis* 23, ed. Duchesne 153).

6. The allusions, much favored in martyrdom protreptics, are to Dan. 3 and to Dan. 6 (and see Fahey 591 ff. for Cyprian's treatment of these figures). Daniel is described as *non consummatus Daniel extitit in suis laudibus:* the *non consummatus* may possibly be intended literally ("Daniel, though he was not devoured, continued to be duly honoured").

7. *quod apud regem . . . pueri praedicaverunt.* By this choice of verb Cyprian hints that the words of the three youths were in fact prophetic, now brought to fulfillment by the present actions of Lucius and his *comites;* he uses later the same verb of John the Baptist, the precursor foretelling the arrival of Christ (*praedicavit Christum venisse,* §4.1).

8. See Dan. 3.16 ff. (Fahey 235 f.).

9. *ut altari Dei adsistat antistes.* For Cyprian's use of *antistes* see *Ep.* 21 n. 24, and on *altare, Ep.* 59 n. 86.

10. *imminente Antichristo.* Cf. in §4.1 *quia cito appropinquavit adventus* [sc. Christi] and *appareat et Dominum iam redire,* and see intro. to *Epp.* 57 and 58 on these millenarian apprehensions. This is in fact almost the last occasion on which Cyprian was prepared to evince such an apocalyptic interpretation of current events (but note touches in *Ep.* 63.18.4 and *Ep.* 67.7, and see d'Alès, *Théologie . . . Cyprien* 78 ff. for a full register of such passages in Cyprian).

11. Note the emphasis on the unexpectedness (*repentina persecutio*) and suddenness (*subito proruperit*) of the recent attacks in Rome (*illic*). There are still no parallel attacks to report in Carthage (*hic*), only prayers of gratitude and entreaty on behalf of the Roman con-

fessors, §4.2. Cyprian now omits to dilate upon the divine warnings about the impending *agon* which had figured so noticeably in his last three letters which we have (*Epp.* 57, 58, 60). That omission is comprehensible under circumstances where immediate danger is visibly and rapidly disappearing. For Cornelius now regarded as martyr (*episcopum Cornelium beatum martyrem*), see *Ep.* 60 intro.

12. *quis episcopus eius unus divina ordinatione delectus.* Cyprian has taken care to emphasise the fundamental point of dispute in the schism with Novatian. This present line of argument—persecution is a distinguishing sign of God's favour—has occurred already in *Ep.* 60.3.2 (where see n. 12). We have to conclude from this passage that neither Novatian nor his clergy have been similarly endangered. On *ordinatio* in Cyprian see the study of van Beneden 94 ff.

13. *qui cum episcopo presbyteri sacerdotali honore coniuncti.* For the strong suggestion here that *presbyteri* have figured amongst Lucius' companions in exile, see n. 3 above; Novatian's following included at least five former Roman *presbyteri* (cf. Corn. *ap.* Euseb. *H.E.* 6.43.20) who, by contrast, have not been so attacked. And being renegades and, therefore, divorced from a genuine bishop, they can have no share with him in the *sacerdotalis honos*. Observe Cyprian's essentially episcopal view of the hierarchy: the status of *presbyteri* is dependent upon their association with a legitimate *sacerdos*, i.e., bishop in his priestly (vs. administrative) aspect. Vilela 281 ff., esp. 284, discusses further the implication of Cyprian's phrasing here, comparing appositely Const. *Lumen gentium* n. 28 from Vatican II: *presbyteri, quamvis pontificatus apicem non habeant, et in exercenda sua potestate ab episcopis pendeant, cum eis tamen sacerdotali honore coniuncti sunt;* and see M. Bévenot, " 'Sacerdos' as Understood by Cyprian," JTS 30 (1979) 413 ff.

14. *vix . . . oculi plebis possunt videndo satiari de adventus vestri gaudio.* The phrase *de . . . gaudio* hangs awkwardly with this sentence: it may indeed belong to the following sentence ("From their jubilation at your arrival the brethren there in Rome now begin to get some notion . . .").

15. Five years later Cyprian was himself to invoke this line of argument in his very last letter, having giving the proconsul's agents (*frumentarii*) the slip just so that his trial and death might take place not in Utica but before his own Carthaginian *plebs*, for their edifica-

tion and glory: see *Ep*. 81.1.1 and cf. *Ep*. 58 n. 2. Although Lucius
in fact died a natural death in early March 254 (figuring, therefore,
in the Roman *depositio episcoporum* and not in the *depositio martirum* of
Chronog. 354, ed. Mommsen, MGH 9.70 f.), Cyprian can rank him
when dead honorifically among the martyrs in *Ep*. 68.5.1, by reason
of his earlier confessional honours (cf. Hummel 26 f.).

LETTER 62

Contents: Eight bishops have written requesting financial assistance
for ransoming their Christian brethren who have been captured by
barbarians. These are circumstances which cause special distress to
Christians, for the captives are their brothers, they are members of
their one body, they are temples of God, they are other Christs now
to be redeemed as He has redeemed them. And human sympathy for
the fate of children, wives, and, above all, dedicated virgins also
helped to spur the faithful readily to donate 100,000 sesterces, knowing that their promised reward will be great hereafter. Should the like
peril occur again (which they pray will not), they will be found
equally generous. A list of the donors is added (along with the names
of bishops who also contributed), so that the recipients can repay
them with their prayers.

Date and circumstances: It has become virtually canonical to date this
letter to 253 (e.g. Monceaux, *Histoire* 2.79; Harnack, *Über verlorene
Briefe* 23, 36; Romanelli, *Storia . . . dell'Africa* 473; Niemer, *Deutsche
evang. Erziehung* 49 (1939) 153; Spanneut, *Tertullien et les premiers moralistes africains* 196; Leipoldt, *Der soziale Gedanke* 183; Howe, *St. Cyprian* 64, etc.). Hinchliff 79 puts the events in 252, and Telfer, *Office*
174, exceptionally (but without argument) opines that it "seems to
belong to the end of Cyprian's life." I am unaware, however, of any
strong grounds for such confident precision.
　　　Ritschl, *De epist.* 29 and *Cyprian von Karthago* 248, did make the
suggestion that the year should probably be 253, for the Christian
captives were in fact victims of the persecution which Cyprian has
been so direfully predicting (*Epp.* 57, 58, 60). That is quite implau-

sible. There is nothing in the text to imply that these captives are confessors for the faith; they are not, in their distress, accruing crowns of glory in heaven. Equally implausible is the view of Keresztes, *Latomus* 34 (1975) 772 and VC 29 (1975) 82, that these captives are fugitives in the time of the Decian persecution who, like their brethren in Upper Egypt (Dionys. Alex. *ap.* Euseb. *H.E.* 6.42.4), fell into barbarian hands as they sought refuge from their persecutor. Cyprian clearly stated his view that such distresses under persecution are to be regarded as the sufferings of martyrs (e.g. *Ep.* 58.4.1 f.), and this attitude must have found some resonance in the text of this letter (which it does not) if only by way of consoling the bishops to whom he writes.

This failure to refer in any way to confession, persecution, and martyrdom also renders totally worthless the (otherwise fanciful) theory of Saumagne, *Cyprien . . . évêque* 168 ff. He regards the barbarian raids as in fact a punitive expedition carried out against Christians only, by detachments of Roman auxiliary cavalry. The hostages are being held awaiting the payment of security money levied on the Christians by the authorities in order to guarantee their quiet behaviour. Cyprian could not have failed to regard this—however unlikely—treatment as persecution. Rachet, *Rome et les Berbères* 246, has a similarly ill-founded suggestion. He surmises that the Bavares may have seized "le prétexte de participer à l'arrestation et aux persécutions des chrétiens, ordonnées par Valérien, dès 253, en procédant à la capture et au rançonnement de leur compatriotes déjà convertis." In seeking to raise the ransom money, the bishops are looking after their own brethren, as they should (it was a mark of outstanding virtue to extend the Church's charitable works to *ethnici* and *gentiles*, Pont., *Vit. Cyp.* 9 f. H.xcix f.); but there is no reason to deduce that Christians only have been victimised in the barbarian raids.

All one can reasonably say is that the letter can be assigned a date anywhere between Cyprian's return from voluntary exile (post-Easter 251) and his relegation to Curubis (August 257); the late summer of 256 should also be excluded—three or four of the bishops concerned were free to journey to Carthage at that season to attend the sessions of the Council that convened on September 1. Even a date *before* the persecution of Decius cannot formally be excluded.

Raids from the hill-tribesmen, nomadic bandits, and desert

sheikhs were always one of the hazards of life in the less protected areas of the North African provinces. In Numidia (where the bishops addressed are to be located: see n. 1 below) life may well have become more hazardous in recent years. For the protecting African legion, 111 Augusta, with its headquarters stationed at Lambaesis, had been disbanded in 238 and its troops distributed on the Rhine and Danube; it had been cashiered for its part in opposing the Gordians and its name was symbolically obliterated on inscriptions. It was not until 15 years later, in the course of 253, that it was eventually reinstated as a reward for the part its men had just played in Valerian's successful bid for empire against Aemilian (see PW 12.2 *s.v.* "Legio" 1336 for *damnatio*, 1339 for *restauratio* [Ritterling]; ILS 531 dates the restoration securely to 253, *e Raet[ia] Gemmell[as] regressi;* cf. ILS 2296, *leg. renovata,* AE 1946.39 *restitutae leg. 111*). It would hardly be surprising if the habitually restless and ill-subdued local *barbari* did not take advantage of this period of military confusion for engaging in their age-old habits of pillage and rapine.

Inscriptional evidence confirms that the 240s and 250s constituted indeed a period of notable disturbance, invasion, and revolt for the province of Numidia and its western neighbour Mauretania Caesariensis. "Barbarian incursions" are mentioned (AE 1950.128), barbarians are "slaughtered and routed" (ILS 3000), and in the 250s there is suppressed a formidable and concerted uprising of the widespread tribesmen of the Bavares as well as of the Quinquegentanei, along with the crushing of a rebel bandit leader Faraxen who was plundering the province of Numidia in guerilla warfare (ILS 1194, 2767). It is in such a context of havoc and unrest that this present letter finds its place. The evidence is set out more fully in my article in *Antichthon* 4 (1970) 78 ff., to which should be added (*inter alios*) Salama, *Revue africaine* 101 (1957) 205 ff. (on the Rusguniae hoard); Loriot in ANRW 2.2.745 ff. (on African defences in the 240s); Bénabou, *La résistance* 214 ff.; Turcan, *Le trésor* 28 ff.; Roxan, *Latomus* 32 (1973) 840 f.; Marcillet-Jaubert, *Bull. d'arch. algér.* 4 (1971) 313 ff.; Leveau, *Antiq. afric.* 8 (1974) 103 ff.; Jarret, *A Study of the Municipal Aristocracies* 117 ff., 188 ff.; Marion, *Antiq. afric.* 12 (1978) 212 ff.; Christol, *Antiq. afric.* 10 (1976) 69 ff.; Fentress, *Numidia* 109 f.; Février, *ZPE* 43 (1981) 143 ff. On the *Limes Tripolitanus*, the monograph of Trousset (1974); Rebuffat in *Armées et fiscalité* (1977) 395 ff.; Trousset, *Roman Frontier Studies 1979* 3.931 ff.; Shaw, *Univ. Ottawa Review* 52 (1982) 25 ff.

It is noticeable that there is no hint of a suggestion in the letter that such troubles, if they should occur again, might ever affect the Carthaginian Church (§4.1). They belonged to the hinterland and to remoter tracts further west; Carthage was itself safely situated down on the coast, with the protecting bulwark of mountains and military forces behind (cf. Haywood in Frank's *Economic Survey* 4.115). But such troubles, of course, continued: note Aug., *Ep.* 111 CSEL 34.642 ff., on the subject of Christians captured by barbarian raiders, and, most dramatically, Aug., **Ep.* 10 CSEL 88.46 ff. (those enslaved have come especially from Numidia, §7.2 p. 50).

Some have placed the tractate *De opere et eleemosynis* in the context of this letter, but that link is not necessary.

1. *Cyprianus Januario Maximo Proculo Victori Modiano Nemesiano Nampulo et Honorato fratribus s.* There can be no doubt that Cyprian is writing to a group of eight Numidian bishops, for all eight names reappear in the list of 18 bishops who are the addressees of *Ep.* 70. That letter is cross-referenced in *Ep.* 72.1.3 by the words *in litteris quas collegae nostri ad coepiscopos in Numidia praesidentes ante fecerunt.* All the present names, with the exception of Victor, figure in that Numidian address-list of *Ep.* 70 in the same order as here (see Benson's table, p. 572). To help confirm matters, two of the names also appear in *Epp.* 76 and 77 (Nemesianus and Victor) in lists of palpably Numidian bishops who have been condemned to the mines. Audollent, *Carthage romaine* 489 n. 5, is, therefore, needlessly agnostic: "ni les noms des évêques à qui s'adresse saint Cyprien, ni le texte même de sa lettre ne fournissent de preuve décisive."

The precise sees of these eight bishops are, however, imperfectly known.

(1) Januarius here heads the list, as he does in *Ep.* 70. His diocese was the legionary and provincial headquarters of Lambaesis (where Privatus still persistently headed his troublesome breakaway church—see *Ep.* 59.10.1 ff.)—and his appears to have been, at this time, the leading see in Numidia. Januarius may well have replaced Privatus after his condemnation. See *Sent. episc.* 6 H.440; von Soden, *Prosopographie* 253 ff., 260; Maier, *L'épiscopat* 157, 337; and (on the

town site) *Princ. Ency. Class. Sites s.v.* "Lambaesis" 478 ff. (Marcillet-Jaubert).

(2) Nemesianus came from Tubunae (Tobna) in the far SW of Numidia, 85 km from Lambaesis; see *Sent. episc.* 5 H.438 (there he has recorded under his name by far the lengthiest *sententia* of that meeting); Maier, *L'épiscopat* 227, 368. On the town, Gascou, *Politique municipale* 204; Fentress, *Numidia* 92. His cultus as martyr appears attested in ILCV 2068 = CIL 8. 20600 (Tocqueville), dated to 359, a *mensa* commemorating *nomina marturu[m]* which include *Cipriani, Nemesiani* (cf. entry in *Kalend. Carth: x[. . .] Kal. Ian. sancti Nemessiani*); and see Y. Duval, *Loca sanctorum* 1.331 ff., 2.713. See further Turner, JTS 2 (1900–1901) 602 ff. (especially on the peculiarities of the biblical text used by Nemesianus).

(3) The Victor here may be the Victor *ab Octavu* of *Sent. episc.* 78 H.459, a town that remains regrettably unidentified. See von Soden, *Prosopographie* 255 ff.

(4) There is a fairly junior bishop Honoratus *a Thucca* in *Sent. episc.* 77 H.458 who might, or might not, be distinguishable from this Numidian Honoratus; he appears here and in *Ep.* 70 in the most junior place. Unfortunately, there were at least two bishops so named—see *Ep.* 70 *init.*—and at least four sites identified by the name Thucca, one of which was indeed Numidian and another on the Numidian-Mauretanian border. But the chances are that the Honoratus who appears elsewhere is Proconsular: see *Ep.* 57 n. 1. See Maier, *L'épiscopat* 220, 333, 335; DACL 9 (1930) *s.vv.* "Listes épiscopales" 1268, 1306 f. (H. Leclercq); PW 7A (1939) *s.v.* "Tucca" 763 ff. (Windberg); PW *Supp.* 7 (1940) *s.v.* "Thugga" 1567 ff. (Windberg).

With the exception of these three (or four), the bishops do not figure at the other synodal gatherings in Carthage for which we have attendance lists. These were the only ones of the eight able to be among the 85 bishops present at the great gathering of September 1, 256. Long distances combined with violent disturbances such as are recorded here would help to explain such absences—as well as the fact that more local, Numidian meetings might also occasionally be convened (cf. *Ep.* 70 and *Ep.* 48 n. 15). One might compare a remark made at the Council of Carthage in 397: the primate drew attention to the fact that the bishops of the *regio Arzugum* in the Tripolitan province could not be expected to participate in the elections that

were held for the other Tripolitan sees "as barbarian tribes lay between the two areas": *interiacere videntur barbarae gentes*, CCL 149.45.
Christianity is now penetrating into this sort of relatively isolated and
marginal area, and is encountering the consequential difficulties in
regular communications.

If a guess needs to be hazarded, the otherwise unknown sees of
these bishops are as likely as not to be located in the remoter and more
southwesterly districts of Numidia towards the Mauretanian border,
a known sphere of military action for the province in the 250s (cf.
Antichthon 4 [1970] 83 ff.)

2. 1 Cor. 12.26 (Fahey 453 f.) followed by 2 Cor. 11.29
(Fahey 469), texts already encountered together in *Ep.* 17.1.1.

3. *cum sit scilicet adunationis nostrae et corpus unum et non tantum
dilectio sed et religio instigare nos debent . . . ad fratrum membra redimenda.*
There is verbal play in the concluding phrase: "the members possessed by our brethren" are to be ransomed as well as "the members
[sc. of the one body of Christ] who are our brethren." There is contemporary evidence for Christians elsewhere being involved in similar, merciful activities: Dionys. Alex. *ap.* Euseb. *H.E.* 6.42.4 (on
Decian refugees who fled in large numbers east of the Nile to "the
Arabian mountain"): "But many in that same Arabian mountain were
reduced to utter slavery by barbarian Saracens. Of these some were
with difficulty ransomed for large sums, others have not yet been up
to this day." Dionysius of Rome sends aid to ransom captive Christians in Cappadocian Caesarea (Basil, *Ep.* MG 32.436), and Gregory
Thaumaturgus deals with the aftermath of raids in Neocaesarea in
Pontus (*Ep. canon.* MG 10.1019 ff.). This is a work of mercy specified
in *Didasc.* 18 = *Const. Apost.* 4.9.2 (Funk 230 f.): *dispertite . . . ad re-
demptionem fidelium, liberantes servos et captivos et vinctos et eos qui vi ab-
ducti* etc.; it is designated by Lactantius, *Div. inst.* 6.12.16 CSEL
19.527 as a proper office of justice (*proprium igitur iustorum opus est . . .
redimere captivos);* and for later, fourth-century ecclesiastical examples, see Gülzow, *Christentum und Sklaverei* 91 f.; Telfer, *Office* 176
ff.; DACL 2.2 (1925) *s.v.* "captifs" 2115 ff. (H. Leclercq). Mac-
Mullen, *Enemies* 192 ff., 255 ff., has parallel evidence for this period
generally. See Osiek, *Harv. Theol. Rev.* 74 (1981) 365 ff., for the early
tradition of ransoming captives in the Christian Church.

4. 1 Cor. 3.16, Fahey 444 f.

5. Gal. 3.27, Fahey 475 f.

6. *ipse qui manet et habitat in nobis de barbarorum manibus exuatur.* Cyprian picks up his biblical allusion to 1 Cor. 3.16 which he quoted in §2.1. On the general connotations of the word *barbari* in such contexts, see Pflaum, *Procurateurs équestres* 131 ff.; Speyer and Opelt, JAC 10 (1967) 251 ff. It rather suggests (but certainly does not establish) incursions by borderland tribes as opposed to acts of internal brigandage or political insurgence; for the word in African inscriptions, note e.g. AE 1939.167 [Tamuda] recording the repulse of *Barbaros [qui T] amudam inrupe [rant]*, perhaps to be associated with Aurel. Vict., *De Caes* 33.3 (invading party of Franks), on which see Fiebiger, *Germania* 24 (1940) 145 f.; Thouvenot, REL 16 (1938) 266 ff.; Pflaum, *Procurateurs équestres* 131 ff., 160 ff.; Tarradell, *Tamuda* (1955) 87 ff.; Blázquez, *Estructura económica* 163 ff.; *idem, Hispania* 28 (1968) 16 ff.; and note also *Flavius Leontius v.p. dux per Africam* who erected his votive offering at Lambaesis *ob reportatam ex gentilibus barbaris gloriam* (ILS 2999: his rank suggests a date later than this present letter, a point neglected by Saumagne, *Cyprien . . . évêque* 162 f.; cf. Pflaum, *Procurateurs équestres* 137 f.; *idem, Carrières* 948 ff.). AE 1950.128 (Ksar-Duib) records the establishment of a *novum centenarium* in 246/47 against *incursib. barba[ro]rum* on the Tripolitanian sector of the Numidian *limes*, and in August 254 the governor of Mauretania Caesarensis could express gratitude *ob barbaros cesos et fusos*, ILS 3000 (Aîn-bou-Dib).

7. *an faciat unusquisque pro altero quod pro se fieri vellet.* Significantly, Cyprian regarded Matt. 7.12 (where his text read *quaecumque volueritis ut faciant vobis homines bona, ita et vos facite illis. Haec est enim lex et prophetae*) as comprising one of the sayings which Christ provided as a concise compendium of his commandments, *praeceptorum suorum . . . grande compendium* (*De dom. orat.* 28 CCL 3A.107 f.). Fahey 287 omits this allusion. A. Dihle has devoted a monograph to the history of this "golden rule" (1962), which enjoyed wide popularity throughout Jewish as well as classical antiquity, especially in its negative formulations.

8. *cum dolore pariter ac vinculi maritalis amore.* Many take this as a hendiadys, thereby rendering the husband more specifically dis-

tressed for the violation of his marriage bed. That interpretation is not necessary, but it does fit in with the theme concerning endangered virgins which follows.

9. *lenonum et lupanarium stupra deflenda sunt ne membra Christo dicata . . . insultantium libidinis contagione foedentur.* For consecrated virginity see *Ep.* 4 n. 5 and cf. *Ep.* 55.20.2. Fear of *lupanaria* for Christian virgins is a common theme in patristic writings and especially in martyr literature: cf. *De mort.* 15 CCL 3A.25: *virgines . . . corruptelas et lupanaria non timentes;* Tert, *Apol.* 50.12 CCL 1.171: *ad lenonem damnandam Christianam potius quam ad leonem putastis* (a famous *bon mot*); *idem, De pudic.* 1.14 CCL 1.1283: *disciplinam quam ipsum quoque saeculum usque adeo testatur ut, si quando, eam in feminis nostris inquinamentis potius carnis quam tormentis punire contendat id volens eripere quod vitae anteponunt;* Greg. Thaum., *Ep. canon.* can. 1 MG 10.1019 ff. (Christian women abused by their barbarian captors); Hippol., *In Daniel* 4.51, SC 14.218 (among the tribulations envisaged at the coming of Antichrist is the rape, abuse, and forced abduction of Christian virgins and women); Euseb. *H.E.* 8.12.3 ff., 8.14.14 ff. (the Great Persecution), etc. For an ample exploration of this very rich *topos*, Augar, *Die Frau in römischen Christenprocess,* TU n.f. 13.4 (1905); also Koch, *Virgines Christi,* TU 31.2 (1907) 62 ff.; DACL 10.2 (1932) *s.v.* "martyr" 2394 f. (H. Leclercq). On the preferred textual reading here (*lupanarum* or *lupanarium?*), Wölfflin, *Archiv. f. lat. Lexikog.* 8 (1893) 145.

10. The citations are from Matt. 25.36 (Fahey 325 f.), which for rhetorical effect Cyprian is prepared to rewrite in an a fortiori cast of argument. On this (for Cyprian) unusual manoeuvre, cf. *Ep.* 3.3.3, where see n. 21. The last clause here (*cum iudicii dies venerit praemium de Domino recepturi*) could conceivably continue the imagined quotation ("expecting to receive your recompense from your Lord when the day of judgment comes").

11. *sestertia centum milia nummorum.* For an explanation of this numerical expression, Callu, *Politique monétaire* 368. This is indeed a sizable sum of money (but hardly to be described as "somma quasi incredibile," Hertling, *Civ. catt.* 3 [1958] 452); and it provides some testimony of at least the size, relative prosperity, and financial resilience of the Christian community in Carthage if one considers that a day-labourer's basic wage at this period could be put somewhere (very approximately) in the vicinity of 30 HS per month. That is to

say, something like the equivalent of the average monthly rations of some 3,000 unskilled workmen has been collected—enough, therefore, to provide one month's food for their (average) family of four, or sufficient for keeping alive 12,000 people for a month. (For computations see Duncan-Jones, *Economy of the Roman Empire* 11 f., 63 ff. [prices in the African provinces], 144 ff.; K. Hopkins in *Trade and Famine* 88, 101; and cf. *Ep.* 13 n. 38; Callu, *op. cit.* 289 ff., esp. 365 ff. and 399 ff. [attested salaries]; Jones, *Lat. Rom. Emp.* 1.438 ff. Note esp. *P. Lond.* 1226 giving the [Egyptian] wages of herdsmen and muleteers in 254 A.D., and *P. Flor.* 321, 322 for similar payments in 256 and 258 A.D. It is only a guess that African salaries were roughly parallel).

12. *ut autem fratres nostros et sorores . . . in mente habeatis orationibus vestris . . . subdidi nomina singulorum.* The appendix has regrettably been lost (no doubt of little interest to copyists); it sounds as if the donors were not too numerous if they could be so specified and that, therefore, the bulk of the donation was made up of some sizable contributions rather than consisted of an accumulation of widows' mites only. This church could boast of brethren in its congregation who were of some substance. On the phrase *in mente habeatis*, which probably figured in liturgical formulae, cf. *Ep.* 79.1.2 (Numidian confessors): *ut nos adsiduis orationibus tuis in mente habere digneris; Act. Fruct.* 3.6 Musurillo 180: *in mente me habere necesse est ecclesiam catholicam ab oriente usque in occidentem;* ILCV 2323-31, to which add e.g. Février, *Riv. di arch. crist.* 48 [1972] 162 f.: *Martyris benedi/cti in men<i>te/habete Quinita/nu);* and see Srawley, *The Early History of the Liturgy* 135 f.; Bishop, *The African Rite* 254 ff.; Renaud, *Eucharistie* 186 ff., 213 ff.

13. *collegarum quoque et sacerdotum nostrorum qui et ipsi cum praesentes essent, ex suo plebis suae nomine quaedam pro viribus contulerunt.* The presence of bishops in Carthage could possibly indicate some conciliar gathering, from which these Numidian bishops were themselves absent; but nothing more than a group of visiting bishops need be implied (cf. *Ep.* 61 n. 1). Many editors (rightly) suspect that the text here should read *ex* [better, *et*] *suo<et>plebis suae nomine* ("on behalf of themselves and of their people").

14. *eorum quoque summulas significavi et misi.* This list has also been lost. The word *summula* is not necessarily derogatory; cf. *Ep.*

5.1.2 (where see n. 9): *summula omnis . . . sit apud clericos distributa . . .
ut haberent plures unde ad necessitates et pressuras singulorum operari possint.*

LETTER 63

Contents: Bishops generally adhere loyally to the gospel teachings but
there are some who either through ignorance or simplemindedness
fail to be faithful to those teachings. Cyprian feels obliged through
divine counsel to warn them that they must imitate the Lord's own
action and offer up a cup that is mixed with wine. This action was,
indeed, already foretold by type and testimony in the Old Testament: by the figures of Noah, Melchizedek, Abraham, Solomon, and
Judah, as well as by the prophecies of Isaiah (§§1–7). And those who
invoke scriptural passages where water alone is mentioned are mistaken. Those texts announce the saving waters of baptism, whereas
the New Testament, both evangelical and Pauline, clearly testifies
that wine was in the Lord's cup, and we are bidden to do the same
in remembrance of Him (§§8–10).

And this is the cup which, as the Psalmist says, intoxicates; to
intoxicate, it must contain wine. The wine is Christ's blood, but the
water symbolises the Gentiles, God's faithful people who are indis-
solubly united with Christ as the water is with the wine in the cup.
Neither wine alone nor water alone will, therefore, fulfill this sacred
mystery—just as the bread can be neither flour alone nor water alone
but must be the two blended together. We must in all this follow not
man-made custom or tradition but what Christ Himself has divinely
instituted (§§11–14).

Some may timidly urge that drinking wine in the morning exposes Christians to danger, but if we shrink from drinking Christ's
blood we cannot shed our own for Christ's sake. Neither will it do to
claim in defence that they do offer up a mixed cup at their evening
meal: the brethren must all be present to express the full truth of the
sacrament. Further, the evening is not the time for holding the Lord's
sacrifice: we celebrate the Lord's resurrection in the morning (§§15–
16).

There can no longer, then, be any excuse for neglecting Christ's authoritative example and explicit instructions; those who corrupt those precepts and steal from the gospel truth are guilty of nothing less than spiritual adultery and robbery. As we are bishops of Christ, it is Christ we must follow and His truth we must preserve, by mixing Christ's cup with wine (§§17–19).

Date and circumstances: There are only slight and inconclusive signs to indicate the date at which this major letter may have been composed. Some have found linguistic grounds for positing an early, pre-Decian date (e.g. Watson 199, 310: two words, favoured by Tertullian, are found here but not elsewhere in Cyprian; he later came to eschew them); that can hardly be cogent by itself (see n. 17 below). Others have similarly found arguments from silence equally convincing for an early date (e.g. Ritschl, *De epist.* 7 ff.: Cyprian fails to emphasise the importance of unity *within* the Church when discussing the symbolism of water commingled with wine in §13.2; that follows dubiously from the text, which duly stresses loyal cohesion as a defining characteristic of the Church: *ecclesiam id est plebem in ecclesia constitutam fideliter et firmiter in eo quod credidit perseverantem).* The unusually forced, clumsy, and awkward allegorical interpretations of Scripture, it is further claimed, corroborate this deduction that *Ep.* 63 is an early, relatively unskilled work *(ista scripturarum interpretatio . . . et tumida et molesta . . . Etiamsi enim temporibus posterioribus allegorice scripturam interpretatur, tamen non ita procul a sana et modesta interpretandi ratione versatur, ut in epistula 63,* Ritschl, *op. cit.* 9). But the typological arguments of *Ep.* 63 are no different in kind—and no less alien to what we might regard as logical deduction—from those to be found in demonstrably later, post-Decian letters (e.g. the figure of Elisha in *Ep.* 64.3.1 f.); there is merely an unusual concentration of them in *Ep.* 63 (Cyprian possibly exploiting an already established catena of *testimonia;* and he has to argue, besides, against the typological exegesis that has been put forward by the opponents he is seeking to combat, §§8.1 ff. where see n. 18).

On the other hand, there are hints which do suggest that a more likely setting is indeed *after* the persecution of Decius: the talk, in §15, of fears and dangers for Christians and of the importance of the Eucharist as a strengthening physic for meeting persecution courageously, and, in §18.4, of the advancing Second Coming are characteristic of Cyprian's post-Decian mood (see nn. 36, 37, 39, 49 below). They do not figure in, nor do they belong naturally to, the period of the *pax longa* which was broken by that persecution of Decius. (But such dangers do not appear to be acutely imminent; the period of threat and apprehension under Gallus is not, therefore, itself a likely context.) Further, Cyprian's opening and confident claim in §1.2 (speaking as a bishop, addressing his episcopal colleagues)— *cum mediocritatem nostram semper humili et verecunda moderatione teneamus*—is another touch that is more compatible with a date when Cyprian had been in his episcopate longer than a matter of months only. Dogmatism is certainly not possible, but so far as these hints can be taken, a date (say) in 254–256 seems to be more plausible than the period 248/249.

There is further discussion in von Soden, *Briefsammlung* 32 f.; Nelke, *Chronologie* 154 ff.; Harnack, *Chronologie* 2.348; Benson 289.

The letter is a remarkable document—our first extant extended study on the nature of the Eucharist. Though addressed to Caecilius personally, it is more in the nature of a circular pastoral letter directed to Cyprian's fellow bishops generally (see n. 1 for evidence). But its special *Tendenz* must not be overlooked: it is not so much concerned with the bread of the Eucharist (briefly treated as an illustrative aside in §13.3 f.) but with the Lord's cup. It is, therefore, rightly listed under the rubric *de calice dominico* in the Cheltenham List (no. 14; Mommsen, *Hermes* 21 [1886] 147); cf. Augustine's generous praise in *De doctr. christ.* 4.125 CSEL 80.153 f: *Beatus Cyprianus summisso dicendi genere utitur in eo libro ubi de sacramento calicis disputat.* For Cyprian is setting out to justify the *traditio* of his church (where the cup has wine mixed with water), a *traditio* which he establishes as impeccably traceable to Gospel origins (§§9 f.), the reality of which was indeed already foreshadowed in the Old Testament by type and prophecy (§§3 ff.). This heavenly-based *traditio* and *veritas* refutes a false and man-made *consuetudo* not so presaged by the Holy Spirit (§8 deals with mistaken biblical exegesis), nor so prescribed by Christ and testified by the Apostle (§11). By this *consuetudo* water alone has been used by some in the Eucharistic cup.

This latter custom can be found assigned as an aberration to a variety of nonorthodox groups. Already in Irenaeus e.g. it is ascribed to the Ebionites, *Adv. haer.* 5.1.3 (SC 153.26): *reprobant itaque hi com-*

mixtionem vini caelestis et sola aqua saecularis volunt esse etc., and in Clement to the Encratites (e.g. *Paed.* 2.2.32 SC 108.68 ff.). It may also possibly be testified as practised by the more orthodox in *Mart. Pionii* 3.1 Musurillo 136 ("when they had prayed and taken the sacred bread and water on the Sabbath"), though Justin *Apol.* 1.65 and 67 MG 6.428 f. is controversial evidence (see Barnard, *Justin Martyr* 177 ff.). Epiphanius provides later testimony (*Adv. haer.* 30.16 [Ebionites], 42.3 [Marcionites], 46.2 [Tatianites], 47.1 [Encratites]). The custom can be traced to ascetic tendencies (e.g. Encratites) as well as to Jewish traditions (veneration for the sacred element of water, e.g. Ebionites). In *Ep.* 63, however, there is no trace of such grounds for the erroneous practice: only false biblical interpretation (§8), mistaken tradition (§14.1), simple ignorance (§§1.1, 17.2), and failure in courage (§15). On the other hand, the criticisms of Irenaeus and Clement as well as other evidence (e.g. the inscription of Abercius 1.16 "giving the mixed drink *[kerasma]* with bread") demonstrate that the use of the *mixed* cup was established widely and early. For *testimonia* and general discussion, Harnack, *Brod und Wasser*, TU 7.2 (1891) esp. 117 ff., 134; DACL 1 (1924) *s.v.* "Aquariens" 2648 ff. (Batiffol); Struckmann, *Die Gegenwart* 278 ff., 306 ff.; Scheiwiler, *Die Elemente* 105 ff., 165; Jülicher, *Zur Geschichte der Abendmahlsfeier* 223 ff.; DTC 10 (1928) *s.vv.* "La messe d'après les Pères, jusqu'à s. Cyprien" 935 ff. (C. Ruch); Klijn and Reinink, *Patristic Evidence for Jewish-Christian Sects* 107, 182. The letter is also analysed at length by R. Johanny in *L'eucharistie des premiers chrétiens* (1976) 155 ff. (though I do not know on what ground he can confidently assign it to the autumn of 253, *op. cit.* 164); B. Renaud, diss. Louvain 1967; Willis, *Downside Review* 339 (1982) 110 ff.; C. W. Crawford, diss. Oxford 1983, esp. 184 ff.

One remarkable feature of the letter is Cyprian's endeavour to find biblical support for the liturgical *traditio* which he loyally upholds—yet there is no explicit New Testament evidence for the *mixed* cup. He is therefore forced to fall back on typological arguments derived from indirect testimony, and this, in turn, induces him to affirm the fundamental symbolism of the mixing of the water with the wine: it is nothing less than the union of Christian believers with their Christ (§13). Cyprian is led thereby to introduce a major and long-enduring theme in Eucharistic theology. It is noteworthy that Cyprian fails to argue from *Jewish* practice that Christ must have used a mixed cup; it would have been uncharacteristic of him so to highlight the Jewishness of Christ. But for the Jewish prescription of tempering wine with water for the cup of benediction, see *Shabbath VIII, Seder Mo'ed, Talmud Bab.* in Epstein (ed.), *The Babylonian Talmud*, pt. 2., vol. 1, 363 f., and cf. *Encyclopaedia Judaica* 16 (1971) *s.v.* "Wine" 539 f.

Another remarkable feature of the letter is the confidence with which Cyprian presents his case (defensively placed as he is behind the impregnable bulwark of divinely vouchsafed admonition and instruction, §§1.2, 2.1, 17.2, 18.4); he shows himself prepared dogmatically to demand conformity in liturgical practice (*morning* service, as well as mixed cup, §16.2) and to impose the "correct" interpretation of the symbolism of the Eucharistic elements (§13): wine alone will not do, therefore, any more than water alone. Hence he can go so far as independently to brand deviants as spiritual adulterers and robbers (§§18.1 f.). We have here important evidence for a growing tendency to require uniformity and to police "discipline" more strictly within the Church. It will now become possible for churches with variant traditions and practices to clash violently, being so persuaded of the utmost importance of maintaining their own (preferably apostolic) traditions (as the rebaptism issue is soon to illustrate, and compare also for this attitude *Ep.* 67.5.1: *diligenter de traditione divina et apostolica observatione servandum est et tenendum quod . . .*). Deléani, *Christum sequi* 148, draws attention to a significant and predominant theme in the letter, of "doing what Christ has done" (e.g. §§1.1, 2.1, 10.2 f., 14.1, 14.9).

Cyprian appears to be acting as "metropolitan," issuing directives to his fellow African bishops, §17.2 (he takes care diplomatically to assign any past errors to honest ignorance but now claims such ignorance to be no longer invincible, §§1.1, 17.2). So sure is he of the crucial importance of his message that he does not seem prepared to make allowance (as he does many times elsewhere, see *Ep.* 30 n. 3, *Ep.* 55 n. 95) for those who may mistakenly choose to differ, but who will still have to render an account of their stewardship hereafter. But it would be reasonable to think that as occasion offered, this virtual tractate would have been also sent abroad (as were e.g. *De unitate* and *De lapsis, Ep.* 54.3.4, and cf. *De bono pat., Ep.* 73.26.2). In other words,

Cyprian would here be reflecting views that we need not suppose remained confined to the North African provinces.

I am grateful to Fr. Charles W. Crawford for allowing me to see his Oxford thesis on the Eucharistic symbolism of the mixed cup (1983) and for commenting so helpfully on a draft of this section.

1. *Cyprianus Caecilio fratri s.* The text of the letter makes it clear that Caecilius is an episcopal colleague (e.g. §17.2: *de antecessoribus nostris;* §19: *officio sacerdotii nostri;* cf. §§14.4: *ille sacerdos . . . vere fungitur,* 18.3: *si sacerdotes Dei et Christi sumus*). He is most reasonably to be identified with the one African bishop of that name whom we know for this period, viz. Caecilius *a Biltha;* he figures as the senior bishop, after Cyprian, present at the Council meeting of *Ep.* 67 as well as that of Sept. 1, 256. For further details see *Ep.* 4 n. 1. But why address this letter to Caecilius *nominatim?* For it also emerges from the text of the letter that *Ep.* 63 is intended to be encyclical in character, directed to episcopal colleagues generally (§17.2: *de hoc quoque ad collegas nostros litteras dirigamus*), with its focus clearly set upon *bishops* (plural) who have erred in their Eucharistic practices (e.g. §1). There is not even the suggestion of a hint that Caecilius may himself have been inclined so to err. We might, therefore, speculatively deduce that the specific address to Caecilius is intended rather by way of an epistolary dedication, honoring by name a leading and trusted colleague in a tractate to be copied and distributed widely.

2. *de hoc ad vos litteras facere.* The *vos* (not *te*) is a further indicator that while Caecilius is technically the addressee of this letter, Cyprian is in fact directing his remarks to the wider audience of his general colleagues (see n. 1 above).

3. *ut si qui in isto errore adhuc tenebatur, veritatis luce perspecta ad radicem adque originem traditionis dominicae revertatur.* The closing sections (§§18 f.) carefully echo these opening motifs of *error,* actions in the past taken out of ignorance or honest simple-mindedness (*simplicitas*), *lux veritatis,* and divine *traditio.* (The phrase *radix adque origo traditionis dominicae* is discussed at length by Wickert, *Sacramentum unitatis* 42 ff.). Where the error has been practised is left vague (*quibusdam in locis* §9.1) and by whom (*quorundam consuetudinem* §14.1, *si quis de antecessoribus nostris* §17.2, *apud quosdam* §19). Perhaps by a

group under rigorist influence (cf. the Montanist Tertullian, *De ieiun.* 1.4 CCL 2.1257: *arguunt nos . . . nec quid vinositatis vel edamus vel potemus*).

4. *sed quando aliquid Deo inspirante et mandante praecipitur*. Cyprian insists that he has been divinely counselled to write this letter of guidance. He closes the letter with remarks made in similar vein (§17.2: *nunc a Domino admoniti et instructi*; §19: *Domino monente corrigere*), even attributing the brighter light of heavenly illumination that is now being received to the more closely approaching Second Coming of Christ (§18.4). For this charismatic aspect of Cyprian's spirituality, see *Ep*. 16 nn. 27 ff.

5. *calix . . . mixtus vino offeratur*. Subsequent discussion makes it clear that this constitutes the fundamental argument of the letter: *wine* is not to be omitted from the water in the Lord's cup. (The corollary, that water is not to be omitted from the wine in the Lord's cup, is touched on but briefly in §13.3; the whole bias of the argument nevertheless shows that Cyprian is addressing his remarks against bishops who do not need to be convinced that water at least should be present in the cup.)

6. John 15.1, Fahey 395.

7. *sanguis . . . qui scripturarum omnium sacramento ac testimonio praedicetur*. Cyprian now proceeds to illustrate his claim by appealing typologically to such O.T. figures as Noah, Melchizedek, Abraham, and Judah as mystically foretelling N.T. truth. For the use here of *sacramentum* (in the sense of "prophetic figure"), Poukens 175 ff. (in de Ghellinck *et al.*, *Pour l'histoire du mot "sacramentum"*).

8. There is allusion to the narrative of Gen. 9.20 ff. For discussion of Cyprian's typology here, see Lewy, *Sobria ebrietas* 138 ff.; Lewis, *A Study of the Interpretation of Noah* 177; Fahey 563 f.—and on the early iconography of Noah in Christian art, Franke, *Riv. arch. crist.* 49 (1973) 171 ff. While it is clear that Noah's drunkenness here figures as a type of Christ's drinking of wine at His *passio* (that word includes the Last Supper in Cyprian, cf. n. 14 below) and the nakedness can be readily related to Christ's being stripped of His garments, the interpretation of other details (the identification of the three sons, the vague *cetera quae necesse non est exsequi*) remains elusive; such opaque "logic" is characteristic of much typological argument. The

theme of Noah's inebriation is elaborated further in §11.2 f., where see n. 27.

9. The quotations are from Gen. 14.18 f. (Fahey 63 f.) and Ps. 109.3 f. (with omissions, Fahey 149). Melchizedek, despite his two fleeting appearances in the O.T., provided a rich typological store in patristic literature (stimulated, of course, by Hebr. 5.10 ff., especially here 7.1 ff.). He was, however, a figure already well developed in Jewish thought (note the 13 fragments of the Melchizedek document from Qumran, for literature on which see Vermes, *The Dead Sea Scrolls* 83, and for translation, Vermes, *The Dead Sea Scrolls in English*[2] 265 ff.) and he continued to enjoy his exegetical role in rabbinic literature, Gnostic writings (observe the Nag Hammadi tractate IX.1, translated in *The Nag Hammadi Library*, ed. J. M. Robinson, 399 ff.), as well as in more orthodox studies. For discussion, Bardy, *Rev. bibl.* 35 (1926) 496 ff.; 36 (1927) 25 ff.; the monograph by Wuttke (1927); Fahey 564 f. (on this passage); and the recent study by Horton (1976, with further bibliography 174 ff.). The theme of Melchizedek is picked up again in §4.3.

10. Gal. 3.6 ff. (with allusions to Gen. 15.6, 12.3), Fahey 474; and for the figure of Abraham in Cyprian generally, Fahey 566 f.

11. Allusion to Matt. 3.9, Fahey 264.

12. Luke 19.9, Fahey 361.

13. Most of the allegorical interpretations to which Cyprian subjects the passage he now proceeds to cite are clear enough. The presence of the apostles, however, he less obviously elicits from the words *misit suos servos* (the Greek *apostoloi* being regarded as the equivalent of *servi missi;* for Cyprian's Greek see *Ep.* 60 n. 11).

14. Prov. 9.1 ff., Fahey 160. On Cyprian's present exploitation of this text, see Mara, *Augustinianum* 20 (1980) 243 ff. Observe here Cyprian's use of *passio* (*in passione dominica id esse gestum quod fuerat ante praedictum*), where clearly the *cena* is regarded as an integral part of the passion of Christ (cf. de la Taille, *Rech. sc. relig.* 21 [1931] 576 ff.; it seems too precise to interpret the word as meaning here "Eucharistic institution," as does Saxer, *Vie liturgique* 253 ff.; further discussion in Renaud, *Eucharistie* 240 ff.).

15. There is allusion to Gen. 49.8 ff. with a direct quotation of Gen. 49.11, Fahey 62 f., 571. It is remarkable in this passage how

the figures of Judah and of Christ are made to merge one with the other. In the concluding sentence of this section (*quid aliud quam vinum calicis dominici sanguis ostenditur?*) the emphasis in the translation given here attempts to reflect the *gravamen* of the argument in this letter, viz. to establish the necessity for *wine* in the Eucharistic cup; cf. §9.2: *vinum fuisse quod sanguinem dixit*; §7.1: *Domini sanguis vino intellegatur*.

16. Isa. 63.2, Fahey 214 f.

17. *torcularis quoque calcatio et pressura taxatur*. Watson 199, 310 sees in the use here of the verb *taxo* (unique in Cyprian) "a sign that when *Ep*. 63 was written he was still under Tertullian's influence" (comparing *laetificare* of §11.3); he concludes on this slender ground that *Ep*. 63 is an early letter, for in it is found vocabulary "which he afterwards avoids." On *taxo* see also Bayard, *Le latin* 115.

18. *quotienscumque autem aqua sola in scripturis sanctis nominatur, baptisma praedicatur*. A bald claim, but what Cyprian appears now to be doing in §8 is addressing himself to texts which have been adduced in support of the Aquarians' case; he proceeds to reinterpret them as referring not to the Eucharist (as claimed) but to baptism. Hence this opening asseveration. Ball, *Nature* 210 f., fantastically sees in this sentence a reference to water supply. He comments on it: "as one goes to the fountain-head to learn the reason for a failing water supply, whether the spring is drying up or a leaking conduit needs repair, so it is necessary to return to the source of divine tradition and thus to avoid human error—Carthage depending on her long aqueducts and well-filled cisterns would find that an especially effective figure".

19. Isa. 43.18 ff. (with omissions), Fahey 207 f.

20. Isa. 48.21, Fahey 207 f., plus, of course, allusion to Jn. 19.34 (omitted by Fahey). For the symbolism of the Rock, cf. Pietri, *Roma christiana* 338 ff.

21. The quotations are from Jn. 7.37 ff., Fahey 386 (Hartel's punctuation here of Jn. 7.37 f. has been modified in the light of the citation in *Test*. 1.22 CCL 3.25). Note the lengthy studies by H. Rahner, *Biblica* 22 (1941) 269 ff., 367 ff., and *Symbole der Kirche* 177 ff., esp. 219 ff. on the rich tradition of this theme of *flumina de ventre* in patristic literature; and for further discussion and parallels of the water from Christ's side symbolising baptism, see *Homélies pascales* 1 (ed. Nautin, SC 27) 100 ff., 181; cf. Hummel 108 f.

22. *per baptisma . . . spiritus sanctus accipitur et sic . . . ad bibendum calicem Domini pervenitur.* Note Cyprian's assumption that the
Holy Spirit is received at *baptism* (cf. *Ep.* 66 n. 21), as well as an incidental indication of the Eucharistic service that normally followed
baptism (cf. *Ep.* 64 n. 12).

23. Mt. 5.6, Fahey 270, followed by Jn. 4.13, Fahey 378. Cyprian is clearly continuing to attack exploitation of these passages cited
in support of the Aquarians' case.

24. Mt. 26.27 ff., Fahey 326. Cyprian introduces the quotation with the temporal phrase *sub die passionis.* Did this come from his
liturgical narrative? Full discussion by Ratcliff, *Stud. patr.* 2.2 (1957)
72 ff. (comparing the *pridie quam pateretur* of the early Roman canon),
and see further Renaud, *Eucharistie* 204 ff. For the theme of the new
wine of paradise, Doignon, *Hommages . . . Renard* 2 (1969) 220 ff. The
bias of Cyprian's argument is manifest here: *calicem mixtum* signifies
"cup with *wine* in the water" (the presence of the latter element not
being disputed). All the mss read, at the end of this paragraph, *et
vinum fuisse quod sanguinem suum dixit* = "and there was wine which
He called His own blood"; *suum* should be restored to Hartel's text.

25. 1 Cor. 11.23 ff., Fahey 459. Observe the unusually ful-
some introduction given to Paul, to emphasise the impeccable credentials for the *traditio* which they ought now to be upholding.

26. Gal. 1.6 ff., Fahey 472.

27. Ps.22.5, Fahey 131. For the *sobria ebrietas* theme (a favourite among patristic writers) which this text is used to introduce, consult the study by Lewy (1929) esp. 123 ff., 138 ff. (on Cyprian); but
Lewy's attempt to make Cyprian here dependent on Origen *In Can-
tic.* 1.111 (ed. Rousseau, SC 37.78) fails to carry conviction; cf. Lebreton, *Rech. sc. relig.* 20 (1930) 160 ff. There is also a lengthy study
of the theme by Chastagnol in *Bonner Historia-Augusta Colloquium
1972/4* (1976) 95 ff., and see further (on Ambrose) Quasten, *Miscellanea . . . Mohlberg* 1.117 ff. See also n. 8 above on the figure of Noah.

28. *exponatur memoria veteris hominis et fiat oblivio conversationis
pristinae saecularis.* There is probably allusion to Ephes. 4.22 ff.
(where Cyprian's text read: *exponite prioris conversationis veterem hominem . . .*). See Fahey 487 (who, however, overlooks this probability).

29. Isa. 5.7. The citation is overlooked by Fahey (instead of
Israel est [the Vulgate reading, which Hartel adopts], most mss have

in fact *erat Israel*, which is to be preferred). It is rare for Cyprian to make such a citation without also providing some identifying formula by way of introduction; cf. *Ep*. 13 n. 18, *Ep*. 58 n. 39, Watson 252 f. There has also been allusion to the marriage feast at Cana, Jn. 2.1 ff; see Fahey 373 f., who discusses the varying interpretations of that episode to be found in patristic writers.

30. Apoc. 17.15, Fahey 549. Hartel, apparently through a misprint, reads *turba* instead of *turbae* of the mss. Note the essay by J. M. Ford in *Donum gentilicium* 215 ff. on the long tradition of portraying the faithless Jerusalem as a harlot.

31. *quia nos omnes portabat Christus qui et peccata nostra portabat videmus in aqua populum intellegi*. Observe a hint of the doctrine of substitution; cf. *De bon. pat*. 6 CCL 3A.121: *aliena peccata portare; De laps*. 17 CCL 3.230: *ille . . . qui peccata nostra portavit; Ep*. 69.5.2: *populum nostrum quem portabat; Ep*. 73.5.2: *Christum . . . qui peccata nostra portaverit;* and see *Ep*. 11 n. 37 for the ultimate Gospel sources (esp. 1 Pet. 2.24, Fahey 521 f.); Kelly, *Doctrines*[3] 178; Turner, *Patristic Doctrine* 104; and more generally Studer, *Augustinianum* 16 (1976) 427 ff. Cf. *Ep*. 55 n. 98, *Ep*. 58 n. 31 for other redemptive views in Cyprian. By Cyprian's version of deductive logic here we are to gather that it has now been proved that water = God's people = sinful nations = those whom Christ bore along with their sins = harlot and the waters she sits upon (Apoc. 17.15), where the interpretation of water is divinely given.

Cyprian now goes on to give some classic interpretations of the symbolism of the water and of the bread used in the Eucharist. For a brief history of the (sometimes heated) debate on the proper interpretation of the water in the wine (prescribed in varying quantities at various places and times), see Jungmann, *Missarum sollemnia* 2.48 ff.; cf. Mersch, *Corps mystique*[3] 2.25 f. For water analogically signifying God's people, cf. Clem. Alex., *Paed*. 2.20.1 SC 108.48: "In the same fashion as the wine is blended with water, so is the Spirit with man."

Cyprian does not tell us in what proportions wine and water are to be mixed, neither does he make it absolutely clear whether it is the wine only (mingled as it is with water) which is consecrated in the cup or it is the wine-with-water. Typically he rides roughshod over such theological niceties (contrast Thomas Aquinas, *Summa theologiae* 3.74.7 [2558] on this letter of Cyprian's).

32. *grana multa . . . panem unum faciunt*. For this image cf. *Ep.* 69.5.2: *panem . . . de multorum granorum adunatione congestum*. Some wish to compare *Didac.* 9.4 (p. 234 Audet): "As this broken bread was scattered upon the mountains and was gathered together and became one . . ."; but the images are not comparable (so, rightly, Cerfaux, *Biblica* 40 [1959] 943 ff.; for a contrary view, Vilela, *Condition collégiale* 318: "ce passage, qui s'inspire nettement de la *Didachè*"; full discussion in Renaud, *Eucharistie* 164 ff.).

33. Jn. 15.14 f. (with omissions), Fahey 396 followed by Matt. 17.5, Fahey 312.

34. Isa. 29.13 (Fahey 201), Mk. 7.9 (Fahey 333 f.), Matt. 5.19 (Fahey 273 f.). The first two texts appear together also in *Ep.* 67.2.1 and *Ep.* 74.3.1 f.

35. *sacrificium patri se ipsum obtulit et hoc fieri in sui commemorationem praecepit*. There are minor textual uncertainties here: (i) Should *primus* be added after *se ipsum* ("He offered Himself the first . . ."), following a number of mss? (ii) Should *commemoratione* be read for *commemorationem* (see Bayard, *Le latin* 359)? Neither problem materially affects the interpretation.

36. *nisi si in sacrificiis matutinis hoc quis veretur, ne per saporem vini redoleat sanguinem Christi*. The expression here is very elliptical but it nevertheless seems clear that Cyprian is now meeting a practical objection that some pusillanimously raise against using the "mixed cup" at the morning Eucharistic services: to be drinking wine at such an unusual hour exposes them to the risk of being detected as Christians and, therefore, to dangers and perils (hence *veretur*). Some mss, in fact, record here variant additions which manifestly incorporate marginal glosses to this same effect (e.g. ". . . feel apprehensive to offer wine lest, after they have tasted that fragrant liquid, the smell of the wine at that morning hour should be detected by unbelievers and they be recognised as Christians" etc.; see Hartel's *ap. crit., ad loc*). For the unusualness of drinking at an early hour, cf. Act. Apost. 2.15: "These men are not drunk, as you suppose; it is only the third hour of the day"; Cic., *Phil.* 2.34.87: *de die . . . bibere* ("to be drinking right from first light").

Observe the implied assumption that the service is characteristically a morning one (*in sacrificiis matutinis*). How and when this Eucharistic sacrifice in fact became separated from an (evening) agape is a wide question and has been much discussed. At least Cyprian is unequivocal that the morning is the proper hour for its celebration (see n. 40 below) and this in turn suggests that a long tradition to this effect had now been well established in his area (cf. Tert. *De coron.* 3.3 CCL 2.1043: *eucharistiae sacramentum . . . etiam antelucanis coetibus nec de aliorum manu quam praesidentium sumimus;* [Novat.] *De spect.* 5.5 CCL 4.173 implies the same customary hour: *festinans ad spectaculum dimissus e dominico et adhuc gerens secum, ut assolet, eucharistiam;* and see further *Ep.* 57 n. 17, *Ep.* 58 n. 7). For *testimonia*, Achelis, TU 6.4 (1891) 183 ff.; Rordorf, *Die Sonntag* 249 ff.; and in addition to the bibliography cited in *Ep.* 57 n. 17 and in n. 40 below, see the bibliographical survey on the question by C. W. Dugmore, *Studies in Church History* 2 (1965) 1 ff.

The objection which Cyprian here confronts has implications for the dating of the letter: it strongly suggests a context *after* the Decian persecution, after there had been broken that spell of the "long peace" which Cyprian represents his church as having enjoyed up to 250 A.D., *De laps.* 5 CCL 3.223 (cf. n. 39 below).

37. *sic ergo incipit et a passione Christi in persecutionibus retardari dum in oblationibus discit de sanguine eius et cruore confundi.* The translation here is forced to be interpretative, as the expression *a passione Christi . . . retardari* appears to be unusually compressed ("ont moins d'ardeur à souffrir comme le Christ," as Bayard construes it). Note again the preoccupation with the Eucharist as a preparation for persecution, which is a sentiment less likely to have found expression in pre-Decian days.

I suspect that the phrase *in oblationibus* is not simply a linguistic variation for *in sacrificiis*, but that it signifies "when they bring their offerings (of bread etc.)" to be used in the Eucharistic celebration. For this use of *oblatio* cf. *Ep.* 34.1: *offerendo oblationes eorum*, and see n. 3 *ad loc.* for supporting evidence; further discussion in Renaud, *Eucharistie* 190 ff.

38. Mk. 8.38 or possibly Lk. 9.26 (with omissions, see Fahey 343 f.) plus Gal. 1.10, Fahey 473 f.

39. *quomodo autem possumus propter Christum sanguinem fundere, qui sanguinem Christi erubescimus bibere.* There are close parallels in *Ep.* 57.2.2 (*quomodo docemus . . . sanguinem suum fundere si eis . . . Christi sanguinem denegamus*) and *Ep.* 58.1.2 (*idcirco se . . . calicem sanguinis*

Christi bibere ut possint et ipsi . . . sanguinem fundere), and see further *Ep.* 57 n. 14. The parallels are suggestive (but no more than that) that *Ep.* 63 may well belong to the period after *Epp.* 57 and 58 were written, i.e. after 253, or, at the least, to a period after persecution has actually been experienced (cf. n. 36 above).

40. *an illa sibi aliquis contemplatione blanditur, quod etsi mane aqua sola offerri videtur, tamen cum ad cenandum venimus, mixtum calicem offerimus?* Cyprian now confronts the objector who may concede that while water alone is offered at his morning Eucharistic services (cf. n. 36 above), yet when it comes to his evening repast (*cena*) he does observe the "mixed cup" precept by offering up a cup that contains both water and wine.

This seems to provide evidence for the continuance in some quarters of an evening ceremonial, but from what follows it is definitely not a congregational but a familial *convivium*. It may well indeed not have constituted formally the same Eucharistic *sacrificium* as in the morning (at least Cyprian is quite firm that it can be no substitute for the community liturgy of the morning); it may have consisted rather of an opening prayer, blessing, the breaking of bread and oblation of the cup (mixed) at the domestic table along with hymns and other devotional exercises (in other words, a survival of a form of the domestic agape). Compare the evening gathering described in *Ad Donat.* 16 CCL 3A.13: *nec sit vel hora convivii gratiae caelestis immunis. sonet psalmus convivium sobrium. . . . magis carissimos pascis, si sit nobis spiritalis auditio;* and in *Act. Marian. et Jacob.* 11.4 f. Musurillo 208 the agape is described as a solemn evening banquet that is full of joyousness (*ista nocte . . . solemne quoddam et laetitiae plenum . . . convivium;* and see *Test.* 3.3 CCL 3.89 ff. for the word *agape* used rather in its more general sense); see also *Ep.* 65 n. 12.

For discussion, DACL 1 (1924) *s.v.* "Aquariens" 2652 (P. Batiffol); Jülicher, *Zur Geschichte der Abendmalsfeier* 230 f.; Hamman, *Vie liturgique* 153 ff., 175 f.; Stam, *Episcopacy* 81 ff.; Lietzmann, *Mass and the Lord's Supper* (ET) fasc. 4, 200 ff.; Jungmann, *Missarum sollemnia* 1.280; Saxer, *Vie liturgique* 46; Dekkers, *Misc. Mohlberg* 246 ff.; Schweitzer, *Archiv. f. Liturg.* 12 (1970), 69 ff. (lengthy study, with references to further literature); Bradshaw, *Daily Prayer* 41 ff.; Renaud, *Eucharistie* 44 ff.

41. *sed cum cenamus ad convivium nostrum plebem convocare non pos-*

sumus, ut sacramenti veritatem fraternitate omni praesente celebremus. Cyprian is insistent that such gatherings around the evening meal must necessarily be private in character, accessible only to a selected circle. (Compare Cyprian's last evening spent *ex more* with *convivae eius et cari in contubernio*, Pontius, *Vit. Cyp.* 15 H. CVII.) They cannot, therefore, replace the morning services, where liturgically Christ and the whole congregation are fully united together; the morning sacrifice, with the mixed cup, must, therefore, still be held also. The defensive objection is, therefore, overruled.

42. *numquid ergo dominicum post cenam celebrare debemus, ut sic mixtum calicem frequentandis dominicis offeramus?* Cyprian is facing a further objection: the evening is indeed the more proper time for the community sacrifice rather than the morning. Now it is no longer a question of some small domestic gathering at the end of the day, but of the fully mustered congregation (*frequentandis dominicis*) at a solemn celebration (cf. Vilela, *Condition collégiale* 322, for a similar reading of the nuances here). For the word *dominicum* (here used in the sense of the "Lord's sacrifice"), see *Ep.* 38 n. 17 and Mohrmann, *Études* 3.223; Janssen, *Kultur u. Sprache* 36 f.; Renaud, *Eucharistie* 14 ff. Cyprian goes on dogmatically to insist that the *morning* is the proper time for Christian brethren to gather together and celebrate their *communal* liturgy. In this section his assumption that the central liturgical act must visibly represent the spiritual unity within the Christian community (*fraternitate omni praesente*) is remarkable.

43. Exod. 12.6, Fahey 69 f., plus Ps. 140.2, Fahey 154. For Cyprian's crisp and dismissive conclusion here (*nos autem resurrectionem Domini mane celebramus*), compare *De dom. orat.* 35 CCL 3A.112: *nam et mane orandum est, ut resurrectio Domini matutina oratione celebretur* (on which see Stadlhuber, ZfKT 71 [1949] 155 ff., and see *Ep.* 64 n. 16); and see further n. 36 above on *sacrificia matutina*.

44. There is, of course, allusion to 1 Cor. 11.26, which had been quoted in §10.1; some mss in fact proceed to quote the verse again. And for discussion of Cyprian's sacrificial view of the Eucharistic liturgy, so strongly expressed here (*passio est . . . Domini sacrificium quod offerimus*), Jungmann, ZfKT 92 (1970) 342 ff.; Walker, *Churchmanship* 37 ff.; and cf. *Ep.* 1 n. 12. Note, too, the implication of the opening words of this section (*passionis eius mentionem in sacrificiis*

omnibus facimus) for the form of the African rite: see W. C. Bishop, JTS 13 (1911/12) 275.

45. In this section Cyprian's language (*de antecessoribus nostris, ad collegas nostros*) reveals that his focus is firmly *episcopal:* both nouns he reserves characteristically for bishops; cf. n. 1 above. And on the divinely-inspired warnings (*nunc a Domino admoniti et instructi*), see n. 4 above; Cyprian is elsewhere equally ready to wield his personally-vouchsafed monitions as knockdown disciplinary weapons; cf. *Epp.* 16.4.1 f., 11.3.1 ff., 66.9.2 ff.

46. Ps. 49.16 ff., Fahey 139 f., a passage Cyprian dexterously exploits to equate neglect of the Gospel detail with adultery and robbery, both of which figure regularly in enumerations of the most heinous of sins, the *capitalia delicta* (see e.g. *Ep.* 50 n. 5).

47. Jer. 23.28, 30, 32 (with omissions), and Jer. 3.9 f., Fahey 220.

48. Jn. 8.12, Fahey 387 (Cyprian's text elsewhere has *lumen mundi*, whereas Hartel reads here *lumen saeculi;* for parallel variation see *Ep.* 58 n. 32; Orbán, *Dénominations du monde* 191 f.). This quotation is followed by Matt. 28.18 ff., Fahey 328 ff. (see *Test.* 2.26 for other texts assembled on the same theme, CCL 3.63 f.).

49. *quia iam secundus eius adventus nobis propinquat, magis ac magis . . . dignatio . . . inluminat.* Observe the bold and confident claim that the Second Coming is close approaching; that attitude is characteristically found in Cyprian's post-Decian writings (see e.g. *Ep.* 58 n. 5 and cf. *Ep.* 22 n. 5) and, therefore, furnishes incidentally a mild pull against the suggestion that *Ep.* 63 might be a pre-Decian composition (cf. nn. 36, 37, 39 above). The mss evidence suggests that *adpropinquat* should be read for Hartel's *propinquat.*

LETTER 64

Contents: Fidus has written to his colleagues about two matters. The first concerns the premature reconciliation of a former presbyter, contrary to the episcopal decree on the question. The bishop involved has been censured, but now that reconciliation has been given, the bishops ruled that it should stand. The second matter concerns the baptism of very young babies before the eighth day of birth. Fidus is of the view that the old law of circumcision entails that they should be baptized no earlier than that day.

The bishops did not support this view. They should not be responsible for the loss of any soul—and there is no difference between souls whether they be of the young or of the old, neither is there any difference in the graces of the Holy Spirit which the Father bestows upon them. The very young infant is not to be regarded as unclean, an object unfit for the baptismal kiss: he comes fresh from the hands of God. The eighth day of circumcision was merely a prefiguring of the eighth day of the Resurrection and the new life of Christianity; that old law is now void. Besides, infants are guilty of sin only insofar as they have inherited contagion from Adam, whereas adults are forgiven in baptism even the gravest of sins. Therefore, the bishops ruled, access to baptism should not be denied to anyone, but especially not to helpless infants.

Date and circumstances: The only indications for establishing a date are in the *salutatio* and in §1. A Council of 66 bishops is in session and Fidus is exercised over the premature reconciliation of a lapsed presbyter contrary to the terms of an episcopal decree which has been laid down regulating the matter.

We know that the Council of 251 established that general regulation on penitence for the lapsed (e.g. *Ep.* 55.17.3). We must, therefore, be after that Council. We also know that the Council of 253 (attended by 42 bishops) modified that regulation so that the remaining penitent lapsed could then be reconciled (*Ep.* 57, where see intro.). It seems eminently reasonable to deduce that this Council meeting should be placed in between these two, when the issue was still a matter of profound concern (cf. n. 3 below).

It is theoretically feasible that there were autumn Council sessions in 251 and 252, but these are neither attested nor necessary. The simplest supposition (and it is that only) is that we have here recorded a letter emanating from the spring Council of 252, which we know was meeting on the Ides of May that year (*Ep.* 59.10.1). So far as I know, there is nothing that precludes such a simple supposition. Cf. Turner, *Studies* 125; Ritschl, *De epist.* 24; Duquenne, *Chronologie* 34; Fischer, *Ann. hist. concil.* 13 (1981) 1 f. Others date variously, e.g. Nelke, *Chronologie* 65 ff. (autumn 251); Colson, *Épiscopat* (autumn 251); Plumpe, *Mater* 89 n. 21 ("in 251 or 253"); Harnack, *Über verlorene Briefe* 36 ("wahrscheinlich Herbst 252", "Ostern 253?"); Monceaux, *Histoire* 2.7 (253, in the autumn, cf. *Rev. de phil.* 24 [1900] 337); Benson 224 f., 231 (autumn 253), etc.

The letter is of great interest for the history of baptism, in particular for the practice of infant baptism. For while Fidus is concerned about the propriety of baptism within the first week of a child's life, he clearly does not object to baptism subsequent to that time—and the 66 bishops of this council have indeed positive reasons in favour of an even earlier ceremony. It does remain unclear whether Fidus himself may possibly have been concerned with the *emergency* baptism of the sickly baby (and not, therefore, with regular practice), but little is said to him in reply on that score; there is nothing about prudential insurance or precautions, about the perils of early death and such like necessities, only that God's mercy and grace is to be denied to no one. While inscriptional evidence may support the conclusion that baptism of the very young was also for the very sick (after all, this testimony comes from *sepulchral* records), there is adequate evidence to support the contrary conclusion that by this time young children of Christian parents were regularly baptised. For Cyprian cf. *De laps* 9 CCL 3.225: *amiserunt parvuli quod in primo statim nativitatis exordio fuerant consecuti; ibid.* 25 *op. cit.* 234 f. (*parvula—in simplicibus adhuc annis*); and for Cyprian's contemporary Origen, *Hom. in Luc.* 14 GCS 49.88: *Et quia per baptismi sacramentum nativitatis sordes deponuntur, propterea baptizantur et parvuli; Hom. in Levit.* 8.3 GCS 29.398: . . . *baptisma ecclesiae pro remissione peccatorum detur, secundum ecclesiae observantiam etiam parvulis baptismum dari; In Rom. comm.* 5.9 MG 14.1047: *Ecclesia ab apostolis traditionem suscepit, etiam parvulis baptismum dare;* and cf. Hippol., *Apost. trad.* 21 (ed. Botte): *baptizate primum parvulos* etc. Most of the relevant literature is reviewed by Jeremias, *Infant Baptism* (with bibliography 101 ff.), and assembled by Didier, *Le baptême des enfants* (see also *idem, Mél. sc. relig.* 6 [1946] 242 ff.), as well as by Kraft, *Texte zur Geschichte der Taufe.* Ferguson, JTS 30 (1979) 37 ff., argues strongly for the recent development of this practice of infant baptism (a precaution in a world of great infant mortality), but this letter certainly provides strong testimony that by now it was a well-established one.

But what appears to have been uppermost in Fidus' mind was not so much overhasty or premature baptism as the essential uncleanness of the very young infant, and it is against such a notion in particular that Cyprian marshals his arguments (§4). We are left to explain Fidus' attitude.

The survival of ritual taboos comes most readily to hand. One such source for this could, of course, be Jewish (§2.1, where see n. 6, §4.3): before the eighth day the child was instinctively felt to be ritually unclean (*unusquisque nostrum adhuc horreat exosculari*, he is reported as having said, §4.1). One could compare *Can. Hippol.* 93–96 (ed. Achelis 88): *mulieres autem puerperae non participentur mysteriis antequam purificentur . . . quodsi ante purificationem domum Dei frequentare desiderat, oret cum catechumenis*, or even Cyprian's contemporary, Dionysius of Alexandria, *Ep. ad Basilid.* §2 (Feltoe, *Letters* 102 f.), forbidding menstruous women from partaking of the Eucharist.

Some syncretistic confusion with the Roman *dies lustricus*, the naming and purificatory day for the Latin child, is also possible. This occurred not before the eighth day from birth (in fact, eighth for a female, ninth for a male child) and might be considered to have left some superstitious residuum concerning the essential uncleanness of the child before its formal acceptance into the family. See Plut., *Quae. Rom.* 102 (*Mor.* 288C ff.); Macrob., *Sat.* 1.16.36; Festus 120M.; Tert. *De anim.* 39.2 (with Waszink's nn. *ad loc.*); Marquardt, *Das Privatleben der Römer* 81 f.; Brind'Amour, *Latomus* 30 (1971) 999 ff.

If Fidus is in fact thinking of *emergency* baptism (by aspersion, cf. *Ep.* 69.12 ff.), then the instinctive repugnance he appeals to might equally well be hygienic and aesthetic, before the ceremony of the first bath had been held. For, by custom, newborn babies could be left, literally, unwashed (e.g. Soranus, *Gynaec.* 2.12 Corp. med. graec. 4.59 f.). But were Fidus arguing that such ceremonies by aspersion left the baptizand still beset by unclean spirits, then we would have expected instead from Cyprian arguments along the lines as those presented in *Ep.* 69.12 ff.

For further discussion see Dölger, *Ant. und Christ.* 1 (1929) 186 ff.; Quasten, *Festschrift J. Pascher* 267 ff.; Thraede, JAC 11/12 (1968/

69) 159 ff.; Didier, *Mél. sc. relig.* 8 (1952) 197 ff.; Nagel, *Kindertaufe und Taufaufschub* 90 ff.; Fischer, *Ann. hist. concil.* 13 (1981) 3 ff.; and my article (from which I have drawn heavily), *Harv. Theol. Rev.* 66 (1973) 147 ff.

Augustine appealed a number of times to this letter, especially in his anti-Pelagian disputes, e.g. *Contr. duas epist. Pelag.* 4.8.23 f. CSEL 60.546 ff.; *De pecc. merit. et remiss.* 3.5.10 CSEL 60.135 ff.; *De gest. Pelag.* 11.25 CSEL 42.78 f.; *Contr. Jul.* 1.3.6 ML 44.644; *Serm.* 294.19 ML 38.1347; *Ep.* 166 CSEL 44.579, etc. There is a Syriac version (Pitra, *Anal. sacr. spic.* 4 [1883] 74 ff.) as well as fragments of an Armenian version (see Dekkers, *Sacr. erud.* 5 [1953] 197 and n. 3 for bibliographical details) strongly suggesting that there was in circulation a Greek version as well (cf. John Damascene with a portion of §5.2 in his *Sacra parallela*, MG 96.516).

1. *Cyprianus et ceteri collegae qui in concilio fuerunt numero LXVI Fido fratri s.* Fidus is undeniably a bishop but his see is unknown. He is likely to come from the vicinity of Therapius, whose reprehensible actions he can report to Carthage. Hence he could be a Proconsular bishop (see n. 3 below) but was prevented by distance (cf. *Ep.* 56 n. 17) or even possibly local disturbance (cf. *Ep.* 62) from attending this Council meeting. See Maier, *L'épiscopat* 319; von Soden, *Prosopographie* 253. On the Council meeting itself, see intro. to this letter.

2. *litteras tuas . . . quibus significasti de Victore quondam presbytero.* Fidus' letter is lost (Harnack, *Über verlorene Briefe* 36); he presumably wrote to Cyprian for his comments and guidance on the two issues he had raised, perhaps asking Cyprian, as the six bishops of *Ep.* 56 had done, that he "discuss the matter fully with a number of colleagues" (*Ep.* 56.3). Cyprian now replies, reporting the *sententiae* of his colleagues on his two questions.

From what follows, it is clear that Victor has lost former clerical rank as a consequence of his lapse: see on such demotion *Epp.* 49 n. 18, 55 n. 52, and cf. *Ep.* 65.1.1: *Fortunatianum quondam apud vos episcopum.* As *libellatici* had been restored to communion by resolution of the Council of 251 (*Ep.* 55.17.3), Victor, who is now reported to have been prematurely readmitted, must have been a *sacrificatus.*

3. *temere Therapius collega noster inmaturo tempore et praepropera festinatione pacem dederit.* At the September meeting of 256, a certain

Therapius a Bulla gave his *sententia* in 61st place, H. 455. This is the only other instance of a bishop Therapius recorded for this period, and the two are presumably to be identified. That still leaves it unclear whether Therapius came from Bulla Regia in the Proconsular province (= Hammam Darradji, 147 km to the SW of Carthage in the rich Bagrada valley) or from further afield, from a second and distinguishable Bulla (= Bulla Minor?) perhaps lying closer towards the Numidian borderlands. See PW 3 (1897) *s.v.* "Bulla" 1047 f. (Dessau); DHGE 10 (1938) *s.vv.* "Bulla," "Bulla Regia" 1203 f., 1205 ff. (Audollent); Benson 231 n. 4, 581; Maier, *L'épiscopat* 118; Thébert, MEFR 85 (1973) 247 ff. (on Bulla Regia); Lepelley, *Les cités* 2.87 ff. It is impossible to tell whether Therapius was actually present among the 66 bishops of the Council. The wording of this conciliar letter rather suggests he was not (contra Benson 232): he would have been expected to put his signature to the letter (cf. *Ep.* 45.4.1).

Note the implication: it was not beyond question that Victor *sacrificatus* should be reconciled, but it had all been done improperly, before the due season (*inmaturo tempore*). See *Epp.* 55 n. 78, 56 n. 9, 57 n. 4, and n. 4 below. Fidus, if he came from a nearby see (cf. n. 1 above), would be under pressure from penitent but impatient lapsed within his own congregation to follow Therapius' example. He may well have sought from the Council authoritative confirmation, and support, that he should not succumb to such pressures.

4. *ante legitimum et plenum tempus satisfactionis et sine petitu et conscientia plebis, nulla infirmitate urgente ac necessitate cogente.* A particularly revealing catalogue of the circumstances in which reconciliation might have legitimately been granted. (1) Deathbed illness (*infirmitas*) was one such, specifically approved, condition: see *Ep.* 55.13.1 and n. 55 *ad loc.*, and *Ep.* 8 n. 25. (2) And *necessitas* was to force the issue of the remaining penitents when a renewal of persecution threatened under Gallus: *Ep.* 57.1.2 (*necessitate cogente*) and n. 10 there, as it had forced Cornelius' hand in dealing with the case of Trofimus, *necessitate succubuit*, *Ep.* 55.11.1. (3) *Ep.* 56 discloses that a *triennium* of penitence might be considered a *legitimum et plenum tempus* for lapsed with unusually mitigating circumstances: see *Ep.* 56.1.1 and n. 9 there, and *Ep.* 4 n. 34. (4) The phrase *sine petitu et conscientia plebis* is, however, without precise parallel, but it might find its nearest illustration in *Ep.* 59.15. There Cyprian reports how he has been

endeavouring to get his *plebs* to agree to admit erstwhile schismatics back into their ranks: *vix plebi persuadeo, immo extorqueo, ut tales patiantur admitti* (§15.3). Sometimes he fails because of popular opposition (*fratres obstinate et firmiter renituntur*, §15.2), at other times he indulgently overrides that opposition (*obnitente plebe et contradicente mea tamen facilitate suscepti*, §15.4). In other words, such readmission procedures were properly regarded as a public hearing in which *plebs* might be canvassed, or cajoled, or scandalised, over candidates; it was a community affair, though with the bishop as the ultimate authority. Correspondingly, popular demand might be taken into serious consideration (cf. *Ep.* 55.11: Trofimus). In *Ep.* 34.4.1, the inquiry into the case of deserting clergy was to be held, similarly, *cum plebe ipsa universa;* and in *Ep.* 49.2.3 ff. the *populus* of Rome is consulted over the readmission of Maximus *et al.*, and the people make their *voluntas* known *ingenti . . . suffragio.* By contrast, Therapius failed to consult the wishes of his own community in the case of Victor—and apparently he even performed the *exomologesis* ceremony without their knowledge—a case not discussed by Mortimer, *Origins of Private Penance* 31 ff., nor by Joyce, JTS 42 (1941–42) 36 ff., though relevant to their inquiries. In the light of what evidence we do have, it would be best to construe *plebis* in *sine petitu . . . plebis* as an objective genitive ("without petitioning, or even informing, his people"). Further discussed by Koch, *Cyp. Unter.* 221 f.; Poschmann, *Paenit. secunda* 385; Galtier, *L'église et la rémission* 356 f.; Daly, *Stud. patr.* 2 (1957) 205; Ritschl, *Cyprian von Karthago* 210 ff. (on the role of the laity).

5. *pacem tamen quomodocumque a sacerdote Dei semel datam non putavimus auferendam.* The important principle seems to be in the process of formation that an episcopal action could be regarded as irregular or unlawful but nevertheless valid. It remains a trifle doubtful, however, whether Cyprian would have been prepared to apply this principle universally to other sacramental acts and episcopal decisions generally, outside this particular case (which was possibly regarded as an extension of those instances where the penitent survived after his emergency reconciliation, *Ep.* 55.13.1). It is, nevertheless, a principle consonant with his general attitude towards the independent *arbitrium* of each bishop (for which he must nevertheless answer to God), on which see *Ep.* 55.21.2 and n. 95 *ad loc.*, and further discussion in Saxer, *Vie liturgique* 19; Daly, *Stud. patr.*

2.2 (1957) 204; Poschmann, *Penance and the Anointing* 60; Walker, *Churchmanship* 51.

     6. *intra octavum diem eum qui natus est baptizandum et sanctificandum non putares.* An interesting case of the strength of the O.T. injunctions on early Christian thinking and an argument not uncharacteristic of some sectors of the African Church where Jewish ideas and practices enjoyed notable life (e.g. Quispel, VC 22 [1968] 93; Frend, *Stud. patr.* 10 [1970] 291 ff.; *idem*, JTS 12 [1961] 280 ff.; *idem*, "Jews and Christians," in *Mélanges . . . Marcel Simon* 189; but for doubts of a Jewish *origin* for the African Church, Barnes, *Tertullian* 273 ff.). On Cyprian's own attitudes see *Test.* 1.8 ff. CCL 3.12 ff., and cf. Taylor, *Stud. patr.* 4 (1961) 504 ff.; Simon, *Verus Israel* 100 ff.; but he, too, is prepared at convenient times to invoke O.T. regulations to help justify N.T. liturgical practices, e.g. *Ep.* 69.12.3 (exploiting Numbers 8 and 19 for baptism by aspersion).

     Fidus' stance is not without parallel elsewhere for such adherence to a more literal interpretation of the O.T. regulations for establishing the proper day of the Christian initiatory ceremony. It is implied e.g. in the Canonical Responses, Book 2, Quest. 4, attributed to Timothy of Alexandria (c. 381): "In the event of approaching death, should a newborn child be received as a catechumen and baptised before the seventh day? Reply: he should" (Whittaker, *Documents of the Baptismal Liturgy* 77); and it can be traced in the *Rituale Armenorum*, where there is to be found the canon for baptising "an 8 days' old child" (Conybeare, *Rituale Armenorum* 86, Greek text 389).

     In Jewish (and very probably in Fidus') line of thinking, the child was considered unclean and ritually taboo *intra octavum diem*; it was excluded from the community until the circumcision ceremony on the eighth day, or later (within minor variations, e.g. Talmud Babli, Shabbath 137a, Mishnah: an infant is to be circumcised on the eighth, ninth, tenth, eleventh and twelfth days, neither earlier nor later. How so? In the normal course it is on the eighth day; if he is born at twilight, on the ninth; at twilight on the Sabbath eve, on the tenth; if a festival follows the Sabbath, on the eleventh; if the two days of New Year follow the Sabbath, on the twelfth. An infant who is ill is not circumcised until he recovers).

     At all events, it is clear that Fidus did not object to child baptism;

he questioned only the propriety of the *very* early baptism of infants. See further intro. to this letter.

7. *nulli hominum nato misericordiam Dei et gratiam denegandam.* This essential verdict is tellingly repeated in §5.1 and again in §6.1 at the conclusion of the letter: *a baptismo atque a gratia Dei . . . neminem per nos debere prohiberi.* It implies clearly a generally accepted view of original sin, for which remittance was necessary: this is stated openly in §5.2 (where see n. 20). Augustine quotes verbatim this section and others of *Ep.* 64 with strong approval in his anti-Pelagian writings (*Contr. duas epist. Pelag.* 4.8.23 CSEL 60.546 f.) and generously refers to this ruling in *Ep.* 166.23 CSEL 44.579.

8. Lk. 9.56, Fahey 345.

9. *illic aequalitas divina et spiritalis exprimitur.* For this somewhat bizarre but ingenious example of typological argument (based on 2 Kings 4.32 ff.), see Fahey 587 who observes: "Typical here is Cyprian's concern for detail and his conviction that even the slightest action of Elisha was meant to communicate typologically a message to the Christian community." Note the closely parallel miracle of St. Martin of Tours, Sulp. Sev., *Vit. mart.* 8.2: *superstratus corpori aliquantisper oravit.*

10. *sanctus spiritus non de mensura . . . aequalis omnibus praebeatur.* A celebrated formulation of Cyprian's pneumatological view, for which *Ep.* 69.14.1 provides a close parallel: *spiritus sanctus non de mensura datur sed super credentem totus infunditur,* and cf. *Ad Donat.* 5 CCL 3A.5: *non . . . capessendo munere mensura ulla vel modus est. Profluens largiter spiritus nullis finibus premitur,* etc. For further comment see *Ep.* 10 n. 18 and Réveillaud, *Stud. patr.* 6 (1962) 181 ff. Cyprian clearly based his view on John 3.34 (*non enim ad mensuram dat Deus Spiritum* [Vulgate]).

11. *Deus ut personam non accipit, sic nec aetatem.* There is biblical allusion in describing God as "not a respecter of persons" (found in Rom. 2.11, Eph. 6.9, Gal. 2.6, Acts 10.34, James 2.1, going back to Deut. 1.17), cf. Fahey 425 (but this passage omitted).

12. *quod vestigium infantis in primis partus sui diebus constituti mundum non esse dixisti, quod unusquisque nostrum adhuc horreat exosculari.* Cyprian is reporting Fidus' argument before producing his colleagues' rejoinder; he may well be repeating some of Fidus' own phrasing. The second *quod* clause is best construed as relative (refer-

ring back to *vestigium*) rather than as causal ("because, as you say
. . .") or substantival ("as for the fact that . . ."); see Thraede, JAC
11/12 (1968/69) 163.

What is particularly puzzling about the present passage is the
phrase *vestigium infantis*. That a kiss (of peace) was associated with the
baptismal ceremony is well established (see n. 14 below), but why
refer to the *vestigium infantis* in particular? Some have argued that
Cyprian (or Fidus) has used the expression in a *pars pro toto* sense, not
a literal sense. He is, therefore, really talking about that kiss of peace
which was given the neophyte after baptism and before the accom-
panying Eucharistic service (see Quasten and Thraede, *art. cit.* in intro., for careful discussion of such a view). It is difficult, however, to
extract such a sense out of the Latin (Sullivan, *Life* 39, translates e.g.
without supporting argument: "The aspect of an infant, as it is in the
first days after its birth, is not clean"). It is best to conclude, therefore, with Watson 265, that *vestigium* is a (well-attested) variant for
pes and that Fidus is referring to a ceremonial kissing of the *foot* which
formed part of the generally accepted African baptismal liturgy.

Such a rite, however, lacks precise parallel. It is by no means
improbable that it was or was to become part of the later-attested (but
controversial) foot-*washing* ceremony. That is documented for Spain
(Council Elvira, can. 48; Hefele-Leclercq, *Histoire* 1.249), for Milan
(Ambros., *De sacr.* 3.1.4 ff. ML 16.451 ff., *De myst.* 6 ML 16.416 f.),
for Gaul (Caesarius of Arles, *Serm.* 204.3 CCL 104.821: *secundum quod
ipsis in baptismo factum est hospitibus pedes abluant*), and for Africa (Aug.,
Ep. 55.33 ff. ML 33.220 ff.); and see, for further parallels, RAC 8
(1972) *s.v.* "Fusswaschung" 765 ff. (Kötting); Beatrice, *Augustinianum*
20 (1980) 23 ff. Small, second baptismal basins may have been used
in such a ceremony: see Davies, *Architectural Setting of Baptism* 26, 40
(Ravenna, Albenga, Fréjus); also Formigé, in *Mélanges . . . Martroye*
177 f. (Fréjus). This act of washing the *planta* of the initiand (derived
from John 13.9) was explained variously but notably as symbolic of
washing away the contagious poison of the serpent who first tripped
up (*supplantavit*) Adam, and of protecting this particularly vulnerable
member of man (cf. Ambrose, *loc. cit.*; Aug., *Contr. duas epist. Pelag.*
4.11.29 CSEL 60.559 f., quoting with approval from the nonextant
commentary on Isaiah by Ambrose: *lavacro pedum, qui in primo lapsi*

sunt homine, sordem obnoxiae successionis aboleri). Hence penitent sinners could be referred to as the "feet of Christ," [Aug.] *Serm.* 83.3 ML 39.1907: *noli hos spernere peccatores quia pedes Christi sunt,* and see Carcopino, *Rendiconti Pontif. Accad. Rom. Arch.* 5 (1928) 79 ff.

Such a foot-washing ceremony, one might speculate, included a kiss as a token of the acknowledged purity which the rite efficaciously achieved over the *contagium mortis antiquae* contracted from Adam (§5.2). But to Fidus' way of thinking, the ritual impurity of the infant, still fresh from childbirth, rendered the first week after its birth an improper and, indeed, repugnant period for holding such a rite. Note Rosenfeld, *Kindesfoot* (1964), for a study of the close folk connexion between child's birth and foot, the foot being a symbol of birth in North European tradition.

13. Tit. 1.15, Fahey 517.

14. *non ita est tamen ut quisquam illum in gratia danda adque in pace facienda horrere debeat osculari.* Note the evidence for a kiss (of peace) in the baptismal ceremony: see the *testimonia* adduced by Quasten in *Festschrift J. Pascher* 267 ff. for two kisses, one concluding the baptismal ceremony, the other as part of the Eucharistic service that normally followed baptism; and cf. Hofmann, *Philema Hagion* 128 ff.; DACL 2 (1925) *s.v.* "Baiser" 127 f. (Cabrol); Dölger, *Ant. und Christ.* 1 (1929) 186 ff. The phrase *in pace facienda* could refer to such a ritual gesture (in addition to *osculari*), with *pax* used as a "Christianism" for *[osculum] pacis,* on which see Pétré, *Caritas* 309 ff.; or *pax* may be used rather in its penitential sense of *remissa peccatorum,* reconciliation from [in this case, original] sin (cf. §5.2 below). Salaville, *Échos* 39 (1941-42) 269 f., discusses whether this passage implies *epiclesis* of the Holy Spirit, comparing *Ep.* 70.2.2 f.

15. *sacramentum est in umbra adque imagine ante praemissum, sed veniente Christo veritate conpletum.* Compare closely *Ad Demet.* 22 CCL 3A.48: *quod ante . . . praecedit in imagine impletur in Christo secuta postmodum veritate.* For the typological use of *sacramentum, umbra, imago,* and *veritas,* note the excursus on Cyprian's vocabulary for typology in Fahey 612 ff. and the references cited there for further literature on this language. To his list of *prae-* verbs on pp. 618 ff. add the present *praemissum,* and on p. 621 add the *conpletum* here as a variant of the *adimpleri* there discussed. Noteworthy in particular is the use of

sacramentum in the sense of "prophetic figure," on which see de Ghellinck *et al.* 175 ff. and cf. *Ep.* 69.14.1: *cuius aequalitatis sacramentum videmus in Exodo esse celebratum.*

For a useful commentary on Cyprian's view of the supersession of Jewish practices by the New Dispensation, see *Test.* 1.8 ff. CCL 3.12 ff.; Justin, *Dial.* 41.4 MG 6.564 f., is particularly close to the present passage on the Jewish prefiguring of the new, spiritual circumcision, on which parallel see Koch, *Rich. rel.* 5 (1929) 156 f.

16. *hic dies octavus id est post sabbatum primus et dominicus praecessit in imagine.* The rich numerological tradition of the figure 8 in Christian thinking (marking the Resurrection, the New Age, the New Creation, a token of the New Kingdom, etc.) is already evidenced in *Epist. ad Barn.* 15.8 f.: ". . . eighth day, that is the beginning of another world. Therefore, we also celebrate with gladness the eighth day on which Jesus also rose from the dead, and was made manifest, and ascended into heaven," as well as in Justin *Dial.* 24.1, 41.4, 138.1 MG 6.527, 564 f., 793 (all connected with baptism and the new circumcision). And for contemporary thinking cf. Origen, *Paschal Homily 3* (ed. Nautin, *Homélies pascales* 2, SC 36) 15, 17 (Nautin 113, 115), again emphasising the connexion of the number 8 with the Lord's Day and the day for being sanctified with the Holy Spirit. The eighth day, i.e. Sunday, thus became the day par excellence for the baptismal ceremony: Eusebius, *Comment. in Ps. 6* MG 23.120. Passages can be gathered from Basil, Greg. Nyssa, Athanasius, Ambrose, Ambrosiaster, and Augustine to illustrate the vitality of the fast-elaborating tradition in the fourth century (see e.g. the assembly of texts by Rordorf, *Sabbat et dimanche* 108 ff., 184 ff.; cf. Daniélou, *Le dimanche* 61 ff.), and the notion appears in Gnostic literature as well (cf. *Hermetica* ed. W. Scott 1.129). For further studies, DACL 4 (1920) *s.v.* "Dimanche" 879 ff. (Dumaine); Dölger, *Ant. und Christ.* 4 (1934) 153 ff.; Daniélou, *Rech. sc. rel.* 35 (1948) 382 ff.; Underwood, *Dumbarton Oaks Pap.* 5 (1950) 80 ff.; Hopper, *Medieval Number Symbolism* 77 f., 85; Staats, VC 26 (1972) 29 ff.; RAC 1 (1950) *s.v.* "Achtzahl" 79 ff. (Schneider); Quacquarelli, *L'ogdoade* (1973); Bacchiochi, *From Sabbath to Sunday* 278 ff.; Odom, *Sabbath and Sunday*, esp. 216 f.; and on the early development of the celebration of Pentecost ($= 7 \times 7 + 1$), Cabié, *La pentecôte* 46 ff. This rich symbolism was translated into the later construction of octagonal-shaped baptisteries, on

which see the works of Dölger, Underwood (131 ff.), and Quacquarelli cited above, adding Sauer, *Symbolik des Kirchen* 78 f.; Krautheimer, *Journ. Warb. Inst.* 5 (1942) 21 ff.; RAC 1 (1950) *s.v.*
"Achteck" 72 ff. (Schneider); Bedard, *Symbolism* (1951).

For evidence on Sunday being regarded (as here) as the day for
celebrating the Lord's resurrection see Dugmore, "Lord's Day and
Easter," in *Festschrift . . . O. Cullmann* 272 ff., and Bacchiochi, *From
Sunday to Sabbath* 204 f., 270 ff. (traceable to Irenaeus, Justin Martyr,
Ep. Barn., etc.), and cf. *Ep.* 63 n. 43.

17. *ea lege quae iam statuta est.* Literally, "by that law which
once was established." There is an interesting African lamp which
iconographically illustrates this overthrow of the Old Law: Christ is
represented as trampling the serpent underfoot, while underneath
both is an overturned seven-branch candelabrum: *Musée Lavigerie (R.
P. Delattre)* 3.37 f.; Ennabli, *Lampes chrétiennes* no. 69 p. 51 and Pl.11.

18. Acts 10.28, Fahey 416.

19. *in Deum multum ante peccantibus cum postea crediderint remissa
peccatorum datur.* Cyprian pointedly illustrates his argument with the
case of converts who have once committed the most heinous sins of
all, sins *in Deum*, i.e. blasphemy, idolatry, adultery, homicide,
which, notoriously, had had a lengthy history of being judged otherwise irremissible, as *peccata aeterna*: see *Ep.* 55 n. 87 (on adultery),
Epp. 55 intro., 8 n. 25, 15 n. 12 (on idolatry), and cf. *Ep.* 73.19.1 f.
(on blasphemy). Note Cyprian's firm view: all past sins, of whatever
character, are forgiven in baptism; cf. *Test.* 3.65 CCL 3.155: *omnia
delicta in baptismo deponi.*

20. *secundum Adam carnaliter natus contagium mortis antiquae . . .
contraxit . . . illi remittuntur non propria sed aliena peccata.* Other early
patristic writers, of course, associated baptism with the cleansing of
sinfulness (especially linked to the process of generation and birth;
cf. Ps. 50.7: *in facinore conceptus sum et in peccatis aluit me in utero mater
mea*, quoted in *Test.* 3.54 CCL 3.141 on the theme *neminem sine sorde
et sine peccato esse*); see e.g. Origen, *In Rom. comm.* 5.9 MG 14. 1047;
Hom. in Luc. 14 GCS 49.87 f. And for the generally accepted view in
antiquity of the foulness of the female womb and the processes of
birth, see also Tert., *De carn. Christ.* 4.1 ff. CCL 2.878 (Marcion's
objections to the Incarnation); Origen, *Contra Celsum* 6.73 SC
147.362 (Celsus' case against the use of the female womb for the In-

carnation), and see further R. Mortley, *Womanhood* 84 f. But Cyprian
is remarkable in linking that sinfulness specifically and exclusively to
Adam; the way in which he presents his argument, however, indicates that this interpretation of "original sin" was no novel but a
widely accepted viewpoint (cf. Aug., *Ep.* 166 CSEL 44.579: *Beatus
quidem Cyprianus non aliquod decretum condens novum sed ecclesiae fidem
firmissimam servans; idem, De pecc. merit. et remiss.* 3.5.11 CSEL 60.
137: *vides quanta fiducia ex antiqua et indubitata fidei regula vir tantus ista
loquatur.*) See also *De op. et eleem.* 1 CCL 3A.55: *Dominus adveniens sa-
nasset illa quae Adam portaverat vulnera,* and cf. *De hab. virg.* 23 H. 204:
*omnes quidem qui . . . hominem illic veterem gratia lavacri salutaris expon-
unt et . . . a sordibus contagionis antiquae iterata nativitate purgantur.*
Hence Pelikan, *Development* 87, can conclude: "Cyprian would thus
appear to have been the first teacher of the Church to connect an explicit argument for the baptism of infants with an explicit statement
of the doctrine that, through their physical birth, children inherited
the sins of Adam and the death that was the wages of sin." (But note
the Cappadocian Firmilian in *Ep.* 75.17.2 on the *antiqua mortis peccata*
which are forgiven in baptism: see *Ep.* 75 n. 75.) For further discussion see Kelly, *Doctrines³* 174 ff.; Lukken, *Original Sin,* esp. 194 ff.;
Pelikan, *Development* 73 ff.; Beatrice, *Tradux peccati* 188 f.; and for Augustine's exploitation of this present Cyprianic notion of *aliena peccata,* see Didier, *Mél. sc. relig.* 9 (1952) 191 ff., and Dubarle, REAug
3 (1957) 113 ff. Despite this notion of *aliena peccata* here, it was without any sense of embarrassment that Cyprian argued against the Novatianist view of sinful pollution (*peccato alterius inquinari alterum
dicunt*) by making the bald claim *secundum fidem nostram . . . unum-
quemque in peccato suo ipsum teneri nec posse alium pro altero reum fieri* (*Ep.*
55.27.2 f.), and see *Ep.* 55 n. 127.

The preceding phrase *prima nativitate* (translated "from that first
birth [sc. in Adam]") could also conceivably be interpreted "[con-
tracted] from the moment he was born." For parallels of these two
senses, see the commentary by J. Molager, SC 291.211, on *De bon.
pat.* 12; and for this phrasing compare *De centesima* ML *Supp.* 1.54:
renovati per lavacrum vitale et delicto primae nativitatis purgati vivamus.

21. *in primo statim nativitatis suae ortu plorantes ac flentes nihil aliud faciunt quam deprecantur.* An embarrassingly fanciful conceit, the
tastelessness only rendered a little more palatable by the fact that it

is a variant on an established rhetorical commonplace that children come weeping into this world because they are facing a life that is nasty, brutish, and short. Augustine did not wince to imitate it, *Serm.* 294.17 ML 38. 1346: *ipsorum infantium lacrimis tamquam fluvio pertrahantur*, though he could also be a little more down to earth on babies bawling throughout the baptismal ceremony, *De bapt. contr. Donat.* 4.30 ML 43. 174: *quin etiam flendo et vagiendo cum in eis mysterium celebratur, ipsis mysticis vocibus obstrepunt.* For classical precedents of the *topos* compare Lucr., *De rer. nat.* 5.224 ff.:

> cum primum in luminis oras
> nixibus ex alvo matris natura profudit,
> vagituque locum lugubri complet, ut aequumst
> cui tantum in vita restet transire malorum.

Also Pliny, *N.H.* 7. *praef.* 2: *hominem tantum nudum et in nuda humo natali die abicit ad vagitus statim et ploratum, nullumque tot animalium aliud ad lacrimas, et has protinus vitae principio.* And see further Aug., *Ennar. in ps.* 125.10 ML 37.1664: *quare a fletu incipit vivere [puer qui nascitur]? Ridere nondum novit; quare plorare iam novit? Quia coepit ire in istam vitam.* For a lengthy exploration of the general *topos*, see A. Goulon, REAug 18 (1972) 3 ff. (Christian reusage, 14 ff.), with further discussion by J. Molager in his commentary (SC 291.210) on *De bon. pat.* 12, where Cyprian evinces a closely parallel sentiment (*unusquisque cum nascitur . . . initium sumit a lacrimis et . . . nihil aliud novit in illa prima nativitate quam flere . . . in exordio statim suo ploratu et gemitu . . .*, CCL 3A.124 f.).

Letter 65

Contents: Cyprian is distressed to learn that a lapsed bishop Fortunatianus is trying to usurp his former position as bishop, to which, being guilty of sacrilege, he is no longer entitled, for he cannot now offer prayers and sacrifices which God can heed. All he is really after, of course, are the opportunities for gluttony and filthy lucre for which in the past he had abused his episcopal position—and for which sins God has now visited such prelates with His censure, effectively driving them away from His altar. If Fortunatianus does not turn to repentance for his sins, every effort must be made to separate the innocent brethren from his error, while the lapsed must not be deceived by his lies into desisting from their necessary acts of penitence.

Date and circumstances: By common consent this letter has been assigned a place out of its due order in the series. The outside limits for its dating can be readily set.

(1) It ought to come after the African Council of 251. Cyprian voices no hesitation about the penitential discipline to which Fortunatianus and his fellow lapsed ought now to be adhering: they can be told of their penitential duties in no uncertain terms (§§1.1, 5.1 f.). The Council of 251 had put an end to hesitation and uncertainty on the issue by establishing that discipline and those duties in firm regulations. And sufficient time ought to have elapsed for Fortunatianus to have been replaced, it may be assumed (see n. 1), by Epictetus (after the persecution had died down?), and that replacement to have been challenged, in turn, by Fortunatianus. The second half of 251 should, therefore, mark the *terminus post.*

(2) There is no hint, however, that there are yet any further threats of renewed persecution under Gallus; when the day of judgment is mentioned (§§1.2, 5.2), it is put matter-of-factly, with nothing of that immediacy which acute fear of persecution in the time of Gallus was to rouse (*Epp.* 57, 58, 60). Neither is there any hint, when he addresses the lapsed in §5.1 f., that reconciliation has now been granted to *sacrificati* who had been doing continuous penitence (as was regulated under fears of coming persecution in the time of Gallus, *Ep.* 57). The first third of 253 (likely date for *Ep.* 57) should accordingly mark the *terminus ante.*

Given those outside limits, there is the mild suggestion that the letter is composed earlier rather than later within that timetable. The need to argue the case for the laicisation of a lapsed bishop (§§2.1 f.), which was laid down by the Council of 251 and universally adopted elsewhere (*Ep.* 67.6.3), suggests that the issue was still fresh. And Cyprian can refer to Fortunatianus' laxist advisers by an anonymous *quorundam* (§§1.2, 2.2); he was inclined so to do while there was still hope of effecting a reconciliation with that party. But events of 252 (appointment of a laxist *pseudoepiscopus* in Carthage) put an end to such diplomatic coyness, and the expression ceases and names are named instead in *Ep.* 59, esp. §§9 ff. (summer of 252); that *pseudoepiscopus* was appointed after the opening of the Council of 252, which met on the Ides of May, *Ep.* 59.10.1. Therefore, the most feasible placing of the letter becomes second half of 251–first third of 252. It ought to be numbered, therefore, immediately after *Ep.* 55. See Koch, *Cyp. Unter.* 177; Nelke, *Chronologie* 156; Turner, *Studies* 124 f.; Réveillaud 11; Duquenne, *Chronologie* 33.

The letter allows us to glimpse Cyprian at work qua "metropolitan," encouraging tactful firmness in his fellow bishop in the face of schism and disharmony. But not only does he uphold and give support to Epictetus; he has his congregation in mind as well (included in his salutation). Fortunatianus clearly enjoys the command of a considerable following and sympathy from among his old congregation (from innocent and lapsed brethren alike, §§4.2 f.). Cyprian is at pains to muster arguments against *sacrificati*, and in particular *sacrificati* bishops, for the benefit of the hearing of that congregation as he tries to prise them away from their old loyalties. And despite the vigorous polemic against worldly bishops (§§3.1 ff.), he takes diplomatic care to leave the way wide open for harmony and settlement; it is left plainly understood that no irrevocable break has yet occurred (§§4.1 f.).

This fleeting insight into local dispute and disarray allows us to imagine the way in which the life of Christian communities was being disrupted all over the Mediterranean world in the wake of the Decian persecution.

Cyprian's attack on bishops dedicated to the pursuit of mammon is notable (§§3.1 f.). He sees them as a cause of the persecution (as in *De laps.* 5 f. CCL 3. 223 f.) but with a somewhat novel twist: the divine *censura* was, through persecution, seeking to remove such sources of corruption away from the altar of God (§3.2.).

1. *Cyprianus Epicteto fratri et plebi Assuras consistenti s.* On this cast of salutation cf. *Ep.* 1 *init.* and see n. 1 *ad loc.* It is the reasonable assumption—but assumption only—that Epictetus is the present

bishop of Assuras. The form of address is standard to a bishop (e.g. *Epp.* 2, 3, 4, etc.).

At the September Council of 256, Assuras was represented by a bishop Victor, *Sent. episc.* LXXXVII. 68 H. 456. He was followed immediately at that Council by Donatulus of Capsa, who appears to have been consecrated bishop in the early months of 253 (see *Ep.* 56 intro. and nn. 1 and 3). We should deduce that Epictetus, *if* he is the bishop, went to his rest from these disquieting wrangles at Assuras within a year or so of receiving this letter, to be replaced by Victor by at least early 253. Epictetus will then have been bishop for about two years at the most. *Mart. Hieron.* for *V. Id. Januar.* (Jan. 9) records *in Africa Epicteti* (*Act. sanct. Nov.* 2.1. [6]), but it would be an *audax coniectura* confidently to claim the two are linked (so, rightly, Delehaye in *Act. sanct. Nov.* 2.2.33). See further von Soden, *Prosopographie* 261 f., 255 ff. (Victor); Maier, *L'épiscopat* 106, 302.

Assuras (= Zanfour) is situated 150 km to the SW of Carthage, some 35 km to the SE of Sicca Veneria: DHGE 4 (1930) *s.v.* "Assuras" 1145 ff. (Audollent); PW 2 (1896) *s.v.* "Assuras" 1749 ff. (Dessau).

2. *cognoverim Fortunatianum quondam apud vos episcopum post gravem lapsum ruinae suae pro integro nunc agere velle.* Some lost communication between Cyprian and Assuras seems to be implied; Cyprian helpfully replies by laying out clearly and authoritatively the principles involved in the dispute. Note that Fortunatianus has forfeited automatically his clerical rank with his lapse; that penalty of laicisation was formally adopted at the Council of 251 (*Ep.* 67.6.3), and see *Ep.* 49 n. 18 for further discussion.

The expression *pro integro agere* is picked up again in §2.1: *agere pro Dei sacerdote*, and §3.3.: *agere pro sacerdote*, and echoed in §5.2: *episcopis sanis et integris.* Cyprian's sacramental theology required that *sacerdotes* should be *integri* if they were to function as efficacious ministers of God; see n. 14 below.

3. *quorundam sacrilega persuasione deceptus.* Cf. §2.2.: *quorundam pectora . . . profunda caligo caecaverit.* It is clear that Fortunatianus favours the laxist party; his advice to the fallen is "not to ask" (*doceat . . . nec rogare*, §1.2), and he is associated with those who deceive the lapsed *falsa et mortali seductione*, §5.1. The *quidam* here are, therefore, laxist leaders (Felicissimus and his five presbyters etc.) who are

falsely encouraging Fortunatianus in his cause. See further intro. to this letter.

4. *audet sibi adhuc sacerdotium quod prodidit vindicare.* Cyprian has verbally moved from Fortunatianus' usurping his *episcopatus* in §1.1 (*episcopatum sibi vindicare*) to his present demand for his betrayed *sacerdotium.* The former word is concerned more with the administrative office of bishop, the latter with the priestly and sacred functions of bishop, upon which Cyprian now proceeds to dilate. See further Bévenot, " 'Sacerdos' as Understood by Cyprian," JTS 30 (1979) 413 ff.

5. *post aras diaboli accedere ad altare Dei.* Note the clear choice of *ara* for pagan, *altare* for Christian sacrifices. See *Ep.* 1 n. 12, *Ep.* 59 n. 86.

6. *fidei et virtutis dux . . . perfidiae et audaciae et temeritatis magister.* For *fides et virtus* as the characteristic twin virtues of the martyr in Cyprian, see *Ep.* 10. n. 3. Cyprian is wishing to give their antonyms in his contrasting phrase: *perfidiae* answers to *fidei* (as again in §3.2: *fidem perfidi*), *audaciae et temeritatis* to *virtutis,* according to the Aristotelian scheme of vicious extremes.

7. Isa. 57.6 (Fahey 211), Exod. 22.20 (Fahey 76 f.), Isa. 2.8 f. (Fahey 190 f.), and Apoc. 14.9 ff. (Fahey 547 f.), a quick collection on the abomination in which God holds anyone who sacrifices to pagan gods. Fortunatianus was a *sacrificatus* (confirmed by §§2.1 f.).

8. *manum suam transferri . . . ad Dei sacrificium et precem Domini.* Note the almost technical use of the singular *prex* to refer to the solemn prayer of oblation (as below in §2.2: *precem pro fratribus facere*), on which usage see *Ep.* 1 n. 26 and Renaud, *Eucharistie* 195 ff. The hands would be used in making the characteristic gesture of the *orans* whilst reciting the *prex,* or would be imposed *in eucharistia* (cf. *Ep.* 70 n. 10) upon the offering (as in the celebrated painting in the Catacomb of Callistus, *cubiculum* A, depicting both an *orans* and a figure imposing hands over bread and fish on a round, three-legged altar table: illustration in Testini, *Le catacombe,* Tav. V).

9. Levit. 21.17 (Fahey 82), Exod. 19.22 and Exod. 30.20 f. (Fahey 75).

10. John 9.31, Fahey 389.

11. *stipes et oblationes et lucra desiderant.* It is unclear whether these three words are merely rhetorical variants or whether they are

intended to denote distinguishable sources of gain (e.g. stipend, donations [in kind?], business profits). They ought somehow to be associated with the office of bishop which Fortunatianus now regrets. For the bishop's position abused for making secular gains, *De laps.* 6 CCL 3.223 f.; on the support and salaries of clerics, see *Ep.* 1 nn. 19 and 21, *Ep.* 34 n. 20, *Ep.* 39 n. 25; and on the interpretation of the present passage, see also Vilela, *Condition collégiale* 327 f.; Watson 274 ("*oblationes* . . . can only have been an irregular source of income"); Janssen, *Kultur u. Sprache* 107 ff., 229 f. (for *oblatio* here, compare *Ep.* 79.1.1: *oblationis nomine quantitatem*).

12. *ventri potius et quaestui . . . servisse.* There is an allusion to Rom. 16.18 (omitted by Fahey), where the Vulgate reads *Christo Domino nostro non serviunt sed suo ventri.* Are we to imagine the scandalous gluttony and carousing to have occurred at Christian *convivia* (on which see *Ep.* 63.16.1 f.; *Ad Donat.* 16 CCL 3A.13: *nec sit vel hora convivii gratiae caelestis immunis. Sonet psalmus convivium sobrium;* cf. *Test.* 3.3 CCL 3.89 on the topic *agapem et dilectionem fraternam religiose et firmiter exercendam;* Hippol., *Apost. trad.* 26 ed. Botte) or merely that these prelates turned the profits derived from their office as bishop to pay for such sensual pleasures? Cf. Lucian *De mort. Pereg.* 13, 16 on sources of revenue, income, profit—and gluttony—available to popular church leaders, and the polemic of Ammianus Marcellinus (writing a century and a half later) against Roman bishops, *R.G.* 27.3.14: "They are enriched with the offerings of matrons *(oblationibus matronarum)* . . . and serve banquets so lavish that their entertainments outdo the tables of kings."

13. *ipsam venisse perspicimus . . . de Dei exploratione censuram.* For persecution regarded as an *exploratio,* cf. *De laps.* 5 CCL 3.223: *hoc omne quod gestum est exploratio potius quam persecutio videretur; Ep.* 11.5.3: *persecutio ista examinatio est atque exploratio pectoris nostri.*

14. *nec oblatio sanctificari illic possit ubi sanctus spiritus non sit, nec cuiquam Dominus per eius orationes . . . prosit.* A clear enunciation of Cyprian's notorious sacramental theology in which the efficacy of the sacerdotal actions is made directly dependent upon the personal sanctity of the *sacerdos.* The baptismal dispute promptly brought out this attitude into full view (e.g. *Ep.* 69.12.3 *ad fin.*). See e.g. the monograph of Navickas (1924); Wiles, *JEH* 14 (1963) 139 ff.; R. F. Evans, *One and Holy* (1972), etc.

15. *ad ecclesiam pulsent ut recipi illuc possint ubi fuerunt.* On this persistent image in Cyprian's penitential discourse, see *Ep.* 30 n. 39.

16. Ephes 5.6 f., Fahey 489 f.

LETTER 66

Contents: Cyprian has discovered to his surprise that Puppianus continues in his wild beliefs about his morals and conduct, even though it is God Himself (who appoints bishops) who has judged his character as worthy. Puppianus prefers, instead, the testimony of renegades and apostates. Moreover, the charge of failing in humility is rebutted by Cyprian's faithful service to the brethren; rather, Puppianus fails in humility by not giving respect to the priest and judge whom God has appointed. Even during the persecution (in which Puppianus was so honoured) Cyprian himself was acknowledged by the devil to be the bishop and was, therefore, singled out for attack (witness the public notice of his proscription). Indeed, the last six years spent in administering baptism, penance, and deathbed rites, and all the other priestly activities of those years, now depend for their legitimacy on Puppianus' personal verdict! Others have not suffered such scruples—neither martyrs, nor fellow bishops, nor confessors, virgins, widows—in short, all of the churches in communion with Cyprian, unless they, too, are all polluted with Cyprian's fatal contagion, leaving only Puppianus unscathed. In fact, the divisions in the Church are caused not by Cyprian but by the chaff which alone can be separated off from the true wheat; the Church herself does not desert Christ and His bishops, and Christ, as He has revealed to Cyprian, will avenge those who deny His appointed bishops.

Date and circumstances: Cyprian has been exercising his functions as bishop now for six years, *iam sex annis* §5.1. That must place the letter, at the earliest, in the last months of 253, or as late as the year 255. Precisely when depends on two unresolvable factors: the commencement date of Cyprian's episcopacy (not known accurately) from which the calculation is to be made, and whether (as he may do) Cyprian is referring to six *completed* years in office as bishop. However,

254 remains the most probable setting for this letter, in view of the fact that earlier, in the course of 252, Cyprian had already talked of his episcopacy as having lasted a *quadriennium* (*Ep.* 59.6.1). See further n. 20 below.

It is interesting to observe that even at such a date Cyprian's personal conduct under persecution continued to be a matter for grave, and provoking, dispute (§§4.1 f.) as well as the controversial circumstances of his original election as bishop (§1.2). His authoritarian style of church government rankled (he failed in humility, §3.1; *he* was responsible for the present schisms, §8.1) and his grand command of privately vouchsafed divine revelations to justify that government could be stingingly ridiculed (§§9.2 ff.). And Cyprian could still be taunted with the special dignities enjoyed by confessors (§§1.2, 4.1 ff.). The old sources of dissension have still not been dammed.

Cyprian's response to these attacks is to pen some notable passages of religious polemic grimly enlivened with touches of salty humour (e.g. the vision of Puppianus all on his own in paradise, §7.3) and trenchant sarcasm (e.g. §5.2), an effective combination seldom encountered elsewhere in Cyprian's writings. He is also stimulated to resort to a particularly strong (but vulnerable) line of argument based on God's choice of only good men as bishops (§§1.2 ff.) and on the divine counsel to which he as bishop enjoys direct access (§§9.1 ff.). But above all he is challenged to state clearly his view of the essential role of the bishops in the structure of the Church, and the respect and obedience which is therefore due to their authority (§§3.2 ff.). The letter thus becomes a significant document for Cyprian's heavy sacerdotalism, as well as for his humanity; Puppianus' criticisms have obviously touched on some raw nerves. Much remains, however, a vigorous *réchauffé* of arguments already rehearsed for the benefit of Cornelius two years earlier in the face of a similar attack (ten of the twelve biblical quotations used in this letter were already exploited in *Ep.* 59). There he had sought to rebut the rival claims of the *pseudoepiscopus* Fortunatus (*Ep.* 59), of whom Puppianus was probably in fact a leading supporter (see n. 10 below). They have not let up their campaign. For a full analysis of Cyprian's techniques in polemic, especially vocabulary, see I. Opelt, *Die Polemik* 116 ff.

There appears to have been a translation into Greek, Watson *CR* 7 (1893) 248.

It is illuminating to compare the response of Dionysius of Alexandria to not dissimilar defamations levelled at his conduct during the persecutions by Germanus: Germanus, like Puppianus, prided himself on his confessions and special vicissitudes (*ap.* Euseb. *H.E.* 7.11.18; cf. n. 4 below). See *ap.* Euseb. *H.E.* 6.40 and 7.11.

1. *Cyprianus qui et Thascius Florentio cui et Puppiano fratri s.*

That Cyprian should thus use double names in his salutation requires explanation, for it is not his custom to employ more than one personal name whether for himself or for others, and on the rare occasions when he does so, there are explanations to hand to account for his break with custom (e.g. clarity of identification: see *Epp.* 1 n. 4, 34 n. 2, and cf. *Ep.* 59 n. 51). In the present case the most readily available explanation is that Cyprian is studiously (and mockingly) reflecting the style of address in the letter from Puppianus to which he is now replying (on which letter see n. 3 below); cf. Watson 273 f. Puppianus had grandly flaunted his own distinguished family names (belonging as he did in all likelihood to a wealthy and locally eminent senatorial family—see below), addressing Cyprian without that respectful deference which Cyprian saw as properly due to his episcopal rank and clearly eschewing for him the actual title of *episcopus* which he denied to Cyprian (§§4.1, 7.1 f.). Cyprian replies accordingly, exceptionally adding his own *agnomen* of Thascius: it is of unknown derivation, in origin presumed (vaguely) "Punic" or "Libyan." It also occurs in the *Act. procos. Cyp.* 3.3 (*"Tu es Thascius qui et Cyprianus?"*) and 4.3 (Musurillo 172) as well as in Pont., *Vit. Cyp.* 15 H. cvii (suggesting this was the name by which he was popularly known). See further Kajanto, *Supernomina* 37, 40, who declares that in African nomenclature "no less than 26% of all the agnomina were barbaric" (p. 23).

As for Puppianus, the combination of inscriptions ILAlg 3069 and 3070 (Theveste) plus CIL 8.26415 (near Uchi Maius) yields the following family tree of which Puppianus, on grounds of nomenclature, was probably a member. The family in Puppianus' generation was domiciled in Uchi Maius, a *pagus* of Carthage near Thugga (Gascou, *Politique municipale* 158 ff.), and had by now risen to senatorial status, having figured in earlier generations as local magistrates and benefactors of Theveste and being still prominent as manufacturers of lamps (branded with the *gens* name *Pullaieni*).

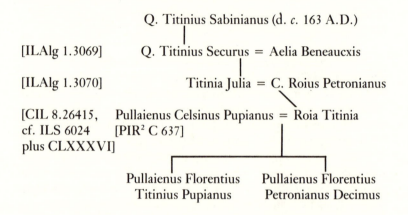

Q. Titinius Sabinianus (d. *c.* 163 A.D.)

[ILAlg 1.3069]   Q. Titinius Securus = Aelia Beneaucxis

[ILAlg 1.3070]   Titinia Julia = C. Roius Petronianus

[CIL 8.26415,   Pullaienus Celsinus Pupianus = Roia Titinia
cf. ILS 6024   [PIR² C 637]
plus CLXXXVI]

Pullaienus Florentius   Pullaienus Florentius
Titinius Pupianus   Petronianus Decimus

(The latter two senators figure as nos. 71 and 70 in Pelletier, *Latomus* 23 [1964] 517; cf. Barbieri, *L'Albo* nos. 832 and 831.)

For discussion of this family see Merlin and Poinssot 108 ff. (plus 54 ff., 113 ff.); Leschi, *Études* 117 ff. (adding the first generation); Pflaum, *Antiq. Afric.* 4 (1970) 112 f. (on the gens *Pullaieni*); Freis, *Chiron* 10 (1980) 383 (also on the *Pullaieni*); Charles-Picard, *La civilisation* 140 ff.; Duquenne, *Chronologie* 170 f.; Gascou, *Politique municipale* 63; and on the additional name *Florentius* (which CIL 8.26415 suggests belonged to at least the last two generations of the above tree), Kajanto, *Supernomina* 48, 82, with other examples 73. It was a name clearly favoured by Christians: compare Boppert's statistics in *Die frühchristlichen Inschriften* 42 (55 out of 117 examples are Christian), and it may have found this special favour from its associations with the flowery crowns of martyrdom and paradise (cf. *Ep.* 10 n. 34, *Ep.* 21 nn. 9 and 21). Is this the reason why *agnomen* (Florentius) and *cognomen* (Puppianus) are reversed from their usual order, Puppianus having stressed the puissant significance of his name? The reversed order occurs in *Act. procons.* 3.3 ("*Thascius qui et Cyprianus*") for Cyprian's own names; cf., on this interchangeability, *P.*

Sakaon 11 (Aurelius Athanasios *kai* Philadelphos, 3–4) with *P. Sakaon* 12 (Aurelius Philadelphos *kai* Athanasios, 7), ed. Parássoglou 28 ff.

If this association of our Puppianus with the above family is valid, we have a rare illustration of a socially eminent Christian in North Africa at this period, and one who, with the additional *gloria* of martyrdom to his dignity (n. 4 below), would be a fitting rival to challenge Cyprian's *auctoritas*.

Was he lay, cleric, or bishop? Though the last status is often assigned to him (e.g. by Vilela 255; Saumagne, *Cyprien . . . évêque* 56; Turner, *Pattern* 331; d'Alès, *Réconciliation* 373 f. n. 4; Younge, *Cyprian of Carthage* 34; Swann, *Relationship* 291), it is altogether most unlikely: the *gravamen* of the letter concerns the respect due to bishops (and to which, manifestly, Puppianus had no claim whatsoever); note especially §§5.1 ff. Equally, Freppel's suggestion (*Saint Cyprien* 138, 229) that Puppianus was one of the five rebel presbyters of Carthage (cf. *Ep.* 14 n. 32) receives no support from the text: Cyprian would surely have dilated on the choice iniquities of such disobedience and disloyalty. Therefore, Puppianus ought to be left as a layman.

2. *ego te, frater, credideram.* It is most unusual for Cyprian not to qualify the vocative *frater;* similar examples do (rarely) occur, but within the body of long letters (e.g. *Ep.* 55.3.1 *ad fin., Ep.* 59.2.1 *init., Ep.* 59.8.1) and after *frater carissime* has preceded. Here and in §9.1 (the only two vocative addresses in the letter) the unqualified *frater* may well have been designed deliberately to suggest a tone of brusqueness, distance, and curtness. But note the Romans use this simple title in *Ep.* 36.1.1, 3.1, and cf. Bastiaenseri 24, Watson 272. At all events it is unwise to conclude simply from his being addressed as *frater* that Puppianus must have been a layman (contra Pell 328; see e.g. *Ep.* 2 *init., Ep.* 3 *init.,* both addressing bishops).

Are we to presume that Cyprian had mistakenly drawn his conclusion (*credideram*) about Puppianus' repentance from a lengthy silence, which has now been noisily broken by his recent, impertinent letter (see next n.)?

3. *in litteris tuis.* Some of the general contents of this lost letter are discernible from Cyprian's rejoinders. (1) Puppianus reported charges he had heard about Cyprian's character and morals (§§1.1, 2.2, 7.1), in particular of his failure in humility (§3.1) and his record under persecution (§§4.1 f.). (2) Questions were raised about his ap-

pointment in the past, and his present status, as bishop (§§4.1 ff.; cf. §§1.2 ff.). (3) Communion with Cyprian involves sharing in his fatal pollution (§§7.3; cf. §§9.1, 1.1). (4) Cyprian is responsible for the present divisions in the church (§8.1). (5) Cyprian places absurd reliance upon the guidance of dreams and visions (§9.1).

4. *ne forte claritatis et martyrii tui dignitas nostra communicatione maculetur.* Puppianus had proudly enumerated his own persecution record (by contrast with Cyprian's?); hence the riposte of §§4.1 ff. and the final rejoinder of §10.3: *de his . . . quae tu egisti vel in persecutione vel in pace.* As a survivor after persecution, Puppianus was strictly a *confessor* (cf. the *confessores* of §7.2 and see *Ep.* 15 n. 1), but instead of *confessio* Cyprian uses here the grander title of *martyrium;* cf. §4.1: *te ad summam martyrii sublimitatem provexit;* that may well be deliberately overblown and ironical grandiosity, or a mocking echo of Puppianus' own arrogant and grandiloquent phrasing. Cf. Hummel 9.

Observe the pollution charge, on which see n. 28 below.

5. *post Deum iudicem qui sacerdotes facit.* For Cyprian's firmly-held view that it is God who appoints bishops, see *Ep.* 3 n. 9, *Ep.* 43 n. 6. In this letter Cyprian does not entertain the possibility, as he does elsewhere, that even such a divine appointment might be rendered void by the disclosure of gross moral failure in the past, committed at a time before that election (e.g. the question of recognising the election of Cornelius, charged with having been a *libellaticus*, *Ep.* 55.10.1 f.), or nullified by the performance of some outrageous and disqualifying act after the election (e.g. the cases of Martialis and Basilides, *Ep.* 67). Cyprian's own appointment as bishop, however, may well have been challenged on both these scores by Puppianus; hence the reporting of *infanda, incesta,* etc., rendering him *indignus* of the office of bishop (§1.2: *credere quod indigni et incesti sint qui ordinantur*), and hence the challenge over his performance under persecution subsequently (§4.1: *post persecutionem sacerdos esse desivi*).

6. Matt. 10.29, Fahey 299 f. (the text has been cited already to support the divine election of bishops in *Ep.* 59.5.2).

7. *credere quod indigni et incesti sint qui ordinantur . . . contendere quod non a Deo nec per Deum . . . constituantur.* The premise upon which Cyprian is basing his argument is clear: the Christian *sacerdos* must be *dignus* and *castus.* If he has been rightfully appointed *sacerdos,*

that proves beyond question that he is *dignus* and *castus*, for God would not appoint someone who is *indignus* and *incestus*. This premise, of course, contributed to Cyprian's difficulties in recognising the exercise of sacramental powers (as in baptism) by those who were outside the Church (and who must, therefore, be *indigni*, *incesti*, etc., for the Lord lets only *eiciendi*, only chaff, be lost outside; see §8.1). Cyprian was not disturbed by circularity in argument.

8. John 5.31 f., Fahey 381 f.

9. *qui iudicio ac testimonio Dei non probantur tantum, sed etiam gloriantur.* The second clause (*sed etiam gloriantur*), which is an unexpected addition, may well have been appended for the benefit of Puppianus, who so freely produced his own testimony on his martyr's *gloria* (see n. 4 above). For the "Christianism" of *glorior* used in the sense of *glorificor*, see *Ep.* 11.8 and n. 56 *ad loc.* and cf. TLL 6.2 *s.v.* "glorior" 11 (*sensu passivo*) 2099 (Knoche).

10. *apud lapsos et profanos . . . de quorum pectoribus excesserit spiritus sanctus.* Puppianus appears to be associated with some breakaway *laxist* group (for *lapsi* figure in its ranks), most economically to be presumed the party of Fortunatus and Felicissimus. This would be consistent with Puppianus' sense of superiority and self-importance derived from his martyr's status (cf. n. 4 above)—the party of Felicissimus was supported by confessors (*Ep.* 43)—and he has certainly broken off communion with Cyprian (cf. §3.1: *cum adhuc . . . mecum communicares*). But some caution is appropriate in making precise deductions in a context of general religious abuse. (Sage 296, less plausibly, regards Puppianus as having "joined the Novatianist faction or some other rigorist splinter group which severely disapproved of Cyprian's more lenient attitude".)

11. *venientes ad ecclesiam singulos . . . suscipio. Veniens* is used as a technical term for one seeking reception into the Church from outside (whether from paganism or from heresy): it is the bishop's task to administer to the *veniens* the sacrament of admission, viz. baptism (cf. §5.2: *novus credentium populus . . . per nos*, and *Ep.* 70.3.1: *nec baptizare venientem potest*). See on *veniens* Janssen 41 f.; Bayard, *Le latin* 182; Watson 263.

12. *tu qui te episcopum episcopi et iudicem iudicis . . . constituis.* The phrase *episcopum episcopi* has become celebrated partly through Cyprian's notable use of a variant on it in *Sent. episc.* LXXXVII *praef.* H.

436 (*neque enim quisquam nostrum episcopum se episcoporum constituit*) as well as through Tertullian's in *De pudic.* 1.6 CCL 2.1281 f. (*pontifex scilicet maximus, quod <est> episcopus episcoporum, edicit . . .*), both of which passages have been subjected to highly controversial interpretations. But the turn of phrase is a common enough rhetorical trope (cf. *Ep.* 31.3: *iudicis . . . iudicem*), on which see e.g. Melin, *Studia* 28 f.; Daly, *Stud. patr.* 3 (1961) 177 f.; Zernov, *Ch.Q.R.* 117 (1933–34) 327 f.

For the bishop regarded as a judge, compare *Ep.* 59.5.1, *ad tempus iudex vice Christi*, where see n. 18.

13. This congeries of texts used to establish divine sanctions for episcopal authority has been culled from Deut. 17.12 f. (Fahey 92 f), 1 Sam. 8.7 (Fahey 104), John 18.22 f. (Fahey 401 f.), and Acts 23.4 f. (Fahey 419), passages all found in the similar context of *Ep.* 59.4.1 ff. and cf. *Ep.* 3.1.1 ff. They represent Cyprian's usual technique of freely applying texts, not originally addressed to apostles or Christian bishops, to the Christian *sacerdotes;* unless one accepts the equivalence of O.T. *sacerdos* with N.T. bishop, they manifest a remarkable lack of relevance. There may also be here a classical literary echo, rare in Cyprian (*umbram . . . nominis;* cf. Lucan, *Phars.* 1.135: *magni nominis umbra*).

14. *nisi si sacerdos tibi fui ante persecutionem . . . post persecutionem sacerdos esse desivi.* Note the unqualified use of *persecutio:* the reference is unequivocally to the persecution of Decius (and to Cyprian's controversial conduct during that persecution—see *Ep.* 5. n. 2). Though the reign of Gallus has now subsequently intervened (cf. n. 20 below), Cyprian clearly does not regard that period as constituting a "persecution" (despite some ecclesiastical historians): see *Epp.* 57 ff. and Introduction. Observe that Cyprian could be regarded in some circles as having forfeited his episcopal *locus* by his disgraceful *fuga:* that would be relevant to the claims of the rival Carthaginian *pseudoepiscopi*, Fortunatus as well as Maximus (*Ep.* 59.9.1 ff.).

15. *cum publice legeretur: SI QVIS TENET POSSIDET DE BONIS CAECILI CYPRIANI EPISCOPI CHRISTIANORUM.* Cyprian is quoting from his official proscription, notices of which would have been prominently posted in the forum and other public places (*publice legeretur*). His argument is that he, too, did in fact suffer under persecution (and suffering is a mark of divine predilection; cf. *Ep.* 55

nn. 38 and 112, *Ep.* 59.7.1 f.), even the devil recognizing him, therefore, as the true bishop (cf. closely *Ep.* 60.3.2). Proscription brought him confessional *gloria* (Pont., *Vit. Cyp.* 7 H. xcvii: *etiam proscriptionis gloriam consecutus est*). For confiscation of goods as a feature of this persecution, see *Ep.* 10 n. 5; it would be a penalty especially imposed upon absent *requirendi*—cf. §7.2: *cum de medio recederent proscripti sunt*, and note *Dig.* 48.17.5 (*bona* of fugitives from justice to be sequestrated for one year, thereafter *in fiscum coguntur*). See further *Ep.* 55 n. 112 on *episcopi . . . in persecutione proscripti*. Though Cyprian had apparently dispersed almost all his personal fortune to the poor (*tota prope pretia dispensans*, Pont., *Vit. Cyp.* 2 H. xcii; Hartel's text is here disputable), he still mysteriously retained his *horti* (*op. cit.* 15 H. cvi *hortos . . . quos inter initia fidei suae venditos et de Dei indulgentia restitutos*) and he continued to have various personal sums at his disposal (e.g. *Epp.* 7.2, 13.7) right until his death; see Pont., *Vit. Cyp.* 13 H. cv. Thus all who were receiving Cyprian's largesse during the persecution—and especially the clergy who held it ready for distribution in Carthage—were endangering themselves (sc. *ipse proscribatur*, or the like, to complete the sentence quoted from the public proscription; the supplement provided by Younge, *Cyprian of Carthage* 68 ["he may keep them"] is entirely implausible). Compare *P. Oxy.* 12.1408, which contains references to an edict of the early third century A.D. ordering search to be made for robbers (with notices of the edict to be posted publicly, 16 f.), shelter is forbidden to the fugitives (22 ff.), and punishments are threatened to those who aid and assist them (25 f.); *Dig.* 48.3.6.1, an edict issued by Antoninus Pius *ut irenarchae, cum adprenderint latrones, interrogent eos de sociis et receptatoribus;* and *P. Oxy.* 47.3364, which refers to further early-third-century edicts (to be posted publicly) threatening with fines those who shelter and protect fugitive and defaulting taxpayers (4 ff., 41 ff.), and see the commentary of J. D. Thomas, *Journ. Egypt. Arch.* 61 (1975) 205, for further parallels; also B. D. Shaw, *Past and Present* 105 (1984) 37.

16. *vel diabolo crederent episcopum proscribenti.* For the devil regarded as the ultimate source of persecution, see *Ep.* 21 n. 35.

17. *ad omnes praepositos qui apostolis vicaria ordinatione succedunt.* For Cyprian's clearly-held view of the apostles as themselves the first bishops, see *Ep.* 3 n. 16, and for his view on the continuous link that joins bishops to those apostles, *Ep.* 33 n. 4. The phrase *vicaria ordi-*

natio (lit. "delegated appointment," "replacing appointment") recurs in *Ep.* 75.16.1 and its precise nuances are explored by van Beneden, *Aux origines* 113 ff.

18. Lk. 10.16, Fahey 346 f.

19. *unde enim schismata et haereses obortae sunt et oriuntur?* The present argument bears close resemblance to *Ep.* 3.3.2 (*haec sunt enim initia haereticorum et ortus adque conatus schismaticorum*) and this in turn suggests that *Ep.* 3 ought to be placed in a post-Decian context (see *Ep.* 3 intro.). *Ep.* 59.5.1 is closely parallel (*neque enim aliunde haereses obortae sunt aut nata sunt schismata quam . . .*); likewise *De zel. et liv.* 6 CCL 3A.78 (*ad haereses adque ad schismata prosilitur dum obtrectatur sacerdotibus*).

20. *ecce iam sex annis nec episcopum nec . . . praepositum nec . . . pastorem nec . . . gubernatorem nec . . . antistitem nec . . . sacerdotem.* A telling crescendo of nouns to signify Cyprian's conception of a bishop's roles, starting with administrative (*episcopum, praepositum*), moving to pastoral and supportive (*pastorem, gubernatorem*), and thence, most importantly, to hieratic (*antistitem*, on which see *Ep.* 21 n. 24, and *sacerdotem*). For illuminating discussion, Bévenot, JTS 30 (1979) 417 ff.

The expression *iam sex annis* ought, at the least, to place this letter within the period 253/54 (see *Letters of Cyprian* 1 [ACW 43] intro. p. 16 and n. 78 for the commencement date of Cyprian's episcopacy in 248/49). Furthermore, well on in summer 252, Cyprian can describe himself as having been bishop for a *quadriennium* (*in episcopatu quadriennio iam probatus, Ep.* 59. 6.1), i.e. for more than three or for four years (cf. *Ep.* 56 n. 8 on *triennium, Ep.* 43 n. 18 on *biennium*). It is most likely, therefore, that the expression *sex annis* should move this letter out of (say, late) 253, which remains formally possible, and into 254 (though Roman inclusive counting, and Cyprian's inclination towards hyperbole, make certainty impossible). In either case the reign of Gallus has ceased (cf. n. 14 above). See Nelke, *Chronologie* 156 f.; Ritschl, *De epist.* 29; Duquenne, *Chronologie* 35.

21. *ne novus credentium populus nullam per nos consecutus esse baptismi et spiritus sancti gratiam iudicetur.* Note the bishop's role as the administrator of baptism (cf. n. 11 above) and Cyprian's instinctive linking of the graces of the Holy Spirit with baptism (a view which was soon to help obfuscate for Cyprian the rebaptism issue; cf. Bé-

venot, *Heythrop Journ.* 19 [1978] 125 ff.). Despite persecution (Decius) and threat of persecution (Gallus), conversions apparently still continued, and in number (*novus . . . populus*).

22. *apes habent regem et ducem pecudes et fidem servant.* The analogies have been confidently derived from Minucius Felix, *Oct.* 18.7 (e.g. Ball, *Nature* 246), which is undeniably close (*rex unus apibus, dux unus in gregibus*), but they figure amongst the hardiest of rhetorical commonplaces (see Spanneut, *Stoïcisme*² 262 ff., and ACW 39.260).

23. *scrupulum tibi esse tollendum de animo in quem incidisti.* Though Puppianus may have been making some biblical allusion (to e.g. Matt. 11.6, 18.6 f., etc.), there are also classical parallels for this notion of being "scandalised," i.e. made to stumble; see Otto, *Sprichwörter s.v.* "lapis" (6), and Häussler, *Nachträge zu A. Otto, Sprichwörter* 29 (on *scrupulus*).

Compare Cyprian's contemporary, Dionysius of Alexandria, using similar imagery: "Gallus . . . did not foresee what it was that had caused Decius to fall but he stumbled over the same stone that was right before his eyes" (*ap.* Euseb. *H.E.* 7.1).

24. Sir. 28.24 (Fahey 180 f.) and Prov. 17.4 (Fahey 165).

25. *martyres . . . qui ad Cyprianum episcopum litteras de carcere direxerunt.* Most probably this refers to the now hallowed Roman martyrs who wrote *Ep.* 31 to Cyprian from their prison. In their salutation, however, they greeted Cyprian as *papas* and not as *episcopus*, but Cyprian may well be alluding to the actual address of their letter, which would have been written *in verso;* cf. Bastiaensen 14 n. 2. On the other hand, the Carthaginian martyrs also wrote to Cyprian (*Ep.* 15.1.2: *cum vos ad me litteras direxeritis*) and in their company figured the highly honoured and imprisoned martyr Mappalicus (*Epp.* 10, 27.1.1).

26. *aut qui in quibusdam locis animadversi caelestes coronas . . . sumpserunt.* The expression *in quibusdam locis* must refer to elsewhere than Africa: there was as yet no episcopal martyr in Africa, that honour being reserved for Cyprian four years hence (Pont., *Vit. Cyp.* 19 H. cix). The vague phrasing is strongly suggestive that the death penalty was unusual in the Decian persecution; for the few known episcopal victims, see *Letters of Cyprian* 1 (ACW 43) Intro. pp. 35 ff.

27. Note the distinction implied between the *martyres* (in n. 25 above), who are now dead, and these *confessores* who, though they suf-

fered physical tortures, actually survived the persecution; see *Ep.* 15 n. 1 and cf. Hummel 30 f., 18 f.

28. *polluto nostro ore polluti sunt.* Why *ore?* Cyprian nowhere appears to have been accused of actually having been a *sacrificatus.* The simplest explanation is that Puppianus was thinking of the communion of prayer: all those in union with Cyprian share in his tainted and unholy worship which, as *sacerdos peccator* and *iniustus sacerdos,* is, necessarily, all that he could offer (cf. closely *Ep.* 67.3.1 f.). By way of defence, therefore, Cyprian retorts in §9.1: *puro adque immaculato ore sacrificia . . . indesinenter offero.*

29. *soli illi foris remanserint qui et si intus essent eiciendi fuerant.* For this confident argument cf. *Ep.* 52.4.2 (*qui plantatus non est praeceptis Dei patris . . . solus poterit de ecclesia ille discedere*), where see n. 25, and *Ep.* 51.2.2. For the biblically-based analogy which follows (the wheat on the threshing floor), see *Ep.* 54.3.1 f. and n. 8 *ad loc.*

30. Rom. 3.3 f. (Fahey 426 f.) followed by John 6.67 ff. (Fahey 385).

31. *utique conexa et cohaerentium sibi invicem sacerdotum glutino copulata.* By deliberately arresting language Cyprian seeks to give expression to the intensity of the tightly bonding power of episcopal unity in cementing together the structure of the Church; cf. *Ep.* 68.3.2: *copiosum corpus est sacerdotum concordiae mutuae glutino adque unitatis vinculo copulatum.* Tertullian had already exploited the same vigorous metaphor in *De pudic.* 5.9 CCL 2.1288: *concorporavit nos scriptura divina, litterae ipsae glutina nostra sunt.*

32. *Christum qui arbitrio et nutu et praesentia . . . praepositos ipsos . . . gubernat.* For this sense of direct guidance and inspiration vouchsafed to the bishops of the Church, cf. *Ep.* 48.4.2: *Dominus . . . sacerdotes . . . gubernanter inspirans et subministrans,* and *Ep.* 16.4.1: *Dominus qui ut secederem iussit* (where see nn. 27 and 30).

33. *prius Dominum meum consulam an . . . te . . . admitti sua ostensione et admonitione permittat.* An outstanding expression of the privileged access to the Lord commanded by Cyprian qua bishop (who, in turn, controls the power to excommunicate or to reconcile, cf. *Ep.* 3 n. 4). For commentary see *Ep.* 16 nn. 27 ff., n. 33, and cf. Walker, *Churchmanship* 45: "Few prelates can ever have had such confidence either in their own inspiration or in the complete wrongheadedness of a schismatic confessor who opposed them. But the im-

portant point in this remarkable epistle is its utterly Christocentric basis." The personal nature of the communication which Cyprian enjoys with his Lord is emphasised by the expression *Dominus meus* (not *noster*), a turn of phrase not at all common in Cyprian. Ignatius of Antioch provides a close general parallel in *Ad Philad.* 7.1 f. As bishop, he considers himself inspired by the Holy Spirit: "I cried out while I was with you, I spoke with a great voice, with the voice of God: 'Give heed to the bishop. . . .' The Spirit was preaching and saying this: 'Do nothing without the bishop. . . .' " And for the ability to command divine visions and signs, compare, too, the soon-to-be-martyred Perpetua, *Mart. Perp.* 4.1 f. Musurillo 110: " 'Honoured sister, you are so greatly privileged that you may ask for a vision and a revelation. . . .' And I, knowing as I did that I could converse with the Lord whose great blessings I had come to experience, faithfully promised to him with these words: 'I shall tell you to-morrow.' And so I asked and this was revealed to me."

34. Gen. 37.19 f., on which Fahey 66 rightly remarks: "This procedure of applying a text from the Pentateuch to himself is very unusual, even unique for Cyprian. Texts which have a prophetic or typological dimension are normally applied either to Christ or to the Gentiles." The explanation for this rare manoeuvre is that Cyprian is under acute attack. Cyprian had used his visions as a knockdown defence of his conduct during the persecution, *Ep.* 16.4.1 (for which conduct Puppianus censured him, §4.1), for commanding obedience from the turbulent confessors, *Ep.* 11.3.1 ff. (of which Puppianus was unrepentently one, §1.2), and for reaching a final solution on the reconciliation of *sacrificati*, *Ep.* 57.1.2 f. (dispute over which formed the *raison d'être* of the breakaway church of Fortunatus and Felicissimus, to which Puppianus apparently belonged—see n. 10 above), and cf. *Ep.* 63 n. 45. To attack Cyprian's reliance on his *somnia* and *visiones*, as Puppianus had done, was, therefore, to assail Cyprian's position at a particularly sensitive and vulnerable point.

35. Cyprian ends his letter brusquely, without any customary formula of farewell as demanded by epistolary politesse. That is unique in the correspondence, and it effectively breaks off the letter on an abruptly hostile and minatory note.

INDEXES

1. OLD AND NEW TESTAMENT

2. AUTHORS AND SOURCES

3. LATIN WORDS

4. GENERAL INDEX